MW01678941

《新概念英语》（新版）辅导丛书

主编 何其莘

顾问 亚历山大（英）

新概念英语自学导读 4

NCE Study Guide 4

Fluency in English

孙玉荣 杜建 编著

外语教学与研究出版社

PEARSON LONGMAN

京权图字：01-2000-1347

图书在版编目（CIP）数据

新概念英语自学导读4 / 孙玉荣，杜建编著. — 北京 ：外语教学与研究出版社，2002（2017.9 重印）
ISBN 978-7-5600-2512-4

Ⅰ. ①新… Ⅱ. ①孙… ②杜… Ⅲ. ①英语－自学参考资料 Ⅳ. ①H31

中国版本图书馆CIP数据核字(2002)第006016号

出 版 人　蔡剑峰
出版发行　外语教学与研究出版社
社　　址　北京市西三环北路19号（100089）
网　　址　http://www.fltrp.com
印　　刷　北京市鑫霸印务有限公司
开　　本　850×1168　1/32
印　　张　17.25
版　　次　2002年2月第1版　2017年9月第39次印刷
书　　号　ISBN 978-7-5600-2512-4
定　　价　21.90元

购书咨询：（010）88819926　电子邮箱：club@fltrp.com
外研书店：https://waiyants.tmall.com
凡印刷、装订质量问题，请联系我社印制部
联系电话：（010）61207896　电子邮箱：zhijian@fltrp.com
凡侵权、盗版书籍线索，请联系我社法律事务部
举报电话：（010）88817519　电子邮箱：banquan@fltrp.com
法律顾问：立方律师事务所　刘旭东律师
　　　　　中咨律师事务所　殷　斌律师
物料号：125120001

外研社 朗文 新概念英语 自学导读 4

NEW CONCEPT ENGLISH *(New Edition)*

STUDY GUIDE 4: *Fluency in English*

This simplified Chinese characters edition first published
in 2002 jointly by Foreign Language Teaching and Research Press
and Pearson Education North Asia Ltd.

合作出版人：李朋义(外研社)　吴天祝(朗文)
主编：何其莘　　顾问：亚历山大(英)
责任编辑：任小玫
执行编辑：周继东　李红玲
封面设计：诸中英

外语教学与研究出版社
培生教育出版北亚洲有限公司 联合出版

《新概念英语》(新版)是《新概念英语》1967 年首次出版以来第一次推出的新版本。现在，由该经典教材的出版者外语教学与研究出版社和培生教育出版北亚洲有限公司独家授权、由原编著者何其莘教授亲自主持编写、亚历山大先生担任顾问的这套《新概念英语》(新版)辅导丛书涵盖自学导读、练习详解、词汇、语法以及录音练习等各方面的内容，是面向中国广大英语爱好者的一套权威的辅导用书，定能满足中国广大读者对《新概念英语》(新版)的全方位的要求，并使英语爱好者在学习过程中最大限度地发挥自己的潜能。

《新概念英语》(新版)辅导丛书包括：

《新概念英语自学导读 1》(*NCE Study Guide 1 : First Things First*)
《新概念英语自学导读 2》(*NCE Study Guide 2 : Practice & Progress*)
《新概念英语自学导读 3》(*NCE Study Guide 3 : Developing Skills*)
《新概念英语自学导读 4》(*NCE Study Guide 4 : Fluency in English*)
《新概念英语练习详解 1》(*NCE Exercise Companion 1 : First Things First*)
《新概念英语练习详解 2》(*NCE Exercise Companion 2 : Practice & Progress*)
《新概念英语练习详解 3》(*NCE Exercise Companion 3 : Developing Skills*)
《新概念英语练习详解 4》(*NCE Exercise Companion 4 : Fluency in English*)
《新概念英语语法手册》(*An NCE Grammar Handbook*)
《新概念英语词汇大全》(*An NCE Complete Vocabulary List*)
《新概念英语词汇自学手册》(*An NCE Pocket Dictionary*)
《新概念英语录音练习手册》(*Recorded Drills for NCE*)

Preface

This Study Guide is intended for all students of *Fluency in English* , but particularly for those working on their own.

Detailed notes are provided for each of the forty-eight texts. These consist of:

- Further notes on the text
- Grammar in use: virtually a systematic survey of the grammatical points concerned as a whole text
- Word study: further notes on the vocabulary
- Key to written exercises

We believe that these additional notes will help students from all background to benefit from the course and to complete it successfully.

Louis George Alexander

前　言

该《自学导读》专为所有使用《流利英语》的学习者而设计，特别适用于自学者。

书中，针对48篇课文中的每一篇均有进一步说明。其中包括：

- 课文详注；
- 语法：实际上整体来讲就是对相关语法点的系统说明；
- 词汇学习；
- 练习答案。

我们确信这些补充材料将使各种起点的学习者从中受益，并顺利学完本课程。

L.G. 亚历山大

目　录

Lesson 1
Finding fossil man
发现化石人

课文详注 Further notes on the text

1. **... read of things that happened 5,000 years ago in the Near East ...**

   read of 读到,获悉。在一定程度上可与 read about 互换使用,但 read about 通常指"读到/获悉有关情况"。此外,使用 read about 时 read 后可用 all、much、a little 等词说明"读到/获悉一般情况",而使用 read of 时 read 后则不能使用类似的词。the Near East 近东,指亚洲西南部和非洲东北部地区。

2. **The only way that they can preserve their history is to recount it as sagas—legends handed down from one generation of storytellers to another.**

   to recount it as sagas 将其作为英雄故事讲述。to recount ... another 为动词不定式短语,在句子中作表语,用来说明主语 way(办法)的情况。应注意动词不定式结构作表语同 be to do 结构即在 be 动词后用一个动词不定式结构作复合谓语之间的不同:前者用来说明主语的内容,而后者则用来表示主语"计划或安排好做"之意,即句子主语即为该动词不定式的逻辑主语。比较:

   We are to send more people to help them with their work.
   我们打算派更多的人帮助他们工作。(*to send ...* 动词由主语 *we* 做出)

   Our task is to send more people to help them with their

work.

我们的任务是派更多的人帮助他们工作。(*to send* ... 动作对主语 *task* 进行说明)

legends 作 sagas 的同位语,其后的 handed down ... another 为过去分词短语,作定语,修饰 legends。hand down 传下来,如:

Their home contains many rare antiques which have been handed down to them from one generation to another.

他们家珍藏了许多世代相传的珍奇古董。

from one ... to another (...)从一……至另一(……)。在此短语中,one 后所随内容与 another 后所随内容相同。由于语义明确,因此通常将 another 后所随内容省略。如文中那样,在 another 后省略了 generation of storytellers。

3. ... but none could write down what they did.

none 没有,代词。既可用来指人,也可用来指物;既可用来指可数名词,也可用来指不可数名词。它往往受 of 引导的介词短语的限制,of 后可接可数名词或不可数名词。当 of 后为可数名词且在句中作主语时其谓语动词多用复数,虽也可用单数,但为不可数名词时其谓语动词只能用单数,如:

None of the drivers have/has turned up.

司机们一个都没来。

None of the money was ever recovered.

一点钱都没有找回来。

此外,none of 后的名词或代词只能用于指 3 个以上的人或物,不能用来指两个以下的人或物。注意 none 与 no one 在使用中的不同。no one 中的 no 为形容词,one 为代词,多用来指人,其意为 not even one(连一个人也不/没有),因此语气较 none 要强。此外,其后不能使用 of 引导的介词短语。用其作主语时,谓语动词只能用单数,如:

No one was killed in the battle.

在那次战斗中没有一个人牺牲。

在简略答语中,none 用来回答对数量的提问(即由 how many/how much 引导的疑问句),而 no one 用来回答对“谁”的提问(即由 who 引导的疑问句),比较:

How many books are there on the desk?
桌子上有多少本书?
None.
一本也没有。

Who is in the room?
谁在屋子里?
No one.
没人。

write down 写下,记下,动词+副词型短语,如:

Make sure that you write down every word the speaker says.

务必把讲话人讲的每句话都记下来。

You'd better write down the address before you forget it.

你最好把地址写下来,免得忘了。

4. ... where the remote ancestors of the Polynesian peoples now living in the Pacific Islands came from.

这里的复数形式 peoples 用来表示多个民族。now living ... Islands 为现在分词短语,作定语,修饰 peoples。

5. But the first people who were like ourselves lived so long ago that even their sagas, if they had any, are forgotten.

the first people 最初的人类,指原始人类。like ourselves 像我们自己这样的,指现代人。so long ago that ... 太久远了以至于……。so ... that ... 引导结果状语从句。if they had any 如果有的话,用作插入语,承上,any 后省略了 sagas。

6. So archaeologists have neither history nor legends to help them to find out where the first 'modern men' came from.

neither ... nor ... 既不……也不……。同 either ... or ... 一样，为表示选择的关联连词，用来连接两个在语法功能上相同、在结构上对称的并列成分。用于连接并列主语时，谓语动词形式需同最邻近的主语（即 nor 后的主语）保持一致，如：

Neither you nor he is wrong.

你和他都没有错。

neither ... nor ... 只用于肯定句式中表达否定意义。用 neither ... nor ... 连接两个结构平行的句子（即将 neither 和 nor 分别置于两个句子的首位）时，如下述最后一例中那样，主、谓语需倒装，如：

It is neither cold nor hot.

天气既不冷也不热。

They neither spoke nor moved, just stared hard at me.

他们既不说话也不走，只是死死地盯着我。

Neither has he heard from her yet nor will he do so before long.

他至今未收到她的来信，最近也不会收到。

7. ... because this is easier to shape than other kinds.

other kinds 其他种类。承上省略了其后的 of stones，即指其他（种类的）石头。

8. They may also have used wood and skins, but these have rotted away.

may + 动词的现在完成时结构用来表示讲话人从目前的角度仍认为过去某事曾发生过，但把握性不大，通常含有"或许/也许发生……了"这样怀疑或推测的意味，如：

The students may have done their exercises yesterday.

学生们也许昨天做完练习了。

He may have talked with her.

他或许同她谈过了。

rot away 腐蚀殆尽,腐烂掉,动词+副词型短语,如:

The soil in the forest is rich with dead leaves and branches that have been rotting away for centuries.

几个世纪以来,一直在腐烂的枯叶和树枝使这片森林中的土壤很肥沃。

9. ... when even the bones of the men who made them have disappeared without trace.

when 尽管,从属连词,在此用来引导让步状语从句。在一定的语境中,when 除了可以引导让步状语从句外,有时还可以用来引导条件状语从句,表示"如果"、"只要"之意。这样使用时,多置于句末,如:

Some of them will make trouble when nothing good is to be expected of it.

即使什么好处都得不到,他们中的一些人也还是要捣乱的。(*when* 引导让步状语从句)

Turn off the switch when anything goes wrong with the machine.

如果机器发生故障,就把开关关掉。(*when* 引导条件状语从句)

语法 Grammar in use

并列句与并列连词

1. 并列句

并列句由若干个连接起来的简单句构成。在并列句中,不存在单独的主句和从句。各小句要根据上下文的要求按逻辑次序排列,但各小句都同等重要,并独立存在。这些小句通常被视为并列句。

2. 并列连词

构成并列句的方法之一是使用并列连词,将要表述的若干小句连接起来。当各小句的主语相同时,通常不再重复。并列连词通常可用来表达几种不同的含义:

(1) 另加/连续

表达此目的时,通常使用的并列连词有:and、both ... and ...、not only ... but ...(too/as well)、not only ... but (also) ...、and then,如:

He washed the car and polished it.

他冲洗了汽车并给它上光。

He not only washed the car, but polished it as well.

他不仅冲洗了汽车,而且还给它上光。

He washed the car and then polished it.

他先冲洗了汽车,然后给它上光。

当句子主语不同时,则要把主语都表达出来,如:

Jim speaks Spanish, but his wife speaks French.

吉姆说西班牙语,而他妻子说法语。

(2) 对比

表达此目的时,通常使用的并列连词有:but、yet,如:

He washed the car, but didn't polish it.

他冲洗了汽车,但没有给它上光。

She sold her house, yet can't help regretting it.

她卖掉了房子,但不禁感到惋惜。

(3) 选择

表达此目的时,通常使用的并列连词有:either ... or ...、neither ... nor ...,如:

He either speaks French, or understands it.

他或是会讲法语,或是懂法语。

He neither speaks French, nor understands it.

他既不会讲法语,也听不懂法语。

(4) 结果

表达此目的时,使用的并列连词是 so,如:

He couldn't find his pen, so he wrote in pencil.

他找不着钢笔,所以他用铅笔写。

(5) 原因

表达此目的时,使用的并列连词是 for,如:

We rarely stay in hotels, for we can't afford it.

我们很少住酒店,因为我们住不起。

词汇学习 Word study

1. preserve *vt.*

(1) (from) 保护,保藏,保存:

The ancient Egyptians knew ways to preserve dead bodies from decay.

古埃及人知道保存尸体不腐烂的方法。

I think these interesting old customs should be preserved.

我认为这些有趣的老传统应当受到保护。

(2) 保持,维护:

He's managed to preserve his independence.

他设法保持了自己的独立性。

It's the duty of the police to preserve public order.

维护公共秩序是警察的职责。

(3) 贮藏:

Boiling with sugar, salting, smoking and pickling are different ways of preserving food.

蜜饯、腌制、烟熏和腌渍是贮藏食物的不同方法。

2. recount

(1) *vt.* (正式)细述(故事),描述:

She recounted her adventures.

她详细讲述了她的冒险经历。

(2) *vt.* 重数,重新计算:

They had to recount the votes.

他们不得不重新计算选票。

(3) *n.* (可数)重新计算,重新数:

The defeated candidate demanded a recount.

被击败的候选人要求重数选票。

3. decay

(1) *vt.* (使)腐败,腐烂:

Sugar can decay the teeth.

糖能蛀牙。

(2) *vi.* 腐败,腐烂:

Stone does not decay, so the tools of long ago have remained.

石头是不会腐烂的,因此远古年代的工具至今尚存。

(3) *vi.* 衰落,衰败,退化:

Each civilization is born, it culminates, and it decays.

每一种文明都要经历诞生、鼎盛和衰落。

Perhaps all nations decay in the course of time.

也许所有的民族都会随着时间的推移而衰败。

(4) *n.* (不可数) 衰落,衰败,退化:

The empty house has fallen into decay.

那所空房子逐渐腐朽了。

(5) *n.* 蛀牙,龋齿:

The dentist used a drill to remove the decay.

牙医用钻拔去了蛀牙。

练习答案 Key to written exercises

1. 关键句型练习答案

A *Tools* (*which were*) *made of stone* were used for scraping and cutting.

Legends (*which have been*) *recorded* in the form of sagas provide some information about the migrations of ancient peoples.

The remains (*which were*) *found* at the back of the cave were dated to about 20,000 years before the present.

B 1 say 2 told 3 say 4 tell

C Do you mind my asking where you *got* it *from*?

I *bought* it *from* a second-hand shop in South London.

D Would you mind *helping me to lift* this box, please?

The children *helped me make* the tree decorations.

E See text.

F 1 Your mother *may have called* when you were out.

2 You *may have left* your umbrella in the waiting room.

3 He *may have changed* his mind.

2. 难点练习答案

A 1 *Part* always refers to a part of a whole: *a part of a country*, *a part of the world*, *parts of this building*, etc.

Place refers to location: *a place in town*, *a place on the shelf*, *places where things are kept*.

2 *History* is an objective account of a series of events: *the history of a country*, *a person's history*, *the history of our times*.

A *story* is an account, possibly fictional or partly so, told from the teller's own point of view: *a bedtime story*, *the story of my life*.

3 *Wonder* means 'ask oneself': *wonder what someone means*.

Wander means 'walk without paying attention to one's direction': *wander around the house / town, trying to decide what to do*.

4 *Like* (preposition) takes a direct object, which can be a noun (*like this job*), a pronoun (*like someone*), or a noun clause (*like what you do*).

As (adverb of manner or of comparison) introduces a clause and could be replaced with 'that which': *do as I say*, or 'in the way that': *think as you do*.

5 *Find out* means 'learn, discover information', and is often intransitive: *How did he find out / find out the truth / find out about this?*

Find means 'come across or discover something that might be lost or not immediately available': *find a missing letter*, *find somewhere to stay*. We also use *find* to express an opinion based on experience: *I find it hard to understand him. I find it best to say nothing*.

6 *Ancient* means 'old in terms of history': *ancient manuscripts*, *ancient customs* (and, giving exaggerated dignity to the idea of age: *ancient friendships*).

Old means 'not new': *old buildings*, *old friendship*, *old injuries*; and not young: *old people*, *old age*.

7 A *tool* is essentially an extension of the hand, and thus applies to processes that are mechanical: *a cutting tool*, *a*

polishing tool, *a machine tool*.

An *instrument* is a device for non-mechanical tasks: *a measuring instrument*, *a surgical instrument*, *a scientific instrument*.

8 *Stone* is the material of which things can be built or made: *building stone*, *stone quarry*, *a stone house*, *a stone bridge*. *Stone* also refers to small accidental pieces of stone: *a stone in my shoe*, *a sharp stone*.

Rock is the material in a state of nature: *bedrock*, *igneous rock*, *a (natural) rock bridge*, *weathered rocks*, *rock cliffs*. *Rock* also refers to a large, free-standing piece of rock: *a round rock*, *rocks on the road*.

9 *Skin* is the natural protective covering of a living person or thing: *my skin*, *tiger skin*, *a banana skin*.

Leather is the material made from the cleaned, dried and processed skin of an animal such as a pig or cow: *leather shoes*, *leather upholstery*.

B 1 Do you happen *to know where he comes from*?

2 It so happens that *he comes from the same town as me*.

3 Can you tell me what *happened in the class yesterday*?

3. 多项选择题答案

1	c	2	a	3	b	4	d	5	d	6	b
7	d	8	a	9	a	10	c	11	a	12	b

Lesson 2

Spare that spider

不要伤害蜘蛛

课文详注 Further notes on the text

1. **Why, you may wonder, should spiders be our friends?**

   Why should ... ？形式的疑问句往往用来表达"不能理解"的含义，如：

   Why should it get colder when we go up a mountain?
   爬山时为什么越往上爬越冷呢？

   此外，这一结构有时也用来表示愤怒和生气，如：

   Give me a cigarette.
   给我一枝烟。
   Why should I?
   凭什么？

   you may wonder 作插入语使用。

2. **Insects would make it impossible for us to live in the world; they would devour all our crops and kill our flocks and herds, if it were not for the protection we get from insect-eating animals.**

   全句为从属连词 if 引导的非真实性条件状语从句。主句中的 would make、would devour 和从句中的 were 均为虚拟语气。本句将主句置前而从句置后，有利于对主句内容的强调，从而加深读者对昆虫给人类带来的危害性的认识。在 would make it impossible ...中，代词 it 为先行词，作句子的形式宾语，而其后带介词 for 的动词不定式为句子的逻辑宾语。if it were not for（如果不是因为/由于）是表示与现实不符的虚拟语气结构，通常用于表示“因为现实这一特定条件而改变了一切”之意，如：

If it were not for his wife's money he'd never be a director.

如果不是他妻子有钱，他永远也不会成为一个董事。

其过去式为 if it had not been for ...，即为表示与过去事实不符的虚拟语气结构，如：

If it hadn't been for your help I really don't know what I'd have done.

如果没有你的帮助，我真不知道我会弄成什么样子。

3. We owe a lot to the birds and beasts who eat insects but all of them put together kill ...

owe ... to ... 为……感激……，把……归功于……。此短语中的 to 为介词，因此其后应使用名词、代词等，而不能使用动词不定式。此外，动词 owe 通常不用于进行时态，如：

If I have improved in any way, I owe it all to you.

如果说我有一些进步，完全归功于你。

We owe to Newton the principle of gravitation.

我们全靠牛顿才知道引力的原理。

在后一例中，the principle of gravitation 为 owe 的直接宾语，由于较长，为使句子保持平衡而将其置后。put together 加在一起，在句子中为过去分词短语，作定语。

4. ... spiders never do the least harm to us or our belongings.

do harm to sb./sth. 与 do sb./sth. harm 均表示“对某人/某物造成损害”。如短语中所示，do 为双宾语动词，harm 为不可数名词。当直接宾语(harm)置于 do 后时，在 harm 与间接宾语之间需使用介词 to，如：

It does more harm to you than good.

这对你害多益少。

Smoking does harm to one's health.

吸烟有害健康。

The drought did a lot of harm to the crops.

干旱使庄稼遭到很多损失。

It will do you no harm.

这对你没害处。

5. **Spiders are not insects, as many people think, nor even nearly related to them.**

as many people think 像人们想像的那样。作插入语。nor even nearly related to them 甚至也几乎与它们毫无关系。此为省略句，省略了are spiders。完整的句子为：nor are spiders even nearly related to them（注意，使用完整句子表达时，由于否定词用于句首，因此主语同谓语动词需构成倒装形式）。当上下文语义明确时，nor 后经常使用省略形式。

6. **One can tell the difference almost at a glance ...**

at a glance（望）一眼（就），如：

It is manifest at a glance.

那是一目了然的。

He saw at a glance that she'd been crying.

他一眼就看出她一直在哭。

7. **How many spiders are engaged in this work on our behalf?**

be engaged in 从事于。介词 in 后可接表示各种活动、工作等的名词、代词或动名词，如：

He has been engaged in the study of cotton-growing for 20 years.

他从事棉花种植的研究已有 20 年之久。

Although he is engaged in writing his memories at this period, he still has other business to attend to.

他虽然这段时间在写回忆录，但仍然有其他事务需打理。

on one's behalf 为某人的利益，为了某人，代表某人。也可为 on behalf of，在美国英语中常用 in behalf of。

8. **One authority on spiders made a census of the spiders ...; that is something like 6,000,000 spiders of ...**

on 为介词，这里作"有关……的"、"从事……研究的"解，它所构成的介词短语作定语，修饰 authority。make a census of 对……进行一次（数据统计）调查。常用来同 census 搭配使用的动词或短语动词有 carry out（进行）和 take（进行）。在表示"有关……方面的调查"时，census 后通常使用介词 of，如：

Last year, that government carried out/took a census of the population.

去年，该政府进行了人口普查。

Some of the doctors in the hospital have made a census of the amount of lung cancer among smokers.

该医院的一些医生已对吸烟者中患肺癌的人数进行了调查。

something like 大约，将近。常用于口语，如：

This book cost me something like $10.

这本书花了我近 10 美元。

有时也用来表达"有点像"，如：

It is shaped something like a ball.

那东西外形有些像球。

9. **Spiders are busy for at least half the year in killing insects.**

be busy in doing sth. 忙于做某事。在表示"忙于某事"时，通常使用 be busy with sth. 这样的结构。句中 busy 后的 for at least half the year 为作时间状语使用的介词短语。本句中 half 为形容词，作名词表达此意义时其结构为 half of the year。

10. **It is impossible to make more than the wildest guess at how many they kill, but they are hungry creatures, not content**

with only three meals a day.

It 为形式宾语,其后的动词不定式短语 make ... kill 为逻辑主语。make a guess at sth. 猜测某事。make a wild guess at sth. 不着边际地猜测某事。其前的短语 more than 为副词短语,修饰形容词 wild 的最高级形式 the wildest,表示"极"、"非常"、"很"、"简直"等。how many they kill 为一名词性从句,作介词 at 的宾语。not content with only three meals a day 并不满足于每日 3 餐。可视为在 not 前省略了 which are,在句中作非限定性定语从句。be content with 对……感到满意,如:

I'm quite content with the offer you've made for the house.

我对你提出的房价感到很满意。

She's now perfectly content with her present salary.

她对目前的工资十分满意。

注意:content 不能作定语。作定语使用时,需用 contented 形式,如:

He has a contented look.

他脸上露出满意的表情。

11. **It has been estimated that the weight of all the insects destroyed by spiders in Britain in one year ...**

句子中的 It 为先行词,其后的连词 that 引导的从句即 that the weight of ... in the country 为逻辑主语。英语中,某些动词(如 believe、estimate、know、say 等)后可以跟随 that 或 whether 引导的宾语从句。如文中的句子,构成主动语态时为:People have estimated that the weight of ... in the country。构成被动语态时,这类由 that 或 whether 引导的宾语从句可提前作主语而整句变为:That the weight of ... in the country has been estimated ... 由于此类被动语态的主语往往太长,为使全句保持平衡,常常使用先行词 it 代替 that

或 whether 从句，而将该从句置于用了被动语态的动词之后，如：

It was not known whether there was gold left in the mine.

不知道矿里是否还有黄金。

本例句中 whether 引导的从句为逻辑主语，而 it 为形式主语。文中 destroyed by spiders in Britain in one year 为过去分词短语，作定语，修饰 insects。

语法 Grammar in use

关系代词、关系副词及关系从句 (1)

关系代词与关系从句

关系从句通常起形容词作用。它以一个短句的形式，置于名词或代词之后修饰该名词或代词。

关系代词通常起到连接复合句中的关系从句与主句的作用，引导关系从句，说明被修饰的名词或代词同该关系从句之间的关系。

关系代词在关系从句中的形式大体为如下几种：

(1) 充当主语：

人：*He is the man who/that lives next door.*

他就是住在隔壁的那个人。

物：*This is the photo which/that shows my house.*

这是我家房子的照片。

所有：*He is the man whose car was stolen.*

他就是那个汽车被盗的人。

(2) 充当宾语：

人：*He is the man (who/whom/that) I met.*

他就是我遇到的那个人。

He is the man (who/whom/that) I gave the money to.

他就是我给钱的那个人。

物: *This is the photo (which/that) I took.*

这是我拍的照片。

This is the pan (which/that) I boiled the milk in.

这就是我煮牛奶的锅。

所有: *It was an agreement the details of which could not be altered.*

这是一项其细节不可修改的协定。

可以看出:(1)"充当主语"部分中,前两个示例中的关系代词 who 或 that、which 或 that 不仅起到连接主句和从句的作用,而且还分别用来修饰名词 man 和 photo,它们在关系从句中起到主语的作用。(2)"充当宾语"部分中,第 1 和第 3 示例中的关系代词 who/whom/that、which/that 同"充当主语"部分头两个示例中的关系代词一样,不仅起到连接主句和从句的作用,而且还分别用来修饰名词 man 和 photo,但是它们在从句中起到宾语的作用。如示例中所示,"充当宾语"部分中的第 1 到第 4 示例中的关系代词,即在关系从句中起到宾语的这些关系代词,均可以省略。然而,此部分第 5 示例介词 + 关系代词结构中的关系代词 which 则不能省略。

在关系从句中使用关系代词时,有以下几点应当注意:

1) 虽然 that 可被用来代替指人的 who,但当动词的主语指人或人们时,通常都用 who。

2) 在表达限定性与非限定性关系从句时,关系代词的使用有较严格的限定:

 a. 在非限定性从句中,指人的关系代词必须用 who 或 whom,无论是作主语还是作宾语都如此,而不能使 that,如:

  The astronauts, who are reported to be very cheerful, are expected to land on the moon shortly.

那些据说是兴高采烈的宇航员们可望不久登上月球。

The author of Rebels, *whom I met at a party last week*, *proved to be a well-known journalist*.

我在上周聚会上所遇到的《叛逆者》的作者被证明是一位著名的新闻记者。

b. 在非限定性从句中,指事物的关系代词必须用 which,无论是作主语还是作宾语都如此,而不能用 that,如:

The Thames, *which is now clean enough to swim in*, *was polluted for over a hundred years*.

泰晤士河现在已很干净,可以游泳,它曾被污染了一百多年。(起主语作用)

The shed in our garden, *which my father built many years ago*, *has lasted for a long time*.

我父亲很多年前在花园里搭的棚子已经有很长时间了。(起宾语作用)

3) 在关系从句中,当关系代词作介词宾语时,应注意:

a. 指人时,介词后只能跟 whom,如:

He is the man to whom I gave the money.

他就是我给钱的那个男人。

但是,当介词挪到句尾时,可以使用 whom、who 和 that 中的任何一个,如:

She is the woman whom / who / that I gave the money to.

她就是我给钱的那个妇女。

b. 指物时,介词后只能跟 which,如:

This is the pan in which I boiled the milk.

这是我煮牛奶的锅。

但是,当介词挪到句尾时,既可以使用 which,也可以使用 that,如:

This is the pan which/that I boiled the milk in.

这是我煮牛奶的锅。

词汇学习 Word study

1. include (不用于进行时) *vt.*

(1) 包括,包含:

Is service included in the bill?

账单里包含服务费吗?

My job doesn't include making coffee for the boss.

我的工作并不包括给老板煮咖啡。

(2) 把……包括在内:

Please include me in the list.

请把我列在此名单内。

There are four of us in the family, or five if you include the dog.

我们家有 4 口人,如果包括狗的话,则是 5 口。

2. devour *vt.*

(1) 吞噬,吞食:

The dog devoured that piece of meat.

那条狗吞食了那块肉。

She devoured the new book she bought yesterday.

她一口气读完了她昨天买的那本新书。(比喻)

(2) (常用被动式)占有,完全吞没:

She was devoured by jealousy.

她妒火中烧。

3. estimate

(1) *vt.* 估计，评价：

The value of the painting was estimated at several thousand dollars.

这幅画据估价值几千美元。

I estimate that we should arrive at 6 o'clock.

我估计我们会6点到达。

(2) *vi.* (for) 出价，估价：

He has asked three or four building firms to estimate for the repair to the roof.

他已找了三四家建筑公司给估算屋顶修缮费用。

(3) *n.* (of)(可数)估计，评定，估价，出价：

His estimate of the cost was about right.

他对费用的估计大体是对的。

They've got three or four estimates before having their house repaired.

找人修房子前他们找了三四家建筑公司估价。

练习答案 Key to written exercises

1. 关键句型练习答案

A 1 *Why should he be* so disappointed?

2 *Why should you be* so unwilling to change your mind?

3 *Why should there be* so many traffic accidents?

B 1 were 2 were 3 were

C See text.

2. 难点练习答案

A 1 *All of them together*: *all of* + pronoun or noun subject means 'every individual in the group'. *Together* is an adverb emphasizing the unity of the whole group: *All of the letters were posted together. All the children came out of school together.*

Altogether is an adverb of degree meaning 'entirely, absolutely': *The two ideas are altogether separate. I'm not altogether surprised.*

2 We use *the other* to refer to the second of two things or groups: *This (one/book) is red, the other (one/book) is black.*

Else, meaning 'additional, more or different', is especially common after indefinite pronouns: *someone / no one / anyone*, etc.: *Let somebody else do it.* We also use *else* after question words: *Who else is coming? Where else would you like to go?*

3 We use *the least* as an intensifier combining with adjectives to form negative superlatives: *the least able*, *the least intelligent*, etc. In this example, however, *the least* is a quantifier, and means 'the smallest amount of'. As a quantifier *the least* combines with uncountable nouns: *the least opportunity*, *the least money*. It also occurs in the adverb phrase *in the least*, meaning 'in the slightest degree': *I'm not in the least impressed.*

The last means 'the final', as opposed to 'the first', 'the second', etc.: *the last emperor of China*, *the last time I saw you*, *the last person in the room*, etc.

4 *Harm* is either a noun: *harm* meaning 'damage, negative effect': *He means no harm. He does no harm to anyone but himself.* Or it is a verb: *harm* + direct object, meaning 'cause damage to, affect negatively': *Pesticides*

harm the soil.

Hurt is a verb meaning 'cause mental or physical pain': *Remarks like that really hurt*. *I fell and hurt my back*. We can also use it intransitively: *My back hurts*. i.e. It causes me pain.

5 *Glance* (noun) means 'a quick look' which is a deliberate action, using the eyes consciously: *Take a glance at yourself in the mirror*. It is also a verb: *He glanced up*. i.e. He looked up.

Glimpse (noun) is 'a quick involuntary sight': *I caught a glimpse of my reflection in the mirror*. i.e. I saw it fleetingly without intending to. *Glimpse* is also a verb: *I glimpsed him hurrying away*.

6 *Work* is uncountable, the act of working or the product of having worked: *I must do some work*. *My work involves a lot of entertaining*.

Job is countable, either the task that one is paid for: *He has a job in a bank*; or a task that one does or may do: *It's a big job and will take at least two hours*. *He never does any household jobs if he can help it*.

7 *Estimate* (verb) means 'make an informed guess': *estimate the number of pages in this book*, *estimate the time needed to complete a job*, etc.

Calculate means 'make an accurate assessment': *calculate how much time you have spent*, *calculate how many people were there*.

B 1 obtain 2 bought 3 fetch 4 received
5 catch/hear 6 understand

C 1 tell 2 telling 3 say 4 say 5 tell

6 said 7 tell

D 1 made 2 do 3 do 4 made 5 made

6 made 7 do

E 1 You can see *at a glance* that nothing has been done for weeks.

2 There are *at least* thirty people still missing after the floods.

3 We may miss the next bus, but *at any rate* we'll be there before midday.

4 They had to move out of the house as quickly as possible, even if it meant selling it *at a loss*.

5 When the auctioneer came, he offered to buy the vase straight away *at sight*.

6 No more than five people may be carried in this lift *at a time*.

3. 多项选择题答案

1 b 2 c 3 b 4 d 5 c 6 a

7 c 8 a 9 a 10 d 11 b 12 c

Lesson 3
Matterhorn man
马特霍恩山区人

课文详注 Further notes on the text

1. **... by a route which will give them good sport, and the more difficult it is, the more highly it is regarded.**

   by a route 沿着一条路。这里的介词 by 为"沿"、"经"之意。the more difficult ..., the more highly ... 为形容词/副词比较级结构 the more ..., the more ...(越……越……)的典型用法,用来表示两个变化的同时发生。

2. **In the pioneering days ...**

   In the pioneering days 在初创时期。这里指登山运动的初创期。

3. **... the easiest way to the top, because the summit was the prize they sought ...**

   to the top 为介词短语,作 way 的定语,即"到达顶峰的路"。they sought 为定语从句,修饰 prize,其间省略了关系代词 which/that,即"他们所追求的目标"。

4. **It is true that during their explorations they often faced difficulties and danger of the most perilous nature, equipped in a manner which would make a modern climber shudder at the thought, but they did not go out of their way to court such excitement.**

   It 在句子中作形式主语,that 引导的从句(从 that 至 at the thought)作句子的逻辑主语,true 为表语。face 面对,遇到,与

be faced with(面对)相比,前者更强调动作,而后者则更注重状态。equipped in a manner ... at the thought 为过去分词短语,作原因状语,修饰 faced,意即“由于/因为以足以使现代登山者一想起来就胆战心惊的简陋装备武装自己”。at the thought 一想起,承上省略了 of the manner。go out of one's way 特意,想尽办法,如:

He has gone out of his way to offer suggestions.

他想尽办法提出建议。

He went out of his way to be rude to me.

他故意对我无礼。

5. **They had a single aim, a solitary goal—the top!**

就语法而言,a solitary goal 同 the top 均为 a single aim 的同位语。这里使用了语义重复法,以达到加强寓意的目的。破折号引出被强调部分。

6. **Except for one or two places such as Zermatt and Chamonix, which had rapidly become popular, Alpine villages tended to be impoverished settlements cut off from civilization by the high mountains.**

except for 除了,主要用于说明整个基本情况后对细节加以的纠正,因而部分地修正了句中的主要意思。可将其用于句末,也可用于句首。它多用于肯定句中,但偶尔也用于否定句中,其后需用名词或代词,如:

Your composition is good except for a few mistakes here and there.

你的作文很好,除了个别地方有些错误。

Except for your presence, I would be bored.

若没有你在这里,我会感到厌烦的。

The park was not worth seeing except for its zoo.

这公园除动物园外不值得一看。

such as 像……一样。当 such 同 as 分开使用时,如文中 one or two places such as 写作 one or two such places as 时,作用相当于 like(像),表示举例。因此文中的 such as Zermatt and Chamonix 可被视为定语,修饰 places。tend to be . . . ,这里用来表示“往往是……”之意。cut off from . . . mountains 为过去分词短语,作定语,修饰 settlements。cut . . . off from . . . 意为“把……与……隔绝”。

7. **Such inns as there were were generally dirty and flea-ridden; the food simply local cheese accompanied by bread often twelve months old, all washed down with coarse wine.**

Such inns as there were 那里(所有)的小客栈。在此短语中,as 为关系代词,引导定语从句,修饰 inns。the food . . . coarse wine 为 Such inns . . . flea-ridden 的并列句。由于上下文语义明确并且为使句子简练,在该并列句 food 后省略了谓语动词 was。all . . . wine 可视为一个独立结构,表示伴随状况,all 为该独立结构中的逻辑主语。对此句进行分析时,应注意句中标点符号的使用(在两个并列句中使用了分号;第 2 个分句中为逗号)。在第 2 个分句中,accompanied by bread 为分词短语,它与其后表示时间的 often twelve months old 均作定语,置后修饰 cheese。

8. **Often a village boasted no inn at all, and climbers found shelter wherever they could—sometimes with the local priest (. . .), sometimes with shepherds or cheese-makers.**

boasted no inn at all 根本没有客栈。wherever 为连词,引导地点状语从句。为使句子更为简练和避免重复,在 they could 后省略了 find shelter,意即“在任何能找到住宿的地方”。sometimes with . . . , sometimes with . . . 有时同……住在一起,有时则同……住在一起。插入语,用来对前文作进一步解释。

9. Invariably the background was the same: dirt and poverty, and very uncomfortable.

dirt and poverty, and very uncomfortable 为 the same 的同位语。

10. For men accustomed to eating seven-course dinners and sleeping between fine linen sheets at home, the change to the Alps must have been very hard indeed.

accustomed to ... at home 为过去分词短语,在句子中作定语,修饰 men。be accustomed to (doing sth.)习惯(做某事),如:

Let the child get accustomed to her new teacher.

让孩子习惯她的新老师。

They got accustomed to taking long walks.

他们习惯了长途步行。

在 accustomed 之后,也可以使用动词不定式,如:

She was not accustomed to be away from home for so long.

她不习惯离家这么久。

The child was accustomed to have her own way.

这孩子任性惯了。

eating seven-course dinners 和 sleeping between fine linen sheets at home 为 accustomed to 后的两个并列的动名词短语。the change to the Alps 变换成阿尔卑斯山山区的生活条件。这里的 change 为名词。无论作为动词还是作为名词使用(如文中那样),表达此意时,该词同 to 的搭配使用不变,如:

The meeting has been changed to Monday.

会议已改为星期一举行。

During the night the rain changed to snow.

在夜间,雨变成了雪。

语法 Grammar in use

关系代词、关系副词及关系从句 (2)

1. 关系副词与关系从句

在表示时间、地点和原因的关系从句中,可以用 when、where 和 why 取代关系代词。它们可被用来代替像 the time、the place 和 the reason 这样的词,如可以说 the time when、the place where 和 the reason why,但不能说 the way how。在使用中,when 只能用于表示时间的名词之后,如 day、occasion、season 等;where 只能用于表示地点的名词之后,如 house、place、town 等;而 why 一般只跟在名词 reason 之后,如:

1981 was the year when my daughter was born.

1981 年是我女儿出生的那一年。

This is the place where I grew up.

这是我生长的地方。

That's the reason why he dislikes me.

那就是他不喜欢我的原因。

它们同样可用于非限定性关系从句中,如:

1981, the year when my daughter was born, was the happiest year for me.

1981 年,对我来说是最幸福的一年,我的女儿在那一年出生。

The small town, the place where I grew up, has been a famous tourist attraction.

我在那个小镇长大成人,它现在已是著名的旅游胜地。

My success in business, the reason why he dislikes me, has been due to hard work.

他因为我事业有成而不喜欢我,但那是我努力工作的结果。

应注意的是,在由 when、where 和 why 引导的限定性关系从句中,可以使用关系代词 that 替代。

2. 关系从句的其他一些重要用法

(1) 当被修饰词为 all、anything、everything、a few、the only one 等,并用来指物时,其后的关系代词通常使用 that(而不是 which),如:

All that remains for me to do is to say goodbye.

剩下我所要做的就是告辞了。

Everything that can be done has been done.

能做的都做了。

但这些词被用来指人时,其后仍需使用 who。

(2) 当被修饰词为形容词最高级形式时,其后的关系代词通常使用 that,如:

It's the silliest argument (that) I've ever heard.

这是我听说的最愚蠢的论点。

Bach is the greatest composer that's/who's ever lived.

巴赫是曾有过的最伟大的作曲家。

(3) 在非限定性关系从句中,可以使用表示数量的名词或代词 + of + whom/which 结构表示数量,如:

Both players, neither of whom reached the final, played well.

两个运动员都未进入决赛,但都表现得很好。

The treasure, some of which has been recovered, has been sent to the British Museum.

这些宝藏已送往大英博物馆,其中一些是失而复得的。

(4) 关系代词 which 可以用来指上述的一个句子,而不仅是一个词。这种用法常见于非限定性关系从句中,此时它通常可以用 and this/that 来代替,如:

She married Joe, which (= and this/that) surprised

everyone.

她嫁给了乔,这使大家都感到意外。

词汇学习 Word study

1. try

(1) *vt*. **试,尝试,试用,试验:**

They have tried using another method.

他们已试了另一种方法。

We've tried our best to do the experiment.

我们已竭尽所能做这项实验。

(2) *vt*. **考验,磨练:**

The great danger they were facing was trying their courage.

他们所面临的巨大危险正考验他们的勇气。

This small print really tries my eyes.

这么小的字体让我看起来真费劲。

(3) *vi*. **尝试,试验,试图,努力:**

We must try to solve the problem.

我们必须努力解决这个问题。

Try and finish the work in a week.

要争取一星期内完成这项工作。

She was trying on a new hat.

她正在试戴一顶新帽子。

You ought to try out the radio before you buy it.

你买这台收音机以前应该试试。

(4) *n*. **(可数)尝试:**

Let me have a try at it.

让我试一试。

2. seek (sought)

(1) *vt*. 寻找,追求,在……中搜索:

They are seeking solutions to the children's psychological problems.

他们正在寻求解决儿童心理问题的方法。

The police are trying hard to seek the truth of the case.

警方正努力寻找这一案件的真相。

(2) *vt*. 征求,要求:

You should seek advice from your lawyer on this matter.

你应当就此问题征求一下你的律师的意见。

(3) *vt*. 自然地移动:

Water seeks its own level.

水自然往下流。

(4) *vi*. 寻找,探索:

They are seeking to reduce the use of water.

他们在寻找减少用水的方法。

He is seeking hard for the answer.

他在努力寻找答案。

He sought out the man who had saved the little child.

他找到了那个救了小孩的人。

3. attain (正式)

(1) *vt*. 获得,取得,达到:

They've at last attained their objectives.

他们最终达到了自己的目的。

(2) *vi*. 达到,到达,获得:

The actions he made in the final attained to perfection.

他在决赛中所做的动作达到了完美的境地。

练习答案 Key to written exercises

1. 关键句型练习答案

A 1 The more *expensive petrol becomes*, the less *people drive*.

2 The more *you try to explain*, the worse *your situation becomes*.

3 The sooner *I finish this job*, the better *I shall feel*.

B See text.

C 1 (*Often*) I am (*often*) in such a hurry (*often*), I (*often*) don't (*often*) have time for breakfast (*often*).

2 We (*often*) buy things we (*often*) don't really need (*often*).

3 He is (*often*) sent abroad (*often*) by his firm (*often*).

D 1 It was impossible for them *to avoid getting wet*.

2 It is difficult *to say the right thing when people are grieving*.

3 It is easy for you *to be cheerful about it, but it was my money*.

E 1 I always find it impossible to refuse *such requests*.

2 *Such freedom* must be balanced by personal responsibility.

3 I had not expected to encounter *such difficulty*.

4 *Such films* as were completed at that time were interesting only in terms of photographic technique.

F 1 I am used to *the baby's waking me in the middle of the night*.

2 Do you object to my *opening the window for a little while*?

3 I am looking forward to *seeing you on the 23rd*.

2. 难点练习答案

A 1 *Situation* means 'position': *In your situation, I would have done exactly as you did.*

Case means 'a particular instance': *In a case like this one, the court usually awards custody to the mother.*

2 We do not use either *specially* or *especially* at the beginning of a sentence. To express 'more than usually', either word is possible: *I think you'll find this article specially/especially interesting.*

But *specially*, not 'especially', means 'for a particular purpose': *I had this desk specially made to suit my height.*

And *especially*, not 'specially', means 'in particular': *I* (*especially*) *wanted to see that production of* Taking Sides (*especially*).

3 *Realize* means 'become aware of': *I realized at once what you meant*; or 'be aware of': *I don't think you realize the seriousness of your situation.*

Understand means 'comprehend': *I understand what you mean.*

In these meanings, both verbs are usually stative, and thus are not usually used in progressive (or 'continuous') tenses.

4 Both *except* and *except for* mean 'with the exception of', and are used especially after *every/any/no*-compounds: *Everyone except* (*for*) *you has already signed the photo.*

Only *except for* can be used at the beginning of a sentence: *Except for last year's party, the summer party has always been out of doors.*

And only *except* in front of a prepositional phrase: *Except in his first job, he had always enjoyed what he did.*

5 We pronounce both *coarse* and *course* in exactly the same way.

Coarse means 'rough, not fine': *coarse salt*, *coarsely-chopped onion*, *coarse speech*, *a coarse joke*.

We use *course* to refer to a phase in a meal: *the first course*, *the meat course*, *a sweet course*, etc.

Course also means 'pathway or direction': *the course we have followed*, *a race course*, *the course of a river*, or it means 'a series of lessons': *I've signed up for a course in navigation*.

6 A *house* is a building for one family to live in. (Buildings divided up into flats for more than one family are known as 'blocks of flats' or 'apartment blocks', not 'houses'.)

Their house is only five minutes from the station.

A house or flat becomes a *home* when you refer to it as the place you live in: *Are you going home now? Is your father at home?* or the place you belong to: *Home is where the heart is.*

B 1 They did not *make any special effort to court such excitement*.

2 Please ask him to *move to where he will not cause an obstruction*.

3 The cottage was *remote from the main thoroughfares*.

4 The table is *inconveniently located*.

5 I'll call in *when I am passing from one place to the other*.

6 We must do this exercise *as/in the manner* we have been taught.

3. 多项选择题答案

1	c	2	a	3	b	4	d	5	a	6	c
7	d	8	a	9	b	10	a	11	c	12	d

Lesson 4
Seeing hands
能看见东西的手

课文详注 Further notes on the text

1. **Several cases have been reported in Russia recently of people who can read and detect ...**

   of people who can ... walls 为介词短语,作定语,修饰主语 cases,即 Several cases of people who ... walls。由于这一定语过长,这样的语序排列使句子显得头重脚轻,为使全句保持平衡,把这一作定语的介词短语放到了全句之后。介词 of 在句中表示"关于"。

2. **... an eleven-year-old school girl, Vera Petrova, who has normal vision but who can also perceive things with different parts of her skin, and through solid walls.**

   Vera Petrova 为 girl 的同位语。who 为关系代词,引导一个非限定性定语从句。and through solid walls 就语法而言与 with different parts of her skin 一样,并列作状语,修饰 perceive。

3. **Suddenly she asked her father why he kept so many old newspapers locked away there, and even described the way they were done up in bundles.**

   kept so many old newspapers locked away there 为 to keep sth. done 的典型用法。在此结构中,done(动词的过去分词形式)即文中 locked away there,为宾语 sth. 即文中 so many old newspapers 的补足语。they were done up in bundles 为定语从句,修饰 way,其间省略了关系代词 that。way 作先行词时,

其后定语从句前的关系代词通常可以省略。do . . . up 此短语根据上下文可表达多种意义，本文中表示“捆”、“包”之意，再如：

They received several presents done up in shiny paper.

他们收到了好几份用亮闪闪的纸包扎起来的礼物。

此外，还可以用来表达“把……扣/扎好”、“把……收拾好”、“使……打扮好”、“使……破产”等含义，如：

This skirt does up at the back.

这条裙子是从后面扣的。

She did her hair up in a bun.

她把头发盘在头上。

Miss Ann came to the party all done up in her best dress.

安小姐穿着最好的衣服来参加聚会。

I've been done up by that dirty trick.

我被那个卑鄙的诡计弄得倾家荡产。

4. Vera's curious talent was brought to the notice of a scientific research institute . . .

bring . . . to the notice of sb. 使……引起某人注意，如：

He brought it to my notice.

他提醒我注意那件事。

The quality of his reports brought him to the notice of his superiors.

他的报告水平很高，引起了上级对他的注意。

The protests in the local newspaper brought the matter to official notice.

地方报纸上的抗议文章促使官方注意到这件事。

5. . . . stranger still, by moving her elbow over a child's game of Lotto she was able to describe the figures and colours printed on it; . . . wearing stockings and slippers, to make out with

her foot the outlines and colours of a picture hidden under a carpet.

stranger still 更为奇怪的是,插入语,促使读者对下文更加注意。by moving . . . of Lotto(通过)在儿童玩的“罗托”纸牌上挪动肘部,介词短语,作方式状语,修饰 was able to describe。printed on it 在它上面印着的,过去分词短语,作定语,修饰 figures and colours。wearing stockings and slippers(在)穿着长筒袜和拖鞋(时),现在分词短语,作时间状语,修饰 make out。承上,在 make out 前省略了 she was able。为保持句子的平衡,将正常语序时应置后的方式状语(with her foot)提到了 make out 的宾语 the outlines and . . . carpet 之前。在该宾语中,hidden under a carpet 为过去分词短语,作定语,修饰 picture。make out 可以用来表示多种意义,但本文中为“辨认出”之意,再如:

I can't make out his handwriting.

我认不出他的字迹。

It was dark, and we could not make out who was coming along the road.

天黑了,我们看不出走在路上的是谁。

6. . . . and, indeed, except when blindfold she lacked . . .

when 与 blindfold 之间省略了 she was。在某些从句中,从句中的主语与主句中的主语相一致且从句主语的谓语为系动词时,可将从句中的主语和其后的系动词省略(如文中形式)。except 除……以外,介词,用于表示将一个或几个特殊的人或物从同一类或者普遍的种类中除去,即意味着从整体里“减去”一部分,即所说的道理或叙述的事实不能适用于该部分。此介词后可使用多种语句成分,包括像文中那样,使用从句,如:

None of us had money, except Tom.

除汤姆外，我们都没带钱。(*except* 后为名词)

We looked for him everywhere except in the bedroom.

除寝室外，我们到处去找过他。(*except* 后为介词短语)

Mary did nothing except clean the dishes.

玛丽除了洗盘子外没干别的事。(*except* 后为省略了 *to* 的动词不定式短语)

Nothing remains for us to do, except to sort up the letters.

除了把信件分分类外，我们没什么事可干了。(*except* 后为带 *to* 的动词不定式短语)

He is a good student except that he is occasionally careless.

他是个好学生，只是偶尔粗心。(*except* 后为 *that* 从句)

He never came except when (he was) in trouble.

除非遇到了困难，否则他决不会来。(*except* 后为 *when* 从句)

I know nothing about the accident except what I read in the paper.

除了我在报上看到的内容外，我对那一事件就再一无所知。(*except* 后为 *what* 从句)

7. ... this ability ceased the moment her hands were wet.

the moment her hands were wet 她的手一湿。the moment 作连词使用，相当于 as soon as(一……就……)。

语法 Grammar in use

被动语态 (1)

1. 主动语态与被动语态

主动语态和被动语态都指动词的形式而言。当句子中表示人或物的主语为动词所表示的动作的施动者时，应用主动语态来

表达,如:

John cooked the food last night.

约翰昨天晚上做了饭。

当句子中表示人或物的主语为动词所表示的动作的受动者时,用被动语态来表达,如:

The food was cooked last night.

饭是昨天晚上做的。

2. 被动语态的构成

被动语态的基本构成形式是:主语 + be 动词(相应的一种时态形式) + 动词的过去分词 + (by + 施动者)。在此结构中,be 动词由于时态及情态助动词等的使用而产生不同的形式;by + 施动者的使用情况则根据文体、语境、习惯等来确定。被动语态的构成形式例示如下:

(1) 时态不同,如:

The food is/was/has been /will be + cooked.

The food is/was being + cooked.

(2) 在含情态助动词的句子中,如:

The food can/may/must be + cooked.

The food can/may/must have been + cooked.

(3) 在动词不定式中,如:

The food is to be/was to be + cooked.

3. 使用被动语态的场合

(1) 被动语态的自然使用与有意使用

在通顺的英语中,被动语态通常被自然而然地使用,有时有些句子很难用主动语态来表达,如:

The origin of the universe will probably never be explained.

宇宙起源问题大概永远不会有答案。

Rome was not built in a day.

罗马不是一天建成的。

当说话人不愿就行为、意见或自己不大肯定的事情表态时，会有意选用被动语态，如：

This matter will be dealt with as soon as possible.

这件事将会尽快处理。

(2) 被动语态的侧重点所在

当说话人侧重点在所发生的事件、认为不必提到行为的主体或避免使用不明确的词（如 someone、a person 等）时，通常使用被动语态，如：

Our roof was damaged in last night's storm.

我家的房顶在昨夜的暴风雨中被毁坏了。

My car's been scratched!

我的车被划了！

Thousands of beaches are polluted.

成千上万处海滩被污染了。

After my talk, I was asked to explain a point I had made.

我发言后，有人要我就我的一个论点加以解释。

(3) 被动语态结构中 by + 施动者结构的使用

当说话人特别强调动作的施动者，即强调有关事件的责任人或物时，通常在被动语态的句子中使用 by + 施动者结构，如：

The window was broken by the boy who lives opposite.

窗子被住在对面的那个男孩打破了。

The window was broken by a stone.

窗子被一块石头打破了。

(4) 被动语态在含 say、believe 等动词的句子中的使用

当说话人对所要陈述的事实没有确切把握而需要把话说得谨慎些时，通常将被动语态用于 it + 被动语态 + that 从句、there + 被动语态 + to be + 补足语或主语 + 被动语态 + to 动词不定

式结构中，如：

It is feared that many lives have been lost in the train crash.

恐怕有不少人在这次列车碰撞事故中丧生。

There is said to be plenty of oil off our coast.

据说我国沿海有大量的石油。

Turner was considered to be a genius even in his lifetime.

特纳生前已被认为是个天才。

(5) 被动语态常用于布告、通告、新闻报道、标题、广告、通知、科技文章等文体之中，如：

Passengers are requested to remain seated until the aircraft comes to a complete stop.

在飞机完全停稳前，请乘客不要离开座位。

The search for the bank robbers continues. Meanwhile, many people have been questioned and the owner of the stolen getaway car has been traced.

搜查银行抢劫犯的工作继续进行。同时，已有许多人被查问，抢劫犯逃跑时所盗的汽车的车主已经找到。

ALL GOODS GREATLY REDUCED!

各种货物大减价！

TRADE AGREEMENTS BROKEN!

贸易协议遭到破坏！

The mixture is placed in a crucible and is heated to a temperature of 300℃. It is then allowed to cool before it can be analysed.

将混合物放入坩埚，加热至摄氏 300 度，冷却后始可分析。

词汇学习 Word study

1. perceive（正式，不用于进行时） *vt.*

(1) 察觉，发觉，看见，看出：

On entering his house, we at once perceived him to be a man of taste.

一进他的房子，我们即刻感觉到他是一个有品味的人。

They perceived that they were unwelcome and left.

他们察觉到自己并不受欢迎，于是就离开了。

We were unable to perceive where the problem lay.

我们看不出问题出在哪里。

I perceived a small trickle of blood coming from the patient's ear.

我发现一小滴血从病人的一只耳朵中流出。

(2) 领悟，理解：

He gradually perceived that his friends had been right.

他逐渐领悟到他的朋友们是对的。

2. describe *vt.*

(1) 描写，叙述：

The woman described the accident in detail.

那个女人详细地描述了那场事故。

Can you describe what he did next?

你能描述一下他接下来做什么了吗？

(2) 形容，把……描绘成：

He described himself as a doctor.

他自称是个医生。

I'd describe the house as run-down.

我会说那座房子破旧不堪。

(3) 作图，描(轮廓)：

He has described a circle with a pair of compasses.

他用圆规画了个圆。

3. concern

(1) *vt*. (不用于进行时)涉及,影响到,对……有重要意义:

This problem concerns everyone.

这个问题涉及所有的人。

(2) *vt*. (不用于被动语态)关于:

The film concerns a woman who goes to China as a missionary.

这部影片是关于一个去中国传教的女人的故事。

(3) *vt*. 担心,忧虑,挂念:

His headaches concern me.

他的头痛令我担忧。

(4) *vt*. 忙于,从事,关心:

He concerned himself with every aspect of the business.

他料理买卖的各个方面。

(5) *n*. (不可数)关心的事,与……有关的事,重要的事:

That problem is of no concern to us.

那个问题与我们无关。

That's a matter of the utmost concern.

那是至关重要的事。

(6) *n*. (不可数)担心,忧虑,挂念:

His concern over his mother's illness kept him awake all night.

他因挂念他母亲的病情而彻夜未眠。

(7) *n*. (可数)公司,商行,企业:

There are many business concerns in that region.

那个地区有许多商务公司。

练习答案 Key to written exercises

1. 关键句型练习答案

A See text.

B 1 I asked him *when he bought that car*.

2 I asked him *where he found that book*.

3 I asked him *why he sent a fax*.

4 I asked him *how he knew I was here*.

5 I asked him *which one he liked best*.

C 1 getting 2 arriving 3 trying 4 persuading

D 1 could 2 could 3 was able to

4 was able to 5 was able to

2. 难点练习答案

A 1 *Normal* means 'standard, exactly as you'd expect': *He grew up in a normal household, just a normal, healthy, reasonably happy child.*

Though *normal* and *ordinary* can seem to be interchangeable, *ordinary* means 'simple, not fancy, not special': *Can I go to the party in my ordinary office clothes? Monday was just like any other ordinary working day.*

2 Both *skin* and *complexion* can be used to refer to the colour and quality of facial skin: *He has an olive complexion/skin*; though *complexion* is the more exact term, and is preferable in formal contexts.

Only *skin* is used to mean 'the outer covering of the body': *The skin ages in response to sunlight.*

3 *Notice* means 'see and become aware of': *Have you noticed that truck at the end of the road?*

Remark means 'comment, say': '*The weather's improved,' she remarked. Remark* meaning 'see' is archaic.

4 An *office* is a room or a building where business is carried out: *I got to the office at nine.*

A *study* is a place in someone's home used for domestic paperwork and private study: *You'll find it on the desk in my study.*

5 A *game* is an activity with rules that people play: *a game of cards, a game of football, a game of chance.* It is also the board and pieces for such an activity: *a game of Monopoly, a board-game.*

A *toy* is an item that someone plays with in his/her own way, and without external rules: *a toy train, a toy car: You can't treat children as if they were toys or dolls and just put them back in the cupboard when you're tired!*

6 *Lack* means 'not have enough': *Lots of children lack the opportunity to learn a foreign language.*

Need means 'require': *How much time will you need?*

7 *Wet* is the opposite of 'dry': *wet weather, wet grass, wet paint,* etc.

Damp means 'very slightly wet', often in a negative or unpleasant way: *a damp house, damp clothes, damp logs that won't burn.*

B 1 tied 2 as good as dead 3 finished

4 decorated it 5 cheated me out of

C 1 numbers 2 shape/outline

3 the shape of the body

D 1 perceive 2 ran away 3 understand him

4 transferred 5 inventing

3. 多项选择题答案

1 a 2 c 3 b 4 a 5 b 6 b

7 c 8 d 9 a 10 a 11 b 12 d

Lesson 5
Youth
青年

课文详注 Further notes on the text

1. People are always talking about 'the problem of youth'.

are always talking about 总是谈论。always 常同进行时态连用表明说话人所说话语中包含的感情色彩(如厌倦等)。

2. If there is one—which I take leave to doubt—then it is older people who create it, not the young themselves.

take leave to do sth. 冒昧做某事,擅自做某事,如:

I take leave to consider the matter settled.

请原谅我认为此事已解决了。

Even if a solid fuel heating system were more economical to run—which I take leave to question anyway—we simply don't have enough space.

尽管固体燃料供热系统用起来更为经济——但恕我冒昧对此质疑——我们根本没有储存的地方。

which I take leave to doubt 前后使用破折号分开,作插入语。take leave to do sth. 为惯用语,leave 后的动词不定式中常用 doubt、question、query 等动词,而作直接宾语的 sth. 常为 it、that 或 story 这类代词或名词。it is ... who ... 为强调句,强调部分为人时也可以用 that 进行连接。not the young themselves,承上省略了 it is 及其后的定语从句(完整部分为:it is not the young themselves who create it)。

3. Let us get down to fundamentals and agree that the young are

after all human beings—people just like their elders.

get down to sth. 认真处理某事,认真做某事。短语中的 to 为介词,因此其后应使用名词、代词或动名词形式,如:

I really must get down to my studies, I've been lazy too long.

我真得安下心来学习了,我懒散的时间太长了。

When we get down to details, the plan seems possible.

当我们认真研究具体细节时,发现这项计划似乎是可行的。

While the weather's fine, I must get down to repainting the house.

天好了,我得再好好粉刷一下房子。

after all 毕竟,终归,终究。介词短语,在句子中作状语,用来加强语气,多用于肯定句中,如:

After all, he has done something good for you.

他毕竟还是为你做了一些好事。

We all thought that he would fail, but he succeeded after all.

我们都认为他要失败,可是他毕竟还是成功了。

After all it is not so hard as it looks.

它毕竟不像看上去那么难。

people just like their elders 像他们长辈那样的人。这里 people 为 human beings 的同位语,置于破折号之后,起到加强语气的作用。

4. ... and maybe that is where the rub is.

that is where the rub is 这就是问题所在。用来引起对所述内容加以注意的话语,从而形成对所述内容的强调。表示相似意思的短语还有 there's/lies the rub、therein lies the rub、that's the rub、the rub is that、the rub lies in (doing) sth. 等。

如：

There's the rub, for it is a claim that can be neither wholly admitted nor wholly dismissed.

那就是问题之所在，因为它是一个既不能完全接受又不能完全放弃的主张。

5. **... and I would have been very pleased to be regarded as something so interesting as a problem.**

would have been 为虚拟语气用法，表示对过去某事的假定推测。so ... as ... 为固定搭配，表示“像……那样……的”之意。由于 something 为不定代词，因此作定语修饰的形容词 interesting 需放在其后。

6. **For one thing, being a problem gives you a certain identity, and that is one of the things the young are busily engaged in seeking.**

for one thing 首先，用来引出某事的原因，如：

I prefer badminton to squash. It's not so tiring for one thing.

与壁球相比，我更喜欢羽毛球。主要是它没有那么累。

有时构成 for one thing, ..., (and) for another (thing), ... (一则……，再则……)这样的结构，如：

For one thing, he drinks; for another, he likes gambling.

一则他酗酒，二则他喜欢赌博。

being a problem 成/作为一个问题。动名词短语，在句子中作主语。that 为指示代词，指代 being a ... identity。the young are busily engaged in seeking 为定语从句，与 one of the things 之间省略了关系代词 that/which。从句中的 be engaged in 表示“忙于”、“从事于”之意。

7. **They have an air of freedom, and they have not a dreary**

commitment to mean ambitions or love of comfort.

have an/the air of 有……模样,呈现……景象,如:

He has an air of a scholar.

他有学者风度。

She has an air of superiority.

她流露出高人一等的样子。

The town has an air of prosperity.

这座城镇呈现出繁荣的景象。

have a/the/one's commitment to 信奉,有……的责任/义务,如:

They have a sincere commitment to religion.

他们虔诚地信奉宗教。

It has the commitment to each of the contracting states.

它对每一缔约国承担义务。

We have our commitment to pay the bills on time.

我们有如期付账的义务。

8. ... and they have no devotion to material things.

have a/the devotion to 对……具有献身精神。to 为介词,后需使用名词、名词性短语或代词,如:

He has an inflexible devotion to an ideal.

他具有对一种理想坚定不移的献身精神。

They have an unselfish devotion to the development of human welfare.

他们有为增进人类幸福而献身的无私精神。

9. It's as if they were, in some sense, cosmic beings in violent and lovely contrast with us suburban creatures.

as if 好像,似乎。短语连词,如文中那样,当其后引出的方式状语从句所表示的情况不是事实而是主观想像或夸大性的比喻时,其从句中的谓语动词(即 were)需用虚拟语气。in some sense 就某种意义上讲/而言，在文中作插入语使用。in contrast with 与……相比，介词 with 也可用 to 替代，如：

In contrast with / to his brother, he was always considerate in his treatment of others.

与他弟弟相比，他总是能体谅他人。

The white half-length figure stood out plainly in contrast with the dark background.

以黑色背景相衬，白色半身像显得一清二楚。

suburban creatures 为 us 的同位语，对 us 作进一步说明。

10. ... but I do not turn for protection to dreary clichés about respect for elders—as if mere age were a reason for respect.

turn to ... for ... 为……而求助于……，如：

One can always turn to music for comfort.

人们总以听音乐寻求慰藉。

He turned to me for help.

他求我帮忙。

We often turn to this handbook for information.

我们经常查阅这本手册寻找资料。

To him she turns for advice in critical moments.

她在关键时刻总是求助于他。

在本句中，由于 about respect for elders 这一作定语的介词短语使宾语 dreary clichés 太长，故将 for 短语提至该宾语之前，以保持语句的平衡。出于修辞和语气表达的需要，to 及其后的宾语的位置相对比较灵活，如上述最后一例中将 To him 提前至全句之前，是为了对该句宾语部分进行语气上的强调。从句 as if 的单数主语 mere age 后的动词 were 为虚拟语气形式。

11. ... and I will argue with him ...

argue with 同……争论，如：

There is no arguing with him.

和他没什么好争论的。

We were arguing with each other about the justice of the war.

我们刚才在争论这场战争的正义性。

Such people should not be argued with.

不应当和这样的人争论。

当介词 with 后指物时,往往表达“用/以……争论”、“以……方式争论”,如:

He argued with much reason.

他辩论得头头是道。

They are arguing with great heat about the justice of the war.

他们正热烈地争论这场战争的正义性。

语法 Grammar in use

被动语态 (2)

需注意的几点

(1) 及物动词和不及物动词

由于只有及物动词才能构成主语(施动者)+谓语动词+宾语(受动者)结构,即只有及物动词后才能有受动者,因此以受动者作主语的被动语态只能用及物动词构成,如:

Someone found this wallet in the street.

有人在街上捡到了这个钱包。(主动)

This wallet was found in the street.

这个钱包是在街上捡到的。(被动)

在英语中,有许多动词既可以作及物动词,也可以作不及物动词,但在语义上往往略有不同,如:

The door opened.
门开了。(可能是自己开的)
The door was opened.
门开了。(可能是被人打开的)

(2) 人称主语和非人称主语

被动语态的主语可以指物,也可以指人,如:

A letter was written.
信写好了。(指物)
Smith has been sent to California for a year.
史密斯被派到加利福尼亚一年。(指人)

(3) 直接宾语和间接宾语

在双宾语动词如 bring、give 等的后面,通常使用两个宾语:间接宾语和直接宾语。主动语态中的间接宾语与直接宾语都可作被动语态中的主语,如:

Tom gave me (间接宾语) *a pen* (直接宾语).
汤姆给了我一枝钢笔。(主动)
I was given a pen by Tom.
我的钢笔是汤姆给的。(被动)
A pen was given to me by Tom.
汤姆给我的是枝钢笔。(被动)

由于人们往往对人比对物更感兴趣,因此使用人称作主语的句子(如:I was given this pen)比用非人称作主语的句子(如:This pen was given to me)的场合要多。

(4) 状态动词

一般情况下,表示状态的动词不能用于被动语态,如:

I love beans on toast.
我喜欢在烤面包片上加一点儿豆子。(只用于主动语态)

在英语中,有时同一个动词既可以被用作状态动词,也可以被

用作行为动词,但是只有当其作行为动词时才能用于被动语态。以动词 measure 为例:

This desk measures 125 × 60 cms.

这张桌子的尺寸是 125×60 厘米。(状态)

This desk has been measured.

这张桌子的尺寸已经量过了。(行为)

(5) 进行时形式

在被动语态中,常用的只有现在进行时和过去进行时两种形式,如:

He is being interviewed now.

他现在正在接受面试。

He was being interviewed at 10.

他 10 点钟时正在接受面试。

进行时形式在被动语态中可以同情态助动词连用,如:

He may be being interviewed at this very moment.

他此刻也许正在接受面试。

(6) 动名词和带 to 的动词不定式

在被动语态中,可以使用动名词和带 to 的动词不定式结构。由于在英语中一些动词之后使用动名词(短语)作宾语,而在一些动词后使用 to 动词不定式作宾语,因此动名词和带 to 的动词不定式除具有自己的构成形式外,还需根据这些动词的使用来确定,如:

Most people don't like being criticized.

多数人不愿意被批评。

He hates to be criticized.

他不愿意被别人批评。

在介词 on、after 等后,可以使用动名词的被动形式,如:

On/After being informed that her mother was seriously ill, she hurried back to England.

她得知母亲病重,连忙回到英国。

(7) 含被动意义的主动动词

在英语中,有少数主动动词作不及物动词用时其自身就含被动意义(如:This surface cleans easily,实际即意味 This surface is/can be cleaned easily),因此其作不及物动词使用时即可表达出被动意义,如:

These clothes wash well.

这些衣服经洗。

This wine is selling quickly.

这种酒卖得正好。

(8) 常用被动语态的动词

有几个动词多用于被动语态,如 be born、be married、be obliged 等,如:

I'm not obliged to work overtime if I don't want to.

我不想加班就可以不加班。

词汇学习 Word study

1. get down

(1) 写下;咽下:

Have you got his telephone number down?

你记下他的电话号码了吗?

The medicine was so horrible that I could hardly get it down.

那药这么难吃,我几乎无法下咽。

(2) (使)沮丧或情绪低落:

This wet weather is getting me down.

这种潮湿的天气使我打不起精神。

2. agree

(1) *vi.* (with, about, on)(不用于进行时)表示同意,表示赞同,持相同意见:

I agree with you about her latest book.

我赞同你对她最近这本书的看法。

We agreed on a price for the car.

我们同意这车的价格。

We agreed to leave at once.

我们同意马上离开。

It is generally agreed that she is the best tennis player in the country.

人们一般都认为她是国内最好的网球运动员。

(2) *vi.* (to)对……表示赞同:

We'll never get him to agree to it.

我们永远不会使他赞同这件事。

(3) *vi.* (with)相符,一致:

The witnesses' statements just don't agree with each other.

证人们的证词不一致。

(4) *vt.* 接受:

The workers have agreed the company's pay offer.

工人们接受了公司的工资提议。

3. feel (felt)

(1) *vt.* 感到,感觉,觉得:

You won't feel the slightest pain.

你不会感到一点儿疼痛。

I felt the house shaking.

我觉得房子在晃。

He felt himself powerfully attracted to the idea.

他觉得自己完全被那个想法吸引住了。

I felt that I was dying.

我觉得自己快要死了。

(2) *vt.* 触摸:

The doctor has felt my pulse.

医生已经给我号了脉。

I felt her forehead to see if she had a fever.

我抚摸她的前额看她是否发烧。

(3) *link v.* 感觉,感到:

I didn't feel very well this morning.

今天早上我感觉不是很好。

I felt at ease with her.

和她在一起我感到很舒服。

练习答案 Key to written exercises

1. 关键句型练习答案

A He's *always changing* his mind. He *always changes* his arrangements at the last minute.

I'*m always making* mistakes like this. I *always make* a point of asking after his family.

People *are always telling* us about things that are bad for our health. We *always tell* our children to come straight home from school.

Everybody'*s always asking* about you. My father *always asks* how you're getting on.

B Only *the rich* can afford to live in that part of town. He must be *a rich man* to live in that part of town.

Caring for *the sick* requires a special kind of temperament. He had been *a sick man* for years.

Uneven pavements and illegal parking make it difficult for *the blind* to go around safely in our city. *A blind man* will often carry a white stick to warn others that he can't see. They say you should never speak ill of *the dead*. Responding to an anonymous call, the police found *a dead man* in the park.

C 1 You would not like *to be accused* of theft.
2 I was astonished *to be told* that all the tickets had been sold.
3 I expect *to be informed* about it tomorrow.

D 1 It is not very pleasant *having* to write so many letters.
2 *Expecting* others to help you and then *not helping* them in return is hardly commendable.
3 It is very enjoyable *teaching* young children.

E 1 He *delighted* in music/in that/in playing the piano.
2 Can I *interest* you in this idea/in this/in joining us?
3 I wish he wouldn't *persist* in such folly/ in this/ in misbehaving in class.
4 Do you *believe* in such things/ in them/ in trying to change the system?

F 1 He doesn't know. There is*n't any* point in asking him.
2 You'll pass your driving test if you do*n't* make *any* mistakes.
3 I do*n't* have *any* faith in him.

2. 难点练习答案

A 1 We cannot use *than* after *elder*: *John is older than I am*. We cannot use *elder* for things: *Which building is older?*
We use either form when comparing two people: *Who is the older/elder?* We use *elder* in front of a noun when referring to two people in a defined group, such as in a

family: *My elder/older brother is a doctor.*

2 *Agree with*: *I agree with you when you say that something must be done.*

Accept + direct object: *I accept your point that something must be done.*

Agree + *to*-infinitive: *I agreed to go with him.*

But we use a noun clause, not a *to*-infinitive, after *accept*: *I accept that these things happen.*

3 *Between* two: *That daft dog hasn't got much brain between his ears.*

Among more than two: *Monet's work is scattered among the many great art galleries of the world.*

4 *Please* means 'give pleasure': *It pleased me very much to be offered a higher salary.*

Beg means 'ask very earnestly', often followed by a *to*-infinitive: *I beg you to think again.*

Also *beg for*: *The prisoner begged for a visit from his wife.*

5 *Regard* means 'look on, consider to be, believe to be' and is generally followed by *as* + noun or *-ing* phrase: *I regard punctuality as (being) the most basic politeness. Many people regard Mozart as (being) the most perfect composer.*

Look at means 'view': *If you look at the situation from her point of view, you will see things differently. The image changes depending on where you look at it from.*

6 *Be interesting to* often (though not invariably) has an impersonal subject and a personal object: *Art galleries are not very interesting to most children.*

Be interested in often (though not invariably) has a personal subject, and, very likely, an impersonal object: *Most children are not very interested in art galleries*. But note: *Someone of my age is hardly very interesting to a young person like you. Children often become less interested in their grandparents in their teens.*

7 *Exciting*: *Young people are exciting*. (That is the effect they have on others.)

Excited: *The writer is excited by young people*. (That is the effect they have on him.) *Excited* combines with *be*, *get*, *feel*, *become*, etc.: *Now, kids, don't get too excited.*

8 *Reason* means 'explanation, justification'. It is normally followed by *for*: *This is the reason for my asking you in particular*, or by a *that*-clause: *This is the reason that I have asked you in particular*, or by a *to*-infinitive: *This is no reason to quarrel with someone.*

Cause means 'the thing that makes something happen'. It is normally followed by *of*: *These changes are the cause of all this trouble.*

B 1 doing (*getting up to* suggests mischievous activity)

2 overcome

3 move from one place to another

4 recovered from

5 escape penalty

6 be excused from (an unwelcome task)

C 1 It seems *ill-advised* to sell the house now when the market is so depressed.

2 The children should not be out on the moor so

ill-protected from the weather.

3 Blaze was an *ill-tempered* horse with a hard mouth and a tendency to kick.

4 The *ill-fated* fishing boat, the *Sapphire*, went down with the loss of four men.

5 I understand that he didn't mean to be unkind, but I still feel *ill-used*.

6 Jennifer considers the children to be *ill-bred* because they are careless about thanking her for her presents.

7 It was a stupid thing to do, but it was *ill-natured* of them to tell us so.

3. 多项选择题答案

1 c 2 a 3 b 4 a 5 b 6 d

7 a 8 c 9 b 10 b 11 d 12 d

Lesson 6

The sporting spirit

体育的精神

课文详注 Further notes on the text

1. ... and that if only the common people of the world could meet one another at football or cricket, they would have no inclination to meet on the battlefield.

that if only ... or cricket 作 saying 的宾语从句。其中的复合从属连词 if only(只要),根据实际语境和语义的需要,可用来引导真实性条件状语从句,或如文中那样引导非真实性条件状语从句。could meet 和 would have 是用来表示与现在事实不符的虚拟语气结构。if only 的用法如下:

We can surely overcome these difficulties if only we are closely united.

只要我们紧密地团结一致,一定能克服这些困难。(真实性条件状语从句)

If only she had had more money, she would have bought some more new clothes.

她那时如果有更多的钱,她就会再买几件新衣服了。(非真实性条件状语从句)

if only 还常单独使用,用来表示诸如"要是……就"、"但愿……"这类含惋惜、愿望等感情色彩的句子。这样用时多用虚拟语气形式,如:

If only they were still alive!

他们要是还活着多好啊!

If only you had come five minutes earlier!

你要是早5分钟到就好了!

此外,不要将 if only(只要)同 only if(只有在……时)相混淆,比较:

We are sure you will succeed if only you try hard.

我们确信只要你努力必定会成功。

We told him he would succeed only if he tried hard.

我们告诉他只有努力他才能成功。

have no inclination to do sth. 不愿做某事,如:

She has no inclination to be a doctor.

她不愿当医生。

2. Even if one didn't know from concrete examples (the 1936 Olympic Games, for instance) that international sporting contests lead to orgies of hatred, one could deduce it from general principles.

Even if 即使,尽管,纵然。它与 even though 表达的语义一样,均作从属连词引导让步状语从句。even if 多在口语中使用,而 even though 多在比较正式的书面语中使用。one 在此用来泛指人,意即"人们"。orgies of hatred 极度仇恨。deduce ... from 从……中推断出,如:

The police deduced the exact spot where the murder took place from a few abandoned items scattered around.

警方从几件四处丢弃的物件准确推断出了杀人现场。

it 在这里指 that 所引导的宾语从句(即指 international ... hatred)中的内容。

3. Nearly all the sports practised nowadays are competitive.

practised nowadays 为过去分词短语,作定语,修饰 sports。

4. You play to win, and the game has little meaning unless you do your utmost to win.

you 在这里如同前文中的 one 一样,用来泛指人,意即“人们”。to win 为动词不定式,这里作目的状语,用来说明做出 play 动作的目的。have little meaning 没有什么意义,little(没什么,没多少)只能用来修饰不可数名词,表示“基本否定”的含义;它要表达“基本肯定”的含义(一点,些许)修饰不可数名词时,则需前加 a。unless 除非,从属连词,引导条件状语从句。unless 引导一般性条件状语从句或该从句带有“附加”意味时,如文中那样,从句通常置于主句之后,再如:

I won't write unless he writes first.

我不会给他写信的,除非他先给我写信。

想加强该条件状语从句的语气时,也可将其放在主句之前,如:

Unless you go with me, I shall not go.

除非你跟我去,不然我就不去。

此外,有时在 unless 后可以使用省略形式,如:

I shall not go unless invited.

除非接到邀请,否则我是不会去的。

In this article the word is used in its original sense unless otherwise stated.

在这篇文章里,这个词永远是照本义用,除非另有说明。

在第 1 句的 unless 与 invited 之间省略了 I am;在第 2 句的 unless 与 otherwise 之间省略了 it is。应当注意的是,只有当从句中使用的主语同主句中的主语一致而且从句主语后使用的是动词 be 时,才能使用上述省略形式。do one's utmost to do sth. 竭尽全力做某事,如:

We must do our utmost to fulfil the task.

我们必须尽最大努力来完成这一工作。

5. **... where you pick up sides and no feeling of local patriotism is involved, it is possible to play simply for the fun and**

exercise: ...

where 为连接副词,在此用来引导非限定性定语从句,修饰 the village green。pick up sides 在这里用来表示"随意组队"之意。pick up 为 gather together 之意。the fun and exercise,这里将 fun 和 exercise 作为一个整体来看待,因此这两个词前共用一个定冠词 the,再如:

The boys and girls in my class are all fond of sports.

我们班里的男女同学都喜欢运动。

不作为一个整体看待时,通常在每个词前都使用定冠词,如:

Our teacher has made a comparison between the English and the German languages.

我们老师已对英语和德语作了一番比较。

6. At the international level, sport is frankly mimic warfare.

At the international level 在国际水平上。作状语。根据上下文,可如译文中所示,译作"在国际比赛中"。

7. But the significant thing is not the behaviour of the players but the attitude of the spectators: and, behind the spectators, of the nations who work themselves into furies over these absurd contests, and seriously believe—at any rate for short periods—that running, jumping and kicking a ball are tests of national virtue.

is not ... but ... 不是……而是……,并非……而是……。spectators 后所使用的冒号表明其后为表示说明、解释或引申的内容。behind the spectators 为介词短语,作定语,修饰 the nations。按照正常语序形式应为:the nations behind the spectators who work ...,即作定语的介词短语应放在被修饰词之后。这里将其提前,一是使 the nations 之后由 who 引导的定语从句同被修饰词 the nations 保持更紧密的关系,二是对该介词短语起到强调的作用,并使全句有更好的平衡感。

此外,起承上作用,在 the nations 前省略了 the attitude,意即“观众背后隐含的国家的态度”。动词 work 在这里被用来表达“使逐渐进入某种状态”之意。表达此含义时,动词 work 后通常使用 *adj*./*adv*./*prep*. 或宾语 + *adj*./*adv*./*prep*. 结构,如:

This little screw has worked (itself) loose.

那个螺丝钉逐渐松了。

He worked himself into a temper.

他越憋火气越大。

They're gradually working round to our point of view.

他们逐渐赞同了我们的观点。

动词 work 和 believe 作 who 引导的定语从句中的并列谓语。at any rate for short periods 至少在短期内。在文中作插入语使用。介词短语 at any rate 用来表达“在任何情况下”、“无论如何”之意,如:

At any rate we can go out when it stops raining.

不管怎样,只要雨一停我们就可以出去了。

that running, ... national virtue 为跟随在动词 believe 后的宾语从句。

语法 Grammar in use

条件状语从句 (1)

1. if 条件句概说

条件是指某一事情完成之后其他事情始能发生。条件状语从句多由从属连词 if 引导。if 引导的条件状语从句不是用来指已经发生的事件,而是用来指能够发生、可能发生或可能发生过的事件。有时这一事件发生的可能性很大,如:

If the price of oil comes down, more people will buy it.

如果油价下跌，就会有更多的人购买。

有时事件是没有或不可能发生的，如：

If my horse had won, I would have made a lot of money.

如果我的马赢了，我早就会赚到许多钱了。

2. 条件句的类型

根据事件有无发生的可能性以及发生的可能性的大小，可以将条件句分为两个类型：真实性条件状语从句和非真实性/虚拟条件状语从句。

3. 真实性条件状语从句的基本结构

真实性条件状语从句最常用的结构是：if + 现在时从句 + 现在将来时主句，如：

If it rains, we'll stay at home.

如果下雨，我们将呆在家里。

应当注意的是，在这一结构中，if 从句中的"现在时"包括所有现在时态，如一般现在时、现在进行时、现在完成时以及现在完成进行时，如：

If he is standing in the rain, he will catch cold.

如果他站在雨里，他会感冒的。

If she has arrived at the station, she will be here soon.

如果她已经到了车站，她很快就会到这儿来。

If he has been travelling all night, he will need a rest.

如果他走了一整夜，他就需要休息一下。

主句中的"现在将来时"包括其他现在将来时，如一般现在将来时、现在将来进行时以及现在将来完成进行时，如：

If he gets the job, he'll be going abroad.

如果他得到那个工作，他就要到国外去了。

If I stay till May, I'll have been working here for 20 years.

如果我呆到 5 月，我在这儿工作就满 20 年了。

4. 真实性条件状语从句的其他表现形式

(1) if + 现在时从句 + 含情态助动词的主句

主句中的 will 用来表达肯定如此或几乎肯定如此。如果觉得其肯定程度达不到使用 will 的程度,或者如果想表达例如“必要”的意思,就可以使用情态助动词来代替 will,如:

If it's fine tomorrow, we { *can* (可以) / *could* (能够) / *may* (可能) / *might* (可能) / *should* (宜于) / *ought to* (宜于) / *must* (必须) } *go out.*

如果明天天气好,我们 { can (可以) / could (能够) / may (可能) / might (可能) / should (宜于) / ought to (宜于) / must (必须) } 出门。

进行时和完成时可以同上述情态助动词连用,如:

If I hear from Tim, I may be leaving tonight.

如果我收到了蒂姆的信,我可能今晚就离开。

If he is in New York, he may not have got my letter yet.

如果他在纽约,他就可能还没收到我的信。

(2) if + 含 should 的从句 + 用祈使语气等的主句

If you (should) happen to see him,

如果你碰巧见到他,

Should you happen to see him,

如果碰巧你见到他,

} *please give him my regards.*

请代我向他问好。

if 从句中含有 should 时,则增加了条件的不确定性。此种结构更常用于想礼貌地提出要求或建议或想委婉地告诉人该做什么的时候,如:

If you should write to her, send her my love.

如果你给她写信,请代我向她致意。

If you should go to Nairobi, go and see the Snake Park.

如果你去内罗毕,你可以到蛇园去看看。

此外，用 should 开头的句子可以不用 if 而表示条件，但这种用法比较正式，常用于诸如公函之中，而不用于日常会话中，如：

Should you not wish our agent to call, please let us know.

若不希望我们的代理人造访，请告知。

Should you be interested in our offer, please contact us.

若对我们的报价感兴趣，请与我们联系。

(3) 用祈使语气的从句＋连词＋主句

当所要表达的内容比 if 从句表示的更为紧迫时，往往可以使用祈使句作为条件状语从句，并根据上下文的含义用连词 and、or、or else 或 otherwise 连接该从句和主句。这种结构常用于提出要求、缔结协议、提供建议或进行威胁等，如：

Provide the materials and we'll do the job.

提供材料，我们就做这活。(要求)

Put that down, or (else) I'll smack you.

把它放下，不然我就揍你。(威胁)

Be there on time, otherwise you'll create a bad impression.

要准时到那儿，否则你会给人一个坏印象。(建议)

词汇学习　Word study

1. arise (arose, arisen)　*vi.*

(1) (旧用法或多用于诗意语言中)起身，起床：

She arose with difficulty from her seat.

她艰难地从座位上站起来。

(2) (from, out of) 出现，呈现，发生：

Some unexpected difficulties have arisen.

出现了一些未料到的困难。

They are discussing the matters arising from the recent

changes.

他们正在讨论由于近来的变化而产生的一些问题。

2. arouse *vt*.

(1)(正式)唤醒:

We aroused her from her deep sleep.

我们将她从熟睡中唤醒。

(2)引起,唤起,激起:

Her behaviour aroused the suspicions of the police.

她的行为引起警方的怀疑。

3. know (knew, known)(不用于进行时)

(1) *vt*. 知道,了解,熟识:

I don't know his phone number.

我不知道他的电话号码.

I know that he is a liar.

我知道他是个骗子。

Do you know what he is looking for the whole morning?

你知道他一上午都在找什么吗?

I know the hostess well.

我与女主人很熟。

(2) *vt*. 会,学会,会做:

He has known the poem by heart.

他已熟记下这首诗。

I don't know how to make cookies.

我不会做小甜点。

He knows French, Spanish and Italian.

他会说法语、西班牙语和意大利语。

(3) *vt*. (from)能识别,区分:

I'd know him if I saw him again.

我再见到他一定能认出他来。

He is old enough to know right from wrong.
他早到了能辨识好坏的年龄了。

(4) *vi*. 知道,了解:

Do you know his name?
你知道他叫什么吗?
I don't know.
我不知道。

(5) *vi*. (of,about) 听说:

Do you know about any good restaurant in this neighbourhood?
这儿附近你听说过有什么好餐馆吗?

练习答案 Key to written exercises

1. 关键句型练习答案

A 1 you will probably play with a lot of aggression
  2 go out every evening, we would go to our favourite restaurant
  3 had more time
  4 practise every day

B 1 makes 2 stop 3 arrives 4 stops 5 move

C See text.

2. 难点练习答案

A 1 *Hear* means 'receive sounds through your ears': *Speak up! I can't hear what you're saying.*
  Listen means 'give attention while hearing': *I like listening to jazz.*
  2 We use *even* (adverb) to express something unexpected or surprising: *Even the younger children enjoyed the concert, so I'm sure the older ones did too.*

Still (adverb) means 'up to now and at this moment': *She's still watching the film, so I suppose she's enjoying it.* It can also mean 'in spite of that', as in: *I know he's admitted putting the money back, but that still doesn't explain how it came to be missing in the first place.*

3 The verb *lead* means 'go first and show the way': *She led us to the small church by the lake.*

The verb *guide* means 'go with someone to show them the way and explain things': *The woman guided us around the big house.*

4 *Principle* and *principal*: these two nouns are pronounced exactly the same, but the meanings are completely different.

A *principle* is a basic rule: *It's one of my principles never to lend my car to anyone.*

A *principal* is the head of a school or college: *He has just become principal of the local college.*

The adjective *principal* means 'highest in importance, chief, main', as in: *His principal source of income comes from acting.*

5 The words *practise* and *practice* are often confused. They are both pronounced in the same way.

However, in British English, *practise* is the verb, and *practice* is the noun: *He practises the piano for two hours a day. The basketball practice lasted two hours.*

In American English, *practice* is both a noun and a verb.

6 In the context of sport, you can *win* a game, a match, a competition, a prize, etc.: *Our team won a silver cup.*

Beat means 'defeat, or do better than' an opponent: *She*

always beats me at chess.

Look: Our team *beat* the best team in France to *win* the competition.

However, *win* (not *beat*) can also be used intransitively: *Who won? Tottenham won*.

7 *Lose* (/luːz/) is a verb which means, in the text, 'not win': *Our football team lost again last Saturday*.

Loose (/luːs/) is an adjective which means 'not firmly fixed': *The screws holding the shelf brackets are very loose. Can you tighten them?*

8 *Arise* is an intransitive verb meaning 'happen, occur, come into being': *An unexpected difficulty has arisen which will necessitate a change of plan*.

Arouse is a transitive verb meaning 'cause to become active': *The children's behaviour at the back of the class aroused the curiosity of the teacher*. (*Arouse* meaning 'wake someone up' is very formal.)

9 A *level* is a position of height in relation to a flat surface, literally or figuratively: *The top of the mountain is at least a kilometre above sea level. This question will have to be discussed at the highest level*.

As a noun, and compared with *level*, *flat* means 'ground level': *That horse is a good runner on the flat*.

B The word *people* can be used in two ways.

As a plural noun it means 'persons, human beings': *Most people seem to like her*.

However, as a countable noun, a *people* means 'a race, a nation' — so plural *peoples* in the sentence means 'races, nations'.

There were about 600 *people* at the concert.

If only the *peoples* of the world all spoke the same language!

C 1 the four o'clock train 2 the 1937 edition

3 The 1944 Education Act 4 The 1917 revolution

D *One* and *you* can both be used as an indefinite pronoun meaning 'everyone/anyone' in general statements.

One is formal, while *you* is informal and preferred in everyday speech.

One might try to discover more about the project before investing money.

Whichever supermarket you go into nowadays, you'll find basically the same things.

E 1 for enjoyment 2 pleasure, amusement

3 without meaning any harm 4 laughed at/ridiculed

3. 多项选择题答案

1 c 2 a 3 c 4 c 5 c 6 a

7 a 8 a 9 d 10 b 11 a 12 a

Lesson 7
Bats
蝙蝠

课文详注 Further notes on the text

1. **Not all sounds made by animals serve as language, and we have only to turn to that extraordinary discovery of echo-location in bats to see a case in which the voice plays a strictly utilitarian role.**

Not all sounds made by animals 并非动物发出的所有声音。在此短语中 made by animals 为过去分词短语，作定语，修饰 sounds。多数情况下 not 与 all 的搭配使用被视为部分否定结构，诸如 every、both、always 等词也可这样使用，如：

Not every one can make music.

并非所有的人都能创作音乐。

The good and the beautiful do not always go together.

善和美的东西并非总连在一起。

但是，在现代英语里，它们有时也被用来表示全部否定的含义，因此在使用中，要根据上下文来确定其确切的含义，比较：

All men can't be first.

不能人人都是第一。(部分否定)

All the blind cannot see.

瞎子都看不见什么东西。(全部否定)

All that glitters is not gold.

闪闪发光之物未必全是真金。(部分否定)

All that come from eggs are not mammals except the

platypus.

除鸭嘴兽外,一切卵生的都不是哺乳动物。(全部否定)

serve as 作为,用作,如:

He has served the company for fifty years, first as office boy and eventually as managing director.

他为公司干了 50 年,最初当勤杂工,最终当上了管理部门的经理。

One room had to serve as both bedroom and living room.

一间屋子只能既作寝室又作起居室使用。

turn to 求助于,如:

They had to turn to the villagers for advice.

他们不得不向村民们求助。

He has given up at last and turned to the dictionary for help.

他最后不得不放弃,转而求助于词典了。

see ... role 为动词不定式短语,在句子中作目的状语。在此短语中,关系连词 which 引导一个定语从句,修饰 case。定语从句中的 play a role in 意为"在……方面起作用",如:

The local police played an important role in settling the regional conflict.

当地警察在解决地区冲突中起了重要的作用。

2. To get a full appreciation of what this means ...

get ... means 为动词不定式,在句中作目的状语。按正常语序应放在句尾,现提前置于句首,起到强调和承上启下的作用。what this means 为名词性从句,作介词 of 的宾语,其中的指示代词 this 指代上段中的 we have to turn to ... a strictly utilitarian role。

3. Everyone knows that if he shouts in the vicinity of a wall ...

that 在此引导一个宾语从句,在此宾语从句中使用了一个由 if

引导的条件状语从句。in the vicinity of 在……附近，如：

Are there any shops in our vicinity?

我们附近有商店吗？

All the ships in the vicinity of the crash joined in the search for survivors.

失事附近的所有船只都加入到对幸存者的搜寻之中。

4. **The further off this solid obstruction, the longer time will elapse for the return of the echo.**

The further off ..., the longer time ...，是由定冠词 the + 形容词（或副词）比较级 + 定冠词 the + 形容词（或副词）比较级形式的特殊使用方法，表示具有因果关系的"越……，越……"的含义，即当一方有变化时另一方也随之变化，如：

The more money you make, the more you spend.

你钱赚得越多，你花得就越多。

The more expensive petrol becomes, the less people drive.

汽油越贵，车就开得越少。

由于语义明确，本句的 obstruction 之后省略了 is。for the return of the echo 为介词短语，在本句中作定语，修饰 time。按正常结构，作定语的介词短语应紧随被修饰词，即 the longer time for the return of the echo ...。这里用较短的谓语动词将其分开，主要是出于修辞的需要，使句子保持平衡。

5. **So was born the echo-sounding apparatus, now in general use in ships.**

本句按正常语序应为：The echo-sounding apparatus was so born, ...这里使用倒装语序，一是出于修辞的需要，使句子不至于显得头重脚轻，二是对方式状语 so 进行强调，再者起到使本句同上文连接得更为紧凑的作用。in general use 普遍使用。这里作 apparatus 的非限定性定语。

6. **Every solid object will reflect a sound, varying according to the**

size and nature of the object.

varying according to ... the object 为现在分词短语,在句子中作方式状语,修饰动词 reflect。

7. **So it is a comparatively simple step from locating the sea bottom to locating a shoal of fish.**

from locating ... a shoal of fish 中,介词 from 与 to 在一起搭配使用,表示"从……到……"之意。由 locating 构成的两个短语为动名词短语,分别作介词 from 和 to 的宾语。

8. **With experience, and with improved apparatus, it is now possible not only to locate a shoal but to tell if it is herring, cod, or other well-known fish, by the pattern of its echo.**

it is now possible ... 中,it 为形式主语,并列连词 not only ... but also ... 后跟随的两个动词短语 to locate a shoal 和 to tell ... 为句子中的逻辑主语。动词 tell 后的 if 引导一宾语从句。这里 if 表达"是否"之意。介词短语 by the pattern of its echo 在句中作方式状语,修饰动词 locate 和 tell,其前的逗号用来将它同 if 从句分隔开,用以说明它是用来修饰 locate 和 tell 的成分,而不是属于 if 从句的成分。

9. **It has been found that certain bats emit squeaks and by receiving the echoes, they can locate and steer clear of obstacles—or locate flying insects on which they feed.**

本句为先行词 it 的使用方法。it 为形式主语,而由 that 引导的从句(即从 that 至全句尾)为句子的逻辑主语。steer clear of 回避,避开,为口语用法,如:

I should steer clear of the fish stew; it's not very nice!

我可不吃焖鱼那道菜,并不特别好吃!

You'd better steer clear of all those doubtful questions.

你最好回避所有那些可疑/含糊的问题。

feed on 靠……生活,以……为食物,如:

What does this bird feed on?

这种鸟吃什么?

Sheep feed mostly on grass.

羊以食草为主。

句中的关系代词用来引导定语从句。

10. This echo-location in bats is often compared with radar, the principle of which is similar.

compare ... with ...用来表达“将……同……相比较”以发现其异同之处。注意它与 compare ... to ...在语义上的不同,后者用来表示“将……比作……”,用以说明两者之间的相似之处。the principle of which ...为非限定性定语从句,用来对前文作进一步说明。

语法 Grammar in use

条件状语从句 (2)

非真实性条件状语从句

(1) 非真实性条件状语从句的概念

真实性条件状语从句用来谈论“将有可能发生的事情,以及其将来的真实结果”;非真实性条件状语从句则用来谈论:(1)想像中的现在情况,以及推测想像中的将来结果;(2) 纯粹想像中的过去事情,以及想像中的过去将来的结果。

(2) 非真实性条件状语从句的结构

在表达非真实性条件状语从句中,由于(1)和(2)表达的概念不同,因此也就需要使用两种不同的结构:

1) if+一般过去时从句+过去将来时主句,如:

If you went by train, you would get there earlier.

如果你坐火车去,你会早些到那儿的。

If you didn't stay up so late every evening, you

wouldn't feel so sleepy in the morning.

如果你每天晚上睡得不那么晚,你早上不会感到那么困的。

2) if + 过去完成时从句 + 过去将来完成时主句,如:

If I had worked harder at school, I would have got a better job.

要是我上学时勤奋一些,我就会有较好的工作了。

If I had lived in the Stone Age, I would have been a hunter.

要是我生活在石器时代,我就会是个猎人。

从上述头一种情形中可以看出,虽然句子使用了过去时,但是并非指过去的时间;而在后一种情形中,虽然句子使用了过去完成时,但是却指的是过去的时间,即过去从未有过的事情。

(3) 非真实性条件状语从句头一种情形中的其他常见结构

除上述头一种情形中使用的主要结构外,还有以下常见的结构形式:

1) if + 过去时从句 + 含情态助动词的主句

当觉得想像的结果可能性较小的时候,或者指能力、可能性等的时候,可以使用相应的情态助动词的过去式替换主句中的 would,如:

If he knew the facts, he could tell us what to do.

如果他知道真相,他能告诉我们该做什么。(能力)

If he were here, he might help us.

如果他在这儿,他可能帮助我们。(可能性)

If he could get the facts, he ought to/should tell us what to do.

如果他能够弄清真相,他应当告诉我们该做什么。(责任)

2) if I/he/she/it were/was ...

在表述非真实性条件状语从句中,在人称代词 I、he、she、it 等后,无论使用 were 还是 was,它们在语义上都没有区别,只是使用 were 时显得更为正式,如:

If I were/was better qualified, I'd apply for the job.

如果我的条件好一些,我就申请那份工作了。

在陈述纯粹想像的事情时,更常使用 were,如:

If I were the Queen of Sheba, you'd be King Solomon.

如果我是希巴女王,你就会是所罗门国王。

3) if I were sb./in one's position ...

当主语为 I,而主语补语为上述词或短语时,必须使用 were。这种用法经常用于提出建议,如:

If I were you/in your position, I'd accept their offer.

如果我是你,我就接受他们的建议。

If I were Jane/in Jane's position, I'd walk out on him.

如果我是珍妮,我就会离弃他。

4) if it were not for/were it not for ...

上述结构中只能使用 were。该结构通常用来说明为什么某事发生或没发生,如:

If it were/Were it not for your help, I would still be homeless.

若非你的帮助,我仍会无家可归。

(4) 非真实性条件状语从句后一种情形中的其他常见结构

除上述后一种情形中使用的主要结构外,还有以下常见的结构形式:

1) 当觉得设想的结果可能性较小时,或者指能力、可能性等时,可以使用相应的情态助动词的过去式代替主句中的 would,如:

If he had known the facts, he could have told us what to do.

如果他了解情况,他就会告诉我们该怎么办了。(能力)

If he had been here yesterday, he might have told us.

如果他昨天在这儿,他就可能告诉我们了。(可能性)

If he could have got the facts, he should have told us what to do.

如果他了解事实,他就应当告诉我们该怎么办了。(责任)

2) if I had been sb./in one's position ...

上述结构常用来描述站在他人的立场上可能会采取的行动,如:

If I had been you/in your position, I'd have accepted their offer.

如果我是你,我早就接受他们的建议了。

If I had been Jane, I'd have walked out on him years ago.

如果我是珍妮,我几年前就离开他了。

3) if it hadn't been for/had it not been for ...

上述结构用来解释某事为什么在过去没有发生,如:

If it hadn't been for the rain, we would have had a good harvest.

要不是有雨,我们本会获得一个大丰收的。

Had it not been for the unusually bad weather, the rescue party would have been able to save the stranded climber.

要不是有反常的坏天气,抢救小组应能救出那个陷入困境的登山者的。

词汇学习 Word study

1. measure

(1) *n*. (不可数)量度,度量衡制;(可数)度量单位,量度器:

give full/short measure 给足/不足量

a measure of weight 重量单位

The ruler is a metre measure.

这把尺子是米量度器。

(2) *n*.(不可数)程度,范围

beyond measure 过度的

in great/large measure 大部分

(3) *n*.(常用复数)方法,步骤,措施:

They tried hard to take measures to solve traffic problems.

他们尽力采取措施解决交通问题。

(4) *vt*. 量,测量(长度、大小、多少等):

She took out a ruler and measured a piece of cloth.

她拿出一把尺子,量了一块布。

(5) *vt*. 有……长(或宽、高等):

The cloth measures 1.5 metres in length.

这块布长1.5米。

2. vary

(1) *vi*. 变化,不同:

Opinions vary on this point.

在这一点上意见各不相同。

Customs vary with the times.

习惯是随时代变化的。

The charge varied from 10 yuan *to 20* yuan.

费用从10元到20元不等。

(2) *vt*. 改变,变更:

Most old men don't like to vary their habits.

大多数老年人都不愿意改变习惯。

3. mean (meant) *vt.*

(1) 表示(意义),意味着:

What does 'lieben' mean in German?

德语中 lieben 是什么意思?

Does this traffic jam mean we'll be late?

交通堵塞意味着我们要迟到吗?

(2) 意欲,决定:

I didn't know my father meant the present for me.

我不知道父亲是要把那个礼物送给我的。

I meant no harm to you.

我无意伤害你。

(3) 对……重要,有价值:

Your advice means a lot to me.

你的建议对我十分重要。

练习答案 Key to written exercises

1. 关键句型练习答案

A 1 To understand *the play thoroughly, you should really read it first.*

2 To enjoy *a good film, you really need to sit back in comfort in a big armchair.*

3 To succeed *in business, many people think you have to be utterly ruthless.*

B See text.

C 1 The old man was deaf, so I managed to make him understand *by shouting.*

2 *By saving* a small amount of money every week for two years, I was able to buy my first computer.

3 In the small village where I was born, they still tell people when there's a fire *by ringing* the church bell.

D 1 with 2 with 3 for 4 with 5 for
6 for 7 to 8 with

2. 难点练习参考答案

A 1 *Sound* can be countable or uncountable and is something that can be heard: *There was a strange sound coming from the box. Sound waves travel at 340 metres per second in air.*

An *echo* (plural *echoes*) is a sound which is reflected or sent back from a solid surface or object: *I whistled three notes, and a few seconds later the echo came back from the hillside.*

2 A *discovery* is the act of finding something that was already there, but not known about before: *The discovery of gas in the North Sea has been very important to Great Britain.*

An *invention* is the creation of something that did not exist before: *The invention of the ball-point pen has meant that a pen is cheap enough for everyone to buy.*

3 *Appreciation* is understanding the good qualities or the worth of something: *She has a genuine appreciation of modern art.*

Estimation refers to esteem or opinion, and in this sense is usually used in the phrase *in my/his/her estimation*: *In my estimation, he has made a complete fool of himself.*

4 An *obstruction* is something that blocks the path of something else: *The man had to have an operation to remove an obstruction from his throat.*

An *obstacle* is something that prevents action, movement or success: *He has overcome lots of obstacles to get where he is today.*

5 The verb *steer* means 'make a boat or a car, lorry, etc. go in a particular direction': *I'd like you to steer the boat into the berth.*

The verb *drive* means 'be responsible for making a vehicle move in a general direction': *We drove from London to Southampton in an open-topped sports car.*

B 1 by 2 in 3 from 4 of

C 1 *Experience* here (uncountable) is the knowledge or skill which comes from practice.

2 An *experienced* surgeon is one who has a great deal of skill and knowledge acquired from years of practice.

3 *Experiences* here (countable) are life events that leave an impression on one.

D Here, *to tell if* means 'to know, or be able to say in advance'.

She is a very good singer, but it is too early to tell if she will be a great singer.

From behind it was impossible to tell if the person was a man or a woman because he/she had long, shoulder-length hair.

E potatoes, pianos, tomatoes, solos

3. 多项选择题答案

1 d 2 c 3 a 4 b 5 a 6 b

7 a 8 c 9 d 10 a 11 a 12 c

Lesson 8
Trading standards
贸易标准

课文详注 Further notes on the text

1. **Chickens slaughtered in the United States, claim officials in Brussels, are not fit to grace European tables.**

本句为报刊中常见的一种直接引语形式,其直接引用语由除 claim officials in Brussels 以外的其他两部分构成。引语中的 slaughtered ... States 为过去分词短语,作定语,修饰 Chickens。claim officials in Brussels 为实现引语部分连接的"连接词语",用来提醒读者该话语为引用语。这样的连接词语可以用"主语+动词"这样的词序,也可如文中那样用"动词+主语"这样的倒装词序。be fit to do sth. 适合做某事,如:

He has recovered from illness quite recently; he is, therefore, not fit to take a long walk.

他的病刚好,所以还不适宜走长路。

He's not fit to tackle such an arduous task.

他不适宜担负这么艰巨的任务。

有关本句的进一步解释见本课后课文注释 1。本课的第 2 句采用了与第 1 句完全相同的句式结构。

2. **... it is differences in national regulations, far more than tariffs, that put sand in the wheels of trade between rich countries.**

本句是由 it is/was ... that/who(m) ... 构成的强调句式。这种分裂句式常用来对句子中的某个词或某个短语进行强调。is/was 后为被强调部分，that/who(m)之后为句子的非强调部分。在 more than 此短语后，不仅可以跟句子，而且可以跟形容词、副词、动词或名词，其语义往往由于后面跟随的成分的不同而不同。如文中那样，其后为名词时，往往表达“不只是”、“不仅仅”之意，如：

A science is more than a large amount of information on some subject.

一门科学不只是有关某门学科的大量资料。

put sand in the wheels of 阻碍，阻挠。有关本句的进一步解释见本课课文注释 2。本课的第 4 句也采用了强调句式。

3. **An electric razor that meets the European Union's safety standards must be approved by ... in Europe.**

that meets the ... standards 为定语从句，修饰 razor。本句为由并列连词 and 连接的并列句。并列连词 and 两边的分句，像课文第 1 和第 2、第 3 和第 4 句那样，采用了相同的句式结构。这样的文体不仅出于语义表达的需要，而且使两种对比条件的相似性更为鲜明，从而有利于读者对作者所要表达语义的更好理解。

4. **As it happens, a razor that is safe in Europe is unlikely to electrocute Americans.**

As it happens 这里作插入语使用，用来对 a razor ... Americans 情况表示强调。

5. **So, ask businesses on both sides of the Atlantic, why have two lots of tests where one would do?**

本句类同于文章的第 1 句，为直接引语的一种表述方法。其中 ask businesses on both sides of the Atlantic 为连接词语，用来连接直接引语的两个部分。有关本句的进一步解释，见本课课文注释 3。

6. **Politicians agree, in principle, so America and the EU have**

been trying to reach a deal which would eliminate the need to double-test many products.

in principle 大体上，在原则上/方面。通常用来说明某事物不完全但基本上符合主语的要求，因而可以接受，如：

We are agreed in principle but not in detail.

我们在原则上是一致的，但在细节上不一致。

The two sides have agreed in principle on the time and place of negotiation.

双方原则上(即大体上)同意了谈判的时间和地点。

have been trying 为现在完成进行时态，用来表明动作发生在过去且一直延续到现在，但更强调现在仍然在进行。which would ... many products 作定语从句，后置修饰 deal。to double-test many products 为动词不定式短语，后置修饰 need。

7. **They hope to finish ... on May 28th.**

hope 为及物动词，但其后不能直接跟名词或代词作宾语，只能跟 that 从句或动词不定式作宾语，如：

I have been hoping (that) I'd have a chance to read the novel.

我一直希望有机会读到这部小说。

We hope to supply each of them with some fresh vegetable a day.

我们希望每天供应他们每个人一些新鲜蔬菜。

8. **Although negotiators are optimistic, the details are complex enough that they may be hard-pressed to get a deal at all.**

although 虽然，尽管。连词，用来引导一让步状语从句。注意使用 although 后，该句主句前不能使用 but。enough 在这里作副词。当 enough 作副词修饰形容词时，通常将其放在该形容词后，如：

He is competent enough to handle this.

他的能力足以处理这件事情。

在 that ... at all 中，that 为连词，这里用来引导结果状语从句，如：

What's the matter that they still haven't answered our telegram?

他们怎么还没有回电报？

What has happened that you all look so excited?

发生了什么事使你们都显得这样兴奋？

9. ... and then hammer out different pacts covering, say, ...

hammer out 通常用来表示“通过不断的或艰苦的努力形成、达成或解决”，如：

They have hammered out an agreement acceptable to both sides.

他们总算达成了一项双方都能接受的协议。

We at last hammered out the differences between us.

我们最终解决了我们之间的分歧。

covering, say, ... manufacturing 为分词短语，这里作定语，修饰 pacts。say 在这里作插入语。

10. ... on general principles, which ... extended to other countries.

which ... to other countries 为非限定性定语从句，修饰 principles。在此从句中，由于动词 extended 与 applied 使用同一个主语(即 which)，并且使用同样的时态结构，因此可如文中那样，省略其前的 could be。用 extend 表达“延伸到/至”含义时，通常与介词 to 搭配使用，如：

Expansionists are now trying to extend their military power to various parts of the world.

扩张主义者正在企图把军事势力扩展到世界各地。

语法 Grammar in use

直接引语和间接引语 (1)

直接引语

(1) 直接引语与直接引语的构成

直接引语是指在书面语中表现口语的方式。说话人实际说的话、引述动词及引述动词的主语构成完整的直接引语。将“说话人实际说的话”置于句尾时,通常使用“主语 + 引述动词”这样的形式;在将“说话人实际说的话”置于句首时,通常既可以使用“主语 + 引述动词”也可以使用“引述动词 + 主语”这样的倒装形式,如:

'This is a serious offence,' the judge said/said the judge.

“这是一种严重的违法行为,”法官说。

但在实际运用中,应当注意以下几点:

1) 将说话人实际说的话置于句首且主语过长时,通常使用“引述动词 + 主语”这样的倒装语序,如:

'Where's this train going?' asked the lady sitting beside me.

“这列火车开往哪儿?”坐在我旁边的一位女士问道。

2) 在上述情况下,当主语为代词时,现代英语中则很少使用倒装语序,如:

'You're right about the meeting,' I said.

“你关于会议的话是对的,”我说。

3) 使用了某些引述动词特别是那些需有宾语的引述动词如 assure(使确信)、inform(通知)、tell(告诉)等后,则不能使用上述的倒装语序,如:

'You haven't got much time,' Tom told me.

“你没有多少时间了,”汤姆告诉我。

(2) 标点符号在直接引语中的使用

1) 在使用直接引语表述中，应将说话人实际说的话用引号括起来，引号既可为双引号，也可为单引号。将“主语 + 引述动词”置于句首时，引述动词后需有逗号（美国英语中有时使用冒号），引语应以大写字母开始，如：

John asked, “Is that you, Bob?”
John asked, ‘Is that you, Bob?’
约翰问：“是你吗，鲍勃？”

2) 将说话人实际说的话置于句首时，在后一引号前应加逗号；但如引用话语为感叹句或疑问句时，感叹号或疑问号之后则无需再使用逗号。当将主语和引述动词置于一引语中间时，在前半部分引语所用的后一引号前需使用逗号，而后半部分引语的头一个字母无需大写，如：

‘It's nice to see you again,’ Mary said.

“很高兴又一次见到你，”玛丽说。

‘A tissue of lies!’ John cried.

“连篇的谎言！”约翰喊道。

‘You think so?’ the inspector asked.

“你是这么想吗？”巡视官问道。

‘Where, in this wretched town,’ John asked, ‘can I get a taxi?’

“在这个糟糕的城市里，”约翰问，“我到哪儿能叫到一辆出租车呢？”

3) 在引语中使用引语时，则需使用两套引号：如外层使用双引号，内层则使用单引号；外层如为单引号，内层则为双引号，如：

Ann said, ‘Just as I was leaving, a voice shouted, “Stop!”’

安说：“就在我要离开时，一个声音喊道：‘站住！’”

(3) 其他一些较常见的使用直接引语但不使用引号的情况

1) 在一些报刊文章中,如本课第 1 段的第 1、2 和第 2 段的第 2 句那样。

2) 在戏剧等的脚本对话中,如:

BOYLE (*agitated*): *A tissue of lies!*

INSPECTOR WILEY: *You think so?*

BOYLE (*sharply*): *Think so? I know it!*

INSPECTOR WILEY: *And no doubt you can prove it.*

博伊尔(激动地):连篇的谎言!

巡视官威利:你是这么想吗?

博伊尔(厉声地):这么想? 我清楚!

巡视官威利:那么无疑你能证明啦。

3) 将像 ask oneself(自问)、think(想)和 wonder(纳闷)这类引述动词用于引述思想时,一般不要求带引号,如:

So that was their little game, he thought.

原来这就是他们耍的小花招,他想。

Where are they now, he wondered.

他们现在在哪儿呢,他纳闷。

词汇学习 Word study

1. hope

(1) *n*. (不可数) 希望,愿望:

There's not much hope that he'll come.

他来的希望不大。

(2) *n*. (可数) 寄予希望的人或事物:

Please help me; you're my last hope.

帮帮我吧,你是我最后的希望了。

(3) *vt*. **希望,期望:**

I do hope (that) you are satisfied, Mr. Smith.

史密斯先生,我真希望你能满意。

We are hoping to visit France next year.

我们希望明年能去法国旅游。

(4) *vi*. (for) **希望,渴望:**

After this dry weather, everyone hopes for rain.

在这样干燥的天气之后,大家都希望能下雨。

2. cover

(1) *vt*. **遮盖,盖住:**

Snow covered the fields.

雪盖住了田野。

Please cover your computer when not in use.

不用时请将电脑盖上。

(2) *vt*. **包住,裹上:**

She covered the baby with a blanket.

她用毯子将孩子裹上。

(3) *vt*. **掩护,保护:**

Our task was to cover the landing of the army.

我们的任务是掩护军队登陆。

(4) *vt*. **包括,包含,论述:**

The book covers 18th-century English history.

这本书论述的是18世纪英国历史。

(5) *vi*. **隐藏,掩盖,掩饰:**

It was obvious that she was trying to cover up a mistake.

显然她在试图掩饰错误。

I covered for her by telling the police she was with me that night.

我为她遮掩,对警察说那晚她同我在一起。

(6) *n*. (可数)盖子,封面,封皮:

He opened the engine cover.

他打开发动机盖子。

I only bought the book because of its beautiful cover.

我买那本书只是因为封皮漂亮。

(7) *n*. (常用复数) 被褥:

He threw off the covers.

他将被褥掀开。

(8) *n*. (不可数) 掩护,掩体,掩蔽处:

The soldiers had no cover from the enemy guns.

在敌人的枪弹面前士兵们没有掩护之物。

When it started raining, we took cover under a tree.

下雨时,我们在一棵树下避雨。

3. apply

(1) *vt*. 应用,实施:

Scientific discoveries are often applied to industrial processes.

科学发明常常用于工业生产程序。

He is now applying his mind to a problem.

他正专注于解决一个问题。

(2) *vt*. (不用于进行时)适用;与……有关:

This rule cannot be applied to every case.

这一规定不适用于每一种情况。

(3) *vt*. 涂;把……用于:

The doctor applied some medicine to his wound.

大夫在他伤口上涂了些药。

Apply the paint evenly to both sides of the door.

均匀地将漆涂在门的两面。

(4) *vi*. (for)(尤指以书面形式正式)申请,请求:

He's going to apply for a job today.
他打算今天去申请一份工作。
They applied to the government for assistance.
他们请求政府给予援助。

(5) *vi*. (不用于进行时)使用;与……有关:
This rule doesn't apply.
这一规定不适用。
This applies to us as much as to them.
这对我们和对他们同样适用。

(6) apply oneself to 致力于,专注于:
They couldn't entirely apply themselves to the research.
他们不能全力以赴地进行这项研究。

练习答案 Key to written exercises

1. 关键句型练习答案

A See text.

B 1 Our fowl are fine, we simply clean them *differently/with a different method*.

2 It is not *only* farmers *that* are complaining.

3 They hope to finish *ahead of* a trade summit...

C 1 say 2 say

D 1 who 2 that 3 that 4 which 5 which

2. 难点练习答案

A 1 *in a different way* = using a different method or manner of doing something

2 *this way* = in this direction

3 *on my way home* = as I was travelling in the direction of my home

4 *In a way* = From one point of view

5 *in my way* = obstructing my path

B 1 *sold* = given or passed to someone in return for money

2 *for sale* = offered to be sold

3 *in the sales* = in the periods when shops offer goods at lower prices than usual

4 *unsold* = that no one has bought

C 1 *on time* = punctual

2 *times* = periods

3 *those times* = that period in history

4 *just in time* = just early enough

5 *at the time* = when this happened

3. 多项选择题答案

1 b 2 d 3 a 4 b 5 d 6 b

7 a 8 a 9 b 10 c 11 b 12 c

Lesson 9

Royal espionage

王室谍报活动

课文详注 Further notes on the text

1. Alfred the Great acted as his own spy, visiting Danish camps disguised as a minstrel.

Alfred the Great 阿尔弗雷德大帝，古英国国王，22 岁登王位。在抵抗丹麦人入侵的斗争中，曾先后与丹麦军交战 6 年未尝胜绩。他后来潜匿于阿塞尔纳岛，终于大败丹麦军。act as 常用来表达两种意义：(1)充当/扮作……的角色，(2)起……的作用，如：

He acted as the public prosecutor when the case was being heard.

法院审理该案时他担任检察官。

She acted as a woman teacher in the film.

在该片中她扮演一位女教师的角色。

An oar often acts as rudder.

桨常常可以起到舵的作用。

visiting ... minstrel 为现在分词短语，在句中作方式状语，修饰 acted。disguised as a minstrel 为过去分词短语，在 visiting ... minstrel 短语中作方式状语，修饰 visiting，这样表达出“扮作吟游歌手到丹麦军队的营地”的含义。

2. While Alfred's ..., the king himself set out to penetrate the camp of Guthrum, the commander of the Danish invaders.

the king himself ... 中 king 指 Alfred the Great。set out 可用

来表示“开始”、“着手”、“出发”等含义，其后需使用动词不定式形式，如：

Then they set out to climb the hill.

随后他们开始爬山。

She usually sets out to write her novel at eight at night.

她通常在晚上8点钟开始写小说。

Guthrum为当时入侵英国的丹麦首领，公元875年5月被Alfred the Great打败后，改信基督教，并认其为教父。the commander of the Danish invaders为Guthrum的同位语。

3. These had settled down for the winter at Chippenham: thither Alfred went.

These这里指the Danish invaders。settle down驻扎，这里使用过去完成时态，用来说明该动作为Alfred做出went动作之前已经完成的动作。thither Alfred went，这里使用了倒装语序，以使上下文连接更为紧密。thither意为to that place(向那里)，旧用法，因为这里描述的是古时发生的事件，作者以此来拉近读者与所发生事件的距离，使之显得更为生动。

4. He noticed at once that discipline was slack: ...

冒号后引出的内容均为说明性文字，用来对discipline was slack进行具体说明。

5. They lived well, on the proceeds of raids on neighbouring regions.

on the proceeds of中的on与动词lived搭配使用，构成live on，表示“靠……生活”之意，如：

Their family lived mainly on the earnings of their parents.

他们家主要靠他们父母的收入生活。

这里因为well与on the ... regions并列作状语，所以用逗号分断。neighbouring regions前的on与raid搭配使用，用来表

示"袭击"之意,如:

Their army made a raid on the enemy coast.

他们的部队突袭了敌方的海岸。

6. There they collected women as well as food and drink, and a life of ease had made them soft.

... as well as ...不仅……而且……。这里应当注意的是,在使用此连词时(与使用 not only ... but also ...不同),其侧重点为 as well as 前(即汉语中"而且"后)的内容,如:

You can not expect her to do the homework as well as look after the children.

你不能指望她又照看孩子又做家庭作业。

a life of ease(一种)安逸/舒适的生活。

7. The force there assembled was trivial compared with the Danish horde.

there assembled 为过去分词短语,作定语,修饰 the force。正常语序应为 assembled there。这里的 there 指 Athelney,现将其提前,有对该地点状语进行强调的意味。compared with the Danish horde 在句中作状语,表示"与丹麦军相比"之意。

compare ... with ...把……同……相比,如:

You may compare this article with that one, and then you'll see which is better.

你可以把这篇文章同那篇文章比一比,那样你就可以看出哪一篇文章好一些了。

horde 在这里用来指军队。

8. But Alfred had deduced that the Danes were no longer fit for prolonged battle: and their ...raids.

that 引导的从句作动词 deduced 的宾语。no longer 不再。be fit for 适应,适合,适宜于。常用来表示资格、能力、条件等适应、适合或适宜于某种目的、某项任务、某种情况等,如:

He has recovered from illness recently; he is, therefore, not fit for such an arduous task.

他的病刚好,因此不适于承担这样艰巨的任务。

本句冒号后的 and their ... raids 起到双重作用:(1)作动词 deduced 的宾语;(2)对 Danes were ... prolonged battle 作附加说明。

9. So, faced with the Danish advancc, Alfred did not risk ... the enemy.

faced with the Danish advance 为过去分词短语,作时间状语,修饰 risk 和 harried,用来表明这两个动作发生的时间。be faced with 面对。多用来表示一种往往不是出于主语意愿的状态,如:

They were faced with many difficulties which, with the help of their neighbours, they overcame one by one.

他们遭遇到很多困难,但是在邻居们的帮助下,他们把困难一个一个地克服了。

Faced with this new turn of events, we decided to revise our original plan.

面对事态的新变化,我们决定修改原定计划。

10. He was constantly on the move, drawing the Danes after him.

drawing the Danes after him 牵着丹麦人的鼻子而让他们跟着他跑。现在分词短语作结果状语,修饰 was constantly on the move。

11. His patrols halted the raiding parties: hunger assailed the Danish army.

冒号后的部分为说明语,表示结果,即表示做出 halted raiding parties 动作后所产生的结果。

12. Now Alfred ...—and within a month the Danes had surrendered.

破折号后引出被强调部分,and ... surrendered 表示结果,即表示做出 began a long series of skirmishes 动作后所产生的结果。

语法 Grammar in use

直接引语和间接引语 (2)

间接引语

(1) 间接引语与间接引语中的引述动词和形容词

把某人所说的或说过的话告诉另一个人时,应当用间接引语结构表达。与在直接引语中一样,间接引语中最常用的引述动词是 say、tell 和 ask。

此外,许多其他可带 that 或 if/whether 或疑问词的动词或形容词(如 certain、sure 等),也可作引述动词或引述形容词。

(2) 间接引语中的变化

1) 间接引语中时态的变化

转述通常发生在过去,所以引述动词通常是过去时。因此,转述从句的时态通常要"倒移"(backshift),主要规则为:一般现在时变为一般过去时,一般将来时变为过去将来时,一般过去时变为过去完成时,现在完成时变为过去完成时,用过去时的情态助动词和过去完成时不变,如:

直接引语:

TOM: '*I need to go to the bank*.'

汤姆:"我需要到银行去。"

PAM: '*I'm waiting for Harriet*.'

帕姆:"我在等哈丽特。"

She said, '*I'll help you*.'

她说:"我会帮助你的。"

He said, '*I lived in Scotland*.'

他说:"我过去住在苏格兰。"

Sylvia said, 'I've moved to another flat.'
西尔维娅说:"我已经搬到另一套房间了。"
Mary said, 'We could see you tomorrow.'
玛丽说:"我们明天可以见你。"
She said, 'I had been waiting for hours before you arrived.'
她说:"我等了好几个小时之后你才来。"
间接引语:
Tom said (that) he needed to go to the bank.
汤姆说我需要到银行去。
Pam said (that) she was waiting for Harriet.
帕姆说她在等哈丽特。
She said (that) she would help me.
她说她会帮助我的。
He said (that) he had lived in Scotland.
他说他曾住在苏格兰。
Sylvia said (that) she had moved to another flat.
西尔维娅说她已经搬到了另一套房间。
Mary said (that) they could see me the next day.
玛丽说他们第2天可以见我。
She said (that) she had been waiting for hours before I arrived.
她说她一直等了好几个小时之后我才到。

2) 间接引语中人称代词的变化

间接引语中人称代词变化与否依转述者的着眼点而定,如:

直接引语:
Ann said, 'I'll send you a card, Sue.'
间接引语:

Ann told Sue (that) she'd send her a card.

安告诉休她将给她寄一张明信片。(别人转述的话)

Ann told me (that) she would send me a card.

安告诉我她会给我寄一张明信片。(休转述的话)

I told Sue (that) I'd send her a card.

我告诉休我将给她寄一张明信片。(安转述的话)

但是,如上所示,在使用间接引语中,必然要涉及到人称代词的变化。主要的人称代词的变化为:

I—he/she *me/you—him/her* *my—his/her*

we—they *us—them* *our—their*

mine—his/hers *ours—theirs* *myself—himself/herself*

3) 间接引语中时间、地点和动词的变化

间接引语中时间、地点和动词的变化与否依转述者的着眼点而定,如:在星期二,A说:

'A card came yesterday saying Sue will arrive tomorrow.'

"昨天收到的明信片上说,休明天到。"

在星期三,B转述这句话时可能会说:

A told me a card had come the day before yesterday/on Monday saying Sue would arrive today/on Wednesday.

A告诉我前天/星期一收到一张明信片,上面说休将于今天/星期三到。

但是,并非总有必要改变时间、地点和动词。例如如果转述上面陈述的时间仍然是星期二,B可能会说:

A told me a card came/had come yesterday saying Sue will/would arrive tomorrow.

A告诉我昨天收到一张明信片,上面说休将于明天到。

但是,时间、地点和动词的改变情况可能如下:

时间：

now—immediately/then

two days ago—two days before/earlier

today—that day

tonight—that night

tomorrow—the next/the following day

yesterday—the previous day/the day before

last night—the night before

地点：

here—there（当所谈地点明确时）

this place—that place

these places—those places

动词：

come—go

bring—take

4）间接引语中情态助动词的变化

在一般情况下，现在时形式的情态助动词变为过去时形式的情态助动词，如：

直接引语：

'I can/will/may see you later,' he said.

他说："我能/愿/可能以后会见到你。"

间接引语：

He said (that) he could/would/might see me later.

他说他能/愿/可能以后会见到我。

使用时还应当注意以下一些情况：

a. shall

用其指对将来的预言、预见等时，在间接引语中需变为 would，而用其指提议、建议或征求意见时需用 should，甚至在第 2 和第 3 人称后也如此，如：

直接引语：

'I shall tell him exactly what I think,' she said.

她说："我将明确告诉他我的想法。"

'Shall I speak to him in person?' she asked.

她问："我亲自对他说好吗?"

间接引语：

She said (that) she would tell him exactly what she thought.

她说她将把她的想法明确告诉他。

She asked whether she should speak to him in person.

她问她是否应亲自对他说。

b. should/shouldn't

用其指可取、义务或可能时，在间接引语中不变；但是例如在直接引语中条件句中用 should 代替 would，则需还原为 would，如：

直接引语：

'You should see a specialist,' he told me.

他告诉我说："你应当找专家看。"

She said, 'If I were you, I should get another lawyer.'

她说："如果我是你，我就请别的律师。"

间接引语：

He told me I should see a specialist.

他告诉我我应该找专家看。

She said (that) if she were me, she would get another lawyer.

她说如果她是我，她就请别的律师。

c. must、mustn't 与 needn't

当 must 指过去并用于表示不可推卸的义务时，在间接引语中可以保持不变，也可以用 had to 代替；用 must 说明将来的必要性时，也可以保持不变，或用 would have to 代替；用 must 表示推论或可能性时，也可以保持不变，并且不能用 had to 来代替，如：

直接引语：

'I must warn you of the consequences,' he said.

他说："我必须警告你会产生什么后果。"

'We must go early tomorrow,' she said.

她说："我们明天必须早走。"

He said, 'George must be a fool to behave like that.'

他说："乔治那样表现一定是个傻瓜。"

间接引语：

He told me he must / had to warn me of the consequences.

他告诉我他必须警告我会产生什么后果。

She said they must/would have to/had to go early the next day.

她说他们第 2 天必须早走。

He said George must be a fool to behave like that.

他说乔治那样表现一定是个傻瓜。

用 mustn't 表示"禁止"时，在间接引语中保持不变或用 couldn't 代替；用 needn't 表示"不必要"时，在间接引语中可以保持不变，也可以用 didn't have to 代替，如：

直接引语：

'You mustn't/can't cross the border,' the guard said.

哨兵说："你们不可越过边界。"

The boss said, ' You needn't/don't have to come in tomorrow.'

老板说:"你明天不必来了。"

间接引语:

The guard said we mustn't / couldn't cross the border.

那位哨兵说我们不可越过边界。

The boss said I needn't /didn't have to come in the next day.

老板说我第2天不必来了。

5) 条件陈述句在间接引语中的变化

只有当条件陈述句的从句为一般现在时而主句为现在将来时时,才使用时态"倒移"的变化方式,其他时态则不变,如:

直接引语:

'If you pass your test, I'll buy you a car,' he said.

他说:"如果你通过考试,我将给你买辆汽车。"

'If you passed/'d passed your test, I would buy/'d have bought you a car,' he said.

他说:"要是你通过/那时通过考试,我就给你买辆汽车/了。"

间接引语:

He said that if I passed my test he would buy me a car.

他说如果我通过考试,他将给我买辆汽车。

He said that if I passed/'d passed my test he would buy/'d have bought me a car.

他说要是我通过/那时通过考试,他就给我买辆汽车/了。

6) 感叹句在间接引语中的变化

其变化主要为词序上的变化,如:

直接引语:

'What a silly boy you are!' she exclaimed.

她惊呼:"你是个多么蠢的孩子啊!"

间接引语:

She told him what a silly boy he was.

她告诉他他是个多么蠢的孩子。

She told him that he was a silly boy.

她对他说他是个蠢孩子。

词汇学习 Word study

1. act

(1) *n*. 行为,行动:

That's a right wing group responsible for several acts of terrorism.

那是一个需对若干恐怖活动负责的右翼团体。

(2) *n*. 法案,法令,条例:

They are now lobbying to amend the Gun Control Act.

他们正游说要求修改《枪支管制法案》。

(3) *n*. (剧)幕:

Hamlet kills the king in Act 5, Scene 2.

哈姆雷特在第2场第5幕中杀掉了国王。

(4) *vi*. (as, on, for) 做;扮演;充当;采取行动:

She acted on our suggestion.

她按我们的建议行事。

He's a lawyer acting for Mr. Miller.

他是为密勒先生作代理的律师。

A trained dog can act as a guide to a blind person.
受过训练的狗可以作盲人的向导。
He acted as if he'd never seen me before.
他表现得就仿佛以前从未见到过我似的。

(5) *vi*. (on, upon) 起作用,见效:
Does the drug take long to act upon the nerve centres?
这种药物需很长时间才能对神经中枢起作用吗?

(6) *vi*. 举动像,装出:
Don't act foolishly!
别装傻!

(7) *vt*. 扮演:
Are you going to act Prince Hamlet?
你打算扮演哈姆雷特王子吗?

2. begin (began, begun)

(1) *vi*. 开始,开始存在:
Work on the new bridge will begin next month.
新桥工程将于下个月开始。
They began on the experiment last Monday.
他们上星期一开始着手那项实验。
Let's begin with a story.
让我们从一个故事开始讲起吧。
We'll begin at the beginning.
我们将从头开始。

(2) *vt*. 开始,开始存在,着手于:
She curled up in bed and began reading the book.
她蜷在床上,开始看书。
It began to rain.
开始下雨了。
She began learning Chinese three years ago.

3 年前她开始学习中文。

3．stay

(1) *vi*. 停留,逗留:

I stayed in bed until ten o'clock.

我在床上一直呆到 10 点。

The teacher asked me to stay behind after class.

老师让我下课后留下。

I'll stay in this afternoon because I'm tired.

我累了,下午就不出去了。

(2) *vi*. 保持:

I tried to stay still.

我尽力保持不动。

(3) *vi*. 暂住:

Which hotel are you staying at?

你住在哪家酒店?

(4) *n*. (可数)居住:

Did you enjoy your stay in London?

您在伦敦过得愉快吗?

练习答案　Key to written exercises

1．关键句型练习答案

A　1　many　2　many　3　much　4　Much of
　5　Many of

B　See text.

C　He broke his right arm *as well as* his right leg.
As well as writing novels, she also writes plays for television.

D　1　No one/Nobody　2　anywhere　3　anything
　4　nothing　5　anyone/anybody

E See text.

2. 难点练习答案

A 1 The verb *wander* (/ˈwɒndə/) means 'walk about without a fixed course or aim': *They wouldn't have got lost if they hadn't wandered from the main path.*

The verb *wonder* (/ˈwʌndə/) means 'ask oneself': *I often wonder what I will do when I leave college.*

2 *Learn* and *teach* are often confused, even by some English people!

Learn means 'acquire knowledge': *I learned a lot from my English teacher.*

Teach means 'give or impart knowledge': *My English teacher taught me a lot about English literature.*

3 *Notice* means 'see and become aware of': *He quickly noticed that she was unwell.*

Remark means 'comment, say': *'It's going to be a nice day,' he remarked.*

4 *Conquerors* are people who take land by force: *The conquerors immediately imposed new laws in the country.*

Winners are people (or animals) who have won competitions, matches, races or prizes: *The winners of all the events in the college games were given medals.*

5 The noun *force* means 'natural or physical power': *If the man doesn't come out soon, the police are going to use force to break in and get him.*

Strength is 'the quality or degree of being strong or powerful': *He used all his strength to carry the child up the cliff to safety.*

B 1 *settled down* = were living

2 *settled* = paid

3 *settled in* = went to live in

4 *settled* = resolved

5 *settled . . . on* = left. . . to

C 1 She is an extremely good public speaker with a great deal of *self-assurance*.

2 Monks and nuns have to practise *self-denial* by giving up life's pleasures.

3 Many countries in the world that used to be governed from London as part of the British Empire are now independent *self-governing* states.

4 She is a very *self-centred* person: she only ever thinks of herself.

D 1 *fit for* = ready for, capable of

2 *Does . . . fit* = Is it the correct size for

3 *fit . . . into* = make them all go in, find enough space for them

4 *fit* = healthy

5 *fit of energy* = burst of energy

6 *fit in with* = agree with

3. 多项选择题答案

1 c 2 d 3 b 4 a 5 a 6 c

7 a 8 b 9 a 10 c 11 a 12 d

Lesson 10
Silicon valley
硅谷

课文详注 Further notes on the text

1. **Carver Mead, a pioneer in ..., notes there are now workstations that enable..., much the way an editor creates a newsletter on a Macintosh.**

a pioneer in ... Technology 为 Carver Mead 的同位语,对其作进一步的说明。there are ... on their desks 为动词 notes 后跟随的宾语从句,动词与宾语从句之间省略了连词 that。that enable ... on their desks 为该宾语从句中的定语从句,修饰 workstations。在 the way an editor ... on a Macintosh 中,the way 前省略了介词 in,整个短语在句中作方式状语。在非正式文体中,in the way 中的介词 in 通常被省略,如:

You're doing it (in) the wrong way.

你做这件事的方法不对。

Do it (in) any way you like.

你想怎样做就怎样做。

an editor ... on a Macintosh 为定语从句,修饰 the way,其前省略了 that。在非正式情况中,that 通常被用来代替 the way 后的 in which 或 by which,而 that 可以被省略,如:

I don't like the way (that) you talk to me.

我可不喜欢你同我谈话的方式。

Let's go the way (that) we went yesterday.

让我们走我们昨天走的那条路吧。

2. As the time and cost of making a chip drop to ..., engineers may soon be free to let ...

句中的 As 为从属连词,用来引导一原因状语从句,表示"因为"、"由于"。be free to do ...结构中,free 为句子的表语,其后跟随动词不定式,表示"可以做",如:

You are free to go anywhere you wish.

你可以到任何你想去的地方。

3. Mead predicts that inventors ... at the office—spawning a new generation of garage start-ups and giving the U.S. a jump on its foreign rivals in getting new products to market fast.

破折号后并列的两个现在分词短语 spawning ... start-ups 和 giving ... fast 为结果状语,作为 that 引导的宾语从句中 inventors ... at the office 所产生的结果。

4. 'We really thrive on anarchy.'

thrive on 靠……而繁荣/发展。不及物动词 thrive 的本意是指生物的"繁殖"、"兴旺",常被引申来表达"繁荣"、"发展"、"生长"之意,如:

Most plants thrive in warm climates.

大多数植物在温暖的气候里生长茂盛。

Babies thrive on their mothers' milk.

婴儿吃母乳长得快。

thrive on 的引申义时常也用来表达不好的意思,如:

Merchants who thrive on smuggling will not end well.

靠走私发迹的商人是不会有好下场的。

5. And on Asians.

本句意为"靠的是亚洲人"。这里用的是个省略句,可以将其视为前一段最后一句的继续。引号中的 We really thrive on anarchy 为 Mead 的观点。本省略句表达出本文作者不但赞成 Mead 的这一观点,而且还补充进了自己的观点。作者将其另起一段，表明作者对自己观点部分的强调。

6. **And Chinese, Korean, Filipino and Indian engineers are graduating in droves from California's colleges.**

in droves 一批批，成群地。drove(批，群)为可数名词，通常用其复数表达，如：

People came in droves to buy lottery tickets.

人们成批地来买福利彩票。

7. **As the heads of next-generation start-ups, these Asian innovators can draw on customs and languages to forge tighter links with crucial Pacific Rim markets.**

as 为介词，经常可用来表示“作为”、“当作”、“处于某地位或身份”之意，如：

We chose him as our monitor.

我们选他作班长。

Speaking as a beginner, I do have much to learn.

作为一个初学者而言，我的确有很多东西需要学。

draw on 凭借，把……作为来源，如：

The newspaper article draws heavily on gossip.

那家报纸的文章主要以流言蜚语为素材。

forge links with 与……建立联系。动词 forge 的本意为“打造”、“打制”，这里为其比喻用法，再如：

They are now trying hard to forge a new unity in their political party.

他们正尽力在其党内促成新的团结。

8. **..., Alex Au, a Stanford Ph.D. from Hong Kong, has set up ...**

a Stanford Ph.D. 在这里为同位语，对 Alex Au 作进一步说明。Ph.D. 为 Doctor of Philosophy 的缩写形式。from Hong Kong 为介词短语，作定语，修饰 a Stanford Ph.D.。

语法 Grammar in use

直接引语和间接引语(3)

1. 间接一般疑问句

一般疑问句中使用的倒装语序在转述中要使用陈述语序(主语+动词),在引述动词与间接引语间要使用连词 if/whether 进行连接,其他变化与将一般陈述句转述为间接引语时相同,如:

'Is he ready?' she asked.
"他准备好了吗?"她问。
She asked me if/whether he was ready.
她问我他是否准备好了。

She asked me: 'Did he went home?'
她问我:"他回家了吗?"
She asked me if/whether he had gone home.
她问我他是否已回家了。

但是,使用连词 if/whether 时应当注意以下几点:

(1) 一般情况下,引述动词后的连词 if 和 whether 可以互换使用,只是 whether 比 if 表示的怀疑程度稍大。但是,当引述动词为 discuss 时,则只能使用 whether。

(2) or not 只能用于 if/whether ... or not 或 whether or not 结构中,但是不能用于 if or not 结构中,如:

直接引语:
'Do you want any dinner or not?'
"你们想不想吃点饭?"
间接引语:
He wants to know if/whether we want any dinner or not.
He wants to know whether or not we want any dinner.
他想知道我们想不想吃饭。(不能用 *if or not*)

2. 间接特殊疑问句

特殊疑问句中使用的倒装语序在转述中要使用陈述语序(主语+动词),在引述动词与间接引语间要使用特殊疑问句中原使用的疑问代词或疑问副词进行连接,其他变化与将陈述句转述为间接引语时相同,如:

直接引语:

'*Where are you going?*'

"你们上哪儿去?"

'*When did you give it to John?*'

"你什么时候把它给约翰的?"

间接引语:

He asked (us) where we were going.

他问(我们)我们上哪儿去。

He asked me when I gave it to John.

他问我什么时候把它给约翰的。

但是,当直接引语为针对主语提问的疑问句时,转述时词序保持不变,如:

直接引语:

'*Who delivered this package?*'

"谁投递的这个包裹?"

'*Which piece fits in this puzzle?*'

"哪一块适合这个拼图玩具?"

间接引语:

Please tell me who delivered this package.

请告诉我是谁投递的这个包裹。

I want to know which piece fits in this puzzle.

我想知道哪一块适合这个拼图玩具。

3. 间接引语中带 to 的动词不定式的使用

(1) 说明祈使语气的动词不定式

直接引语为祈使句时，在转述为间接引语时，可以用适当的动词 + 带 to 的动词不定式构成，但应当注意的是，引述动词必须符合祈使句的功能(如要求、告诉、劝告等)，如：

直接引语：

She said, 'Remember to switch off all the lights.'

她说："记着把所有的灯都关掉。"

间接引语：

She reminded me to switch off all the lights.

他提醒我把所有的灯都关掉。

直接引语为否定祈使句时，在转述为间接引语时，应当使用适当的动词 + not to 不定式构成，如：

She told/asked/warned him not to make a mess in the kitchen.

她叫/要求/警告他别把厨房搞得乱七八糟。

有时也可以用 be to 来转述，如：

直接引语：

'Wait for me.'

"等等我。"

间接引语：

He says I am/was to wait for him.

他说我应等他。

(2) 疑问词后的动词不定式

Shall I ...?、Should I ...?、Do you want me to ...? 等表示建议和征询意见情况的直接引语可以使用两种方式转述，如：

直接引语：

'Shall/Should I phone her?'

"我应该给她打电话吗?"

间接引语:

He wanted to know if/whether he should phone her.

他想知道他是否应该给她打电话。

He wanted to know whether to phone her.

他想知道是否应该给她打电话。

含有疑问词的征询也可以用两种方式转述,如:

直接引语:

'*How shall I prepare the sauce?*'

"我应怎么配制调味汁呢?"

间接引语:

He wanted to know how he should prepare the sauce.

他想知道他该怎样配制调味汁。

He wanted to know how to prepare the sauce.

他想知道怎样配制调味汁。

但是,在 why 或 if 之后不能跟动词不定式。

词汇学习 Word study

1. create *vt.*

(1) 创造:

The wealth of society is created by the labouring people.

社会财富是劳动人民创造的。

(2) 引起,造成:

The visitors created a lot of troubles.

参观者们制造了许多麻烦。

It's very important to create a good impression when you meet a client.

和客户见面时留下好印象是非常重要的。

(3) 建立，组建：

The local government created several new divisions.

地方政府组建了几个新的部门。

2. design

(1) *vt.* 设计，画草图，设计图案：

They've designed a new plane.

他们已设计出了一架新飞机。

The engineer hopes to design a new bridge.

那位工程师希望设计一座新桥。

She designed a new dress for the fashion show.

她为服装表演设计了一套新服装。

(2) *vt.* 构思，设想：

The author has designed a good plot.

那个作家想出一个好情节。

(3) *vi.* 设计服装：

He designed for many wealthy clients.

他为许多有钱的顾客设计服装。

(4) *n.* (可数)设计图样，草图：

He showed us a design for a new bike.

他向我们展示了一种新自行车的设计图样。

(5) *n.* (不可数)设计，布局，图案：

He's now studying art and design at college.

他现在正在大学学习艺术和设计。

I like the colours but not the design.

我喜欢它的色彩，可是不喜欢它的图案。

3. produce

(1) *vt.* /prəˈdjuːs/ 生产，制造：

That factory produces household electronic appliances.

那家工厂制造家电产品。

(2) *vt*. /prə'djuːs/ 产生，引发：

Hard work produces success.

努力工作才能成功。

(3) *vi*. /prə'djuːs/ 生产，制造，产生：

The bakery hasn't begun to produce yet.

那家面包房还没有开始生产。

(4) *n*. /'prədjuːs/ (不可数)产品，农产品：

The farmers are selling produce of their own.

农民正在销售农产品。

练习答案 Key to written exercises

1. 关键句型练习答案

A See text.

B 1 speaking 2 telling 3 driving 4 buying 5 smoking

C 1 arrives 2 gets 3 arrives 4 collect

2. 难点练习答案

A 1 Did you *notice* what the man was wearing?

2 'This is just what we want students to do,' *observed* the visitor as he inspected students at work in the laboratory.

3 'This is a beautiful village,' she *remarked*, 'I'd like to live here.'

B A lot of people in Britain like *chips* so much that they eat them with everything.

C 1 *set off* = began their journey

2 *set in* = begun, started

3 *set by* = save

4 *set out* = leave

5 *set to* = begin (work) eagerly or with determination

3．多项选择题答案

1 c	2 a	3 a	4 b	5 d	6 c
7 b	8 b	9 d	10 c	11 a	12 a

Lesson 11
How to grow old
如何安度晚年

课文详注 Further notes on the text

1. **In the young there is a justification for this feeling.**

In the young 在年轻人身上。介词+表示人的名词或代词,即 in sb. 这样的结构,可以表达"在某人身上"这样的概念,如:

In her I see a future leader.

在她身上我看到了一个未来领导者的气质。

That's really an unusual ability in such a young child.

这样年幼的孩子具有这样一种能力的确不寻常。

this feeling 指前一句中所说的 oppressed by the fear of death。

2. **Young men who have reason to fear that they will be killed in battle may justifiably feel bitter in the thought that they have been cheated of the best things that life has to offer.**

who have reason to fear ... 中的关系代词 who 引导一定语从句,修饰 men。此从句中的 have reason to do sth. 表示"有做某事的理由",其中的 reason 作为不可数名词使用,其后所跟随的动词不定式作定语,修饰 reason,再如:

In view of her behaviour, you had good reason to be suspicious.

就她的行为而言,你完全有理由怀疑她。

本句结构稍微有些复杂,使用了 3 个语法功能各异的 that 从句:动词 fear 后的 that 引导一宾语从句,为 fear 的宾语;介词短语 in the thought that 中的 that 引导一同位语从句,说明名词 thought 的内容；最后一个 that 引导一定语从句，修饰 things。in the thought that 想到，如：

We accepted his idea in the thought that it would bring benefit to both sides.

考虑到他的想法会给双方带来好处，我们采纳了。

cheat sb. of sth. 从某人那里骗取某物，如：

A swindler cheated her of one hundred dollars by selling her a watch which did not work.

一个骗子卖给她一只不走的表，骗走了 100 美元钱。

常见的类似结构还有：rob sb. of sth.（从某人那里抢走某物）、deprive sb. of sth.（从某人那里剥夺走某物）等，如：

They robbed me of my money.

他们抢走了我的钱。

That will deprive me of my chance to visit France.

那将使我失去到法国访问的机会。

但应注意，在表达“从某人那里偷走某物”时，应使用 steal sth. from sb. 形式，如：

He stole a bicycle from me.

他偷走了我的一辆自行车。

3. But in an old man who has known ... , and has achieved whatever work it was in him to do, the fear of death ...

in an old man 中的介词 in 同第 2 句 in the young 中的 in 表达同样的概念。作者在这里采用同样的结构形式，对年轻人和老年人的状况进行对比。句中的 who 为关系代词，引导一定语从句，修饰 an old man。has known 和 has achieved 为 who 的并列谓语。whatever work it was in him to do 一切他能做的，作动词 achieved 的宾语从句。其中代词 it 作形式主语，其逻辑主语为动词不定式 to do，而 whatever work（= any work）作动词不定式的宾语。在 in sb. to do 这样的结构中，介词 in

通常用来表达“在(性格/能力)中”这一含义,如:

It's not in me to lie.

我(生来)不会说谎。

She doesn't have it in her to break her word.

她不会不遵守诺言。

4. **The best way to overcome it—so at least it seems to me—is to make your interests gradually wider and more impersonal, until bit by bit the walls of the ego recede, and your life becomes increasingly merged in the universal life.**

to overcome it 此动词不定式作定语,修饰 way。so at least it seems to me 作插入语,使用的是倒装语序。其正常语序为:at least it seems so to me,其中的代词 it 用来指整个句子的内容。to make ... impersonal 此动词不定式作主语 the best way 的补足语。bit by bit 一点一点地。在 the walls of the ego 中,walls 是暗喻用法,这一短语表示出“像一堵高墙的自我”含义。becomes increasingly merged in 逐渐融于……之中。

5. **An individual human existence should be like a river—small at first, narrowly contained within its banks, and rushing passionately past boulders and over waterfalls.**

like a river 像一条河流,为明喻。破折号后的插入语用来对 river 作进一步说明。此说明语使用了延伸比喻(extended metaphor)的手法,即对原明喻 like a river 所作的延伸说明。

6. **Gradually the river grows ... lose their individual being.**

与上一句中的 small ... waterfalls 相同,这里作者使用的仍然是延伸比喻的手法,是对明喻 like a river 的进一步延伸说明。不同点在于,前一延伸比喻是由一系列短语构成,而本延伸比喻则由一系列短句构成。

7. **The man who, in old age, can see his life in this way, ..., since the things he cares for will continue.**

句中 who . . . in this way 和 he cares for 为两个定语从句,分别修饰 the man 和 the things。since 因为,由于,从属连词,引导原因状语从句。

8. **And if, with the decay of vitality, weariness increases, the thought of rest will be not unwelcome.**

with the decay of vitality 随着精力的衰退。介词短语作状语,修饰 increases。这里将其提前是为了对其进行强调。在 the thought of rest 中,用 rest 指 death,使用的是一种称作委婉语(euphemism)的修辞格。这种修辞格常用来取代粗鲁或令人感到不快的话语,使之听起来委婉一些。再如:

It's ten years since her husband passed away.

她丈夫去世已 10 年了。(句中指 *died* 的短语 *passed away* 即为委婉语)

not unwelcome 未尝/并非不是好事。这是由 not + 否定形容词构成的双重否定形式,表达出肯定意义。这里用其表达一种委婉语气。

9. **I should wish to die while still at work, knowing that others will carry on what I can no longer do, and content in the thought that what was possible has been done.**

I should wish . . . 我倒希望……虚拟语气用法,这里用来表示委婉的语气。在 while still at work 中,while 为从属连词,引导一时间状语从句,while 和 still 之间省略了 I am。应注意的是,只有当时间状语中的主语与主句中的主语相同或为代词 it 且其后均为系动词时,方可构成句中这样的省略形式,如:

She doesn't like to be disturbed while (she is) at work.

她工作时不喜欢被打搅。

They'll try their best to help you when (it is) necessary.

必要时他们会尽力帮助你的。

knowing that . . . has been done 为现在分词短语,在句中作原

因状语,修饰 wish to die。that others ... no longer do 中的 that 引导一宾语从句。在此宾语从句中,关系代词 what 引导一名词性从句,作短语动词 carry on 的宾语。content in the thought ... has been done 与 knowing ... 并列作原因状语。可以认为在 content 前省略了现在分词 being。名词 thought 后的 that 引导一同位语从句,对 thought 作进一步说明。该同位语从句中的 what was possible 为一名词性从句,作主语。

语法　Grammar in use

名词性从句 (1)

在句子中其作用相当于一个名词的从句被称为名词性从句。像任何名词一样,名词性从句在句子中可以起到主语、宾语和补语的作用。

由陈述句构成的名词性从句

(1) 一般性的 that 从句(有时为 what 从句,但连词 that 常被省略)

That money doesn't grow on trees should be obvious.

金钱不会从树上长出来该是显而易见的。(主语)

Everybody knows (that) money doesn't grow on trees.

众所周知,金钱是不会从树上长出来的。(宾语)

但名词性从句作主语或宾语时,应当注意以下几点:

1) 在一般情况下,应当避免使用作主语的名词性从句,而往往用先行主语 it 的同位语结构形式,如:

It is obvious (that) money doesn't grow on trees.

显而易见,金钱是不会从树上长出来的。

以 that 引导的作主语的名词性从句中的连词 that 不能省略,但是如上所示,在许多形容词前和诸如 pity、shame 等少数名词之后,可以将 that 省略。

2) 名词性从句作动词宾语时,特别是在非正式语体中,前面的连词 that 常被省掉。许多动词(如 believe、know、think 等)之后的连词 that 皆可用可不用。某些动词(如 answer、imply 等)之后则一般需要使用连词 that。在诸如 assure、inform 等这样的“引述动词”之后,通常也要使用连词 that。此外,在较长的句子里,特别是在 that 从句与动词隔开时,连词 that 一般都不可省,如:

The dealer told me how much he was prepared to pay for my car and that I could have the money without delay.

那个商人告诉我他准备出多少钱买我的汽车,并说我会立即收到那笔款。

3) 介词之后不能使用 that 从句,如可以说:

He boasted about his success.

他夸耀他的成功。

He boasted that he was successful.

他夸耀他成功了。

但不能说:

* *He boasted about that he was successful.*

(2) 若干名词/介词/介词短语等 + that 从句

在名词 the fact、the idea 等后使用 that 从句可以避免直接用 that 开头这样笨拙的句子结构。同样,这样的形式也可以用于介词或介词短语之后,如:

The fact that his proposal makes sense should be recognized.

应当承认他的建议是有道理的。

The idea that everybody should be required to vote by law is something I don't agree with.

主张由法律规定每个人都要投票的意见是我所不能赞同的。

His love of literature was due to the fact that his mother read poetry to him when he was a child.

他对文学的爱好是由于他母亲从小就给他朗读诗歌的缘故。

In spite of/Despite the fact that hotel prices have risen sharply, the number of tourists is as great as ever.

尽管酒店收费猛涨,旅客的人数还是同以往一样多。

(3) 描述个人情感或确信无疑的形容词 + that 从句

afraid(害怕的)、glad(高兴的)、happy(幸福的)、pleased(愉快的)等,或 certain(可靠的)、sure(确实的)等之后皆可跟 that 从句,如:

I'm afraid (that) we've sold out of tickets.

对不起,我们的票已经卖光了。

(4) 否定词从主句至从句的转移

在表示思想和感觉的动词之后,如 believe(相信)、imagine(设想)、suppose 等动词之后,否定词从主句转移至 that 从句后,意思不变,如:

I don't believe (that) she'll arrive before 7.

我不相信她会在 7 点以前到达。

I believe (that) she won't arrive before 7.

我相信她 7 点以前不会到达。

词汇学习 Word study

1. fear

(1) *n*. (可数)恐惧,敬畏:

There is a look of fear in her eyes.

她的眼神流露出一丝恐惧。

(2) *n*. (可数)忧虑,担心(的事):

There is no reason for your fears.

你的忧虑毫无道理。

(3) *vt*. 害怕,恐惧:

I fear mice.

我怕耗子。

She feared to speak in her father's presence.

她害怕在她父亲面前讲话。

She feared flying.

她害怕飞行。

(4) *vt*. 恐怕,担心:

I fear I must go now.

恐怕我必须得走了。

(5) *vi*. 恐惧:

Never fear!

千万别怕!

(6) *vi*. (for) 为……担心:

We feared for her safety.

我们为她的安全担心。

2. grow (grew, grown)

(1) *vi*. (体积或数量的)变大,增加:

You must invest if you want your business to grow.

要想使生意扩大,必须投资。

(2) *vi*. 生长,发育:

Rice does not grow in a cold climate.

水稻在寒冷的气候下不能生长。

(3) *link v*. 变得,成为:

It's growing dark; we must go home soon.

天就要黑了,我们必须赶快回家。

I've grown accustomed to looking after myself.

我已经逐渐习惯自己照顾自己了。

It has grown out of fashion.

这已过时了。

She's growing to be more and more like her mother.

她长得越来越像她妈妈了。

(4) *vt*. 留(头发、胡子等);种植(庄稼):

She's grown her hair long.

她已留了长发。

The farmers grow corn in that region.

那个地区的农民种植玉米。

3. lose (lost)

(1) *vt*. 失去,遗失,损失:

He lost his keys.

他的钥匙丢了。

She lost her father in the accident.

她在这次车祸中失去了父亲。

(2) *vt*. (常用于被动语态) 失踪;死,死去:

The plane and all its crew and passengers were lost.

飞机及其机组全体成员和所有乘客都遇难了。

(3) *vt*. 输,失败:

The delay lost the battle for them.

The delay lost them the battle.

时间迟误使他们战斗失利。

(4) *vt*. 未赶上:

I lost the bus.

我没赶上汽车。

(5) *vt*. 没听见,没看见:

I lost some of your words because of the noise.

由于噪音,你说的有些话我没听到。

(6) *vt.* 专注,沉浸于:

He was lost in the book.

他沉浸于书中。

(7) *vt.* 浪费(时间、机会、努力等):

You should lose no time.

你不该浪费时间。

(8) *vi.* 受亏损,蒙受损害:

Will the company lose by the transaction?

公司在这项交易中会遭受损失吗?

(9) *vi.* (钟表)走得太慢:

My watch never loses.

我的表从来不慢。

练习答案　Key to written exercises

1. 关键句型练习答案

A　See text.

B　1　finds　　2　arrives　　3　changes

C　1　ought to/should　　2　must　　3　ought to/should
　　4　must

D　See text.

E　See text.

2. 难点练习答案

A　The regular verb *flow* (*flowed*, *flowed*) means 'move smoothly (as if) in a stream': *The river flowed gently down to the sea. The morning traffic flows past our house in a steady stream.*

The irregular verb *fly* (*flew*, *flown*) means 'move through the air with wings or in an aircraft': *All of these birds will fly south in the autumn.*

B There was a dispute about foreign fishermen fishing in our territorial *waters*.

C In sentence 1, *since* is a conjunction meaning *as*, *as it is a fact that*, *because*.

In sentence 2, *since* is a preposition meaning *from a point in the past until now*.

D I can *no longer* support our representative because I don't agree with his policies.

I can't support our representative *any longer* because I don't agree with his policies.

3. 多项选择题答案

1 a	2 a	3 b	4 d	5 d	6 d
7 a	8 d	9 d	10 b	11 d	12 b

Lesson 12
Banks and their customers
银行和顾客

课文详注 Further notes on the text

1. **When anyone opens a current account at a bank, he is lending the bank money, repayment of which he may demand at any time, either in cash or by drawing a cheque in favour of another person.**

open an account 开一个户头(即账号)。a current account 一个活期户头(即账号)。repayment of which ...在句中为非限定性定语从句,which 代表前面的 money,而 repayment of which 在此定语从句中作动词 demand 的宾语。in cash 用现金,以现金的方式。draw a cheque 开一张支票。in favour of 为介词短语,这里用来表示"以……为收款人"之意。在该介词短语之后,通常接人、事物或动名词作宾语。除根据本课课文所表达的上述含义外,此介词短语更常用来表示主语"赞同/支持(某人或某人的建议、意见等)",无被动含义,有时还用来表示"有利于"的意思,如:

Are they in favour of her suggestion?

他们赞成她的建议吗?

He is not in favour of giving votes to young people.

他不赞成投年轻人的票。

We're glad to see that more and more laws have been changing in favour of the poor.

我们高兴地看到越来越多的法律正向有利于穷人的方面

改变。

2. **Primarily, the banker-customer relationship is that of debtor and creditor—who is which depending on whether the customer's account is in credit or is overdrawn.**

指示代词 that 在这里指代前面的 the relationship，意即 the relationship of debtor and creditor。这里 who ... overdrawn 为定语从句，which ... overdrawn 为此定语从句中的主语 who 的表语。depending on ... overdrawn 为现在分词短语，同 which 一起构成独立主格结构，which 是该分词短语的逻辑主语，代表 debtor 或 creditor，意即“谁是债务人而谁是债权人”。whether ... overdrawn 为一个名词性从句，作介词 on 的宾语，其中的 be in credit 表示“有结余”之意。破折号后的整个解说性内容都用来进一步说明其前的句子。

3. **But, in addition to that basically simple concept, the bank and its customer owe a large number of obligations to one another.**

in addition to 除……以外还(有)。注意该介词短语同表示“除……以外其余的都”含义的介词短语 with the exception to 在语义上的不同，比较：

In addition to books, the delegate presented our university with other valuable gifts.
除了书籍以外，那位代表还赠送给我校一些其他珍贵的礼品。(包括那些书籍)
With the exception of that book, all his works have been translated into Chinese.
除了那本书以外，他其余的著作都已经译成了中文。(不包括那本书)

owe ... to ... 对……负有……。介词 to 后要接表示人的名词。除根据本课课文表达的这一含义外，还可用其表达诸如“欠……的……”、“把……归功于……”之意，如：

He owes $100 to his father.

他欠他父亲100美元。

If my child has improved in any way, he should owe it all to his teacher.

如果说我的孩子有了一些进步,完全归功于他的老师。

4. ... can give rise to problems and complications but a bank customer, unlike, say, a buyer of goods, cannot complain that the law is loaded against him.

give rise to 引起,导致。在介词 to 后,通常接表示不良结果的词,如:

These poor living conditions have given rise to disease.

这些糟糕的生活条件引起了疾病的发生。

unlike 为介词,同其后的 a buyer of goods 构成介词短语作 customer 的非限定性定语。该介词短语中插入的 say 为插入语,表示"比如"、"比方说"之意。在动词 complain 后的 that 宾语从句中,be loaded against 表示"与……不利"。

5. The bank must obey its customer's instructions, and not those of anyone else.

这里的指示代词 those 指代 instructions,以避免重复。

6. When, for example, a customer ... to debit his account only in respect of cheques drawn by himself.

for example 比如,例如。这里用作插入语。in respect of 为介词短语,常用来表达"关于"、"就……而言",其后接名词、代词或从句,如:

He is senior to me in respect of service.

在工作资历方面,他比我深。

In respect of what you say, there is nothing more that we can say.

就你的发言来讲,我们再没什么可说的了。

该短语在商业用语中还可用来表示“作为”、“根据”之意，如：

They should give her $ 200 in respect of the work she has done.

他们应付给她200美元作为她的工作报酬。

drawn by him 为过去分词短语，作定语，修饰 cheques。

7. . . . , and there is a very firm rule that the bank has no right or authority to pay out a customer's money on a cheque on which its . . .

这里的 that 从句为同位语从句，对 rule 作进一步说明。to pay out . . . forged 为动词不定式短语，作定语，修饰 right or authority。

8. It makes no difference that the forgery may have been a very skilful one: . . .

这里的代词 it 作形式主语，全句的逻辑主语是后面的 that 从句。make no difference 表示“没有差别”，意即“不起作用”之意。that 从句中的 may have been，即情态助动词 may + 动词的完成时结构，通常用来表示讲话人认为过去发生的事情从目前看来仍抱有可能性，但把握性不大，往往含有怀疑或推测的意味，如：

The students may have done their exercises yesterday.

学生们也许昨天做好练习了。

He may have talked with her.

他或许同她谈过了。

代词 one 后的冒号引出说明性内容。

9. For this reason there is no risk to the customer in the practice, adopted by banks, of printing the customer's name on his cheques.

这里的过去分词短语 adopted by banks 和介词短语 of . . . cheques 均作 practice 的定语。就正常的句子结构而言，该介词短语应紧随 practice 之后。这里将 adopted by banks 提前是使句子显得更为紧凑。

10. ..., it is the bank which will lose, not the customer.

这里的 it is ... which ...结构为强调用法。但应注意的是，在一般情况下，通常多使用 that，而不是 which。

语法 Grammar in use

名词性从句 (2)

由疑问句构成的名词性从句

(1) 由一般疑问句构成的名词性从句

一般疑问句构成的名词性从句由 if/whether + 陈述句语序的句子构成，可以起到主语、表语、动词/介词宾语的作用，如：

Whether he has signed the contract doesn't matter.

他是否在合同上签字无关紧要。(主语)

The question is whether he has signed the contract.

问题是他是否在合同上签了字。(表语)

I want to know whether/if he has signed the contract.

我想知道他是否在合同上签了字。(动词宾语)

We're concerned about whether he has signed the contract.

我们很关心他是否在合同上签了字。(介词宾语)

但是，在使用中应当注意，此类名词性从句在作主语、表语和介词宾语时只能使用 whether，而不能使用 if；在动词和少数否定形容词如 not certain 和 not sure 之后，whether 和 if 均可使用。

(2) 由疑问词疑问句构成的名词性从句

疑问词疑问句(即由 wh-词构成的疑问句，也称特殊疑问句)构成的名词性从句由 wh-疑问词 + 陈述句语序的句子构成，句子中起到的作用同如下所示：

When he did it is a mystery.

他什么时候干的这件事是个谜。(主语)

The question is when he did it.

问题是他什么时候干的此事。(表语)

I wonder when he did it.

我不知道他什么时候干的此事。(动词宾语)

It depends on when he did it.

这取决于他什么时候干的此事。(介词宾语)

此外,可以用关系代词 what 代替定语从句中的 that/which 结构形式,构成名词性从句,比较:

What matters most is good health.

最要紧的是有个好身体。(名词性从句)

The thing that matters most is good health.

最要紧的是有个好身体。(定语从句)

词汇学习 Word study

1. owe

(1) *vt.* 欠(债等),应该向……付出:

I owe her ten dollars.

我欠她 10 美元。

I still owe the garage for those repairs.

我还欠那家修车厂那些修理费。

(2) *vt.* 应把……归功于,感激:

We owe it to you that we finished our work in time.

幸亏有你帮助,我们才及时完成了工作。

I really owe a lot to my parents.

我真的很感激我的父母。

(3) *vi.* 欠钱:

Robert still owes for his shoes.

罗伯特还欠着买鞋的钱。

2. demand

(1) *vt*. 要求：

We demand justice.

我们要求公正。

She demanded to see the person in charge.

她要求见负责人。

She demanded that he return the dictionary he borrowed from her.

她要他归还从她那儿借的那本词典。

(2) *vt*. 需要：

This job demands patience.

这项工作需要耐心。

(3) *n*. (可数)要求：

The police is unlikely to agree to the kidnapper's demands.

警方不可能同意绑架者的要求。

(4) *n*. (可数)需要：

He has many demands on his time.

他有许多工作要花时间去做。

The demands of nursing an elderly sick person are too great for many people.

对许多人来说护理一位年老的病人太难了。

(5) *n*. (不可数)需求：

Good teachers are always in great demand.

总是很需要好教师。

3. instruct *vt*.

(1) 教导，教授：

The teacher instructed his students in how to do the chemical experiment.

教师向他的学生讲授如何做这个化学实验。

(2) 命令,指示:

We were instructed to leave one by one.

我们被命令一个一个地离开。

练习答案 Key to written exercises

1. 关键句型练习答案

A 1 The bank has no right or authority to pay out a customer's money on a cheque *on which* its customer's signature has been forged.

2 The source *from which* I obtained this information is very reliable.

3 We have certain principles *on which* we should act.

B 1 I am not referring to our policy but to *that of* our opponents.

2 The only system I know which will help you to remember what you have heard at a lecture is *that of* keeping notes.

C 1 The exhibition consists entirely of *pictures painted* by young children.

2 *The report* on education *prepared* by a government committee will soon be published.

3 According to the regulations, *income earned* overseas will be taxed.

2. 难点练习答案

A 1 The two words *current* and *currant* are pronounced the same.

The adjective *current* means 'belonging to the present, of the present day': *That word is no longer in current use.*

As a noun, a *current* is 'a continuously moving mass of liquid or gas' or 'the flow of electricity past a fixed point': *The current is strongest in the middle of the river. This button switches the current on.*

A *currant* is a 'small dried seedless grape, especially used in baking cakes': *My mother always puts a kilo of currants into a cake like this.*

2 The verbs *lend* and *borrow* are easily confused.

To *lend* something to someone (or *lend* someone something) means 'give someone the possession or use of something on the condition that it will be returned later', while *borrow* means 'take or receive something from another person, usually with permission, and with the understanding that it will be returned after a certain time'.

I lent a book to James./I lent James a book.

James borrowed a book from me.

3 *In favour of* means 'approving of, on the side of, in support of': *She is very much in favour of women managers.*

For the sake of means 'in order to help, improve or bring advantage': *He was advised to go and live near the coast for the sake of his health.*

4 *Whether* and *weather* are pronounced the same, but are very different in meaning.

Whether is a conjunction meaning 'if ... or not': *I*

don't know whether to go swimming.

The noun *weather* is the condition of wind, temperature, rain, sunshine, snow, etc., at a certain time or over a period of time: *If the weather is fine, we'll have the party outside in the garden.*

5 *Loaded* is the past tense of the verb *load* meaning 'put (a load) on or in (a vehicle, structure, etc.)': *They loaded their furniture into the van.* It also means 'put bullets into a gun or film into a camera': *This gun is loaded.*

Laden is an adjective meaning 'heavily loaded': *The lorry was fully laden. The apple trees are laden with fruit this year.*

6 The adverb *else* after question words and some pronouns means 'besides, also': *We need another helper. Can you find anyone else?*

The pronoun *other* means 'the second of two, the remaining one of a set': *One of you is right; the other is wrong.* It also means 'an additional person or thing': *Are there any other problems?*

7 A *specimen* is 'a piece or amount of something for being shown, tested, etc.': *The doctor will need a specimen of your blood.*

An *example* is 'something taken from a number of things of the same kind, which shows the usual quality of the rest or shows a general rule': *Can you give me an example of an adjective that ends in '-ive'?*

8 A *customer* is 'a person or organization who buys goods or services from a shop, business, etc.': *That man*

spends £20 a week in our shop and is one of our best customers.

A *client* is 'a person who gets help and advice from a professional person, for example from a lawyer, accountant, etc.': *That young accountant hasn't been in business long, but he already has 50 clients.*

9 The two words *cheque* and *check* are pronounced the same, but in British English have different meanings.

A *cheque* is 'a written order to a bank, on special printed paper, to pay a certain sum of money from one's bank account to oneself or to another person': *I haven't got enough cash, I'm afraid, so will you take a cheque?*

A *check* is 'an examination or inspection to make certain that something is correct or in good condition': *They gave the car a thorough check before they bought it.* (The verb *check* means 'test, examine or inspect to see if something is correct, true, in good condition, etc.': *Their bags were checked by security guards as they entered the building.*)

In American English, the spelling *check* is used for the British English *cheque*.

10 The verb *adopt* (/ə'dɒpt/) means 'take and use as one's own': *We adopted their production methods because they were so much better than our own.*

The verb *adapt* (/ə'dæpt/) means 'make suitable for new needs, new conditions': *When they moved to France, the children adapted to the change very well.*

11 The verb *print* means 'press letters or pictures onto paper by using shapes covered with ink, or copy letters,

etc. onto paper by using photographic methods': *This new machine can print 60 pages a minute.*

The verb *type* means 'operate a (typewriter or word processor) keyboard with your fingers': *I can only type with two fingers.*

B 1 *account* = a sum of money kept in a bank, which may be added to and taken from

2 *account* = a bill, statement of money owed

3 *account for* = explain, give a satisfactory explanation for

4 *account* = a written or spoken report or description

5 *on my account* = for my advantage or benefit

6 *on account of* = because of

C I don't know what to ask for my old bicycle, but how about, *say*, \$100?

Farmers, unlike, *say*, office workers, are bound to get dirty at work.

D When they *entered* the house, no one said a word.

Let's *discuss* the problem like adults.

As soon as we *reached* the top of the mountain, we all had a drink.

I wouldn't *leave* your car here if I were you.

E *In addition to* giving practice in speaking, the course also aims to help students improve their writing skills.

A large number of people attended the concert at our local hall last Saturday.

The spelling of German, *unlike* English, is very easy to understand.

You will be paid £250 *in respect of* the work you have done so far.

She has been ill for a month, and *for this reason* she has had to stay away from work.

3. 多项选择题答案

1	c	2	a	3	b	4	a	5	c	6	c
7	d	8	a	9	c	10	a	11	a	12	b

Lesson 13

The search for oil

探寻石油

课文详注　Further notes on the text

1. The deepest holes of all are made for oil, and they go down to as much as 25,000 feet.

在 The deepest holes of all 中，代词 all 指代 all holes。在 they go down to as much as ... 中，代词 they 指代前面所述 the deepest holes。短语 as much as 在这里表示“多达”、“达到”之意，就语义而言 much 相当于 deep，即表达出 as deep as 之意。

2. ... as we must with other mineral deposits.

这里的连词 as 引导出一方式状语从句，表示“像……那样”。由于上下文语义明确和为了使文章简练，在 must 后省略了 send men down。介词 with 在这里表示“对于”之意。整个从句表达出“就像开采其他矿藏一样，必须派人下去”。

3. ... and the search for oil has done more to improve deep drilling than any other mining activity.

名词性短语 the search for oil 在句中作主语。这里 has done more than ... 表示“比……做得更多”之意，而动词不定式 to improve deep drilling 在这里作状语，修饰 has done，意即“在改进深井钻探方面”。由于语义明确，这里在 any other mining activity 之后省略了 has done。

4. When it has been decided where we are going to drill, we put up at the surface an oil derrick.

在本句 When 引导的时间状语从句中，代词 it 起到形式主语的作用，而名词性从句 where ... drill 为逻辑主语。短语动词 put up 在这里表示“竖起”之意，表示与短语动词 set up 相同的语义。在表达上述意义时，这两个短语动词可以通用，而 put up 较 set up 更常见些。但不能用 put up 表示“建立/成立(某一机构或团体)”，如：

They are determined to set up a complete modern industrial system.

他们决心建立一个完整的现代化工业体系。(不用 *put up*)

The factory set up a night school last year.

这家工厂去年成立了一所夜校。(不用 *put up*)

an oil derrick 为 put up 的宾语，而介词短语 at the surface(在地面上)为地点状语。这里将地点状语提前，起到对该地点状语强调的作用。

5. It has to be tall ..., and we have to lower into the ground and haul out of the ground great lengths of drill pipe which are rotated by an engine at the top and are fitted with a cutting bit at the bottom.

这里的代词 It 指代 an oil derrick。great lengths of drill pipe 在这里作动词 lower 和 haul 的宾语。就正常的结构安排而言，其表达形式应为 ... we have to lower great lengths of drill pipe into the ground and haul them out of the ground，这里将其置于两个状语短语 into the ground 和 out of the ground 之后，主要起到使句子结构更为紧凑简练和更利于同其后由 which 引导的定语从句进行连接的作用。介词短语 at the top 和 at the bottom 指 at the top 和 at the bottom of the drill pipe。在并列连词 and 和 are fitted with 之间省略了关系代词 which。这里 be fitted with 表示“装配着”之意。

6. The geologist needs ..., so every so often a sample ...

The geologist 中的定冠词 the 在这里并非用来特指某一位 geologist，而是用来泛指 geologist 这一类人。短语 every so often 作频率状语，表示“时常”之意，类似的频率状语还有：every now and again、every now and then、every once in a while、now and again 等，如：

Every so often they go to the countryside.

他们常常下乡。

John comes to visit us every now and then.

约翰时常来看望我们。

7. **..., from which can be seen the strata the drill has been cutting through.**

本句为非限定性定语从句。本从句中使用了倒装语序结构，按正常语序为：from which the strata the drill has been cutting through can be seen。其中 the drill has been cutting through 为定语从句，其前省略了关系代词 that (which)。可以看出，这里由 the strata 和定语从句 the drill has been cutting through 构成的主语太长，使句子显得头重脚轻。为了避免这种情况，这里使用了倒装语序。

8. **Once we get down to the oil, it usually flows to the surface because great pressure, either from gas or water, is pushing it.**

Once 一旦。连接词，引导一时间状语从句。get down to 达到。此为一个及物动词词组，to 为介词，除表示本课课文中的意思外，更常用来表达“认真对待”、“致力于”等含义，后接工作、任务、学习等名词或动名词，如：

Now let's get down to business.

现在让我们言归正传。

It's no good shirking the job; it will have to be got down to.

推卸这份工作是没有用的，你得认真去干。

either from gas or water 作非限定性定语，置后修饰 pressure。

9. **This pressure must be under control, and we control it by means of the mud which we circulate down the drill pipe.**

under control 含被动意义，表示“被控制住”之意，作表语，通常与动词 be、bring、keep 等词连用，如：

Keep your temper under control.

忍住性子，别发火。

My son is no longer under my control.

我的儿子已不再服我的管教了。

本句中的 it 指代 pressure。by means of 以……方式，靠……手段。which 为关系代词，后置修饰 mud，这里用来引导一个定语从句，在从句中起宾语作用。

10. **We endeavour to avoid the old, romantic idea of a gusher, which wastes oil and gas.**

endeavour to do sth. 设法/尽力去做某事。正式用法，在动词 endeavour 后使用作宾语的动词不定式。本句中的介词 of 表示“关于”之意。这里的关系代词 which 用来引导一非限定性定语从句，后置修饰 the old, romantic idea。

11. **We want it to stay down the hole until we can lead it off in a controlled manner.**

本句中所用的两个 it 均指 oil。动词不定式 to stay down the hole 用作宾语补足语，其中 down 为介词。这里使用的 lead ... off 表示“让……流出”之意。

语法 Grammar in use

情态助动词 must、have to (或 have got to)和 need 的用法

就所表达的意义而言，must、have to 和 have got to 这 3 种形式一般可以互换使用。但在用于第 1 人称且指外在权力时，多使用

have to 和 have got to,如:

We have to/'ve got to send these VAT forms back before the end of the month.

在月底之前我们必须把增值税表送回。(即:法律要求我们这样做)

然而,当说话人认为自己有权做某事时,多使用 must,如:

I/We really must do something about the weeds in this garden.

我/我们确实必须除去花园里的杂草了。(即:假如我/我们不去做,也不必对任何人说明原因)

用于其他人称时,must 在表示不可推卸的责任方面,其迫切性和语气均比 have to 要强,如:

You must phone home at once. It's urgent.

你必须立即给家里打电话。事情很紧急。

指单一动作时,have to 和 have got to 可以互换使用,如:

I have to/have got to check the oil level in the car.

我必须检查汽车中的油量。

然而,指习惯性动作时,have to 和 have got to 不一定都可以互换。可互换的情况如:

I have to/have got to leave home every morning at 6.

我每天早上 6 点钟就得离开家。

可是,在同某些表示经常性的副词,如 always、sometimes 等连用时,have to 比 have got to 使用更多,如:

I often have to get up at 5. Do you ever have to get up at 5?

我经常得 5 点钟起床。你在 5 点钟起过床吗?

在表示"难道你不能不做……吗?"的意思时,一般要使用 must you ...? 而不用 do you have to ...? 或 have you got to ...? 形式,如:

Must you always interrupt me when I'm speaking?

你难道总是非要打断我说的话才行吗?

也可以用 must 表示恳切的邀请,如:

You really must come and see us sometime.

你什么时候务必来看看我们呀。

还可以将 must 用于表示强调劝告,如:

You really must have a holiday this year.

你今年一定得休假。

然而,need 只具有情态助动词的部分特征,一般仅在某些疑问句和否定句中使用。用于一般疑问句时,问者往往希望得到否定的答复,如:

Need you leave so soon?

你有必要这么早走吗?(=当然不必/希望不必)

由 need ... ? 构成的一般疑问句,在其肯定回答中通常使用 must,而在其否定回答中通常使用 needn't,如:

Need I type this letter again?
这封信需要我再打一遍吗?
Yes, you must.
是的,你必须再打一遍。
No, you needn't.
不,你不必了。

对于由 need + have + 过去分词...? 构成的表示"有必要做(曾做过的)……吗?"意义的一般疑问句,肯定回答中通常使用 had to,而否定回答中通常使用 needn't have,如:

Need you have told him about my plans?
你有必要把我的计划告诉给他吗?
Yes, I had to.
是的,我必须这样做。(无可选择)
No, I needn't have.
不,我不必这样做。(有可选择)

作为情态助动词的 need 还可以和否定副词（如 hardly、never、seldom、rarely、scarcely 等）连用，表示实际否定含义，如：

You need never know what he has just told me.

你根本不必知道他刚才告诉我的话。

I need hardly tell you how badly I feel about her departure.

我不必对你说我对她的离去有多么难过。

此外，need 还可用于否定主句后的从句中，如：

I don't think you need leave yet.

我认为你还不必走。

总之，作为情态助动词使用的 need 多用于否定结构，表示没有必要，如：

I needn't go.

我不必去。

除此之外，need to 一般只作完全动词使用，如：

I need to go to the dentist this morning.

今天上午我需要去看牙。

She doesn't need to go to the dentist.

她不必去看牙。

Why did you need to go to the dentist?

你为什么要去看牙?

词汇学习　Word study

1. decide

(1) *vt.* 解决，判决，裁决：

The committee is designated to decide an argument.

该委员会被指定裁决一场辩论。

(2) *vt.* 决定：

He decided that he would stay.

他决定留下来。

(3) *vt*. 使决定：

What decided you to take the job?

什么使你决定接受这个工作?

(4) *vi*. 解决,判决,裁决：

The committee decided on/for/in favour of the cheapest option.

委员会裁定采用最便宜的那种。

(5) *vi*. 决定：

You have to decide by next Friday.

你必须在下周五之前做出决定。

In the end we decided to go to the theatre.

最终我们决定去剧院看戏。

2. avoid *vt*.

(1) 避免,防止：

To avoid an accident, you should drive more carefully.

为避免发生意外,你应当把车开得更小心些。

(2) 避开,回避：

He had to walk more slowly to avoid the puddles in the road.

他不得不走得更缓慢些,以避开路上的水坑。

3. reach

(1) *vt*. 到达：

He reached the station at 9.00 a.m.

他早晨9点到达了车站。

(2) *vt*. 伸,伸出：

He reached his hand out for the book.

他伸手拿书。

(3) *vt*. 与……取得联系：

He was trying to reach her last night.

他昨晚试图与她取得联系。

(4) *vt*. 达成,达到:

They finally reached the agreement.

他们最终达成共识。

The bookshelf reaches the ceiling.

书架一直顶到天花板。

The cost will reach millions.

成本将达成数百万。

(5) *vi*. 伸手去抓,摸,够:

I can't reach to the top of the wall.

我够不着墙顶。

The man reached for his gun.

那个人伸手去够他的枪。

(6) *n*. (可数)伸,伸出:

The climber made a reach for the rope.

登山者伸手去够绳子。

(7) *n*. 能及的范围:

It is out of my reach.

这是我力所不及的。

练习答案 Key to written exercises

1. 关键句型练习答案

A See text.

B See text.

C 1 are going to 2 will 3 will be 4 will
5 is going to

D 1 Tell me where *he lives*. (Direct question: Where does

he live?)

2 I don't know why *he went there*. (Direct question: Why did he go there?)

3 Ask him how *he knows so much about the town*. (Direct question: How do you know so much about the town?)

4 Did he tell you when *he was born*? (Direct question: When was he born?)

E She *allowed* me to have the day off.

Can you *ask* him to go shopping for me?

Can you *teach* me to write Chinese?

The police still don't know what *caused* the driver to swerve off the road.

They *warned* me not to stay too long.

I *advise* you to leave as soon as possible.

2. 难点练习答案

A 1 The words *hole* and *whole* are pronounced the same, but have different meanings.

A *hole* is an empty space inside something solid: *There was a large hole in the field and at the bottom of the hole was the entrance to a cave.*

The adjective *whole* means 'all (the) or the full amount of': *When I was ill the last time, I took a whole week off college.*

2 An *engine* is 'a piece of machinery with moving parts which changes power from steam, electricity, oil, etc. into movement': *A jet engine is extremely noisy.*

A *machine* is 'any instrument or apparatus which uses power, such as electricity, to perform work': *They've just bought a new washing machine. We've got a drinks machine in our office*.

3 The verb *fit* means 'be the right size or shape (for)': *These shoes fit me perfectly*.

The verb *suit* means 'match or look good on (someone)': *She should never wear red: the colour doesn't suit her at all*.

4 The adjective *clean* means 'free from dirt' (*I must put on a clean shirt this evening*) or 'having a smooth edge or surface' (*The surgeon made a clean cut in the patient's arm*).

The adjective *clear* means 'easy to hear, read or understand': *The lecturer was a very clear speaker*.

5 The noun *control* means 'the power to command, influence or direct': *They have no control at all over their children*.

The noun *check* means 'an examination or inspection, to make certain that something is correct or in good condition': *You should keep a check on the oil level in your car*.

B 1 construct 2 extinguish 3 tolerate

4 postponed

C 1 From the moment that/When/As soon as

2 one time

3 Some time ago/A long time ago

4 occasionally

5 immediately

6 Suddenly and unexpectedly

D Don't worry—everything is *under control*.

That woman's children are so badly-behaved they are almost

out of control.

I couldn't help the family because the situation was completely *beyond my control*.

E The young man got into his car and *drove off* without looking to see if anything was coming.

I know he lost his temper, but he'll *cool off* soon.

As soon as the film finished, they came out of the cinema and *hurried off* home.

Can you *switch off* all the lights before you go to bed?

My mouth is feeling all tingly now that the injection *is wearing off*.

3. 多项选择题答案

1	a	2	c	3	d	4	a	5	c	6	b
7	d	8	a	9	b	10	c	11	a	12	d

Lesson 14
The Butterfly Effect
蝴蝶效应

课文详注 Further notes on the text

1. **Beyond two or three days, the world's best weather forecasts are speculative, and beyond six or seven days they are worthless.**

   Beyond two or three days 超出/超过两三天。这里 beyond 表示"超出/超过……范围"的含义,在句中作状语。这里将其提前,用来表示强调。代词 they 用来指代 the world's best weather forecasts。

2. **For small pieces of weather—and to a global forecaster, small can mean thunderstorms and blizzards—...**

   此处破折号中的内容为插入语,对前面短语 For small pieces of weather 中的形容词 small 作进一步的解释说明。

3. **..., cascading upward through a chain of turbulent features, from dust devils and squalls up to continent-sized eddies that only satellites can see.**

   这里 cascading ... features 为分词短语,在句中作方式状语,对主句谓语动词 multiply 作具体说明。from ... to ... . 从……到/至……。这里由 from ... to ... 构成的介词短语在句中作非限定性定语,置后修饰 a chain of turbulent features。此短语中的 that 为关系代词,引导一定语,它用来指代 eddies,在从句中起主语作用。

4. **... work with a grid of points of the order of sixty miles**

apart, and even so, ... since ....

这里 work 含有“起作用”的意义。介词短语 with ... apart 在句中作方式状语。其中 apart 作定语,置后修饰 sixty miles。even so 即便如此,这里的 so 为代词,指代前面整个句子所表述的意义。since 因为,由于,连词,用来引导一原因状语从句。

5. **But suppose the earth could be covered with sensors spaced one foot apart, rising at one-foot intervals all the way to the top of the atmosphere. Suppose every sensor ... a meteorologist would want.**

这两个句子由 suppose(假设)引导的两个条件状语从句构成,提出两个假定条件。在这两个从句中,could 和 would 表明使用的是虚拟语气。在 suppose 引导的条件状语从句中,既可以使用一般语气,也可以使用虚拟语气。当认为所假设的条件具有更多的不确定性时,通常可以使用虚拟语气。在 be covered with(布满/覆盖着)中,可将 covered 视为一个形容词,表明状态。spaced one foot apart 为过去分词短语,作定语,后置修饰 sensors。rising at ... the atmosphere 为现在分词短语,在句中作方式状语,说明 could be covered with 的方式。a meteorologist would want 为定语从句,其前省略了关系代词 that/which。

6. **At noon the spaces between the sensors will hide fluctuations that the computer will not know about, tiny deviations from the average.**

between the sensors 传感器之间的,介词短语,作定语,修饰 spaces。that 为关系代词,引导一个定语从句,在这里指代 fluctuations,作介词 about 的宾语。这里 tiny deviations from the average 是 fluctuations 的同位语,对其作进一步的说明。

语法 Grammar in use

分词结构在句子中的使用 (1)

代替从句的现在分词结构

分词结构在句子中具有多种功能。起到多种从句的作用就是其诸多功能中的一种。分词结构更常使用于正式语体中。现将分词结构形式和其可替代的从句形式分别列出,对它们在句子中的构成形式进行比较。

(1) 代替时间状语从句

Since I phoned you this morning, I have changed my plan.(时间状语从句)
Since phoning you this morning, I have changed my plan.(分词结构)
从我今天早上给你打了电话以后,我就改变了计划。

When I found the front door open, I became suspicious.(时间状语从句)
On finding the front door open, I became suspicious.(分词结构)
当发现大门开着,我就起了疑心。

While I tried to open the can, I cut my hand.(时间状语从句)
In trying to open the can, I cut my hand.(分词结构)
在试图打开罐头时,我划破了手。

注意:

1) 现在分词可以用于时间连词 after、before、since、when 和 while 之后,但不能用于 as、as soon as、directly 和 until 等时间连词之后。

2) 上述第 2、3 例中的介词 on 和 in 可以作 when 和 while 解。

3) 当 since 相当于 because(因为)时,不能使用分词结构。

(2) 代替原因状语从句

As I was anxious to please him, I bought him a nice present.(原因状语从句)
Being anxious to please him, I bought him a nice present.(分词结构)
因为我急于讨好他,我给他买了一件精美的礼品。

(3) 代替条件状语从句

If you are travelling north, you must change at Leeds.(条件状语从句)
If travelling north, you must change at Leeds.(分词结构)
如果你要去北方旅行,你必须在利兹换车。

Unless you pay by credit card, please pay in cash.(条件状语从句)
Unless paying by credit card, please pay in cash.(分词结构)
请付现金,除非(你)使用信用卡。

注意:

现在分词结构通常只用于连词 if 和 unless 之后。

(4) 代替让步状语从句

While he admitted that he had received the stolen jewellery, he denied having taken part in the robbery.(让步状语从句)
While admitting that he had received the stolen jewellery, he denied having taken part in the robbery.(分词结构)
尽管(他)承认收受了盗窃的珠宝,但他否认参与了抢劫案。

注意：

现在分词结构可以用于 although、even though、though 和 while 之后。

(5) 代替定语从句

The train which is arriving at Platform 8 is the 17.50 from Crewe.（定语从句）

The train arriving at Platform 8 is the 17.50 from Crewe.（分词结构）

即将进 8 号站台的列车是 17:50 从克鲁开来的。

注意：

现在分词结构可以用来代替其关系代词后用一般现在时或现在进行时表达的限定性定语从句。

词汇学习 Word study

1. guess

(1) *vt.* 猜测，猜出：

He guessed the answer to the teacher's question.

他猜出了老师所提问题的答案。

I didn't know for certain, but I guessed that he was over forty.

我说不准，但我猜他有四十多岁了。

(2) *vt.* (口)想，估计：

I guess you don't have time to go out now that you have young children.

我想你既然有了小孩，就没时间出去了。

(3) *vi.* 猜测：

I don't really know, I'm just guessing.

我并不知道，我只是在瞎猜。

(4) *n*.（可数）猜测，估计：

I took a guess at the answer.

我猜了一下答案。

At a guess, there are 100 people at the birthday party.

凭估计，生日晚会上有 100 人。

(5) *n*. 猜想：

My guess is that he didn't come because he was angry with us.

我猜想他没来的原因是他生我们的气了。

2. hide (hid, hidden)

(1) *vt*. 躲藏，隐蔽：

The trees hid the house from view.

树木把房屋遮挡住了。

(2) *vt*. 隐瞒，掩饰：

Don't hide your feelings; say what you think.

不要隐瞒你的感受，你想到什么就说什么。

(3) *vi*. 躲藏，藏：

The boy ran swiftly up the stairs and hid in the bedroom.

小男孩飞快地跑上楼，躲到了卧室里。

3. multiply

(1) *vt*. 乘：

4 multiplied by 7 is 28.

4 乘以 7 等于 28。

(2) *vt*. 增加：

The factory has tried hard to multiply its production.

那家工厂已做出极大努力来增加产量。

(3) *vi*. 有乘的能力，做乘法：

The little girl can't multiply yet.

那个小姑娘还不会乘法呢。

(4) *vi*. 增加：

Their production multiplied quickly when they adopted the new approach.

采用了新方法后，他们的产量增长得很快。

(5) *vi*. 繁殖：

This kind of animals never multiplies fast.

这种动物不会繁殖得很快的。

练习答案 Key to written exercises

1. 关键句型练习答案

A 1 There's a fault in the earth's crust *running* (= and it runs) along the west coast of the U.S.A.

2 The hurricane hit Florida, *sweeping away* (= and it swept away) everything in its path.

3 I noticed the lights were on, *assuming* (= and I assumed) they were at home.

4 The President emerged from the airport *waving* (= and he waved) to the reporters.

B 1 You can go home early, providing (that) *you finish your work*.

2 We can offer you a job on condition (that) *you start next Monday*.

3 You can come in any time you like tomorrow morning so long as *you come in on Saturday as well*.

4 I won't phone you unless *I need some help*.

5 He'll definitely win even if *he gets a slow start*.

C 1 *a* He will not get the fax tomorrow morning.

b He will have the fax tomorrow morning. In fact, it will reach him sometime between now and then.

2 *a* He will wait in Beijing. The message will arrive. Then he will leave.

b He will leave Beijing. Then this message will arrive. But he won't be there to receive it.

3 *a* When next June comes, the new motorway will be ready. (We don't know exactly when they will complete it, but it will be sometime between now and next June.)

b This sentence stresses the fact that next June is the earliest date for the completion of the new motorway.

2. 难点练习答案

A 1 *since* = because

2 *since* = from the time when

3 *since* = from then until now

4 *since* = from (eight o'clock) until now

5 *Since* = As, As it is a fact that

B 1 Whether 2 whether 3 if/whether

4 whether 5 if/whether

3. 多项选择题答案

1 d 2 b 3 d 4 c 5 c 6 a

7 c 8 c 9 b 10 d 11 b 12 d

Lesson 15
Secrecy in industry
工业中的秘密

课文详注 Further notes on the text

1. **Two factors weigh heavily against the effectiveness of scientific research in industry.**

weigh against 不利于。表达此意义时,这一短语动词不用于被动语态,并且通常仅用于一般时态,如:

Evidence will weigh against him.

证据将对他不利。

His frequent lateness will weigh heavily against him when new appointments are being decided.

新决定任命时,他经常迟到将对他极为不利。

weigh ... against 形式通常表达"根据……权衡/考虑"的含义,如:

The quality of the product must be weighed against its cost.

必须根据其成本考虑产品的质量。

2. **... the general atmosphere of secrecy in which it is carried out, the other the lack of ...**

这里关系代词 which 引导一定语从句,其中的代词 it 用来指代 scientific research。由于语义明确,在 the other 与 the lack of ...之间省略了动词 is。

3. **In so far as any inquiry is a secret one, it naturally limits all those engaged in carrying it out from effective contact with ...**

在英语中，短语连词 as far as 和 so far as 均可表达"就……而言"的意义，对主句的行为或状态加以限制，说明先行或后随事项所适用的范围，如：

As far as I could see, they were all satisfied.

依我来看，他们都是满意的。

So far as the quality of tone goes, the radio is excellent.

就音质而论，这收音机好极了。

但同介词 in 连用表达同一概念时，只能使用 in so far as 这一形式，其语气比单独使用 so far as 或 as far as 要强，如：

In so far as it served to foster new forces in the field of scientific research, I think we are justified in considering our experiment a great success.

至少在培养科研新生力量这一点上，我想我们有理由说我们的实验是极为成功的。

本句主句中用了两个 it，第 1 个指 secrecy，第 2 个指 inquiry。to limit ... from ... 表达"限制……不使……"之意。engaged in ... the same firm 为过去分词短语，作定语，修饰 those。这里 those 指 those research workers。be engaged in 表示"从事"，介词 in 后需使用名词、代词或动名词形式，如：

He has been engaged in the study of this field for 30 years.

他从事这一领域的研究已有 30 年了。

4. ... in researches which are of such general and fundamental nature that it is a positive advantage to them not to keep them secret.

which 为关系代词，引导一定语从句。be of 具有，如：

Mary is of a such gentle nature.

玛莉有着那样温柔的性格。

关联连词 such ... that ...（太……以至于……）用来引导结

果状语从句或程度状语从句，如：

Scientific evidence must be gathered in such a way that other scientists can be sure of its accuracy.

科学的论证必须这样收集，别的科学家才会确信其精确性。

It is such treatment that I cannot enjoy it.

这样的待遇是不能使我感到愉快的。

在此结果/程度状语从句中，对非谓语部分进行否定的特指否定成分即 not to keep them secret 为该从句的逻辑主语，先行代词 it 为形式主语。该从句中使用的两个 them，第 1 个指代 the bigger firms，第 2 个指代 researches。

5. Yet a great many processes depending on such research are sought for with complete secrecy until the stage at which patents can be taken out.

depending on such research 为现在分词短语，作定语，修饰 processes。这里 seek for 用来表达"探索"之意。with complete secrecy 极端秘密地，为方式状语，修饰 are sought for。at the stage 在这一阶段。which 为关系代词，用来引导定语从句。

6. Even more processes are never patented at all but kept as secret processes.

at all 表达"完全"、"根本"意义时，主要用于否定句(包括同含否定意义的词连用)中，如：

He doesn't know French at all.

他根本不懂法语。

but 除……以外，介词，意义与 except 相近，但 but 更强调意义上的几乎完整性，而 except 则更强调例外。此外，如文中那样，其后可以使用相当于名词的动词原形(即一般为省略了 to 的动词不定式)，如：

I have written all my letters but one.
我只差一封信就全写完了。(强调完整性)
I have written all my letters except one.
我还差一封信没写。(强调例外)

They could do nothing but wait for the doctor to come.
他们别无它法,只有等医生的到来。(其后使用省略了 *to* 的动词不定式)

本句中的 kept 前省略了 are。

7. This applies particularly to chemical industries, where chance discoveries play a much larger part than they do ...

这里指示代词 This 指 to keep as secret processes。在短语动词 apply to 中,根据使用结构来看,to 既可能是介词也可能是不定式符号。作介词使用时,该短语通常表示"向……提出申请"或如文中那样表示"适用于",而作不定式符号时,则表示"申请做"之意,如:

She has applied to that organization.
她已向该组织提交了申请。

What he has said doesn't apply to you.
他所说的话对你不适用。

They applied to return to the college last year.
他们去年申请要回校。

where 为关系副词,在这里用来引导一非限定性定语从句。play a part in ... 在……中起作用。they do 中的代词 they 用来指代 chance discoveries,do 用来指代 play a part。

8. Sometimes the secrecy goes to such an extent that ...

such an extent that ... 到了这样的程度以至于……。这里 such ... that ... 为关联连词,用来引导一结果状语从句。

9. Many firms, for instance, have great difficulty in obtaining ... to have their names entered as having taken out such and

such a book, for fear ... they are likely to be undertaking.

have difficulty in ... 在……方面有困难。使用此短语时,有两点应注意。首先,difficulty 之后要使用介词 in,再于其后使用名词、代词或动名词,不能在 difficulty 后直接使用动词不定式。其次,表达上述意义时,difficulty 为不可数形式,如:

They have no difficulty in solving the problem.

他们在解决这个问题方面没有困难。

We may have some difficulty in getting there by six o'clock.

我们 6 点以前到达那里可能有点困难。

to have their names entered 使用了 to have sth. done(过去分词)这样的使役结构。在这一结构中,sth. done 在句子中起复合宾语的作用。过去分词用来表明 sth. 所处的状态。as having taken out such and such a book 中的 as 为介词,having taken out 为动名词的完成时结构,所构成的介词短语在句中作方式状语。such and such a book 某某书。在英语中,想不指名地提到某个人时,常说,如:Mr. so and so,即"某某先生"。想不具体地说出某人或某事的名字或特征时,常用:such and such a girl (或 place、date)等。在 for fear ... to be undertaking 中,for fear 为复合连词,其后省略了 that。有人将其引导的部分视为消极性的目的状语从句,但就其意义而言,将其归类为原因状语似乎更为合理。在其引导的从句中,通常使用 should(或 would、might) + 动词原形或直接使用动词原形这样的虚拟语气结构。在现代英语中,有时也使用 may + 动词原形,但通常用来表达"预防某种可能性"的含义,如:

He handled the instrument with care for fear that it should be damaged.

他小心地摆弄那仪器,(因为)怕把它毁坏了。

Take an umbrella with you for fear that it may rain.

带上雨伞,(因为)恐怕要下雨。

they are likely to be undertaking 为定语从句,置后修饰 the kind of research,其前省略了关系代词 that 或 which。

语法 Grammar in use

分词结构在句子中的使用 (2)

代替从句的过去分词结构

过去分词结构在正式及文学体裁中比在会话中更为常见。

(1) 代替被动语态

过去分词结构之前可以不使用任何连词,直接用其代替被动语态,如:

When it was viewed from a distance the island of Nepenthe looked like a cloud.(时间状语从句中使用了被动语态结构)

Viewed from a distance, the island of Nepenthe looked like a cloud.(过去分词结构)

从远处眺望,尼彭西岛就像一朵云。

(2) 代替状语从句

过去分词结构之前也可以用相应连词代替被动语态,如:

Although it was built before the war, the engine is still in perfect order.(让步状语从句中使用了被动语态结构)

Although built before the war, the engine is still in perfect order.(与表示让步状语从句的连词 *although* 连用的过去分词结构)

虽然发动机是战前制造的,但仍性能良好。

If you are accepted for this post, you will be informed by May 1st.(条件状语从句中使用了被动语态)

If accepted for this post, you will be informed by May 1st.(与表示条件状语从句的连词 *if* 连用的过去分词结构)

如果同意你任此职,5 月 1 日前你将得到通知。

注意:在 after、before、since、on 和 in 之后不能直接使用过去分词结构,而需用 being + 过去分词结构,如:

After/When we were informed the flight would be delayed, we made other arrangements.

After/On being informed the flight would be delayed, we made other arrangements.

我们得知飞机要推迟起飞后,我们另作了安排。

(3) 代替关系从句

将定语从句中的关系代词 which 和其后的 be 动词删去,即可构成代替关系从句的过去分词结构,如:

The system which is used in this school is very successful.(关系从句中使用了被动语态)

The system used in this school is very successful.

这所学校所实施的制度是非常成功的。(代替关系从句的过去分词结构)

词汇学习 Word study

1. weigh

(1) *vt*. 称,量,掂:

I often weigh myself.

我常常称体重。

She weighed a pound of sugar in the grocery.

她在杂货店称了一磅糖。

(2) *vt*. 掂量,考虑,权衡:

He always weighs his words before speaking.

他总在说话前斟词酌句。

(3) *vi*. 重若干,称分量:

Feathers weigh light.

羽毛称起来很轻。

This box weighs six kilogrammes.

这只箱子重6公斤。

(4) *vi*. 有分量,有影响:

The loss weighs heavily with me.

损失对我关系很大。

2. likely (likelier, likeliest)

(1) *adj*. 可能的:

Is it likely that he won't come?

可能他不来了吧?

(2) *adj*. 会有结果的:

It is the likeliest time to find him at home.

这是最可能在家里找到他的时间了。

(3) *adv*. (常用于 most likely、very likely 等短语中)可能地:

They'll very likely refuse the invitation.

他们很可能拒绝邀请。

(4) as likely as not 可能,多半:

He'll come as likely as not.

他多半会来。

3. limit

(1) *vt*. (to)限制,限定,作为……界限:

You must limit yourself to ten minutes.

你必须限定自己在10分钟之内做完。

(2) *n*. (可数) 界限,边界:

In the election, they set a limit to the candidates' age.

在选举中,他们给候选人的年龄定了个界限。

(3) the limit 无法忍受的人或事:

You are the limit! Can't you be quiet for a while!

你真叫人受不了! 难道你就不能安静一会儿吗?

(4) within limits 适度地;有限度地:

I'd like to give you my help, within limits.

我愿意有限度地帮助你。

练习答案 Key to written exercises

1. 关键句型练习答案

A 1 See text.

B 1 carrying 2 obtaining

C 1 He was engaged in *looking for a cure for the common cold.*

2 He was prevented from *publishing the results of his research.*

3 He insisted on *telling his colleagues what he had discovered.*

4 If you persist in *consulting with your old colleagues, we shall have to take action.*

D 1 He told me *not to mention* it to you.

2 Please tell him *not to call* in the morning.

3 Didn't I beg you *not to write* to him?

E 1 We are going to *have* this room *decorated* soon.

2 I *had* this watch *repaired* last year.

3 Will you *have* the television *installed* in this room?

F 1 *Lest* anyone should worry that this will lead to price increases, let me reassure them that it will not.

2 Mother bought a lot of milk *for fear* we wouldn't be able to get any for a few more days.

2．难点练习答案

A 1 He is such a kind person that he is always thinking of ways to help his *fellow men*.

2 I try to do as much work as all my *fellow students*.

3 The leader of the trade union tried to persuade his *fellow workers* not to go on strike.

B 1 I'll help you *in so far as* I can. (in so far as = to the extent that)

2 She goes to the city *often enough* to know where the best places are to eat.

3 The temperature rose *to such an extent* that the firemen had to leave the burning building.

4 There have been so many complaints about the department that *the whole nature of* their business will have to be investigated.

C 1 performing it, completing it

2 go on, continue

3 filled with a strong feeling or excitement

4 bring to a successful end

D The phrase *such and such a* means 'a certain (time, amount, etc.) not named':

If they tell you to come on such and such a day, don't come if it's not convenient.

3．多项选择题答案

1 c　2 a　3 d　4 c　5 d　6 d

7 b　8 a　9 c　10 a　11 c　12 a

Lesson 16
The modern city
现代城市

课文详注 Further notes on the text

1. In the organization of industrial life the influence of the factory upon the physiological and mental state of the workers . . .

the influence upon/on . . . 对……的影响。在表达“对……有影响”的意义时，名词 influence 常与动词 have 连用，构成 have influence upon/on 这样的结构形式。应注意的是，在此短语中，influence 常作不可数名词使用，但 influence 前有修饰语时有时也可作可数名词，如：

It is said that in that country ten big families have great influence on its affairs.

据说在那个国家里，10 大家族对其事务颇有影响。

Religion has a great influence on man's behaviour.

宗教对人们的行为颇有影响。

2. . . . the conception of the maximum production at lowest cost, in order that . . .

at lowest cost 以最低成本的。介词短语，作定语，修饰 production。in order that 为复合连词，相当于 so that，后接从句，表示“为了”、“以便”、“目的在于”。其从句中常使用 may、might、can、could、should 等情态助动词，一般在正式书面用语中使用，如：

She will send them her proposals in order that they may have time to consider them.

她要把她的建议交给他们,以便他们有时间考虑这些建议。

In order that there might be no time lost, I oiled the machine myself.

为了节省时间,我亲自给机器上了油。

3. It has expanded without any idea of the human beings who run the machincs, and without giving any consideration to the effects produced on the individuals and on their descendants by the artificial mode of existence imposed by the factory.

It 这里指代 modern industry。without any idea of 根本不想/完全忽视。关系代词 who 用来引导一定语从句。without giving any consideration to 根本/完全不考虑。由于 without 为介词,因此其后的动词 give 需使用其动名词形式 giving。give consideration to 对……给予考虑。consideration 表示"考虑"时通常为不可数名词,如:

This requires some consideration.

这需要考虑一下。

They haven't taken this into consideration.

他们没有考虑到这一点。

在 the effects produced on the individuals and on their descendants ...中,由 produced ...构成的过去分词短语在句中作定语,修饰 the effects。短语 produce effects on ...表示"对……产生/造成影响"之意。过去分词短语 imposed by the factory(由工厂强加给的)在句中作定语,修饰 the artificial mode of existence。

4. The great cities have been built with no regard for us.

with no regard for us 不考虑我们。show/ pay regard for 对……关心,如:

She shows no regard for the feelings of others.

她根本不关心别人的感受。

You must have regard for our safety.

你必须关心我们的安全。

5. **The shape and dimensions of the skyscrapers depend entirely on the necessity of obtaining the maximum income per square foot of ground, and of offering to the tenants offices and apartments that please them.**

depend on/upon 依照,依赖,如:

Our plans depend on the weather.

我们的计划全依仗天气了。

of obtaining ... ground 和 and of offering ... that please them 同为定语,修饰 the necessity。offices and apartments 作 offering 的宾语,that please them 为定语从句,修饰 offices and apartments。这里 them 指代 tenants。

6. **This caused ... buildings where too large masses of human beings are crowded together.**

where 引导的是定语从句,修饰 buildings,意即"大厦内众多的人挤在一起"。

7. **While they enjoy ..., they do not realize that they are deprived of the necessities of life.**

that 引导一宾语从句,作动词 realize 的宾语。be deprived of 被剥夺,如:

We will be deprived of most of our basic rights by this new law.

我们将被这条新法律剥夺掉大部分的基本权利。

8. **The modern city consists of monstrous edifices and of dark, narrow streets full of petrol fumes and toxic gases, torn by the noise of the taxicabs, lorries and buses, and thronged ceaselessly by great crowds.**

consist of 包括，由……组成，如：

Our province consists of thirty counties.

我们省由 30 个县组成。

of dark, narrow ... 也与动词 consists 搭配，与 of monstrous edifices ... 为并列成分。full of ... gases 作定语，修饰 streets。torn by ... buses 和 thronged ... crowds 都是过去分词短语，作定语，修饰 streets。

9. Obviously, it has not been planned for the good of its inhabitants.

it 指 the modern city。the good 作名词，意即“利益”。

语法 Grammar in use

状语从句 (1)

状语从句，或称副词从句，是以从句形式修饰谓语、定语、状语或整个句子的结构形式。如同可以用 When?、Where?、How?、Why? 等提问及其答语来识别副词那样，状语从句也往往可以用同样的方法加以识别。

1. 时间状语从句

时间状语从句一般回答 When? 提出的问题，并可以用下列从属连词来引导：when(当……时候)、after(在……之后)、as(当，一边……一边)、as long as(达……之久，长达)、as soon as(一……就)、before(在……之前)、by the time (that)(到……的时候)、directly(一……就)、during the time (that)(在……期间)、immediately(一……就)、the moment (that)(一……就)、now (that)(既然)、once(一旦)、since(自从)、until/till(直到)、whenever(无论何时)、while(在……期间)等，如：

You can keep these records as long as you like.

这些唱片你愿保留多久都行。

He hasn't stopped complaining since he got back from his holidays.

自从他休假回来,就不停地抱怨。

Once you've seen one penguin, you've seen them all.

一旦你看见一只企鹅,就能看到它们全体。

时间状语从句放在句首时,如例3所示,其后常用逗号同主句分开。时间状语从句表示将来的意味时,在 after、as soon as、before、by the time、directly、immediately、the moment、till/until、when 等词后面不用一般将来时而用一般现在时,不用将来完成时而用现在完成时。这两种现在时态在时间连词后面常常可以互换,如:

The Owens will move to a new flat when their baby is/has been born.

孩子出生以后,欧文斯全家将搬到一套新的公寓去住。

现在完成时常常用于 once 和 now that 之后,如:

Now that we have decorated the house, we can move in.

现在我们把房间装饰好了,我们可以搬进去了。

2. 地点状语从句

地点状语从句一般回答 Where? 提出的问题,可以由 where(在……地方)、wherever(无论什么地方)、anywhere(无论何处)、everywhere(到处)等连词引导,如:

You can't camp where/wherever/anywhere you like these days.

如今你可不能随意在哪儿都宿营。

地点状语从句一般置于主句之后,但根据强调的需要,anywhere、everywhere 和 wherever 也可以放在句首,但 where 一般不可以,如:

Everywhere Jenny goes she's mistaken for Princess Diana.

无论詹妮走到什么地方,她都会被误认为是戴安娜公主。

where一般表示一个确定的但非特指的地点，而wherever、anywhere和everywhere通常表示“任何地方”，比较：

The church was built where there had once been a Roman temple.
那座教堂建在一度是罗马神庙的地方。
With a special train ticket you can travel wherever/anywhere/everywhere you like in Europe for just over £100.
你如持有专车票，仅花100英镑多一点儿，就可以到欧洲各地旅行。

词汇学习 Word study

1. earn *vt.*

(1) 挣得，赚：

How much do you earn each month?
你每月挣多少钱？
He earns $30,000 a year by writing stories.
他每年写小说可挣3万美元。

(2) 赢得：

His honesty earned him respect.
他的诚实使他得到尊敬。
He earned a lot of praise from the papers for the way he handled the strike.
他由于处理那次罢工的方式赢得了报界的赞扬。

(3) 使得到：

Her success in the exam earned her a place at university.
她在考试中取得的好成绩使她在大学获得了一席之地。
His skill in negotiating earned him a reputation as a

shrewd tactician.

他谈判的技巧为他赢得精明的策略家的名声。

2. obtain

(1) *vt.* 得到,获得,取得:

It's difficult to obtain a ticket for this concert.

这场音乐会的票很难搞到。

He said the police obtained this information by illegal means.

他说警方是通过不合法的手段获取这一情报的。

(2) *vi.* (正式,不用于进行时)通行,流行:

This regulation still obtains here.

这条规定在此仍然有效。

Those conditions no longer obtain.

那些状况已不再存在。

3. consist (不用于进行时) *vi.*

(1) (of) 由……组成,由……构成:

This bread consists mainly of sugar, flour and butter.

这种面包主要成分是糖、面粉和黄油。

The United Kindom consists of Great Britain and Northern Ireland.

联合王国是由大不列颠和北爱尔兰组成的。

(2) (in) 在于,存在于:

For her, happiness consists in watching television and reading magazines.

对她来说,幸福存在于看电视和杂志之中。

The beauty of Venice consists in the style of its ancient buildings.

威尼斯之美在于其古建筑的风格。

✍ 练习答案 Key to written exercises

1. 关键句型练习答案

A See text.

B 1 He is attending English classes in order that *he may make himself understood in Australia*.

2 She works very hard in order that *she may gain promotion soon*.

3 The Prime Minister has gone abroad in order that *he may consult directly with the leaders of other countries*.

C 1 I didn't know how many mushrooms my mother wanted, so I collected *as many as possible*.

2 *As far as possible* the company tries to deal with each individual complaint on its merits.

3 She didn't want everyone to know she was leaving, so she told *as few people as possible*.

4 She always wants to pay *as little as possible* for anything she buys.

D 1 Most teachers exert considerable *influence upon* their students.

2 All of his judgments are *based on* a lifetime of experience in the profession.

3 You might think that the students are noisy and badly-behaved but that's not *the true nature of* most of them.

4 When he became rich, he changed his whole *mode of* life.

5 I have very little *regard for* people who live on state benefits.

6 His answers to your requests will *depend on* how he's feeling.

7 They are faced with *the necessity of* buying a new car because their old one breaks down so often now.

8 The public transport system is *deprived of* the money needed for modernization.

9 What does the United Kingdom *consist of*? It consists of Great Britain and Northern Ireland.

10 The office was *full of* people all talking at the same time.

E 1 While we are less concerned *with large profits than we were, we have still not forgotten what we are in business for.*

2 While modern cities have grown in size, *they haven't improved their transport systems.*

3 While factory conditions have improved, *the same cannot be said for conditions in farming.*

2. 难点练习答案

A 1 The adjective *physiological* refers to the working of the body: *A stroke can have quite serious physiological effects on a person.*

The adjective *psychological* means 'of or connected with the way the mind works': *There might be some psychological reason for her behaviour over the past weeks.*

2 The verb *neglect* means 'give too little attention or care to': *She's been neglecting her college work.*

The verb *ignore* means 'take no notice of, or refuse to pay attention to someone or something': *When he came into the room, he completely ignored me. The government is rather unwisely ignoring the mood of the country.*

3 *Modern* means 'of the present time or typical of the most

recent times': *What do you think of modern art?*

Contemporary means 'belonging to the present time or of or belonging to the same (stated) time': *Contemporary reports of past events are often more interesting than a modern historian's view of them.*

4 The verb *earn* means 'get money by working': *How much does he earn a month?*

The verb *win* means 'gain or receive as the result of victory or success in any kind of competition': *I won £10 on the Lottery last week.* It also means 'be the best or first in a battle, competition, race, etc.': *He finally won the tennis match after two hours.*

5 The verb *please* means 'make someone happy': *The girl in the shop is always eager to please everyone.*

The verb *beg* means 'ask (for) with great eagerness or anxiety': *She begged her mother to allow her to go to the pop concert.*

B 1 The firm pays its company representatives a car mileage allowance which at the moment is 45p *per mile*.

2 I once drove my old car at 95 miles *per hour*.

3 If we all go on the trip, the cost *per person* will work out at exactly £10.

4 This particular material costs £5 *per yard*.

5 That restaurant has a 10 *per cent* service charge.

C 1 pressed

2 came together in large numbers

3 put, pushed, filled

D necessities, masses, buses, gases, lorries, taxicabs/taxis, cities

3. 多项选择题答案

1	a	2	b	3	c	4	c	5	a	6	d
7	d	8	b	9	a	10	b	11	a	12	c

Lesson 17
A man-made disease
人为的疾病

课文详注 Further notes on the text

1. **This rabbit had no natural enemies in the Antipodes, so that it multiplied with that promiscuous abandon characteristic of rabbits.**

   natural enemies 天敌。so that 引导结果状语从句。it 指 rabbit,该句的意思是“因此便以兔子所特有的杂乱交配迅猛繁衍后代”。with that promiscuous ...of rabbits 作方式状语。that 在此处作副词,表示程度,意即“那么”、“那样”,如:

   Don't take that much.
   别拿那么多。

2. **... the herbage which might have maintained millions of sheep and cattle.**

   关系代词 which 引导定语从句,修饰 herbage。该从句使用的是虚拟语气,表示“如果那些牧草不被兔子吃掉的话就可以饲养数百万头牛羊”。但是牧草被兔子吃掉是事实,所以这是不可能的,故使用虚拟语气结构。sheep 和 cattle 这两个单词的单复数形式相同。

3. **... was susceptible to a fatal virus disease, *myxomatosis*.**

   be susceptible to 易受……感染的,易受……影响的,如:

   She is so susceptible to cold.
   她容易得感冒。

4. **By infecting animals and letting them loose in the burrows,**

local ... created.

By infecting animals ... burrows 作方式状语。let loose 让乱跑。them 指受感染的动物。

5. **Later it was found that there was a type of mosquito which acted as the carrier of this disease and passed it on to the rabbits.**

it 为先行主语,真正的主语是 that 引导的主语从句。which 引导的是定语从句,修饰 a type of mosquito。act as 充当,担任,如:

She acted as our interpreter.

她担任我们的翻译。

pass ... on to 把……传给,如:

Please pass the information on to your co-workers.

请将这个消息传给你的同事们。

6. **So while ... to get rid of mosquitoes, ... Australia was encouraging this one.**

while 引导的是时间状语从句。get rid of 摆脱,如:

Finally we got rid of the insect problem.

最终我们摆脱了昆虫问题。

this one 指 a type of mosquito。

7. **It later became apparent that rabbits were developing a degree of resistance to this disease, so that the rabbit population was unlikely to be completely exterminated.**

It 为先行主语,真正的主语是 that 引导的主语从句。a degree of 某种程度的,如:

To do it well you have to achieve a high degree of proficiency.

要把它做好,你得达到很高的熟练程度。

注意名词 resistance 后面跟介词 to, 意即"对……的抵抗力",

如:resistance to a disease(对疾病的抵抗力)。so that 引导的是结果状语从句,意即“所以兔子不可能完全被消灭”。

8. **There were hopes, however, that the problem of the rabbit would become manageable.**

that 引导的是名词 hopes 的同位语从句,用来对 hopes 作进一步的说明。

9. **Ironically, Europe, which had bequeathed the rabbit as a pest to Australia, acquired this man-made disease as a pestilence.**

which 引导非限定性定语从句,修饰 Europe,意即“将这种兔子作为有害动物传给澳洲的欧洲”。bequeath ... to ... 把……遗赠给……,如:

She bequeath her fortune to him.

她把遗产赠送给他。

10. **A French physician ... and introduced *myxomatosis*.**

该句虽然在结构上是个由连词 and 连接的并列句,但是前后两个部分的关系是因果关系。

11. **It did not, however, remain within the confines of his estate.**

It 指这种多发性黏液瘤疾病。

12. **..., and it spread to Britain where wild rabbits are regarded as a pest but where domesticated rabbits, equally susceptible to the disease, ... fur industry.**

句子中 where 引导的两个句子都是定语从句,修饰 Britain。equally susceptible to the disease 作定语,修饰 rabbits。

13. **The question became one of whether Man could control the disease he had invented.**

one of whether ... 中的 one 代替 the question,以避免重复。whether 引导一宾语从句,作介词 of 的宾语。Man 在此处大写,指“人类”。he had invented 中,he 前省略了关系代词 that,作定语从句,修饰 the disease。he 指“人类”。

语法 Grammar in use

状语从句 (2)

1. 方式状语从句

此类从句一般回答 How? 提出的问题。引导方式状语从句的连词可以为:as(以……方式,按照)、in the way (that)(以……方式)、as if(仿佛,好像)、as though(仿佛,好像),如:

Type this again as I showed you a moment ago.

把这份材料按我刚才告诉你的那样再打一遍。

It sounds as if/as though the situation will get worse.

听起来好像情况会恶化似的。

She acted as if she were mad.

她的举动像疯了一样。

在口语中,可以用 how 和 the way 代替 as, 如:

This steak is cooked just how/the way I like it.

这牛排正是按我喜欢的那样做的。

当方式状语从句由 (in) the way (that)、the way in which、in the same way、(in) the same way as 等词语引导时,也可以用来表示比较,如:

She's behaving (in) the same way her elder sister used to.

她的举止和她姐姐过去一模一样。

此外,如上所示,方式状语一般置于主句之后。

2. 原因状语从句

此类从句一般用来回答 Why? 提出的问题,通常可以用下述从属连词引导:because(因为)、as(因为)、seeing (that)(由于)和 since(既然),如:

As/Because/Since there was very little support, the strike was not successful.

由于支持很少,罢工未获成功。

使用原因状语从句时，在主句与从句的使用位置上需注意下述几个方面：

(1) 一般情况下，被强调部分应当放在句尾。

(2) as 或 since 引导的原因状语从句一般放在句首，因为它们所表达的原因通常是已知的，因此没有必要再予以强调，如：

As/Since you can't type the letter yourself, you'll have to ask Susan to do it for you.

既然你自己不能打这封信，那你就请苏珊替你打吧。

(3) because 引导的原因状语从句一般放在主句之后，因为它通常为被强调的部分，如：

Jim's trying to find a place of his own because he wants to feel independent.

吉姆在设法找一个属于他自己的住处，因为他想要有自立感。

此外，because 在任何时候都可以代替 as、since 和 for 来说明一种或几种原因，而后者却不一定总能代替 because。

词汇学习 Word study

1. cause

(1) *n*. (可数)原因，起因：

Ice on the road was the cause of the accident.

路上的冰是造成这起事故的原因。

He is the cause of all my unhappiness.

他是造成我所有不幸的根源。

(2) *n*. (不可数)理由：

Don't complain without cause.

不要无缘无故瞎抱怨。

She showed us cause for dismissing him.

她向我们说明了开除他的原因。

(3) *n*. (可数)事业：

She devoted herself to the cause of women's liberation.

她一生致力于妇女的解放事业。

(4) *vt*. 使发生，引起，促使：

What caused the accident?

是什么导致了这起事故？

His illness caused him to miss the match.

他的病使他错过了这场比赛。

The car has caused me a lot of trouble.

这辆车给我找了许多麻烦。

They believe inflation is caused by big wage increases.

他们认为通货膨胀是由大幅度提高工资引起的。

2. maintain *vt*.

(1) 保持，维持，继续：

He maintained his leading position until the end of the game.

他一路领先，直到比赛结束。

Part of her job is to maintain good relations with our suppliers.

她的部分工作是保持好同我们的供应商的关系。

(2) 赡养，供养：

He is too poor to maintain his family.

他太穷，无力赡养家人。

The supplies of food were scarecely enough to maintain life.

供应的食物不足以维持生计。

(3) 维修，保养：

The railway lines have to be constantly maintained.

这些铁路线得不断进行维修保养。

That's the well-maintained house he mentioned just now.

那就是他刚才提到的那所维护得很好的房子。

(4) 坚持,主张:

He maintained his opinion that we should go immediately.

他坚持认为我们应该马上走。

He maintained that he had been home all night.

他坚持说他整个晚上都呆在家里。

3. spread (spread)

(1) *vt.* 展开,摊开:

The bird spread (out) its wings and flew away.

鸟展翅飞走了。

Spread the map out on the floor.

把地图铺在地板上。

(2) *vt.* 涂抹:

Spread some butter on the bread. (= Spread the bread with butter.)

把黄油涂在面包上。

(3) *vt.* 散布,传播:

One of his staff is spreading rumors about his past.

他的一名职员在散布有关他过去的谣言。

Rats spread diseases.

老鼠传播疾病。

(4) *vi.* 展开,扩展:

In the last five years the city has spread out rapidly in all directions.

在最近的5年中,该城市快速向四周延伸。

(5) *vi.* 弥漫,扩散:

The fire quickly spread to other parts of the building.
大火很快就蔓延到大楼的其他部分。

(6) *vi.* 流传,传播:

How do such rumours spread?
这样的谣言是怎么传开的?

(7) *n.* (可数,常用单数)传播,普及;范围,广度;散布,蔓延:

The spread of knowledge makes the society more and more progressive.
知识的传播使社会越来越进步。

The rapid spread of the disease is alarming the medical departments.
这场疾病的蔓延使卫生部门如坐针毡。

练习答案 Key to written exercises

1. 关键句型练习答案

A 1 In the early days of the settlement of Australia, enterprising settlers (unwisely) introduced the European rabbit. (ll.1-2)

2 (Later) it was found (later) that there was a type of mosquito which acted as the carrier of this disease and passed it on to the rabbits. (ll.7-8)

3 (Effectively) it (effectively) spread the disease all over the continent and (drastically) reduced (drastically) the rabbit population (drastically). (ll.9-10)

4 (Later) it (later) became apparent (later) that rabbits were developing a degree of resistance to the disease, so that the rabbit population was unlikely to be (completely) exterminated (completely). (ll.10-11)

5 (Ironically,) Europe, which had (ironically) bequeathed the rabbit as a pest to Australia, (ironically) acquired this man-made disease as a pestilence. (ll. 13-14)

B 1 He could not drive very well, *so that* he had an accident the second time he went out on the roads.

2 She learned a little Italian *so that* she could ask for things when she went there on holiday.

C 1 While Tom was doing his homework, his sister *was watching a video*.

2 While my wife was seeing to the evening meal, I *was writing some letters*.

D See text.

2. 难点练习答案

A 1 The verb *discover* means 'find out a fact, an answer to a question or problem, etc.': *Scientists have now discovered that this disease is carried by rats*.

The verb *invent* means 'make or produce (especially a new or useful thing or idea) for the first time': *Alexander Graham Bell invented the telephone in 1876*.

2 A *disease* (/dɪˈziːz/) is 'an illness or unhealthy condition caused by infection, a disorder, etc., but not by an accident': *She has suffered from a rare heart disease for many years*.

The noun *decease* (/dɪˈsiːs/) is a formal or legal word meaning 'death': *Upon your decease the house will pass to your wife*.

3 A *basis* is 'the facts, principles, statements, ecially. from which something is formed, started or developed': *The series of lectures he gave finally formed the basis of the*

book he wrote on the subject.

A *base* is 'the lowest part of something, especially the part on which something stands': *There was some strange carving on the base of the marble column*.

4 *Apparent* means 'easily seen or understood': *It soon became apparent why he had left the area so suddenly*.

Obvious means 'easy to see and understand, clear, must be recognized': *There were disadvantages to his plan which were obvious to us all*.

(*Apparent* and *obvious* are often interchangeable.)

5 The verb *acquire* means 'gain or come to possess, especially by one's own work, skill or action, and often over a long period of time': *How did you acquire your skill of using a keyboard?*

The verb *obtain* means 'become the owner of, especially by means of effort or planning': *I haven't been able to obtain that CD anywhere*. (The verb tends to be a little formal.)

6 One meaning of *degree* is 'a point on an imaginary line used for measuring or comparing qualities, feelings, abilities, etc.': *The minister expressed a degree of optimism about the state of the economy*.

A *rank* is 'a level of relative value, ability, importance, etc., on a scale, especially the official position someone holds in the army, navy, etc.': *That man attained the rank of captain after only a few years in the navy*.

B We were woken *in the early hours* of the morning by cats fighting in the street.

In the early years of the king's reign, the country enjoyed a period of peace.

The great violinist Yehudi Menuhin learned to play *at a very early age*.

C The old barn on that farm is *overrun* with rats.

You can't *overtake* on that bend: you can't see what's coming from the other direction.

She's very tired because she's been *overdoing* things at work.

The teacher *overlooked* my rudeness once, but warned me never to be rude again.

D 1 Don't *spread the butter* too thickly on my sandwiches.

2 This butter *spreads* very easily straight from the fridge.

E The spelling of *-able* words is always a problem. When, to create an adjective, we add *-able* to a verb or a noun which ends in a silent 'e', we usually drop the 'e' (*value—valuable*, *love—lovable*). However, in British spelling, the 'e' is kept in words ending in '-ceable' and '-geable' where the final 'e' affects the sound of the preceding consonant: *trace—traceable*, *manage—manageable*.

movable, lovable, peaceable, knowledgeable, changeable, serviceable, believable

F This CD is not the one I borrowed from you: it's *my own*.

I didn't stay with the others all the time because I wanted to spend some time *on my own*.

I don't need an umbrella because I've got one *of my own*.

3. 多项选择题答案

1	b	2	b	3	a	4	d	5	a	6	b
7	b	8	d	9	c	10	d	11	c	12	a

Lesson 18
Porpoises
海豚

课文详注 Further notes on the text

1. **There has long been a superstition among mariners that porpoises will save drowning men by pushing them to the surface, or protect them from sharks by surrounding them in defensive formation.**

   has long been 为现在完成时,表示该迷信一直流传到现在并还在流传。that 所引导的是名词 superstition 的同位语。动词 save 和 protect 为该同位语从句的并列谓语动词。by pushing them to the surface 和 by surrounding them in defensive formation 为方式状语,其中的代词 them 指 drowning men。

2. **Marine Studio biologists have pointed out that, however intelligent they may be, it is probably a mistake to credit dolphins with any motive of lifesaving.**

   that 引导宾语从句。however 引导的是该宾语从句中的让步状语从句。it 作该宾语从句的先行主语,真正的主语是动词不定式 to credit dolphins with。credit ... with ... 相信……具有……;在(贷方)记入……,如:

   I credit his parents with common sense.

   我相信他父母亲是通情达理的。

   He credited the account with fifty dollars.

   他在账户的贷方记入了 50 美元。

3. **On the occasions when they have pushed to shore an unconscious**

human being they have much more likely done it out of curiosity or for sport, as in riding the bow waves of a ship.

when 引导的是定语从句,修饰 occasion。much more likely 更大的可能。out of curiosity 出于好奇心。out of 出于,如:

I helped him out of kindness.

我帮助他是出于善心。

The boy did it completely out of ignorance.

那个男孩子做那件事纯属无知。

as in riding the bow waves of a ship 就像它们追逐被船首犁开的浪花一样。as 后面省略了 they did, 该短语在此句中作方式状语,修饰 have much more likely done it . . . 。

4. **In 1928 some porpoises were photographed working like beasers to push ashore a waterlogged mattress.**

photograph . . . doing sth. 拍摄到……做某事,如:

Tom was photographed leaving the building.

汤姆被拍摄到离开那座大楼。

5. **If, as has been reported, they have protected humans from sharks, it may have been because curiosity attracted them and because the scent of a possible meal attracted the sharks.**

as has been reported 中的 as 为关系代词,代替 they have protected humans from sharks,引导非限定性定语从句。it may have been 中的 it 指 they have protected humans from sharks。may have been 表示对过去发生的事情的推测,表示可能。句子中的两个 because 引导的是表语从句。

6. **It is possible that upon such an occasion a battle ensued, with the sharks being driven away or killed.**

It 为先行主语,that 引导的主语从句为真正的主语。with the sharks being driven away or killed 该短语为独立主格结构,表示伴随状况。短语中的 the sharks 作现在分词短语 being driven or killed 的逻辑主语。

7. **Whether it be bird, fish or beast, the porpoise is intrigued with anything that is alive.**

Whether it be bird, fish or beast 中,whether 作连词,引导一个让步状语从句,用以列举两个或更多的可能,句中的 it 指后面的 anything that is alive。此句中使用的是虚拟语气,意即 It is not important if it is a bird, fish or beast, 又如:

Whether you like it or not it's going to happen.

不管你喜欢不喜欢,它都要发生。

Let's face it—you're going to be late whether you go by bus or train.

让我们来正视它——不管你乘公共汽车还是乘火车你都要迟到。

be intrigued with 对……感兴趣,如:

The little girl is intrigued with whatever she sees.

那个小姑娘对看到的任何事情都很感兴趣。

that 引导的是定语从句,修饰 anything。

8. **They are constantly after the turtles, who peacefully submit to all sorts of indignities.**

after the turtles 追逐海龟。who 引导的是非限定性定语从句,修饰 the turtles。submit to 屈从于,如:

The people in that country did not submit to the invaders.

那个国家的人们不向入侵者屈服。

9. **Almost any day a young porpoise may be seen trying to turn a 300-pound sea turtle over by sticking his snout under the edge of his shell and pushing up for dear life.**

trying to turn ... 作主语 a young porpoise 的补足语。by sticking... and pushing up ... 作方式状语,修饰 turn ... over。该短语中的第 1 个 his 指"海豚的",而第 2 个 his 则指

"海龟的"。for dear life 拼命地，如：

He hung on to the slippery rope for dear life.

他拼命地抓住那根滑溜溜的绳子。

10. ..., and may require two porpoises working together.

working together 为现在分词短语，作宾语 two porpoises 的补足语。

11. In another game, as the turtle swims across the oceanarium, the first porpoise swoops down from above and butts his shell with his belly.

as 引导的是时间状语从句。from above 中的 above 为名词，而不是介词。该句中的第 1 个 his 指"海龟的"，而第 2 个 his 指"海豚的"。

12. He no sooner recovers his equilibrium than the next porpoise comes along and hits him another crack.

He 指 the turtle。该句使用的是 no sooner ... than ... 结构，意即"刚……就……"，如：

No sooner had he come into the room than the bell rang.

他刚进房间，电话铃就响了。

13. Eventually the turtle has been butted all the way down to the floor of the tank.

all the way 作状语，修饰 down to the floor of tank，意即"一直"，如：

It was so late that we had to walk all the way home.

天太晚了，我们只好一直走回家。

14. He is now satisfied merely to try to stand up, but as soon as he does so a porpoise knocks him flat.

does so 指 stands up。knock ... flat 将……击倒。

15. The turtle at last gives up by pulling his feet ...

by pulling his feet ... 作方式状语，修饰 gives up。

语法 Grammar in use

状语从句 (3)

1. 条件状语从句

此类从句通常可以由下述连词引导：assuming (that)(假定)、if (如果)、on condition (that)(在……条件下)、so/as long as(只要)、unless(除非，若不)等。(有关此部分语法内容和示例，见本册第6～7课后的语法部分。)

2. 让步状语从句

让步状语从句具有对比因素，因此有时也称为对比状语从句。此类状语从句一般由下述连词引导：although(虽然)、considering (that)(就……而论，考虑到)、though(虽然)、even though/if(即使)、much as(虽然很……)、while(虽然)、whereas(鉴于)、however much/badly/good, etc.(无论多么多/多么坏/多么好等)、no matter how(不管如何)、no matter how much (不管有多少)等，如：

Although/Though/Even though I felt sorry for him, I was secretly pleased that he was having difficulties.

虽然我为他感到惋惜，但因他有困难而暗自高兴。

Much as I'd like to help, there isn't a lot I can do.

虽然我很乐意帮忙，但没有多少我能出力的事。

While I disapprove of what you say, I would defend to the death your right to say it.

尽管我不赞成你说的话，我还是要拼命维护你这样说的权利。

连词 however 可以与许多形容词/副词连用；no matter 可以与疑问词(who、when、where 等)连用；而带后缀-ever 的复合词也可以像 no matter 那样引导让步状语从句，如：

However far it is, I intend to drive there tonight.

不管有多远，我今晚也要开车到那儿去。

Whatever (= No matter what) I say, I seem to say the wrong thing.

无论我说什么，都似乎说得不当。

在正式语体中，所有引导让步状语从句的连词后面为现在时时，其动词前都可以使用 may；而当 as 和 though 用来表达"不管到什么程度"的意思时，均可将其用于某些形容词、副词或动词之后引导让步状语从句，如：

However brilliant you are / may be, you can't know everything.

不管你有多聪明，也不可能什么都知道。

Unlikely as it sounds / may sound (= Though it sounds / may sound unlikely), what I'm telling you is true.

不管听起来怎样不可能，我告诉你的话都是真的。

Beautiful though the necklace was (= Though the necklace was beautiful), we thought it was over-priced so we didn't buy it.

不管项链如何漂亮，我们还是认为价钱太贵，没有买它。

Try as he might (= Though he tried), he couldn't solve the problem.

尽管他努力了，还是未能解决问题。

词汇学习 Word study

1. save

(1) *vt.* 搭救，挽救：

The soldier saved a child from drowning.

这名士兵救了一个溺水儿童。

(2) *vt.* 节省，省去：

We should save some money for future use.

我们应该为将来之用而攒点钱。

The computer will save you the trouble of having to type your paper again.

电脑省去了你将论文再打一遍的麻烦。

(3) *vt*. **储蓄,贮存:**

The clerk always saves 10 percent out of his monthly pay.

那个职员每月储蓄月薪的1/10。

(4) *vi*. **节省,储蓄,存钱:**

We'll just have to save for college.

我们得为上大学而存钱。

We should save on every penny.

我们应该节约每一分钱。

They are saving up to take a trip abroad.

他们正在存钱准备出国旅游。

2. push

(1) *vt*. **推,推动:**

He had to push his bicycle up the hill.

他不得不把自行车推上山。

He pushed the door open.

他将门推开。

(2) *vt*. **使伸出,使突出:**

He pushed the drowning boy to the surface of the water.

他将溺水的男孩推到水面。

(3) *vt*. **推进,催迫:**

His parents pushed him to get a job.

他父母催促他找个工作。

(4) *vt*. **提拔(人);推销(产品):**

The company is pushing its new product.

这个公司在推销它的新产品。

(5) *vi*. 推：

They were pushing and shoving.

他们连推带挤的。

(6) *vi*. 努力前进，努力工作：

He is pushing too hard at his new job.

他过分努力地干着他的新工作。

(7) *n*. (可数) 推，推动：

Give the car a hard push.

用力推一下车。

(8) *n*. 奋力：

We must make a push to finish making the plan.

我们必须加把劲把计划搞出来。

(9) push ahead with 推动，推进：

They tried to push ahead with their work.

他们努力推动工作的进程。

(10) push around 摆布：

He was pushed around by his mother.

他受他母亲摆布。

(11) push oneself forward 出风头：

He likes to push himself forward in class.

他喜欢在班里出风头。

(12) push through 挤过去：

He pushed through the crowd.

他从人群中挤过去。

3. credit

(1) *n*. (不可数)荣誉，称赞：

Most people are happy to take all the credit, but none of the blame.

多数人都乐于接受赞扬而不愿意接受谴责。

(2) *n*. (可数,常用单数)光荣,获得荣誉的人或事物:

Those table tennis players were a credit to our nation.

那些乒乓球运动员是我们国家的光荣。

(3) *n*. (可数)银行存款:

Please deposit this sum to my credit.

请把这笔款存入我的账上。

(4) *n*. (不可数)信任,相信:

It is unwise to place credit in hearsay.

相信道听途说是不明智的。

(5) *n*. (不可数)学分:

He took a course for three credits.

他选修了一门可得3个学分的课程。

(6) *vt*. 相信,信任,信赖:

It was hard to credit some of the stories we heard about her.

有关她的一些传言令人很难相信。

(7) *vt*. 把……存入:

He credited $200 to my account.

他将200美元存入我的账户。

(8) *vt*. 相信有:

He'd always been credited with understanding and sympathy for his patients.

人们一直认为他对病人既善解人意又有同情心。

练习答案 Key to written exercises

1. 关键句型练习答案

A See text.

B 1 I can't remember *posting that letter last week, although I'm sure I did.*

2 You should avoid *speaking to those girls if you don't get on with them.*

3 Will you stop *asking me so many questions*?

4 Fancy *meeting you here!*

5 I can't imagine him *going to a disco*.

6 Pardon my *asking, but are you related to John*?

C We commonly use the conjunction *no sooner... than* with the past perfect: I had *no sooner* put the phone down from ringing her *than* she rang me back.

(The same idea can also be expressed with *hardly... when*: He has *hardly* recovered his equilibrium *when* the next porpoise comes along...)

2. 难点练习答案

A 1 The verb *drown* means 'die by being under water and unable to breathe': *When the ship sank, only two people drowned, the rest of the passengers survived.*

The verb *choke* means 'have great difficulty in breathing or stop breathing because of blocking or damage to the breathing passages': *He almost choked to death on a fish bone.*

2 The adjective *unconscious* refers to 'having lost consciousness': *She hit her head as she got into the car and was unconscious for a few minutes.*

Insensitive, however, is 'lacking thoughtfulness and sympathy': *He's always great fun, but he's often total insensitive to the feelings of other people.*

3 *Curiosity* is 'a strong desire to know or learn': *We were*

burning with curiosity to know what had happened.

Strangeness, on the other hand, is an unfamiliar quality: *We were all struck by the strangeness of all the old people who lived in the house.*

4 *Indignity* is 'a state or situation that makes one feel ashamed or feel loss of respect': *I suffered the indignity of having to apologize in front of all those people.*

Disrespect is 'a lack of respect or politeness': *I'm sorry to say that he often shows disrespect for his elders.*

5 The verbs *raise* and *rise* are commonly confused.

Raise is a regular transitive verb meaning 'lift, push or move upwards': *She raised her finger to her lips as a sign for silence.*

The irregular vereb *rise* (*rose*, *risen*) is intransitive and means 'move from a lower to a higher level or position, go up, or get higher': *The river is rising after the rain.*

6 A *game* is 'a form of play or sport, or an example of this': *Let's have a game of cards.*

A *play* is 'a piece of writing performed by actors in a theatre or on TV or radio': *The college drama society are going to perform a play written by one of the students.*

7 The two adverbs *eventually* and *finally* are very close in meaning, both mean 'at last, in the end'.

However, *eventually* implies that 'at the end of a continuing process': *After many attempts she eventually managed to get promotion.*

And *finally* means 'at last, after a long period of time or after a series of difficulties': *After several delays, the plane finally left at six o'clock.*

B 1 *likely* = probably

2 *unlikely* = improbable

3 *likely* (here) = not at all probable, since it is said to show that one disbelieves what someone has said

4 *likely* = suitable to give good results or to succeed

C The men in the castle finally *drove off* their attackers.

When the sheep got into the shop, it took four people to *drive* them *out*.

The defending army *drove* the attackers *back* into the sea.

The shortage of bread will probably *drive* prices *up*.

D 1 They *are* constantly *after*... = They are constantly chasing...

2 The game *is over*. = The game is finished.

3 He's *out*. = He is away./He is not here.

4 When will he *be back*? = When will he be returning?

5 The match *is off*. = The match has been cancelled.

6 The fire *is out*. = The fire is no longer burning.

7 What'*s on*... = What film is showing...

E 1 When the police surrounded the house, the two men finally *gave themselves up*.

2 The chemical compound *gave off* an awful smell.

3 I wish my friend would *give back* the money he owes me.

3. 多项选择题答案

1 b　2 a　3 b　4 c　5 d　6 c

7 d　8 c　9 c　10 c　11 b　12 a

Lesson 19
The stuff of dreams
话说梦的本质

课文详注 Further notes on the text

1. **It is fairly clear that the sleeping period must have some function, and because there is so much of it the function would seem to be important.**

   It 作先行主语,真正的主语是 that 引导的从句。该句中的情态助动词 must 用来表示"肯定",如:

   You must be wrong here.

   在这点上你肯定错了。

   在 so much of it 中, much of 常用于代词 it、this 或 that 等前面,表示许多,如:

   I still remember much of it in some detail.

   我仍然记着这件事的许多细节。

   在文中,该处的 it 指 sleeping period。情态助动词 would 在此处表示"可能"。

2. **..., and one odd finding that makes the problem puzzling is that it looks very much as if sleeping is not simply a matter of giving the body a rest.**

   odd 奇特的。that 引导定语从句,修饰 finding。后面的 that 引导的是表语从句。动词 looks 在此处作系动词,as if 引导的是表语从句,意思是"好像"。

3. **'Rest', in terms of muscle relaxation and so on, ...**

   in terms of muscle relaxation and so on 从使肌肉得到放松等方

面来看。in terms of 从……方面看。

4. ... to a degree, and function best when more or less continuously active.

to a degree 在一定的程度上。when 引导的是时间状语,其后省略了 the body's tissues are。

5. In fact a basic amount of movement occurs during sleep which is specifically concerned with preventing muscle inactivity.

which 引导定语从句,修饰 movement,意即"防止肌肉活动停止的运动"。

6. This might be a plausible hypothesis were it not for two factors.

were it not for two factors 如果不是下面两个因素的话。该句为条件状语从句,在英语中可以省略 if,将从句中的 were 或 should 置于句首,构成条件状语从句。但这种用法通常只用于正式文章或公函中,如:

Should you be interested in our offer, please contact us.

你若对我们的报价感兴趣,请与我们联系。

Were it not for your help, I would still be homeless.

若非你的帮助,我仍会无家可归。

7. First the electroencephalograph (...) shows that while there is a change in the pattern of activity during sleep, there is no evidence that the total amount of activity is any less.

that 引导宾语从句,该从句的主句是 there is no evidence ...。while 在该宾语从句中引导一让步状语从句。最后的 that 引导的是名词 evidence 的同位语从句。

8. Some years ago ... experiments dealing with the recording of eye-movements during sleep.

dealing with 作定语,修饰 experiments,意即"涉及记录睡眠期间人的眼睛活动的实验报告"。deal with 处理,对付,论述,

如:

We deal with many customers every day.

我们每天跟许多顾客打交道。

This chapter deals with the problem of inflation.

这一章论述通货膨胀的问题。

9. **... is punctuated with peculiar bursts of eye-movements, some drifting and slow, others jerky and rapid.**

punctuate ... with/by ... 用……不停地打断……,如:

The President's speech was punctuated by constant applause.

总统的讲话不停地被掌声打断。

some drifting and slow 和 others jerky and rapid 是两个独立主格结构,作 eye-movements 的同位语。可视为在这两个结构中省略了现在分词 being。

10. **People woken during these periods of eye-movements generally reported that they had been dreaming.**

woken ... eye-movements 为过去分词短语,作定语,修饰 people。that 及其之后内容均为动词 reported 的宾语从句。

11. **When woken at other times they reported no dreams.**

When 引导的时间状语从句中省略了 they were。reported 后面跟随的是宾语从句,省略了 that they had。

12. **If one group of people ... for several nights on end, and another group ... but when they were not exhibiting eye-movements, ...**

on end 连续地,如:

He used to lock himself in his bedroom for hours on end and refuse to talk to anyone.

他过去常常连续几个小时将自己锁在卧室里,不同任何人讲话。

when 引导的是时间状语从句,意即“在眼球没活动时”。

13. **...were that it was not the disturbance of sleep that mattered, but the disturbance of dreaming.**

that 引导的是表语从句。该从句中使用了强调结构。所强调的部分是句子的主语 the disturbance of sleep 和 the disturbance of dreaming。按正常结构应该是:The disturbance of sleep did not matter, but the disturbance of dreaming mattered. 在 but the disturbance of dreaming 后面省略了 that mattered。

语法 Grammar in use

状语从句 (4)

1. 目的状语从句

此类状语从句通常可以用来回答 What for(为什么)? For what purpose(为什么目的)? 这样的问题,一般可以用下述连词引导:so that(以便)、in order that(以便)、in case(以免)、lest(免得)、for fear (that)(以免)等。但使用这类状语从句时,需就下述各点对其动词的结构形式和句子的时态予以注意:

(1) 当主句中的动词为一般现在时、现在完成时或一般将来时时,so that 和 in order that 引导的从句中可以使用 may(可以)、can(能够)或 will(会),也可以使用一般现在时,如:

I've arrived early so that/in order that I may/can/will get a good view of the procession.

我到得很早,以便可以/能够/会好好看看那游行的队伍。

Let us spend a few moments in silence so that/in order that we remember those who died to preserve our freedom.

让我们默哀片刻,以缅怀那些为维护我们的自由不受侵犯而牺牲了的人们。

(2) 当主句中的动词为一般过去时、过去进行时或过去完成时，so that 和 in order that 引导的从句中可以使用 should(可以)、could(能够)、might(可以)或 would(会)，如：

I arrived early so that/in order that I should/could/might/would get a good view of the procession.

我到得很早，以便我可以/能够/会好好看看那游行的队伍。

(3) 构成 so that 和 in order that 从句中的否定式时，可以使用 should、would 和 might，但是不能用 could，如：

I arrived early so that/in order that I might not miss anything.

我到得很早，以免错过什么。(*should not* 和 *would not* 均可使用，但不能使用 *could not*)

(4) in case 引导的状语从句用将来时态时，从句中必须使用 should、might 或现在时态，如：

We've installed an extinguisher next to the cooker in case there is/there should be/might be ever a fire.

我们在炉灶旁边安装了一个灭火器，以防着火。

(5) 在 lest 引导的状语从句中，should 可有可无，也可以使用虚拟语气，如：

We have a memorial service every year lest we (should) forget our debt to those who died in battle.

我们每年举行一次悼念仪式，以不忘缅怀阵亡将士。

I avoided mentioning the subject lest he be offended.

我回避提及这个问题，以免触犯他。

(6) 在 for fear 引导的状语从句中通常使用 might，但在 in case 引导的从句中使用过去时结构更为常用，如：

I bought the car at once for fear (that) he might change/in case he changed his mind.

我马上买下那辆汽车，以免他变卦。

(7) 用 to、so as to 和 in ordr to(其否定式分别为 not to、so as not to 和 in order not to)也可以表示目的，但它们是不定式形式，而不是连词。由于它们的结构简单得多，显得更为自然，故更为常用。

2. 结果状语从句

此类状语从句描述结果。它们可以由表示“太……以至于”意义的 so + 形容词/副词 + that 引导从句，或由 such (a) + 名词(或形容词 + 名词 + that)引导从句。分别用来回答 How + 形容词/副词...? 和 What's ... like? 这类的问题，如：

His reactions are so quick/He reacts so quickly (that) no one can match him.

他的反应/他反应如此敏捷(以致)无人比得上他。

They are such wonderful players (that) no one can beat them.

他们都是出色的运动员，没有人能战胜他们。

注意：由于在结构上，目的状语从句与结果状语从句均可以用连词 so that 引导，因此有必要对其加以区分。区分方法大体如下：

(1) 在目的状语从句中，任何时候都可以用 in order that 代替 so that，而在结果状语从句中则不可以。

(2) 在目的状语从句中，通常需要使用相应的情态助动词；而在结果状语从句中则通常不使用情态助动词。

(3) 结果状语从句总是用于主句之后；而目的状语则可以置于主句之前。

分别示例如下：

We arrived early so that/in order that we could/should/might/would get good seats.

我们到得早，以便找到好座位。(目的状语从句)

We arrived early, so (that) we got good seats.

我们到得早,因此我们找到了好座位。(结果状语从句)

So that I shouldn't worry, he phoned me on arrival.

为了不让我担心,他一到就给我打了电话。(目的状语从句)

词汇学习 Word study

1. achieve

(1) *vt*. 完成,实现:

They will achieve nothing if they don't work harder.

如果他们不更努力地工作,他们将一无所获。

She finally achieved her goal of becoming Vice President.

她最终实现了成为副总统的目标。

(2) *vt*. 达到,得到:

The company has achieved a 100% increase in profit.

这家公司的赢利增长了100%。

(3) *vi*. 做得好,取得成功:

Some smart children still do not achieve at school.

一些机灵的孩子在学校仍做得不尽如人意。

2. show (showed, shown/showed)

(1) *vt*. 出示,显示,展出:

Let me show you how to handle this.

让我来告诉你怎么来掌握这个。

Let me show you the work we've been doing.

我来给你展示一下我们一直在做的工作。

Please show the photograph to me.

请让我看一下那张照片。

(2) *vt*. 演出,放映:

The cinema shows five films each day.

该电影院每天放映 5 部电影。

(3) *vt*. 表明,证明,指出:

Plenty of evidence shows that he is the right choice for the job.

足够的证据表明他是这个工作的合适人选。

Could you show me the way, please?

你能给我指指路吗?

(4) *vt*. 解释,使了解:

He showed us an easier way to solve the problem.

他给我们讲解了解这道题的一个更简便的方法。

(5) *vi*. 出现,出席:

It's getting late; do you think they'll still show up?

天渐晚了。你认为他们还会来吗?

(6) *n*. (可数)表示,显示:

The occupying army staged a big military parade as a show of strength.

占领军进行了一次庞大的军事阅兵,以显示其力量。

(7) *n*. (可数)展览(会):

There is a flower show at Beihai Park.

北海公园有一个花卉展。

(8) *n*. (可数)演出:

There is a film show tonight.

今晚有场电影。

(9) *n*. (可数)外观;景象;奇观:

He is making a sorry show.

他作出遗憾的样子。

(10) *n*. (不可数)炫耀:

She is fond of show.

她喜欢炫耀。

(11) show off 炫耀:

The child is showing off in front of guests.

那个孩子在客人面前炫耀。

(12) show up

1) 揭露,使知道:

That report showed up the manager's mistakes.

那份报告揭露了经理的错误。

2) 到来,到达:

I wonder if he'll show up now.

我不知道他是否现在会来。

3. report

(1) *vt.* 报告,报道:

It is reported that the sun has come into an active period.

据报道太阳已经进入活跃期。

He just reported the facts.

他报告的仅是事实。

(2) *vt.* 告发:

He reported the student for stealing.

他告发那个学生偷东西。

(3) *vi.* 报到:

Reporting for duty, sir.

前来报到,长官。

(4) *n.* (可数) 报告,报道:

He wrote five reports last month.

他上月写了 5 份报告。

(5) *n.* 传言,谣传:

According to reports it is going to be hotter next year.

据说明年会更热。

(6) *n*. 成绩单：

My daughter has a good report this term.

我女儿本学期成绩优良。

练习答案 Key to written exercises

1. 关键句型练习答案

A 1 See text.

B 1 since 2 for 3 since 4 since

C Your car *needs cleaning*. (= Your car needs to be cleaned.)

Do these shoes *need mending*? (= Do these shoes need to be mended?)

The house *wants decorating*, I think. (= The house wants to be decorated, I think.)

D 1 *If it were* possible, I would leave tomorrow.

2 I would take action at once *if it were not* too late.

3 *If this allegation were* true, he would be arrested.

2. 难点练习答案

A 1 The adverb *fairly* (like *quite* and *rather*) means 'to some degree'. It is the weakest of the three words and is placed in front of the adjective it modifies: *It's a fairly difficult exercise, but not <u>too</u> difficult.*

The determiner *enough* means 'as much or as many as may be necessary': *The exercise is not difficult enough to worry me.*

2 If something is *puzzling*, it 'makes someone feel helpless and uncertain in the effort to explain or understand something': *All the doctors who have treated Jane have found her illness very puzzling.*

If something is *confusing*, it makes you feel mixed up (in your mind): *The instructions were so confusing that I couldn't understand them.*

Remember: Something is *puzzl**ing*** or *confus**ing***, someone is *puzzl**ed*** or *confus**ed***.

3 A *factor* is 'any of the forces, conditions, influences, etc., that act with others to bring about a result': *An important factor in the success of the project is the president's support.*

A *fact* is 'something that has happened or is happening, the truth, reality': *Don't give me a long account, just give me the facts.*

B 1 *dealing with* = about, having as its subject

2 *dealing with* = doing business with

3 *deal with* = take action about, tackle

C 1 *on end* = without a break, continuously

2 *on purpose* = by design

3 *On the whole* = Generally, Considering everything

4 *on duty* = at work

5 *on leave* = on holiday from government or army service

6 *on any account* = for any reason

7 *on my way* = going, leaving

3. 多项选择题答案

1	b	2	b	3	c	4	a	5	d	6	a
7	a	8	b	9	d	10	d	11	b	12	c

Lesson 20
Snake poison
蛇毒

课文详注 Further notes on the text

1. **How it came about that snakes manufactured poison is a mystery.**

   How 引导的是主语从句。it 在主语从句中作先行主语，真正的主语是 that 引导的主语从句。is a mystery 是整个句子的谓语部分。come about 发生，如：

   How did such a mess come about, anyway?

   到底这乱七八糟的是怎么发生的？

   come about 常用于 it + comes about + that 结构中，如：

   It came about that he had to cancel his vacation.

   所发生的事使他不得不取消假期。

2. **Over the periods their saliva, a mild, digestive juice like our own, was converted into a poison that defies analysis even today.**

   Over the periods 经过很长时间。a mild, digestive juice like our own 作名词 saliva 的同位语。convert into/to 把……改成，把……转换成，如：

   The plant converted to microchip production.

   该厂转产微集成电路。

   They converted their money from marks into pounds.

   他们将马克兑换成英镑。

   that 引导定语从句，修饰 a poison。defy 向……挑战，激(某人做某事)，如：

She defied them to prove her guilty.

她倒要看看他们能不能证明她有罪。

课文中该句的意思是"至今仍无法分析清楚的毒液"。

3. ...; they could have caught and lived on prey without using poison, just as ... still do.

could have caught and lived on 是虚拟语气结构，用来陈述与事实不符的情况。live on/off 靠……生活，以……为食，如：

The whole family lived on her salary.

整个一家子都靠她一个人的工资生活。

He didn't want to live off his parents.

他不想靠他的父母生活。

without using poison 为介词短语，作条件状语，意即"如果不用毒液的话"。这种结构称作含蓄条件句，也就是不用 if 直接引导的条件句，如：

With luck, we'll be there by tomorrow.

幸运的话，我们明天将到达那儿。(= *if we are lucky*)

Given time, they'll probably agree.

给时间的话，他们可能会同意。(= *if we give them time*)

But for his pension, he would starve.

要不是他有养老金，他就挨饿了。(= *if he didn't have his pension*)

just as 引导方式状语从句。

4. Poison to a snake is merely a luxury; it enables it to get its food with very little effort, no more effort than one bite.

to a snake 作状语，意即"对蛇来说"。to get its food ...为动词不定式，作宾语 it 的补足语。no more effort than one bite 是 little effort 的同位语，对其作补充说明。

5. And why only snakes?

这是一个省略句,完整的句子应该是:And why do only snakes have poison?

6. Cats, for instance, would be greatly helped; no running fights with large, fierce rats or tussles with grown rabbits—just a bite and no more effort needed.

这是两个分句。两个分句都省略了条件句 if they had poison。后一个分句还省略了 they would have。破折号后面的部分强调说明"如果有毒液的话,咬一口就足矣,毫不费劲"。

7. ..., it would be an assistance ... a two-edged weapon ...

it 指 poison。a two-edged weapon 双刃剑。意即"既有利又有弊"。该句的意思是"如果食肉动物都有毒液,就会造成食肉动物之间的互相残杀"。

8. But, of the vertebrates, ...

of the vertebrates 等于 among the vertebrates,意即"在脊椎动物中"。

9. One wonders also why Nature, with some snakes, concocted poison of such extreme potency.

One 在此处作代词,泛指"人们"。with some snakes 作状语,指"在某些蛇的身上"。该句中将其提前,放在其所修饰的动词 concocted 之前,是为了强调大自然在某些蛇身上调制出如此高效的毒液。concoct 调制,一般指"调制食品",如:

> *She concocted a meal from leftovers.*
>
> 她用剩菜剩饭做出了一顿饭。

该动词还可以转义为"编造",如:

> *He concocted an excuse for being late for work.*
>
> 他为上班迟到而编造了个借口。

of such extreme potency 为介词短语,作定语,修饰 poison,意即"如此高效的"。

10. In the conversion of saliva into poison, one might suppose that a fixed process took place.

In the conversion . . . poison 为介词短语,作状语,表示"在唾液转变成毒液的过程中"。该句使用的是虚拟语气结构,情态助动词 might 用来表示某种可能性。

11. It did not; some snakes manufactured a poison different in every respect from that of others, as different as arsenic is from strychnine, and having different effects.

It 指 a fixed process,did not 后面省略了短语动词 take place。different in . . . from that of others 作 poison 的定语。in every respect 作状语,修饰 different,意即"在各方面"。that of others 中的 that 指 poison,意即"其他蛇的毒液"。be different from 与……不同,如:

She is quite different from her elder sister.

她与她的姐姐截然不同。

as different as . . . 作非限定性定语从句,第 1 个 as 前面省略了 which is。as arsenic is 后面省略了 different。该从句的完整结构应该是:which is as different as arsenic is different from strychnine。and having different effects 与 different in every respect . . . 为并列结构,作定语,修饰 poison。

12. One poison acts on the nerves, the other on the blood.

act on 作用于,对……起作用,如:

The aspirin acted on the pain.

阿司匹林止痛。

on the blood 前面省略了动词 acts。如果并列结构中的动词相同,后一个动词可以省略。

13. Both poisons are unpleasant, but by far . . .

Both poisons 指 blood poison 和 nerve poison。by far 作状语,意即"……得多"、"显然",常用来修饰比较级或最高级,强调

数量或程度,如:

She is by far the better player.

她显然比别的运动员强得多。

This melon is by far the ripest of all.

这个西瓜显然是这些西瓜中最熟的。

14. It is said that ..., that the blood poison is, so to speak, ...

It为先行主语,that ... of the two和that the blood ... an improved formula为两个并列的主语从句。so to speak为插入语,意即"打个比方说"、"可以这样说",如:

We lost our shirt, so to speak.

可以这么说,我们丢了衬衣。

15. Be that as it may, the nerve poison does its business with man far more quickly than the blood poison.

Be that as it may是一个倒装的让步状语从句,相当于however that may be,意即"尽管如此"。does its business with man,意即"在人身上起作用"、"要人的命"。

16. Snakes did not acquire their poison for use against man but for use against prey such as rats and mice, and the effects on these of viperine poison is almost immediate.

Snakes did not acquire their poison for use against man but for use against prey意即"蛇的毒液不是为了对付人的,而是对付它的猎物的"。such as相当于like,用来列举,如:

My doctor told me to avoid fatty foods such as bacon or hamburgers.

我的医生告诫我避免食用诸如咸肉或汉堡这样的高脂肪食物。

the effects是主语,of viperine poison为其定语。on these中的these指rats and mice。名词effect与介词on搭配,指"对……所起的作用"。

语法 Grammar in use

状语从句 (5)

1. 比较状语从句

此类状语从句通常用来回答 How(怎么样)? 这样的问题,往往暗含 in relation to/compared with(较之于)之意。比较状语从句中往往包含下述这样的结构:as + 形容词(原形)/副词(原形) + as(像……一样)、not so/as + 形容词(原形)/副词(原形) + as(不像……一样)、形容词比较级/副词比较级 + than(比……更)、more/less ... than(比……更多/更少)、the + 比较级 + the + 比较级(越……越)等。此外,还包含诸如 as/so much/many + 名词 + as(像……一样多)这样的结构。根据所要表达的意义,其前还可以使用诸如 half(一半)、nearly(几乎,差不多)、nothing like(根本不像)等词语。有关比较状语从句的用法,见下述示例:

He is as quick in answering as his sister (*is*).

他回答得和他妹妹一样快。

He is not so/as quick in answering as his sister (*is*).

他回答得不如他妹妹那样快。

He moves more slowly than his sister (*does*).

他行动起来比他妹妹缓慢。

The more you practice, the better you get.

你练得越多,效果就越好。

He didn't sell half as/so many videos as he thought he would.

他售出的录像带还不到他设想的一半。

如上所示,当主句中与从句中所使用的动词及其时态相同时,从句中的动词往往可以省略;当主句和从句中所使用的主语、动词和时态相同时,可以将从句中的主语和动词省略,如:

When I spoke to him on the phone this morning, he was more agreeable than (*he was*) *last night.*

今天早上我用电话跟他通话时,他比昨天晚上要随和。

此外,在使用 as/so many/much + 名词 + as 结构时,如其前使用诸如 just(正好)、twice/ten times(两倍/10 倍)这类词语,其后只能使用 as 结构,而不能使用 so 结构,如:

You've made just as (不用 *so*) *many mistakes as I have.*

你犯的错误正好和我犯的一样多。

2. 限定性状语从句

主句受到由 in that(因为)、in so far as(在如此程度)和 in as much as(在如此程度)所引导的从句的修饰或限制,如:

The demonstration was fairly peaceful in that/in so far as there were only one or two clashes with the police.

该示威是相当和平的,与警察只发生了一两次冲突。

3. 缩略状语从句

这里指可以将从句中的主语和动词 be 省略的句子形式,如:

While (*she was*) *at college, she wrote a novel.*

她上大学时写了一部小说。(时间)

Where (*it is*) *necessary, improvements will be made.*

哪儿需要,就在哪儿改进。(地点)

He acted as if (*he was*) *certain of success.*

他的举止就像一定会成功一样。(方式)

If (*it is*) *possible, please let me know by this evening.*

如果可能的话,请你今天晚上以前告诉我。(条件)

Though (*he was*) *exhausted, he went to bed very late.*

虽然他已精疲力竭,但还是很晚才上床。(让步)

但原因状语从句不能用这种方法来省略,它们常被分词结构代替,也同样起到缩短从句的作用。

词汇学习 Word study

1. catch (caught)

(1) *vt*. 捉住,接住,握住,使缠住:

The dog caught the ball in its mouth.

那条狗用嘴接住了球。

The police caught him by the arm while he was stealing.

他行窃时,警察抓住了他的胳膊。

A nail caught his sleeve while he was getting into the hole.

他钻那个洞时,钉子挂住了他的衣袖。

(2) *vt*. 无意中发现:

This kind of cancer can be cured, provided it is caught early.

如果发现得早,这种癌症是能够治愈的。

The fans waited at the airport, hoping to catch a glimpse of their idol as he got off the plane.

球迷们在机场等候着,希望在他们的偶像走下飞机时能看上他一眼。

The police caught him stealing a car.

警察看到他正在偷汽车。

(3) *vt*. 赶上,及时赶到:

If we go home now, we might just catch the 10 o'clock news.

如果我们现在回家,我们可能正好赶上10点钟的新闻。

(4) *vt*. 染上,感染:

She caught a cold/fever yesterday.

她昨天伤风/发烧了。

(5) *vt*. (不用于进行时)听清楚,领会:

What did she say? I didn't catch it.
她说的什么？我没听清。

(6) *vt*. 吸引,迷住:

The idea caught her imagination.
她摆脱不了这个想法。

The unusual picture on the wall caught our attention.
墙上那幅不寻常的画吸引了我们的注意力。

(7) *vi*. 被钩(或挂、缠)住:

Her skirt caught in the door.
她的裙子挂在了门上。

(8) *vi*. 燃着,点着:

The wind was so strong that the fire caught quickly.
风很大,火很快烧起来。

(9) *n*. (可数)抓,捉;捕获物:

The boat brought back a big catch of fish.
那只船捕回了大量的鱼。

(10) *n*. (可数)闩(钩/扣):

The catch on this door is broken.
这扇门的门扣坏了。

(11) *n*. (可数,常用于口语中)圈套;诡计:

That house is extremely cheap; there must be a catch in it!
那所房子太便宜了,这里面肯定有什么鬼把戏!

(12) catch on

1) 流行起来,受欢迎:

It was a popular style in Britain, but it never really caught on in America.
这在英国是很受欢迎的式样,但在美国它真的很难流行起来。

2) 懂得,理解:

It was a long time before the police caught on to what he was really doing.

过了很长时间警方才搞清他到底在干些什么。

(13) catch up

1) (with) 赶上,追上:

At the moment our technology is more advanced than theirs, but they are catching up with us fast.

现在我们的技术比他们的要先进得多;但是他们正飞快地追上来。

2) (on) 赶完,弥补:

They have to catch up on their work tonight, so they can't go out.

他们今晚要赶完工作,因此他们出不去。

3) (in)(常用于被动语态)(被)缠住,陷入:

The government was caught up in a bitter dispute between the miners and their employers.

政府陷入了矿工与其雇主间的激烈争执中。

2. need

(1) *modal v.*(没有时态和人称变化,用于疑问句或否定句时后接不带 to 的不定式)必要,必须:

Need I stay here?
我一定要呆在这儿吗?
No, you needn't.
不,你不必呆在这儿。

You needn't have watered the flowers. It's raining now.

你没必要浇花的,现在在下雨。

(2) *vt.* 需要,要:

Fish need water.

鱼需要水。

The lawn needed mowing.

草坪需要修剪了。

I need more people to help.

我需要更多的人帮忙。

The desk needs to be cleaned.

桌子该擦一擦了。

(3) *n.* (of) (不可数) 缺乏,缺少,需要:

Our school is now in great need of teachers.

我们学校现在很缺老师。

(4) *n.* (常用复数)要求,需要之物:

The mother worked hard to satisfy the needs of children.

那位母亲努力工作,以满足孩子们的需要。

(5) *n.* (不可数)贫穷,不幸,逆境:

A friend in need is a friend indeed.

患难之交才是真正的朋友。

(6) if need be 如果需要:

I'll stay here overnight if need be.

如果需要的话,我会在这儿呆一整夜。

3. take (took, taken) *vt.*

(1) 携带;拿,拿走;偷:

Take the coat with you, it's cold outside.

外面很冷,你带上外衣。

He took a pen and began to write.

他拿起一枝钢笔,开始写起来。

Somebody took my bicycle.

有人把我的自行车偷走了。

(2) 运载:

Bob took me to the hospital yesterday.

昨天鲍勃带我去了医院。

(3) 握;抓:

She took the baby in her arms.

她把孩子抱在怀里。

(4) 需要,花费(时间):

The journey took four hours.

路上用了4个小时。

This wood takes three coats of paint.

这木料需要涂3遍漆。

It took me just two minutes to solve that problem.

我只用了两分钟就解开了那道题。

(5) 乘车;吃,喝:

I took a taxi to the hospital.

我是坐出租车去医院的。

I took the medicine.

我把药吃了。

(6) 同意接受;视为,理解为:

The restaurant doesn't take cheques.

这家餐馆不收支票。

He took her remark as an insult.

他把她的话视为一种侮辱。

I take your silence to mean that you agree.

我认为你的沉默表示你同意了。

(7) 做;进行;写下:

She enjoyed taking a hot bath after work.

她喜欢工作后洗个热水澡。

You'd better take notes in class.

在课堂上你们最好记笔记。

(8) take after (相貌、行为)像:

She takes after her mother.

她很像她母亲。

(9) take on

1) 雇用：

The factory is taking on new workers.

那家工厂正在雇用新工人。

2) 开始：

He had to take on extra work to pay the bills.

他不得不开始干额外的活以支付账单。

(10) take over 接管：

Peter took over the farm after his father died.

父亲去世后，彼得接管了农场。

(11) take to

1) 沉溺于：

He took to drink.

他沉溺于喝酒。

2) 开始喜欢：

They took to each other at once.

他们立刻一见钟情。

(12) take up

1) 使用，占用时间/空间：

The bed took up half of the room.

这张床占了半间屋子。

2) 从事：

She took up medicine as a career.

她从事医学这一行。

✍ 练习答案 Key to written exercises

1. 关键句型练习答案

A If my parents had given me some encouragement, I think *I could have succeeded* as a professional musician.

If they hadn't had to catch the 6.30 train back, they *could have stayed* an hour or two longer.

If she had taken more money with her, she *could have bought* some new clothes.

B They are not going to *force* the new changes *on/upon* us.

Vegetarians *live on* a diet that does not contain meat.

There are a number of important processes in the *conversion* of coal *into* gas.

Studying at a college or university is very *different from* attending school.

As soon as the police get the information they want, they will *act on* it and surround the house.

The *effect on* the audience of the composer's first symphony was indescribable.

C Even though he has retired, he still gets up early just as he always *did*. (did = got up early)

He certainly enjoys music as much as you *do*. (do = enjoy music)

If you act as he *does*, you won't be very popular. (does = acts)

D 1 Of the two books, I found the horror novel *the more* entertaining.

2 Janet was *the most* intelligent girl in the class.

E 1 The concert tickets were *much more expensive* than I had been told.

2 The test was *far more difficult* than I thought it was going to be.

3 The game was *far less exciting* than John told me to expect.

4 The computer course this year is *much less interesting* than the one last year.

2. 难点练习答案

A 1 The adverb *merely* means 'only, simply': *I merely suggested that you should do it again; there's no need to get annoyed.*

The adverb *only* means 'nothing more than, with no one or nothing else added or included': *I only saw him yesterday.* (= and no longer ago)

2 The adjectives *fierce* and *furious* can easily be confused. *Fierce* means 'angry, violent and likely to attack': *The house is guarded by a fierce dog.*

Furious, on the other hand, means 'very angry in an uncontrolled way', as in: *I was furious at being kept waiting.*

3 The phrase *take place* means 'happen': *Where is the meeting taking place tonight?*

Take part means 'participate': *Five hundred people took part in the procession through the town.*

4 The two words *prey* and *pray* are pronounced in the same way: /preɪ/.

The uncountable noun *prey* refers to 'an animal that is hunted and eaten by another animal': *The lions pursued their prey until it was too exhausted to run any farther.*

(The verb *prey on* means 'hunt and eat as prey': *Cats prey on birds and mice.*)

The verb *pray* means 'speak, often silently, to God or a god, privately or with others': *The whole family went to the temple to pray.*

B 1 *came about* = happened, in a way that seemed impossible to prevent

2 *came over* = took hold of suddenly and strangely

3 *came up with* = thought of; produced

4 *came across* = met by chance

C 1 This ticket will *enable* me to fly first class.

2 The boys from the two schools were always having *running fights* with each other.

3 We did a lot of shopping yesterday: *in fact*, we visited every clothes and shoe shop in our small town.

4 The two girls might be sisters, but they are totally different *in every other respect*.

5 I feel as exhausted as a middle-aged businessman on a ten-mile walk, *so to speak*. (*so to speak* = as one might say: we tend to use 'so to speak' after a novel or unusual expression.)

6 I really think that acting is a very precarious profession. *Be that as it may*, I still wouldn't stop my daughter going onto the stage if she wanted to. (*be that as it may* = even if that's true, in spite of that)

D See text.

3. 多项选择题答案

1	b	2	c	3	a	4	d	5	c	6	c
7	c	8	b	9	d	10	b	11	c	12	a

Lesson 21
William S. Hart and the early 'Western' film
威廉·S.哈特和早期的"西部"影片

课文详注 Further notes on the text

1. **..., for unlike Gary Cooper and John Wayne he appeared in nothing but Westerns.**

for 在此处引导一个原因状语从句。它所引导的原因状语从句主要是给出新的信息,原因只是捎带说一下。该连词引导的从句从不出现在句首,而且也不能单独使用,且常用于较正式的文体,如:

I decided to stop and have lunch—for I was feeling hungry.

我决定停下来,吃午饭——我觉得饿了。

在课文中是说明一下为什么他是西部影片明星中的佼佼者。Gary Cooper,加里·古柏(1901~1961),美国电影演员,以演西部片中的牛仔著称。John Wayne,约翰·韦恩(1906~1980),美国电影演员,擅长演西部片中的牛仔英雄。nothing but 仅仅,只是,如:

I could see nothing but flowers everywhere.

我到处看到的只有花。

Westerns 西部电影。

2. **It was Hart who created the basic formula of the Western film, and devised the protagonist he played in every film he made, the good-bad man, the accidental-noble outlaw, or the**

honest-but-framed cowboy, or the sheriff made suspect by vicious gossip; in short, the individual in conflict with himself and his frontier environment.

该句为强调句结构,所强调的部分是该句的主语 Hart。正常结构应该是:Hart created the basic formula ... and devised the ...who 引导的是定语从句,修饰 Hart。he played in every film he made 作定语,修饰 protagonist。he made 作定语,修饰 every film,意即"在他自己拍摄的影片中他所塑造的主人公"。the good-bad man, ... the individual ... environment 为 protagonist 的同位语。made suspect by vicious gossip 为过去分词,作定语,修饰 the sheriff,等于 who was made suspect by vicious gossip,该短语中的 suspect 作主语 who 的补足语。in conflict with ... environment 为介词短语,作定语,修饰 the individual。in conflict with 与……发生矛盾,与……冲突,如:

He is in conflict with his relatives about the terms of a will.

他就遗嘱的条款与亲属发生矛盾。

in short 总而言之,一句话。

3. **Unlike most of his contemporaries ..., Hart actually knew something of the old West.**

the old West 指密西西比河以西的地区。

4. **He had lived in it as a child when it was already disappearing, and his hero was firmly rooted in his memories and experiences, and in both the history and the mythology of the vanished frontier.**

it 指 the old West。as a child 孩提时期。when 引导时间状语从句,该从句中的 it 也指 the old West。从句中使用过去进行时表示当时西部的拓荒生活已经开始消失。his hero 指他所塑造的影片主人公。be rooted in 扎根于,根源在于,如:

They are rooted in poverty.

他们深陷在贫困之中。

the vanished frontier 指 the old West。

5. **And although no period or place in ..., myth and reality did join hands in at least one arena, the conflict between the individual and encroaching civilization.**

although 引导的是让步状语从句,用否定词 no + 副词的比较级 more absurdly 强调"只有西部拓荒时期才被荒谬地浪漫主义化了",如:

No one else has ever had a greater influence on my life (than him).

任何其他人都没有(他)对我的一生有过更大的影响。(即他的影响最大)

join hands 携手联合,如:

They joined hands in fighting tyranny.

他们联合起来与暴政作斗争。

the conflict between ... civilization 作 arena 的同位语,意即"神话和事实至少在某一个舞台上共存,也就是存在于个人与渐渐闯入的文明这两者的冲突之中"。

6. **Men accustomed to struggling for survival against the elements and Indians were bewildered by ..., and unhorsed by fences, ...**

accustomed to ... Indians 作定语,修饰 Men。be accustomed to 习惯于。该短语中的 to 是介词,后面只能跟名词或动名词,如:

He is accustomed to hard work.

他已习惯于艰苦的工作。

The old man was accustomed to walking long distances.

那位老人习惯于长途跋涉。

I'm not accustomed to the cold weather.

我不习惯寒冷的天气。

against the elements and Indians 为介词短语，作定语，修饰 struggling。be bewildered by 被……所困惑，如：

She was bewildered by his departure.

他的离去使她不知所措。

and unhorsed by 与 were bewildered by 为该句的并列谓语，unhorsed 前面省略了 were。由于西部英雄都是骑在马上的，所以在此处 unhorsed by 指"被赶下了马"，也就是说"被击败"。19 世纪初期，美国西部地区处于开拓时期。牛仔们骑马放牧畜群，广阔的地区任他们驰骋。为了生存，他们与大自然斗，与土著印第安人斗。可是随着文明的渐渐渗入、经济的发展，开始有了政治家、商人、银行家等，同时也出现了划分疆界的藩篱以及相应的法律和外来的清规戒律。所有这些使他们失去了过去自由自在的生活，所以说他们被击败了。

7. **Hart's good-bad man was always an outsider, always one of the disinherited, and if he found it necessary to shoot a sheriff or rob a bank along the way, his early audiences found it easy to understand and forgive, especially when it was Hart who, in the end, overcame the attacking Indians.**

an outsider 局外人。the disinherited 被剥夺继承权的人。英语中定冠词 the + 形容词常用来表示"某类人"，如：the rich(富人)、the poor(穷人)、the blind(盲人)。he found it necessary to shoot a sheriff or rob a bank 以及 his early audiences found it easy to understand and forgive 中的 it 为先行宾语，后面的动词不定式为真正的宾语。it 后面的形容词 necessary 和 easy 为宾语补足语。in the end 最终，相当于 finally。

8. **Audiences in the second decade of the twentieth century found it pleasant to escape to a time when life, though hard, was relatively simple.**

in the second decade of 为介词短语，作定语，修饰 Audiences。

found it pleasant to escape to a time 中的 it 为先行宾语，真正的宾语是动词不定式 to escape to a time，形容词 pleasant 为宾语补足语。when 引导的是定语从句，修饰 a time。though hard 作让步状语，though 和 hard 之间省略了 life was。

9. We still do; living in a world in which ...our daily lives, we all want a code to live by.

We still do 指前句中的 found it pleasant ... simple。意即“我们今天仍有这种感觉”。living in a world in which ... our daily lives 为现在分词短语，作原因状语。a code 准则。to live by 作定语，修饰 a code，意即“靠……过活”，如：

We must live by certain principles.

我们必须遵循某些原则生活。

语法 Grammar in use

动词不定式用法 (1)

省略了 to 的动词不定式的用法 (1)

(1) 动词 let 和 make 与动词不定式连用

在动词 let(允许)和 make(迫使)后，无论其后是否使用名词或代词作宾语，均需跟省略了 to 的动词不定式结构，如：

Please let us have more time, will you?

请多给我们一点儿时间好吗?

I won't let you ride my bicycle.

我不让你骑我的自行车。

That beard makes you look much older than you are.

你的胡须使你看上去比你的年龄大得多。

就结构而言，区别是：

1) let 后可以使用一个被动形式的不定式；而 make 表达上述意义(迫使)时其后绝不可使用被动形式的不定式，只有在其表达其他意义时其后方可使用被动形式的不定式，如：

He let it be known he was about to resign.

他宣称他即将辞职。

Rules were made to be broken.

规则是为打破而制定的。

注意：上述第2例中的动词make不表示"迫使"之意，而表示create（制定）之意，因此其后跟随了动词不定式的被动形式。

2) 动词let本身一般不用其被动形式表达"被允许"的含义，而动词make自身则可用于被动语态，但其后需使用带to的动词不定式结构，如：

We were not allowed to speak.

我们没有被允许讲话。

He was made to work twenty hours a day.

他被迫一天工作20小时。

注意：上述第1例中的动词通常不使用动词let。

此外，英语中还有许多含有动词let和make的固定短语动词使用省略了to的动词不定式，常见的有：let fall（无意中说出）、let go（放开）、let me see（让我想想看）、live and let live（自己活同时也让别人活）、make believe（假装）、make do（凑合着用）等，如：

The dog's got a stick between his teeth and he won't let go.

那狗叼着一根棍子不放。

You'll have to make your pocket money do. I can't give you more.

你必须将就着用你的零花钱，我不能再给你了。

(2) would rather 等与动词不定式连用

这类的短语形式通常有用来表达“宁愿”、“宁可”的 would/'d rather、would/'d sooner、had/'d rather 和 had/'d sooner 以及用来表达“最好”的 had/'d better 和 had/'d best。在这些短语之后,需使用省略了 to 的动词不定式结构,如:

I'd rather work on the land than work in a factory.

我宁愿在田里干活,不愿在工厂工作。

We'd better/best be going.

我们最好走吧。

Yes, we'd better/best be.

是的,我们最好走。

在这些说法之后,可以使用被动语态结构,如:

I'd rather be told the truth than be lied to.

我宁愿听真话,也不愿被欺骗。

构成其否定形式的 not 需用于这些短语之后,如:

You'd better not go near the edge.

你最好别走近边缘。

(3) Why? 和 Why not? 与动词不定式连用

why 和 why not 后用省略了 to 的动词不定式结构,分别表达“不值得费力去……”、“我认为你应该”以提出某种建议的,如:

You're fully insured, so why worry?

你已经全部保险了,那何必还担心呢?

Why not wait till the winter sales to buy a new coat?

为什么不等到冬季大甩卖时再买一件新外衣呢?

词汇学习 Word study

1. appear *vi.*

(1) 出现,露面:

A car appeared over the hill.

一辆汽车出现在山头上。

If I don't appear by 8, I won't be coming at all.

如果到8点钟我仍未来,那么我就不会来了。

(2)(不用于进行时,后跟作表语的名词或形容词)看起来像;似乎:

They appeared rather upset about something.

他们似乎对什么事情感到很不安。

It now appears certain that the fire was caused deliberately.

现在看起来那场火显然是故意放的。

They appear to be sincere but I don't completely trust them.

他们看起来挺真诚,但是我并不完全相信他们。

There appears to have been a mistake over the numbers.

似乎数字有些不对头。

It appears (that) she won't be coming after all.

好像她根本就不会来。

(3)产生,开始存在:

Children's speech ability appears in their first or second year.

儿童的说话能力在他们一两岁时形成。

2. accustom *vt.*

(1)(to)使习惯于:

Finally he accustomed himself to the new job.

他最终使自己习惯了那个新工作。

You have to accustom yourself gradually to using metric measurements.

你得使自己慢慢习惯使用公制计量单位。

3. escape

(1) *vt*. 逃走,避免:

He narrowly escaped death.

他九死一生。

He escaped being punished.

他逃脱了惩罚。

(2) *vt*. 未被注意:

Nothing escaped his attention.

一切都没有逃过他的注意。

(3) *vi*. 逃走,跑掉:

Finally, he escaped from the enemy's prison.

最终,他从敌人的监狱里逃了出来。

(4) *n*. (不可数)逃跑,逃脱:

Escape is not easy.

逃脱不容易。

(5) *n*. (可数)漏出,流出:

There is an escape of water in the kitchen.

厨房里漏水了。

练习答案 Key to written exercises

1. 关键句型练习答案

A See text.

B I promise to tell the truth, the whole truth, and *nothing but* the truth.

That boy has been *nothing but* trouble ever since he came to the school.

I've just looked through that box and there is *nothing but* rubbish in it.

C See text.

D 1 I *did mention* it to him, but he wasn't impressed.

2 You *did post* my letter, didn't you?

3 We *did enjoy* ourselves at the party.

E 1 Her speech, *though* quite short, was excellent and very entertaining.

2 There wasn't really time to visit the old castle. I wish we had found time *though*.

F 1 They all thought that it was a good cause *to fight for*. (= for which to fight)

2 The story gave them all something *to talk about*. (= about which to talk)

3 The police couldn't arrest the man because they didn't have quite enough information *to act on*. (= on which to act)

4 He keeps changing his mind so he's an impossible man *to work with*. (= with whom to work)

2. 难点练习答案

A 1 The verb *appear* means 'become able to be seen, come into sight or become noticeable': *The car appeared over the hill*. It can also mean 'perform publicly e.g. in a play or a film': *The first time he appeared on the stage was in a school play*.

Appear and *seem* can both be used to mean 'give a particular idea or feeling e. g. about one's character, feelings or intentions': *He appears/seems to be sincere*, but I don't completely trust him. (In this sense, neither verb can be used in the continuous form.)

2 Point out the clear difference in pronunciation between

these two words.

The verb *devise* (/dɪˈvaɪz/) means 'plan or invent, especially cleverly': *They devised a plan for getting the jewels out of the country.*

A *device* (/dɪˈvaɪs/) is 'a piece of equipment intended for a particular purpose': *The missile has a heat-seeking device which enables it to find its target.*

3 While the word *suspect* is a noun, it is also an adjective. It means 'of uncertain truth, quality, legality, etc.': *His fitness is suspect, so we can't risk including him in the team.*

Suspicious means 'suspecting guilt or wrongdoing, not trusting': *His strange behaviour made the police very suspicious.*

4 The uncountable noun *memory* refers to 'the ability to remember events and experiences': *She played the tune from memory.*

As a countable noun, it means 'an event or experience that one remembers from the past': *I have a very clear memory of going to the beach for the first time.*

Remembrance can mean 'something kept or given to remind one or the act of remembering': *A church service was held in remembrance of those killed in the war.*

5 *History* is 'the study of events in the past, such as those of nation, arranged in order from earlier to later times': *She has a degree in Chinese history.*

A *story* is 'an account of events, real or imagined': *He wrote a short story about a teenage pop star.*

6 The verbs *rob* and *steal* can easily be confused.

Rob is used in the construction 'rob someone of something/rob a place': *The thief robbed the lady of her watch. The gang robbed the bank.*

Steal means 'take what belongs to someone else without any right to it': *The thief stole the lady's watch. They stole £1m from the bank.*

B 1 Unlike most of his contemporaries, *the painter never experimented with abstract art.*

2 Unlike some people, *I never pass on any gossip I might hear.*

3 Unlike yourself, *I have never been interested in football.*

C This was the party's most disastrous and embarrassing defeat ever: *in short*, it was a fiasco.

On this particular issue the Prime Minister is *in direct conflict with* many of his colleagues in the Government.

Although she is normally right, she has been wrong on *at least* one occasion this week.

He tried several times to pass his driving test, and *in the end* he succeeded.

3. 多项选择题答案

1	b	2	d	3	b	4	b	5	a	6	a
7	d	8	d	9	a	10	b	11	c	12	a

Lesson 22
Knowledge and progress
知识和进步

课文详注 Further notes on the text

1. **Why does the idea of progress loom so large in the modern world?**

   loom large 赫然出现，显得突出，如：

   Her possible candidacy loomed large in the future plans of the party.

   将来她极有可能被该党推举为候选人。

2. **Knowledge began to increase as soon as the thoughts of one individual could be communicated to another by means of speech.**

   communicate ... to ... 向……传达……，如：

   She tried to communicate her thoughts to her children.

   她设法把她的想法告诉给她的孩子们。

   by means of 用，依靠，如：

   By means of borrowing money from the bank he bought his new house.

   靠着从银行借的钱他买了新房子。

3. **With the invention of writing, a great advance was made, for knowledge could then be not only communicated but also stored.**

   with the invention of writing 为原因状语，with 是"由于"的意思。for 引导的是原因状语从句。

4. **Libraries made education possible, and education in its turn**

added to libraries: the growth of knowledge followed a kind of compound interest law, which was greatly enhanced by the invention of printing.

possible 作 education 的宾语补足语。education in its turn added to libraries 教育反过来也丰富了藏书。in one's turn 轮到某人。compound interest law 复利法则,又称雪球法则,意即利上滚利,增长速度很快。which 引导非限定性定语从句,修饰 the growth of knowledge。

5. **All this ..., with the coming of science, the *tempo* was suddenly raised.**

   with the coming of science 中的 with 表示"随着",作状语。the tempo 指 the growth of knowledge 的速度。

6. **The trickle became a stream; the stream has now become a torrent.**

   该句采用比喻的手法,将知识积累的过程比作水从 trickle(涓涓细流)到 stream(小溪)又汇集成 torrent(奔腾的江河)的过程。

7. **Moreover, ..., it is now turned to practical account.**

   turn ... to account 利用。该句中的副词 now 表示"立刻"的意思。

8. **What is called 'modern civilization' is not the result of a balanced development of all man's nature, but of accumulated knowledge applied to practical life.**

   What 引导的是主语从句。of a balanced ...和 of accumulated knowledge...都作 result 的定语。applied to practical life 为过去分词短语,作定语,修饰 knowledge。apply ... to 把……应用于,如:

   We must apply theory to practice in our work.

   在工作中,我们必须把理论付诸于实践。

9. As is so often pointed out, knowledge is a two-edged weapon which can be used equally for good or evil.

As 作关系代词,引导非限定性定语从句,指 knowledge is a two-edged weapon ... evil。which 引导定语从句,修饰 a two-edged weapon。for good or evil 作目的状语。

10. Could any spectacle, for instance, be more grimly whimsical than that of gunners using science to shatter men's bodies while, close at hand, surgeons use it to restore them?

该句的结构是疑问句,但实际上起到一个加强语气的陈述句的作用,这种疑问句常被称为修辞疑问句。修辞疑问句中的一般疑问句的否定形式常表示肯定的意思,而肯定形式的则表示否定的意思,如:

Are we going to let them do this to us? (= *We aren't* ...)

我们能让他们这么对待我们吗?

Didn't I tell you it would rain? (= *I told you* ...)

我难道没告诉你要下雨吗?

that 代替 spectacle。using science to shatter men's bodies 作定语,修饰 gunners。while 在该句中不用来引导时间状语从句,而相当于连词 but,意即"而",引出与前面提到的截然相反的事情,如:

Fred gambled his money away while Julia spent all hers on dresses.

弗雷德把钱都赌光了,而朱丽娅却把钱都花在衣着上。

close at hand 在手边,在近旁。it 指 science。them 指 men's bodies。

11. We have to ask ourselves very seriously what will happen if this twofold use of knowledge, with its ever-increasing power, continues.

what 引导的是宾语从句，作动词 ask 的直接宾语。if 引导的是宾语从句中的条件状语从句。this twofold use of knowledge 指知识可以用来造福，也可以用来为害。with its ever-increasing power 作名词 knowledge 的非限定性定语。its 指 knowledge 的。

语法 Grammar in use

动词不定式用法 (2)

省略了 to 的动词不定式的用法 (2)

(1) 动词 help 和 know 与动词不定式连用

在动词 help 和 know 后可以使用省略了 to 的动词不定式形式，也可以使用带 to 的动词不定式形式，但在具体使用中应注意它们在使用结构中的不同：

1) 可以将动词 help 用于 help do (to do) sth. 和 help sth. do (to do) sth. 这样的结构中，如：

Everyone in the village helped (to) build the new Youth Centre.

村子里的每一个人都曾帮助建造新的青年活动中心。

Mother helped me (to) do my homework.

妈妈帮助我做家庭作业。

但当 help 之后需使用动词不定式的否定形式时，通常需使用带 to 的动词不定式结构，如：

How can I help my children not to worry about their exams?

我怎样才能帮助我的孩子们不为他们的考试着急呢？

2) 通常只可将动词 know 用于 know sb. to do sth. 中，即在该动词后使用带 to 的动词不定式结构。但当动词 know 用于完成时时，其后则可以使用省略了 to 的动词不定式结构，如：

I've never known her (*to*) *be late before.*

我以前从不知道她迟到过。

I've never known her not (*to*) *be late!*

我从不知道她没有迟到过！

3) 当动词 help 和 know 本身为被动形式时，其后的动词不定式则只能使用带 to 的动词不定式形式，如：

She was helped to overcome her fear of flying.

她被帮助克服了恐飞症。

He was known to have/to have had a quick temper as a boy.

人们都知道他在孩提时代脾气就暴躁。

(2) and 与 but 等词与动词不定式连用

在 and、but、except、or 和 than 后，可以使用省略了 to 或带 to 的动词不定式结构，如：

Which would you prefer: to win a million pounds or (*to*) *have a brain like Einstein's?*

你喜欢哪一样：赢得 100 万英镑？还是有一个像爱因斯坦似的头脑？

这些词后的动词不定式如为进行时或完成时时，可以下述形式连接：

I'd like to be flying over the Alps and (*to be*) *looking down/and be looking down at the mountains.*

我喜欢飞越阿尔卑斯山并俯瞰那些山峦。

I'd like to have been offered the job and (*to have been*) *given/and been given the opportunity to prove myself.*

我但愿当时有人给我这项工作，让我有机会证明我自己。

当句中第 2 个动词不定式与第 1 个动词不定式连接紧密时，第 2 个动词不定式通常用省略了 to 的动词不定式结构，如：

I'd like to lie down and go to sleep.

我想躺下睡觉了。

词汇学习 Word study

1. enhance *vt.*

(1) 提高,增强,加强:

The new dress enhanced her elegance.

这套新服装使她显得更加典雅。

Good secretarial skills should enhance your chances of getting a job.

好的文秘技巧会增加你找工作的机会。

A fine wine will enhance a delicious meal.

美酒会使佳肴增辉。

2. progress

(1) *n.* (不可数) 进步,上进,发展:

He made no progress with her.

他与她的关系没有什么进展。

(2) *n.* 前进,行进:

The car made slow progress.

车慢慢地向前开。

(3) *vi.* 改进,发展:

He is progressing in his studies.

他的学习正在进步。

(4) *vi.* 前进,行进:

Time is progressing.

时间在推移。

3. undergo (underwent, undergone) *vt.* 经历,经受,忍受:

She's undergoing treatment at the hospital.

她正在医院接受治疗。

The company has undergone some major changes in the last five years.

该公司在最近的5年里经历了一些很大的变化。

For years they underwent starvation.

他们忍受了多年的饥饿。

练习答案 Key to written exercises

1. 关键句型练习答案

A See text.

B The fact that the girl suddenly returned made the search for her *unnecessary*.

All the different features of this house make it very *desirable*.

By the time the people in the workshop had finished, they made my old car *unrecognizable*.

C 1 *People emigrating* this year will benefit from a special payment from the government.

2 *All aeroplanes arriving* after 16.00 will be required to pay an additional landing fee.

3 *Ships sailing* from this port must register their port of destination before they sail.

D 1 *Photographs taken* inside the building must be authorized by the Manager.

2 *Passports issued* from this office will be valid for all parts of the world.

3 *Passengers delayed* overnight are always given free accommodation.

2. 难点练习答案

A 1 *Surely* is used in English to mean 'I believe, hope or expect' and usually implies some surprise and sometimes indignation. Often as not, it begins a sentence and is stressed in speech: *Surely he's not suggesting that I did it on purpose!* (= I sincerely hope he's not suggesting this and I don't think he ought to.)

Certainly means 'it is certain': *He's certainly not suggesting that I did it on purpose.* (= I know for certain that he is not suggesting this.)

2 The adjective *extraordinary* means 'unusual, surprising, special, more than what is ordinary': *He has an extraordinary tenor voice for such a young man.*

The adjective *outstanding* is more than 'extraordinary', it means 'much better than most others, very good': *Academically she is outstanding: at the age of 13 she has just gained a place at Oxford University.*

3 A *spectacle* is 'a grand public show or scene or an unusual thing or situation to be seen and noticed': *The military parade was a magnificent spectacle. I have witnessed some strange spectacles in my life.*

A *view* is 'something seen from a particular place, especially a stretch of pleasant country': *I'd like a room with a view, please.*

B 1 It is becoming *more and more* obvious that Jack will not become an artist.

2 Some of the prisoners managed to speak to each other *by means of* a series of taps on pipes.

3 The propeller-driven aircraft made commercial flight

possible, and the jet engine *in its turn* led to today's generation of aircraft.

4 I had *a kind of* a feeling that she might call me today.

5 These particular birds are still *comparatively* rare in the south of England.

6 Those people live their lives *according to* laws laid down hundreds of years ago.

7 Don't worry. I'll be *at hand* to help you if you get into trouble.

C The small amount of knowledge grew to a large amount, and now that large amount has increased to a massive amount—enough perhaps to drown us?

D The prefix *ever-* before an *-ing* adjective means 'constantly, all the time', as in *ever-decreasing circles*.

Some scientists say that the universe is an *ever-expanding* universe.

We live in an *ever-changing* world.

The company faced *ever-diminishing* profits for four or five years before they finally closed up.

3. 多项选择题答案

1 c 2 d 3 a 4 c 5 b 6 a

7 d 8 b 9 c 10 d 11 a 12 b

Lesson 23
Bird flight
鸟的飞行方法

课文详注 Further notes on the text

1. ... the varieties are infinite; ...

the varieties 指 the varieties of flight,意即"飞行方式"。

2. Any ship that crosses the Pacific is accompanied for many days by the smaller albatross, which may keep company with the vessel for an hour without visible or more than occasional movement of wing.

that crosses the Pacific 为定语从句,修饰 any ship。which 引导的是非限定性定语从句,修饰 the smaller albatross。keep company with 陪伴着,如:

Whenever my husband went away on business my parents would come and keep company with me.

每当我丈夫外出出差,我父母就来跟我作伴。

visible 和 more than occasional 作并列定语,修饰 movement of wing。more than 在这里作副词,表示"非常",相当于 very,如:

I was more than a little curious about the whole business.

我对整件事都非常好奇。

We will be more than glad to help you in any way we can.

我们将非常高兴地尽我们所能来帮助你。

3. The currents of air that the walls of the ship direct upwards, as well as in the line of its course, are enough to give the great bird with its

immense wings sufficient sustenance and progress.

that 引导定语从句,修饰 the currents of air,意即"沿着船体上升的气流"。as well as in the line of its course 也作定语,修饰 the currents of air。its course 指"船的航线"。the great bird 作动词 give 的间接宾语,sufficient sustenance and progress 作动词 give 的直接宾语。with its immense wings 作定语,修饰 the great bird。the great bird 指 albatross。

4. **The albatross is the king of the gliders, the class of fliers which harness the air to their purpose, but must yield to its opposition.**

the class of fliers . . . opposition 是 gliders 的同位语。which 引导定语从句,修饰 the class of fliers。its 指 the air 的。yield to 屈服于,服从于,如:

They finally yielded to our demand.

他们最终同意了我们的要求。

5. **In the contrary school, the duck is supreme.**

该句中的 school 指"类"、"群"。the duck 指野鸭类。

6. **It comes nearer to the engines with which man has 'conquered' the air, as he boasts.**

It 指 the duck。comes nearer to the engines 近乎于……的发动机。with which 引导定语从句。conquered 用引号引上,表示这是一种夸张的说法。人类所谓的征服空气只是能够靠着发动机的动力在空气中飞行。as he boasts 作状语,意即"正像人们所自夸的那样"。he 指 man。

7. **Duck, and like them the pigeons, are endowed with steel-like muscles, that are a good part of the weight of the bird, and these will ply the short wings with such irresistible power that they can bore for long distances through an opposing gale before exhaustion follows.**

like them 为介词短语，作定语，修饰 the pigeons，them 指 duck。该句中 duck 前既没有定冠词也没有不定冠词，表明该词泛指野鸭类，故 like them 中使用复数代词 them。endow with 捐……给，赋予……以，如：

They endowed the hospital with a large sum of money.

他们给医院捐了很多钱。

She is endowed with the finest qualities.

她天资优良。

that are a good part of the weight of the bird 为非限定性定语从句，修饰 muscles，但用关系代词 that 引导非限定性定语从句非常罕见。these 指 muscles。and these will ... 与 Duck, ..., are endowed with ... 是两个并列的句子。ply ... with 向……供应，如：

They plied him with liquor.

他们给他酒。

The little boy plied his father with questions about their new house.

那个小男孩不断地向他的父亲问有关他们新房子的问题。

that they can bore for long distances through an opposing gale before exhaustion follows 为结果状语从句。该结构是典型的 such ... that ... 结构，如：

It was such a hot day that we went to swimming.

天气那么热，我们就游泳去了。

bear 在此处的意思是"行进"，如：

Please bear left at the traffic light.

在红绿灯处向左走。

8. Their humbler followers, such as partridges, have a like power of strong propulsion, but soon tire.

humbler 是形容词 humble 的比较级,指"次于野鸭和鸽子的鸟"。such as partridges 是插入语。like 作形容词,意即"类似的"。but soon tire 中动词 tire 的主语也是 their humbler followers。

9. **You may pick them up in utter exhaustion ...**

in utter exhaustion 为介词短语,作定语,修饰 them,表示"精疲力竭的"。

10. **The swallow shares the virtues of both schools in highest measure.**

share 分享,共同具有,如:

The two chemists shared the Nobel prize.

那两位化学家分享这项诺贝尔奖。

both schools 指前面提到的以滑翔方式飞行的信天翁类的鸟和以钢铁般的肌肉的力量飞行的野鸭类的鸟。in highest measure 作状语,意即"最大程度地"。

11. **It tires not, nor does it boast of its power; but belongs to the air, travelling it may be six thousand miles to and from its northern nesting home, feeding its flown young as it flies, and slipping through a medium that seems to help its passage even when the wind is adverse.**

It tires not 中未采用助动词 + 否定词句式,所采用的是古英语或诗歌中使用的句式。连词 nor 为否定连词,故句子应该倒装,即 nor 后面跟随助动词 does,而将主语 it 置于其后。boast of /about 夸耀,如:

He boasted of his law school.

他夸耀自己(所在)的法学院。

but belongs to the air 中的主语与前一分句相同,也是 it,指"燕子"。belong to 属于,如:

The scarf belongs to me.

这条围巾是我的。

travelling it may be six thousand miles . . . 为倒装句,倒装是为了强调 travelling 的生动逼真。按正常语序是: it may be travelling . . . 该句使用 may + 进行时结构,也是为了强调燕子能一直飞行 6,000 英里。nesting home 意为 home for nesting。feeding . . ., and slipping . . . adverse 作状语,并列修饰 travelling,表示伴随状况。its flown young 中的 flown 意为"已会飞的"。as it flies 作时间状语从句。a medium 指 air。

12. Such birds do us good . . .

do sb. good 对某人有好处,对某人行善,如:

It will do you good to have a holiday.

休假会对你有好处。

He has done a lot of good for the community.

他为社区做了很多好事。

语法 Grammar in use

动词不定式用法(3)

省略了 to 的动词不定式的用法(3)

(1) 感知动词与动词不定式连用

在感知动词如 feel(感到)、hear(听到)、listen to(听)、look at(瞧)、notice(注意)、observe(观察)、perceive(觉察)、see(看)、smell(嗅)、watch(观看)后,既可以使用动名词形式,也可以使用省略了 to 的动词不定式形式,但使用时应当注意下述各点:

1) 这类动词后使用的省略了 to 的动词不定式通常用来指整体动作,而动名词形式通常用来指正在进行的动作,如:

I watched a pavement-artist draw a portrait in crayons.

我看到一位马路画家用彩色粉笔画了一幅画。(指从开始画到结束)

I watched a pavement-artist drawing a portrait in crayons.

我看到一位马路画家在用彩色粉笔画一幅画。(指正在画)

2) 无论使用动名词形式还是使用省略了 to 的动词不定式形式,都可用来描述短暂的动作,但描述极短暂的动作时只能用省略了 to 的动词不定式形式,如:

I heard someone unlock the door/unlocking the door.

我听到有人开门/在开门。

I heard him cough.

我听到他咳嗽。(一次)

I can hear him coughing.

我能听到他在咳嗽。(反复地)

3) 如在上述动词后使用一系列动词时,其后的动词应当为省略了 to 的动词不定式形式,如:

The crowd watched the firemen climb the ladder, break a window on the third floor, and enter the building.

人们看到消防队员爬上梯子、打碎 4 层楼的窗子并进入楼房。

4) 在上述感官动词后,不能使用被动形式的动词不定式,但可以使用被动形式的动名词,如:

I saw him being taken away by the police.

我看到他正被警察带走。

但在上述感官动词后可直接使用过去分词形式,如:

I saw him taken away by the police.

我看到他被警察带走了。

5) 当上述感官动词自身为被动形式时,其后通常可使用动名词形式,也可以使用带 to 的动词不定式形式,如:

They were seen waiting on the corner.

有人看到他们正在街角上等候。(动名词形式为进行中的动作)

They were seen to climb through the window.

有人看到他们爬进了窗户。(带 *to* 的动词不定式形式为已完成的动作)

(2) have 与动词不定式连用

用动词 have 可以构成 have sb. do sth. 这样跟随省略了 to 的动词不定式形式,表达"使某人做某事"之意,如:

He wanted a job, so I had him paint the kitchen.

他想干活,所以我就让他粉刷厨房。

Have the next patient come in now please, nurse.

护士,现在请让下一位患者进来。

(3) rather/sooner than 与动词不定式连用

在表达"宁愿"之意的 rather than 和 sooner than 之后,既可以使用动名词形式,也可以使用省略了 to 的动词不定式形式,如:

Rather than waste/wasting your time doing it yourself, why don't you call in a builder?

为什么你宁愿浪费时间自己干而不去请一个包工呢?

词汇学习 Word study

1. accompany *vt.*

(1) 陪伴,陪同:

She accompanied me on that journey.

那次旅行她一直陪伴着我。

(2) 伴随,与……一同发生:

Rain accompanied the thunder.

雨伴随着雷声。

(3) 为……伴奏/伴唱:

I accompanied her on guitar.

我用吉他为她伴奏。

2. yield

(1) *vt*. 生产,生:

A tree yields fruit.

树结果子。

(2) *vt*. 让与,放弃:

The enemy yielded a fortress.

敌军放弃了要塞。

(3) *vi*. 出产:

This land yields well/poorly.

这块土地产量高/低。

(4) *vi*. (to) 服从,屈服,投降:

You'd better yield to persuasion.

你最好听从劝告。

The enemy yielded to us.

敌人向我们投降了。

(5) *n*. (可数/不可数)产量,产额,收获量:

How to increase the yield is a serious problem we should solve.

如何增产是我们应当解决的严重问题。

What is the yield per mu*?*

每亩产量多少?

3. endow

(1) *vt*. 大笔捐赠:

The millionaire endowed a college.

这个百万富翁捐款建造了一所大学。

(2) endow with 赋予:

She is endowed by nature with beauty and intelligence.

她具有与生俱来的美丽和聪颖。

练习答案 Key to written exercises

1. 关键句型练习答案

A See text.

B 1 If you have ever driven at a hundred miles an hour, *you may understand why I would like to drive a racing car.*

2 If you have never been to New Zealand, *you may like to know that it is well worth a visit.*

3 If you have finished your work, *you may like to read this magazine article.*

C See text.

2. 难点练习答案

A 1 *Quite* and *quiet* are easily confused, not only because of their spelling, but also because of the way they are pronounced.

The adverb *quite* (/kwaɪt/) means 'completely' when used with ungradable adjectives like *dead*, *unique*, *lost*, etc., or 'strong' words like *amazing*, *astonishing*, *happy*, etc.: *Our first sight of an albatross was quite amazing.*

It means 'less than' when used with gradable adjectives and adverbs: *The lecture was quite good. He lectured quite well.* (Note that this use of *quite* is not very common in American English.)

The adjective *quiet* (/ˈkwaɪət/) means 'with little noise': *The latest model has a new quieter engine.*

2 A *wing* is a movable limb which a bird or insect uses for flying: *The bird spread its wings and flew away.*

A *feather* is 'any of the many parts of the covering which grows on a bird's body, each of which has a stiff rod-like piece in the middle, with soft hair-like material growing from it on each side': *When we visited the bird sanctuary, the children picked up lots of coloured feathers to take home.*

3 The words *course* and *coarse* are pronounced in the same way (/kɔːs/ or /kɔːrs/), but are quite different in meaning.

A *course* is 'the path along which something moves, or the direction of movement taken by someone or something': *The plane changed course to avoid the storm.*

The adjective *coarse* means 'not fine or smooth; lumpy or rough': *The sand on the beach on the north side of the island was very coarse, whereas on the south beach it was very fine.*

B 1 What *sort* of bicycle did you buy?

2 How many *sorts* of snakes did you see at the zoo?

C 1 *roughly* = about, not exactly

2 *rough* = uneven, not smooth

3 *Roughly* = About, Approximately

4 *rough* = stormy and violent, not calm

D If you *keep company with* drug addicts, you might become

one yourself.

As well as Jane's father, the rest of her family were there to greet us, too.

Men no longer *take off their hats to* ladies as they used to many years ago.

E 1 It takes me *a good fifteen minutes* to walk home from work.

2 I didn't measure it, but we must have walked *a good twenty miles* yesterday.

3 There must have been *a good five hundred people* at our village concert.

4 I have *a good many* friends on the Internet now.

5 We've been there *a good few* times.

F They planted lots of different flowers, *such as* roses, carnations and poppies.

Many professional thieves only steal light things *such as* jewellery and money.

G Do: do your duty, do wrong, do harm, do the shopping, do a lesson, do some work, do a job, do your best, do business, do an experiment, do (someone) a favour, do some homework

Make: make an excuse, make a fortune, make an attempt, make a bed, make a proposal, make sense, make a speech, make a problem, make a difference, make a copy, make an announcement, make an agreement, make money, make a mistake, make a living, make fun of, make friends with, make trouble, make sure, make a will, make a noise

H We often use the phrases *good morning*, *good afternoon*, etc. when reporting speech and with the verbs *wish* and *say*.

Note that we can *wish someone luck*, *well*, *good morning*, *good afternoon*, *good evening*, *good night*; and we can *say good morning*, *good afternoon*, *good evening*, *good night*, *hello*, *goodbye to someone*.

Wish me luck in the exam! I think I'm going to need it!

As I left on my trip to America, all my friends *wished me well*.

She *wished me good night* as I left her at her door.

3. 多项选择题答案

1	c	2	a	3	d	4	c	5	c	6	d
7	c	8	a	9	b	10	c	11	a	12	c

Lesson 24
Beauty
美

课文详注 Further notes on the text

1. **A young man sees a sunset and, unable to understand or to express the emotion that it rouses in him, concludes that it must be the gateway to a world that lies beyond.**

   sees a sunset 和 concludes that ... 为并列谓语动词,它们的主语是 A young man。unable to understand or to express ... 作原因状语,表示"由于无法理解和表达日落在其心中激起的感情"。that it rouses in him 作定语从句,修饰 the emotion。该从句中的 it 指 a sunset。that it must be ... 作动词 concludes 的宾语从句。that lies beyond 作定语从句,修饰 a world,意即"遥远的"。beyond 作副词。

2. **It is difficult for any of us in moments of intense aesthetic experience to resist the suggestion that we are catching a glimpse of a light that shines down to us from a different realm of existence, different and, because the experience is intensely moving, in some way higher.**

   It 为先行主语,真正的主语是动词不定式 to resist the suggestion ...。for any of us 这一介词短语实际是动词不定式 to resist 的逻辑主语。in moments of intense aesthetic experience 作状语,意即"在强烈感受到美的时候"。that we are catching ... existence 为名词 suggestion 的同位语从句。该从句中的 that shines down ... existence 作定语,修饰 a light。different and, ... higher 作非限定性定语，其中 different 和 higher 为并列成分，同时作定语，修饰 realm of existence。because ... moving 作原因状语从句，意即“由于美感的强烈感染”。in some way 在某种程度上。

3. **And, though the gleams blind and dazzle, yet do they convey a hint of beauty and serenity greater than we have known or imagined.**

though the gleams blind and dazzle 作让步状语从句，blind 和 dazzle 为不及物动词，作该从句的并列谓语，意即“令人眼花缭乱”。yet do they ...中的助动词 do 起强调作用，放在主语前面更具有强调的作用。a hint of /about... ……的启示，……的提示，如：a hint of suspicion(有点怀疑)、a hint about the answer(有关答案的提示)等。greater than ...作定语，修饰 beauty and serenity。than 引导的是比较状语从句。

4. **Greater too than we can describe; for language, which was invented to convey the meanings of this world, cannot readily be fitted to the uses of another.**

Greater too than we can describe 是省略句，greater 前面省略了 The beauty and serenity is。than 引导的是比较状语从句。for 为连词，引导原因状语从句，意即“由于”。which 引导的是非限定性定语从句，修饰 language。该从句中的动词不定式作目的状语。be fitted to 适合于。

5. **That all great art has this power of suggesting a world beyond is undeniable.**

That all great art ... beyond 作主语从句，is undeniable 是该句的谓语部分。of suggesting a world beyond 作定语，修饰 this power。

6. **In some moods, Nature shares it.**

In some moods 在某种状态下。Nature 在这里指“大自然”，作专有名词，故大写。it 指前面一句中的 this power of suggesting a world beyond。

7. **There is no sky in June so blue that it does not point forward to a bluer, no sunset so beautiful that it does not waken the vision of a greater beauty, a vision which passes before it is fully glimpsed, and in passing leaves an indefinable longing and regret.**

该句采用排比结构(parallel structure 或 parallelism)，即把结构相同或相似、意义相关、语气一致的几个词组或句子并列使用的句子。排比句便于表达强烈的感情，突出所强调的内容，增强语言的气势。与此同时，由于句子整齐，节奏分明，也增强了语言的韵律美，如：

Harson liked to swim in the summer, to ski in the winter, and to hunt in the fall.

哈森喜欢在夏天游泳、冬天滑雪、秋天打猎。

该句中采用 3 个动词不定式 + 介词短语结构，构成排比结构。该句中相同的结构是 no sky ... so blue that it does not ... 和 no sunset so beautiful that it does not ...。由于采用了这种排比结构，使该句对大自然的描写更为生动感人。a bluer 更加蔚蓝的苍穹。a vision which passes ... regret 作 the vision of a greater beauty 的同位语，其中的 which 作定语，修饰 a vision。passes 和 leaves 同作 which 的谓语。in passing 作状语，修饰 leaves。

8. **But, if this world is not merely a bad joke, life a vulgar flare amid the cool radiance of the stars, and existence an empty laugh braying across the mysteries; if these intimations of a something behind and beyond are not evil humour born of indigestion, or whimsies sent by the devil to mock and madden us, if, in a word, beauty means something, yet we must not**

seek to interpret the meaning.

该句也是一个典型的排比结构,由 3 个并列的条件状语从句构成。主句是 yet we must not seek to interpret the meaning。在第 1 个条件状语从句中,life 和 existence 前面省略了 if,后面省略了 is not merely。braying across the mysteries 为现在分词短语,作定语,修饰 an empty laugh。第 2 个条件句中 evil humour 和 whimsies 为该条件句中的并列表语。born of indigestion 和 sent by the devil to mock and madden us 作定语,分别修饰 humour 和 whimsies。a something 中的 something 作名词,故其前用不定冠词。behind and beyond 玄妙的。in a word 总而言之。

9. **If we glimpse the unutterable, it is unwise to try to utter it, nor should we seek to invest with significance that which we cannot grasp.**

it 为先行主语,真正的主语是动词不定式 to try to utter it。其中的 it 指 the unutterable。nor 为否定词,置于句首,故该句为倒装句。that 指 the unutterable,作动词 invest 的宾语。which 引导定语从句,修饰 that。invest sb. with sth. 授予某人某物,把某物赋予某人,如:

The President invested him with authority.

总统赋予他权利。

10. **Beauty in terms of our human meanings *is* meaningless.**

in terms of 关于,根据,如:

In terms of salary, the job is terrible.

就薪水而言,这个工作太糟糕了。

语法 Grammar in use

动词不定式用法 (4)

带 to 的动词不定式的用法 (1)

(1) 用来表示目的的动词不定式 to/in order to/so as to 结构

用上述词+动词构成的动词不定式结构在句子中可以起到目的状语的作用,如:

She was sent to England to / in order to / so as to be educated.

她被送到英国去受教育。

用否定词 not 构成的 not to 和 so as not to/in order not to 形式,可分别表示"取舍"和"反面的目的",如:

I went to France not to study French, but to study architecture.

我去法国不是为了学法语,而是为了学建筑。

I shut the door quietly so as not to wake the baby.

为了不把宝宝惊醒,我轻轻地关上门。

当动词不定式所表示的动作由宾语而不是由主语做出时,通常使用 for+宾语+带 to 的动词不定式结构。常见的使用上述结构的动词有:apply(应用)、arrange(安排)、ask(要求)、call(号召)、plan(计划)、plead(请求)、phone(打电话)、pray(祈祷)、ring(按铃)、send(叫,派)、vote(投票)、wait(等待)、wish(希望)等,如:

How long have you been waiting for the train to arrive?

你等火车到站有多长时间了?

I bought a second car (in order) for my son to learn how to drive.

我买了第 2 辆车,以便让我的儿子学习驾驶。

有时带 to 的动词不定式结构(不包括 in order to 和 so as to)用

于某些动词如 bring(带来)、buy(买)、need(需要)、take(拿)、use(用)、want(想要)等的宾语之后,这时它们往往起补足语的作用,用来对其前的宾语作进一步的说明,如:

I want something to cheer me up.

我需要一点能提神的东西。

I brought a chair to sit on.

我带了一把椅子来坐一坐。

(2) 表示结果的动词不定式

带 to 的动词不定式被置于句子的后半部分,往往用来说明出乎意外的结果。这类动词不定式前使用 only 或 never 后,往往表达出该结果是不受欢迎的含义,如:

We came home after our holiday to find our garden neat and tidy.

我们度假归来,发现我们的花园又干净又整齐。

He returned after the war, only to be told that his wife had left him.

战后他归来,听到的只是他的妻子已离他而去的消息。

She left home, never to return.

她离开了家,再没回来。

(3) 表示将来或虚构的过去的动词不定式

带 to 动词不定式的一般式用于 hope(希望)、intend(打算)、mean(意欲)、(would) like to(愿意)等动词之后时,表示"将来"的含义;而使用动词不定式的完成式时,则表示"虚构的过去",如:

I would like to see that film.

我愿意去看那部电影。(表示现在或将来)

I would like to have seen that film.

我但愿看了那部电影。(表示虚构的过去)

I would have liked to see that film.

我曾想看那部电影。(表示虚构的过去)

词汇学习 Word study

1. understand (understood)

(1) *vt.* 理解,了解,通晓:

Do you understand Russian?

你懂俄语吗?

I don't understand what you mean.

我不明白你的意思。

I can't understand him leaving so suddenly.

我不明白他为何走得那么突然。

She doesn't know how to look after you.

她不知道该如何照顾你。

(2) *vi.* 懂得,取得理解:

Eventually he will understand.

他终会理解的。

(3) make oneself understood 表达自己的意思,使旁人理解自己的意思:

Can you make yourself understood in French?

你能用法语表达自己的意思吗?

2. rouse *vt.*

(1) 惊起(猎物等):

The gunshot roused the birds.

枪声把鸟惊走了。

(2) 激怒,激励:

His words roused her.

他的话激怒了她。

(3) 唤起,使觉醒:

The book roused the boy's interest in the universe.

那本书引起了男孩对宇宙的兴趣。

3. resist *vt.*

(1) 抵制,抗拒:

This little girl found it difficult to resist the charms of H.O.T.

这个小姑娘觉得难以抵制 H.O.T. 的魅力。

They couldn't resist peeking through the keyhole.

他们不由自主地从锁孔窥视。

(2) 抵抗,对抗:

They have made up their minds to resist the enemy's attack.

他们决心抵抗敌人的进攻。

(3) 禁止,忍住:

I never resist an invitation of going fishing.

我从不拒绝钓鱼的邀请。

练习答案 Key to written exercises

1. 关键句型练习答案

A Remember that we can use *must* in different ways:

- *must* for obligation and *must not* for prohibition: *We must be home by 5.00. We must not be late.*
- *must* for assumption or deduction: *She dresses so well she must have a lot of money.*

Must could be replaced by *has to* in items 2 and 3 (where *must* expresses an obligation).

Must in items 1 and 4 expresses an assumption or deduction.

B 1 *It* must have been after one o'clock when I arrived home.

2 *There* must have been a large number of accidents over the Christmas holidays.

3 You might be asked to make a speech, but I think *it* is highly unlikely.

4 *It* will be difficult to dissuade him now that he has made up his mind.

5 *There* will be difficult times ahead.

C 1 *That he wrote this story himself* is unbelievable.

2 *That you should believe this to be true* is astonishing to me.

3 *That we all feel depressed sometimes* is quite true.

D If we glimpse the unutterable, *we should not attempt to utter* (*or describe*) *what we have seen*.

2. 难点练习参考答案

A 1 *Unable* and *enable* are understandably and easily confused, but are quite different.

The adjective *unable* (/ʌnˈeɪbəl/) simply means 'not able' and is normally followed by the *to*-infinitive: *He seems unable to understand the simplest instructions*.

The verb *enable* (/ɪˈneɪbəl/) means 'make able, give the power, means, or right to do something': *The albatross's large wings enable it to glide for long periods*.

2 The irregular verb *rouse* means 'waken': *The servant roused them from their rest in time to eat before they set off*.

The regular verb *raise* means 'lift, push or move upwards': *When the soldiers reached the top of the hill, they raised their flag*.

3 The irregular verbs *lie* (*lay*, *lain*) and *lay* (*laid*, *laid*) are often confused.

Lie means 'be or remain in a flat position on a surface': *They just lie on the beach all day*.

Lay means 'place, put, especially carefully, in a flat position': *We must lay the injured woman carefully on the stretcher before we put her into the ambulance*.

Remember too that the regular verb *lie* means 'tell lies': *Don't believe the girl: she lies to everybody*.

4 The adjective *indefinable* refers to something that cannot be defined: *As soon as I arrived, I felt an indefinable air of tension in the house*.

Undefined refers to something that can be defined but has not been: *When he first started in the new job, he felt a little awkward because his position in the company was undefined*.

5 *Vulgar* means 'showing a lack of fine feeling or good judgment in the choice of what is suitable or beautiful': *Their house was full of expensive but vulgar ornaments*.

Common can mean 'found or happening often or in many places, usual': *Rabbits and foxes are common in Britain*. It can also mean 'of no special quality or rank': *Common salt is very cheap*.

B 1 The meeting usually *concludes* with questions from any visitors.

2 That was the most embarrassing *experience* I have ever had.

3 She doesn't usually like this kind of music, she still

came *though*.

4 *a* The couple *invested* their life's savings in their son's business.

b As we parted, he *grasped* my hand and shook it warmly.

5 British schools, colleges and universities have three *terms* in the academic year.

C 1 I'm sure the young man doesn't *fully realize* how serious his crime is.

2 He may be young, but he is *fully capable* of lifting that box of books.

3 Before you make your first parachute jump, an instructor will *explain fully* exactly what you must do.

D As I was walking past the woods, I *caught a glimpse* of a fox among the trees.

I don't know why, but when I left the building I felt *in some way* easier in my mind.

Many famous people didn't *seek to* become famous, it just happened.

3. 多项选择题答案

1	a	2	a	3	c	4	c	5	b	6	c
7	a	8	d	9	d	10	a	11	c	12	d

Lesson 25
Non-auditory effects of noise
噪音的非听觉效应

课文详注 Further notes on the text

1. **Many people in industry and the Services, who have practical experience of noise, regard any investigation of this question as a waste of time; they are not prepared even to admit the possibility that noise affects people.**

the Services 军队。who 引导一非限定性定语从句,修饰 Many people in industry and the Services。regard ... as 把……看作,如:

He regards my younger brother as his friend.

他把我弟弟看作是他的朋友。

this question 指 noise。be prepared to do sth. 愿意做某事,如:

Would you be prepared to help me get things ready for the party?

你愿意帮我将聚会的事情安排妥当吗?

People are not prepared to talk about these kinds of personal problems.

人们不愿意谈论这类个人问题。

that noise affects people 为名词 possibility 的同位语从句。

2. **This is a pity, ..., and it is likely to be discredited if it gets to be associated with bad science.**

it 指 noise abatement。discredit 怀疑,如:

Evidence of links with drug dealers has discredited the

President.

与毒品贩子有关系的证据使总统受到怀疑。

get to do sth. 开始做某事，成功做某事，如：

If you get to see her, you may receive some help.

如果你能见到她，你也许能得到一些帮助。

If you get to know her, you'll like her.

如果你了解她，你会喜欢她的。

associate with 与……交往，与……联系在一起，如：

We associate with all sorts of people.

我们与各种各样的人们交往。

3. **One allegation often made is that noise produces mental illness.**

often made 作定语，修饰 one allegation。that 引导的是一表语从句。

4. **A recent article ..., was headed with a striking illustration of a lady in a state of considerable distress, with the caption 'She was yet another victim, reduced to a screaming wreck'.**

be headed with(文章的)标题是，以……开头，如：

The article was headed with 'How to cut your heating bills'.

文章的标题是"如何降低你的供暖费用"。

in a state of considerable distress 作定语，修饰 a lady，意即"一位表情沮丧的女子"。with the caption 作定语，修饰 illustration，意即"带有……解说词的插图"。reduced to a screaming wreck 为过去分词短语，作定语，修饰 victim，意即"成了一只会尖叫的可怜虫"。reduce to 使变成，使陷入，如：

She was reduced to poverty.

她陷入了贫困。

I reduced the problem to a few simple questions.

我将那个问题分解成了几个小问题。

5. **On turning eagerly to the text, one learns that ...**

该句中 on 的意思是 on the occasion of。directly after 一……就……。turn to 转换到，如：

Let's turn to a more pleasant topic.

我们转到另一个愉快点儿的话题吧。

6. **Another patient might equally well complain that her neighbours were combining to slander her and persecute her, and yet one might be cautious about believing this statement.**

might well 和 may well 可以表示"十分可能"，如：

You might well be right.

你可能是对的。

You may well get lost, so take a map.

你可能会迷路，所以带上一张地图。

that 引导的是宾语从句。combine to do sth. 联合做某事，如：

They are normally harmless substances which combine to form a highly poisonous gas.

它们一般是无害物质，合成起来却构成剧毒气体。

one 指"人们"。this statement 指 her neighbours were combining to slander her and persecute her。

7. **What is needed in the case of noise is a study of large numbers of people living under noisy conditions, to discover whether they are ... are.**

What is needed in the case of noise 为主语从句。living under noisy conditions 为现在分词短语，作定语，修饰 people。to discover ... 作目的状语，修饰谓语部分 is a study of large numbers of people ...。whether 引导的是动词不定式 to discover 的宾语从句。

8. **Some time ago ..., examined a very large number of men working on aircraft carriers: the study was known as Project Anehin.**

working on aircraft carriers 为现在分词短语，作定语，修饰 men。aircraft carriers 航空母舰。冒号后面的部分是对前面所提到的调查作的补充说明。

9. **It can be unpleasant to live even several miles from an aerodrome; if you think what it must be like to share the deck of a ship with several squadrons of jet aircraft, you will realize that a modern navy is a good place to study noise.**

   It 作先行主语，真正的主语是 to live ... aerodrome。what 引导一宾语从句，该从句中的 it 是先行主语，真正的主语是 to share the deck ... jet aircraft。that 引导的是动词 realize 的宾语从句。

10. **This result merely confirms earlier American and British studies: if there is any effect of noise upon mental health, it must be so small that present methods of psychiatric diagnosis cannot find it.**

   冒号后面的部分是 American and British studies 的同位语，是对该研究的内容所作的具体说明。if 引导的是条件状语从句。句中的两个 it 都是指 effect of noise。that 引导的是一结果状语从句。

11. **That does not prove that it does not exist; but it does mean that noise is less dangerous than, say, being brought up in an orphanage—which really is a mental health hazard.**

   That 指前句中的 this result。后面的 that 是关系连词，引导动词 prove 的宾语从句。该从句中的 it 指 the effect of noise。but 后面的 it 指 this result。其后的 does 表示强调。that noise is ... hazard 为动词 mean 的宾语从句。say 作插入语，意即"比方说"。being brought up in an orphanage 为动名词短语，作比较状语从句中的主语，该从句中省略了 is dangerous。破折号后面引出的是非限定性定语从句，修饰 being brought up in an orphanage。使用破折号是为了对该从句进行强调。

语法 Grammar in use

动词不定式用法 (5)

带 to 的动词不定式的用法 (2)

(1) 作动词宾语的动词不定式

在英语中,有许多动词同带 to 的动词不定式固定搭配使用,用于这类动词后的动词不定式在句子中起到宾语的作用。常见的这类动词包括:attempt(试图)、begin(开始)、bear(忍受)、care(想)、cease(停止)、commence(开始)、compete(竞争)、consent(同意)、continue(继续)、dare(敢)、deserve(值得)、dislike(厌恶)、fail(不能)、hasten(催促)、hate(讨厌)、have (got)(得,不得不)、help(帮助)、hurry(赶紧)、like(喜欢)、long (渴望)、love(爱)、manage(设法)、need(需要)、neglect(疏忽)、offer(提供)、prefer(喜欢)、refuse(拒绝)、scheme(计划)、seek (寻求)、start(开始)、stop(停止)、struggle(奋力)、try(试图)、unite(联合)、wait(等)、want(想)、wish(希望)等,如:

I want to leave.

我想离开。

I need to be left alone for a while.

我需要一个人待会儿。

(2) 普通否定式与动词不定式的否定式的比较

将否定词 not、never 置于带 to 的动词不定式之前构成动词不定式的否定形式。可以就下述两个句子,将动词不定式的否定形式同普通句子的否定形式进行语义上的比较:

I soon learnt not/never to swim near coral reefs.

我很快就知道不可/决不可在珊瑚礁附近游泳。

I didn't learn/never learnt to swim when I was a child.

我小时候没有/从没有学过游泳。

对许多动词如 advise(建议)、ask(要求)、instruct(指导)、remind(提醒)、tell(告诉)、warn(警告)等以及形容词/名词+动词不定式结构而言,否定词的位置会有极大的影响。试比较:

He told me not to feed the animals.
他叫我别喂动物。(做出了 *tell* 的动作)
He didn't tell me to feed the animals.
他没有叫我喂动物。(未做 *tell* 的动作)

Ask Rex not to phone, I don't want to be disturbed.
让雷克斯别来电话,我不想被打搅。(要做 *ask* 的动作)
Don't ask Rex to phone. I'll ring him myself.
别让雷克斯来电话,我将亲自给他去电话。(不要做 *ask* 的动作)

I was sorry not to go.
我后悔没去。(未做 *go* 的动作)
I wasn't sorry to go.
我不后悔去了那儿。(做出了 *go* 的动作)

It was a surprise not to hear from him.
没收到他的信使我感到惊讶。(未做 *hear from* 的动作)
It wasn't a surprise to hear from him.
我收到他的信并不感到惊讶。(做出了 *hear from* 的动作)

(3) 分裂动词不定式

所谓"分裂动词不定式"即将动词不定式中的 to 与其后的动词之间插入一个副词或类似 please 这样的结构形式。常见的这类副词有:completely(完全地)、fully(全面地)、really(真地)、truly(真实地)等,如:

I want you to clearly understand what I'm telling you.
我希望你清楚地理解我告诉你的事。

It's difficult to really understand the theory of relativity.

真正理解相对论是不易的。

虽然这种结构形式在口语中常见,但在具体使用中最好还是尽力避免这样的结构形式。

词汇学习 Word study

1. prepare

(1) *vt*. 准备,预备:

She's preparing her lessons.

她正准备功课。

She has prepared a nice meal for him.

她为他做了一顿好饭。

(2) *vt*. 筹备:

They couldn't prepare the meeting well on time.

他们未能按时筹备好会议。

(3) *vt*. 为……作准备:

She prepared her child to be a dancer.

她培养女儿成为舞蹈家。

(4) *vi*. 预备,作好准备:

He is now preparing to sit an examination.

他正在为参加考试作准备。

2. combine

(1) *vt*. /kəmˈbaɪn/ 使结合,使联合,团结;兼有:

She combined flour, sugar, egg, and water to make a cake.

她把面粉、食糖、鸡蛋和水和在了一起做蛋糕。

His new plan boldly combines practicality and originality.

他的新计划大胆地结合了实用性和创造性。

(2) *vt*. /kəmˈbaɪn/ 化合:

What do we produce when we combine copper with iron?

把铜和铁化合在一起会产生什么？

(3) *vi*. /kəmˈbaɪn/ 联合，结合，团结：

Two factions combined to object the proposal.

两派联合起来反对该提议。

(4) *vi*. /kəmˈbaɪn/ (with) 化合：

Two atoms of hydrogen combine with one of oxygen to form water.

两个氢原子与一个氧原子化合而成水。

(5) *n*. /ˈkɔmbaɪn/ (可数) 团体，组合，集团；联合收割机

3. worry

(1) *vt*. 使烦恼，使焦虑，使担忧：

What's worrying you?

什么事使你烦恼？

I am much worried.

我非常着急。

It worries me that you might not pass the exam.

令我烦恼的是你可能通不过这次考试。

It worries me to think of you going home alone every night.

一想到你每天晚上独自回家我就担心。

(2) *vt*. 困扰，折磨：

Her daughter is now worrying her for a new dress.

她的女儿正缠着她要身新衣服。

(3) *vi*. 烦恼，担心，发愁：

Don't worry.

别着急。

All the teachers are now worrying about the students' safety.

所有的老师都正在为学生们的安全担心。

Don't worry over her health.

不要为她的健康担心。

(4) *n*. (不可数)烦恼,担心;(可数,常用复数)烦恼事

练习答案 Key to written exercises

1. 关键句型练习答案

A 1 *Many roads which we use* were not built for such heavy traffic.

2 *The heavy snow which fell last week* has now begun to melt.

3 *The party of tourists which we had in our hotel at the weekend* left this morning.

4 *The clerk who took the original telephone call* apologized for the mistake.

B 1 A large animal *frequently seen* near our village has proved to be a black panther.

2 One ridiculous argument *sometimes heard* is that failure is a necessary part of progress.

3 One sight *generally considered* worth visiting is the old church on the cliffs.

C 1 Have you written back to your penfriend *yet*?

2 I haven't told them about the concert *yet*.

3 I don't know how many old girlfriends he has, but Gail is *yet another* in a long line.

D 1 *On opening* the door, I got a surprise.

2 *On seeing* me approaching, he ran towards me.

3 *On being asked* to leave the meeting, he got very angry.

4 *On arriving* at the station, she bought a ticket.

E At the sight of the bank robbers with their guns, the girl was *reduced to* a quivering jelly.

The police are still trying to establish the *cause of* the accident.

The local Health Officer has received lots of *complaints about* the standard of hygiene in that café.

Most spokesmen for government departments are extremely *cautious about* saying anything which can be understood too easily.

At the youth hostel, Karla had to *share* a room *with* a girl she had never met.

It's been said that such horrific sights on television news can have dreadful *effects upon* young children.

Modern *methods of* tracing the source of a disease do not always seem to be very effective.

2. 难点练习答案

A 1 While the verb *regard* can mean 'look at in a stated way', it tends to be used to mean 'consider in a stated way': *I have always regarded him with the greatest admiration.*

Look at means 'turn the eyes so as to see something': *What are you looking at?*

2 The words *affect* and *effect* are easily confused.

The verb *affect* means 'cause some result or change in; influence': *Will the miners' strike affect the price of coal?*

Effect is a noun meaning 'a result or condition produced by a cause or something that happens when one thing acts on another': *Fortunately the miners' strike had little effect on the price of coal.*

3 A *plea* is 'an urgent or serious request': *The British government has sent India a plea for mercy for the man accused of drug smuggling.* (The verb closely associated with the noun *plea* is *plead* ⟨*for*⟩.)

The verb *please* means 'make... happy, or give satisfaction (to)': *The assistants in that store are eager to please all their customers.*

4 The word *objective* is both an adjective and a noun. As an adjective, it means 'existing outside the mind, real, not influenced by personal feelings': *You must try to be more objective in dealing with these problems.*

As a noun, an *objective* is 'an aim, especially one that must be worked towards over a long period': *Our objective is to achieve full, or near-full employment over the next ten years.*

An *objection* (from the verb *object*) is 'a statement or feeling of opposition or disapproval': *If you have no objection, I'll lock up now.*

5 The verb *confirm* means 'give support or certainty to (a fact, etc.) e.g. by providing more proof or by stating that something is true or correct': *He said he would accept the job, so we have asked him to confirm his acceptance in writing.*

The verb *assure* (not to be confused with *ensure* or *insure*) means 'tell firmly and with confidence, especially with the aim of removing doubt': *She assured me that the medicine was safe to take.*

B like (*v.*)—*dislike* (l.3) adequate—*inadequate* (l.3)
credit (*v.*)—*discredit* (l.5) pleasant—*unpleasant* (l.17)

C 1 *brought up* = educated and cared for
2 *brought up* = asked, mentioned
3 *bring him round* = cause him to regain consciousness
4 *brought back* = reminded me of
5 *brought the house down* = caused great admiration, probably with a lot of applause (and possible whistles and shouting)
6 *bring to mind* = remember
7 *bring out* = cause to be seen, make clear

3. 多项选择题答案

1	d	2	b	3	a	4	d	5	d	6	c
7	a	8	c	9	d	10	b	11	c	12	a

Lesson 26
The past life of the earth
地球上的昔日生命

课文详注 Further notes on the text

1. **It is animals and plants which lived in or near water whose remains are most likely to be preserved, for one of the necessary conditions of preservation is quick burial, and it is only in the seas and rivers, and sometimes lakes, where mud and silt have been continuously deposited, that bodies and the like can be rapidly covered over and preserved.**

该句结构比较复杂,整个段落为一个句子。这个句子的基本结构是两个并列复合句。这两个并列句都是强调句,第 1 个是 It is animals and plants ..., for ... burial,第 2 个是 and it is only in the seas and ... preserved。第 1 个强调句所强调的部分是 animals and plants which ... water。将该句还原为非强调句后,其结构应该是 The remains of animals and plants which lived in or near water are most likely to be preserved, for ... burial。第 2 个强调句所强调的部分是地点状语 in the seas and rivers。将该句还原为非强调句后,其结构应该是 and bodies and the like can be rapidly covered over and preserved in the seas and rivers, and sometimes lakes, where mud and silt ... deposited。which lived in or near water 作定语从句,修饰 animals and plants。for one of the necessary conditions ... burial 作原因状语从句,作补充说明。where mud and silt have been continuously deposited 作非限定性定语从句,修饰 the seas and rivers, and sometimes lakes。the like 相当于 such like,类似的东西,如:

There's a big sports hall for tennis and badminton and the like/and such like.

有一个打网球、羽毛球这类项目的大型体育馆。

First class travel is not for the like of us.

坐头等舱旅行可不是我们这类人的事。

cover over 遮没。

2. But ... only a small fraction of the creatures that die are preserved in this way before decay sets in or, ... them.

that die 作定语,修饰 creatures。set in(常用来表示不好的事情)开始,到来,如:

We need to have the roof repaired before the bad weather sets in.

我们需要在坏天气到来之前把屋顶修好。

After a few days, exhaustion set in and the climbers were forced to give up their attempt to reach the top of the mountain.

几天过后,疲劳袭来,登山者不得不放弃登上顶峰的打算。

3. After all, all living creatures live by feeding on something else, whether it be plant or animal, dead or alive, and it is only by chance that such a fate is avoided.

live by 靠……生活,遵循,如:

The boy lived by selling newspapers.

那个男孩靠卖报纸为生。

For several years she lived by begging.

数年来她靠乞讨为生。

I always try to live by what I believe in.

我总是试图遵循我的信仰而生活。

whether it be plant or animal, dead or alive 是一个让步状语从句,用的是虚拟语气。it 指 something else。and it is only by chance that ...为强调句,被强调的部分是状语 by chance。还原为非强调句应该是 and such a fate is avoided only by chance。such a fate 指"被吃掉的命运"。by chance 偶然,如:

I got this job completely by chance.

我得到这份工作纯属偶然。

4. When you think of the innumerable birds that one sees flying about, not to mention the equally numerous small animals like field mice and voles which you do not see, it is very rarely that one comes across a dead body, except, of course, on the roads.

think of 想起,想像,如:

She thought of her bitter past and could not help sobbing.

她想起了自己悲惨的过去,不禁泣不成声。

that one sees flying about 为定语从句,修饰 birds。one 泛指"人们"。flying about 作宾语补足语。not to mention ... see 为补充说明部分。not to mention 为固定词组,意即"更不用说"、"更不屑说",主要用来强调所要补充说明的部分,如:

He is one of the most intelligent, not to mention handsome, among the people I know.

他是我认识的人中最聪明的人之一,更甭说有多英俊了。

注意该词组与 don't mention it 的区别。don't mention it 用于别人对你表示感谢而进行回答时,意即"不必客气",如:

Thanks for your help.
十分感谢你的帮助。
Not at all, don't mention it.
没什么,不必客气。

it is very rarely that ... roads 中的 it 是先行主语,that 引导的

是真正的主语。come across 遇到,偶然碰到,如:

If you come across my glasses, can you let me have them, please?

如果你看到我的眼镜,请你交给我,行吗?

5. **It is almost always due to some very special circumstances that traces of land animals survive, as by falling into inaccessible caves, or into an ice crevasse, like the Siberian mammoths, when the whole animal is sometimes preserved, as in a refrigerator.**

该句为强调句,强调部分是原因状语 almost always ... circumstances。as 引导方式状语从句,as 后面省略了 they survive。when 意即"这时",补充说明动物掉进冰河裂缝里,有时就像被保存在冰箱里一样。as in a refrigerator 的 as 后面省略了 it is preserved。

6. **This is what happened to the famous Beresovka mammoth which was found preserved and in good condition.**

what 引导表语从句。which 引导定语从句,修饰 the famous Beresovka mammoth。preserved and in good condition 作主语补足语。

7. **In his mouth were the remains of fir trees—the last meal that he had before he fell into the crevasse and broke his back.**

In his mouth were the ... 是倒装句。该句之所以倒装,是因为主语即 the remains of fir trees 及后面由破折号引出的同位语 the last meal 和其定语从句 that he had before ... back 过长。

8. **Apparently what happened was that water collected on these tar pits, ... ventured out on to ..., and were promptly bogged in the tar.**

what happened 为主语从句,that 引导的是表语从句。

9. And then, when ..., came out to feed and suffered exactly the same fate.

the same fate 指 were promptly bogged in the tar,意即“也掉进沥青坑”。

语法 Grammar in use

动词不定式用法 (6)

带 to 的动词不定式的用法 (3)

(1) 作表语的带 to 的动词不定式

可以将带 to 的动词不定式用于动词 be 之后,作表语使用,如:

Your mistake was to write that letter.

你的错误是写了那封信。

注意:当置于 be 动词之后的动词不定式为前文 do 动词动作的引申或说明时,作表语使用的动词不定式既可为带 to 的动词不定式,也可为省略了 to 的动词不定式,如:

What you do is (to) mix the eggs with flour.

你要做的是把面粉和鸡蛋搅合在一起。

All I did was (to) press this button.

我所做的只是按这个电钮。

此外,有时作表语的动词不定式可以用主动语态来表达被动的含义。然而,有时则只能用被动语态来表达被动的含义,如:

This house is to let/to be let.

此房出租。

Who is to blame/to be blamed?

该怪谁?

He's (only) to be admired/envied/pitied.

他(真)值得尊敬/羡慕/同情。

但是，在使用上述结构时，切忌同表示将来时间的 be to do sth. 这一结构形式相混淆。表示将来时间的 be to do sth. 的用途十分有限，一般仅用于表示“正式的安排/公务”，如：

OPEC representatives are to meet in Geneva next Tuesday.

石油输出国组织代表将于下星期二在日内瓦进行会谈。

(2) 固定词组中的带 to 的动词不定式

有些已形成固定搭配的带 to 的动词不定式结构，其中使用的任何成分通常均不能更改或省略。常见的这类词组有：to be honest（老实说）、to begin with（首先）、to cut a long story short（简而言之，长话短说）、to get (back) to the point（回到主题）、not to make too much of it（别太小题大作）、to put it another way（换句话说）、to tell you the truth（跟你说实话吧）等，如：

To tell you the truth, I've never heard of such a thing.

说实话，我从来没有听说过这种事。

词汇学习 Word study

1. feed (fed)

(1) *vt.* 喂，喂养：

What does she feed the baby on?

她用什么喂她的婴儿？

The little girl was feeding the pigeons some breadcrumbs.

那个小姑娘在给鸽子喂面包屑。

You could feed breadcrumbs to pigeons.

你可以给鸽子喂面包屑。

(2) *vt.* 供原料(给)：

This lake is fed by two rivers.

这个湖的水是由两条河注入的。

(3) *vi*. (on)(牲畜等)吃:

The cattle feed chiefly on grass.

牛主要吃草。

(4) *n*. (可数)(动物的)一餐,一顿饭:

(5) *n*. (可数,口语,幽默的说法)饱餐:

That was a great feed we had last night.

昨天晚上我们饱餐了一顿。

(6) *n*. (不可数)饲料:

He carried a bag of chicken feed into the room.

他扛着一袋鸡饲料走进屋子。

2. destroy *vt*.

(1) 摧毁,破坏,损坏:

The bomb has destroyed several buildings in the area.

炸弹毁坏了这个地区的几幢楼房。

You must destroy all these documents for purposes of confidentiality.

为了保密,你必须将所有这些文件销毁。

(2) 消灭,歼灭:

They destroyed the invaders.

他们歼灭了入侵之敌。

(3) 使破灭,使失败:

I felt destroyed by the thought that she no longer needed me.

一想到她不再需要我了,我就觉得彻底失落了。

3. venture

(1) *n*. (不可数/可数)冒险,冒险行动:

Only a brave man would undertake such a venture.

只有勇敢的人才会冒这样的险。

He declined the venture.

他拒绝了去冒险。

(2) *n*. (可数)冒险事业,商业冒险,投机:

He has failed in his ventures.

他投机失败了。

(3) *vt*. 冒……的危险:

He ventured his life to rescue the drowning child.

他冒着生命危险抢救那个落水的孩子。

(4) *vt*. 拿……进行投机:

The gambler will venture all his money on the final try.

这个赌徒准备孤注一掷。

(5) *vt*. 大胆提出:

He ventured an objection at the meeting.

他在会上大胆提出反对意见。

I venture to say we'll need help.

我敢说我们将需要帮助。

(6) *vi*. (on, upon)冒险,敢于,鼓起勇气前进:

They are determined to venture on the dangerous journey.

他们决心冒险去进行一次危险的旅行。

练习答案 Key to written exercises

1. 关键句型练习答案

A 1 The archaeologists are waiting *until* the weather improves before they continue digging.

2 *After* they die, most land animals decompose or they are eaten by other creatures.

3 I will telephone you *as soon as* I get to London.

4 They have promised to phone us *when* they have some definite news.

B 1 The old lady does not go out in the winter, *for* she feels the cold a great deal.

2 I've got a present *for* you.

C See text.

2. 难点练习答案

A 1 The adjective *favourable* (in the text) means 'advantageous': *The company will lend you money on very favourable terms.*

The adjective *favourite* means 'most loved': *My favourite snack is a small bar of chocolate.*

2 *Alive* and *living* are easily confused.

The adjective *alive* means 'having life, not dead' and, like similar adjectives *asleep*, *awake*, *alight*, etc., cannot be used before a noun: *Are your grandparents still alive? He's the only man alive who could do it.*

(Note that we must use *alive*, not *living*, in the expression *dead or alive*.)

The adjective *living* means 'alive now': *She has no living relatives.*

(Remember that the noun *living* is 'a means of providing oneself with what is necessary for life': *What do you do for a living? She earns a living as a writer.*)

3 *Avoid* means 'keep away from, or keep out of the way of': *I had to swerve to avoid the old man who was walking in the road.*

The verb *prevent*, however, means 'stop (something) happening or stop (someone) doing something'.

It is often used with the preposition *from*: *What can we do to prevent this disease (from) spreading?*

B 1 Can you ask your father to move his car? It's *in the way*.

2 I stopped *on the way* here to visit my uncle.

3 *In a way* I can see what you mean, but I can't agree with you completely.

4 Oh, *by the way*, while we're talking about old college friends, have you heard from John lately?

C 1 *due to* = because of, caused by, as a result of

2 *due to* = expected or supposed to

3 *due* = what rightfully belongs to somebody, especially something non-material

4 *due* = directly, exactly

D 1 Please do *as* I say.

2 He was white *as* a sheet.

3 He left *as* suddenly *as* he came.

4 Don't act *like* a baby.

5 The carnivores, *like* sabre-toothed cats, ...

3. 多项选择题答案

1	c	2	b	3	c	4	b	5	a	6	c
7	d	8	d	9	a	10	b	11	a	12	c

Lesson 27
The 'Vasa'
"瓦萨"号

课文详注 Further notes on the text

1. **For nearly three and a half centuries she lay at the bottom of ... until her discovery in 1956.**

   she 指"瓦萨"号帆船。有关说明见书中课文注释 1。英语中多用代词 she 指代船只。her discovery 指 the discovery of *Vasa*。

2. **King Gustavus Adolphus, 'The Northern Hurricane', then at the height of his military success in the Thirty Years' War, had dictated her measurements and armament.**

   'The Northern Hurricane'是 King Gustavus Adolphus 的同位语。at the height of 在……高度,在……顶峰,如:

   It flew at a height of ten thousand feet.

   它在一万英尺的高空飞行。

   the Thirty Years' War 三十年战争。参见书中课文注释 2。her 指"瓦萨"号的。

3. **She was intended to play a leading role in the growing might of Sweden.**

   intend to do sth. 打算做某事,如:

   I don't think she intended me to hear the remark.

   我认为她不打算让我听到这话。

   play/perform a role in 在……中发挥作用,扮演角色,如:

   She plays a leading role in this play.

   在这个话剧中她扮演主角。

Education plays a very important role in economic development.

教育在经济发展中起着非常重要的作用。

4. **As she was prepared for ... 1628, Stockholm was in a ferment.**

in a ferment 处于激动的状态。

5. **From the Skeppsbron ... the people watched this thing of beauty begin ...**

this thing of beauty 指"瓦萨"号。

6. **They had laboured for three years to produce this floating work of art; ...**

this floating work of art 指"瓦萨"号,意即"水上艺术品"。

7. **The high stern castle was a riot of carved gods, demons, knights, kings, warriors, mermaids, cherubs; and zoomorphic animal shapes ablaze with red and gold and blue, symbols of courage, power, and cruelty, were portrayed to stir the imaginations of the superstitious sailors of the day.**

该句由两个并列分句组成,这两个分句由分号分开。a riot of 许多,主要指色彩丰富,如:

Jim's roses are a riot of colours.

吉姆的玫瑰花五颜六色。

ablaze with 闪耀……的(ablaze 是形容词),如:

The city was ablaze with lights.

城市里灯火辉煌。

Her face was ablaze with anger.

她满面怒容。

ablaze with 在课文里作定语,修饰 zoomorphic animal shapes。symbols of courage, power, and cruelty 作 zoomorphic animal shapes 的同位语。zoomorphic animal shapes 作第 2 个并列分

句的主语,该分句的谓语是 were portrayed。to stir the imaginations ... day 作目的状语。of the day 当时的。

8. **Then the cannons of the anchored warships thundered a salute to which the *Vasa* fired in reply.**

to which the *Vasa* fired in reply 作定语从句,修饰 a salute。in reply 作为回答,如:

The teacher nodded in reply.

老师点头作为回答。

9. **As she emerged from her drifting cloud of gun smoke with the water churned to foam beneath her bow, her flags flying, pennants waving, sails filling in the breeze, and the red and gold of her superstructure ablaze with colour, she presented a more majestic spectacle than Stockholmers had ever seen before.**

As 引导的是时间状语从句。该从句中的 with the water churned ..., her flags flying, pennants waving, sails filling ..., and the red and gold ... ablaze with colour 为 5 个独立主格结构,均作方式状语,修饰动词 emerged。这 5 个独立主格结构生动形象地将当时"瓦萨"号刚起航时的壮观场面表现出来。该句的主句是 she presented ... before。than 引导比较状语从句,该连词后面省略了 that。

10. **As the wind freshened there came a sudden squall and the ship made a strange movement, listing to port.**

there came a sudden squall 该句为 there 引导的句子。通常 there 与 be 动词连用,表示"存在"。此外 there 还可以同其他动词连用,如:arise、come、exist、rise、go、lie、live、remain、seem、stand 等动词连用,如:

There seems to be a problem.

好像有一个问题。

There came the crack of a shot.

传来一声枪响。

listing to port 作结果状语，修饰 made a strange movement。

11. The Ordnance Officer ordered all the port cannon to be heaved to starboard to counteract the list, but the steepening angle of the decks increased.

to be heaved to starboard 作宾语 all the port cannon 的补足语。to counteract the list 作目的状语，修饰 to be heaved。

12. Then ... shore, as cargo, ballast, ammunition and 400 people went sliding and crashing down to the port side of the steeply listing ship.

as 引导的是时间状语从句。sliding and crashing ... 作方式状语，修饰 went。

13. In that first glorious hour, the mighty *Vasa*, which was intended to rule the Baltic, sank with all flags flying—in the harbour of her birth.

which 引导的是非限定性定语从句。with all flags flying 为独立主格结构，作方式状语。破折号用来起强调作用，强调就是在她诞生的港口沉没。in the harbour of her birth 为介词短语，作地点状语。

语法 Grammar in use

动词不定式用法 (7)

带 to 的动词不定式的用法 (4)

(1) 动词 + 带 to 的动词不定式

在许多常用动词之后可以直接使用作宾语的带 to 的动词不定式。这些动词包括：afford(提供)、aim(意欲)、agree(同意)、decline(拒绝)、fail(未能)、hasten(急忙)、hurry(急忙)、long(渴望)、manage(设法)、offer(提议)、prepare(准备)、refuse(拒

绝)、seek(谋求)、shudder(发抖)、strive(争取)、struggle(努力)等,如:

I can't afford to buy a car.

我买不起汽车。

I hesitate to disagree with you.

我不愿意与你的意见相左。

在使用上述动词时,有两点需注意:(1)在这些动词后不能使用动名词或 that 从句;(2)在这些动词后很少使用动词不定式的完成时形式。

(2) 动词 + (名词/代词) + 带 to 的动词不定式

在某些动词与动词不定式之间加或不加作宾语的名词/代词均可。当该动词与其后的动词不定式之间使用名词或代词后,该名词或代词同其后的动词不定式构成复合宾语结构。经常这样使用的这类动词包括:ask(询问)、beg(乞求)、choose(选择)、expect(期待)、hate(憎恨)、help(帮助)、intend(打算)、like(喜欢)、love(热爱)、need(需要)、prefer(宁愿)、prepare(准备)、promise(保证)、want(想要)、wish(希望)等,如:

I want you to speak to the manager.

我希望你去同经理谈话。

I like you to keep everything tidy.

我希望你将每件东西都保持整洁。

应当注意动词 promise 与上述其他动词在语义上的不同。比较:

The teacher asked the boy to answer the question.

那位老师要那个男孩回答问题。(*answer* 的动作由男孩做出)

The teacher promised the boy to solve the problem.

那位老师答应那个男孩去解决那个问题。(*solve* 的动作由老师做出)

当上述动词用于 would 之后时，往往表示提出具体的建议、要求等，如：

I'd like you to find him a job.

我希望你给他找个工作。

(3) 动词＋名词/代词＋带 to 的动词不定式

还有很多动词与动词不定式中间必须加作宾语的名词或代词。常用的这类动词包括：advise（建议）、allow（允许）、assist（协助）、bribe（贿赂）、cause（使）、caution（警告）、challenge（挑战）、charge（责令）、command（命令）、compel（强迫）、condemn（注定）、dare（挑战）、direct（指引）、drive（强迫）、enable（使能）、encourage（鼓励）、forbid（禁止）、force（逼迫）、impel（推动）、implore（恳求）、incite（激励）、induce（诱使）、instruct（指示）、invite（邀请）、oblige（迫使）、order（命令）、permit（允许）、persuade（劝说）、press（催促）、recommend（推荐）、remind（提醒）、request（要求）、teach（教）、tell（告诉）、temper（引诱）、urge（催促）、warn（警告）等，如：

I advise you to leave.

我劝你离开。

What he said encouraged me to go on.

他的话激励我继续下去。

词汇学习 Word study

1. watch

(1) *vt.* 观看，注视：

The children are watching television/ a football game.

孩子们正在看电视/一场足球赛。

He watched them eating.

他看着他们吃饭。

I watched him get into his jacket.

我看见他穿上了夹克。

I watched the typewriter carried out of the door.

我看见打字机被搬出了门。

(2) *vt*. **看管,看守,监视,注意:**

Can you watch the baby for an hour?

你能照看这婴儿一个小时吗?

Watch that you don't fall off!

注意别摔下来!

(3) *vt*. **守候,等待:**

The wolf is behind the tree and is watching his time.

那只狼躲在树后,在窥伺时机。

(4) *vi*. **观看,注视:**

Are you going to play or only watch?

你将参加比赛还是只是观看?

(5) *vi*. **看守,监视,注意:**

There is a policeman watching outside the house.

有一名警察在屋外监视着。

(6) *vi*. **(for)守候:**

They are watching for a chance.

他们正在等待时机。

(7) *vi*. **整夜守护:**

The nurse watches with the sick.

护士在晚上看护病人。

(8) *n*. **(可数)手表,挂表**

(9) *n*. **(不可数/可数)看守,守卫,守护,照管,注意:**

Some soldiers are keeping close watch over the enemy.

一些战士正密切注意敌人的行动。

I'm on the watch for them.

我正在监视他们。

Everybody here should keep watch against the thief.

这儿的每个人都应当谨防小偷。

That man is just under close watch.

那个人正被严密监视。

2. fire

(1) *n.* (不可数)火,炮火:

There is no smoke without fire.

无风不起浪。

They are now under fire and cannot move.

他们正在炮火监视下,不能挪动。

(2) *n.* (可数)炉火;火灾:

There is a warm fire in the room.

房间里的炉火温暖。

(3) *n.* (喻)炙热的感情,激情:

The young man is full of fire.

这个小伙子充满了激情。

(4) *vt.* 点火,引燃:

It took several matches to fire the wood.

用了几根火柴才将木柴引燃。

(5) *vt.* 激起:

The teacher's remark fired my interest in history.

老师的话激起我对历史的兴趣。

(6) *vt.* 发射(子弹),射击,开枪:

The policemen are firing their pistols at the suspect.

警察正向嫌疑犯射击。

(7) *vt.* 开除:

She was fired for spending too much time on the phone.

她因花太多时间打电话而被开除。

3. labour

(1) *n*. (不可数)劳作,劳动:

Much labour went into making that model.

制造那个模型花费了大量的劳力。

(2) *n*. (不可数)劳动阶级,劳工:

A meeting will be held between labour and management to avoid a strike.

劳资双方将开会洽谈,以避免罢工。

(3) *n*. (可数)一件工作:

This is a labour that calls for both exertion and precision.

这是一件既花力气又要求精确的工作。

(4) *n*. (可数/不可数)分娩时的阵痛:

Labour can take hours.

分娩有时会持续数小时。

(5) *vi*. (辛劳地)工作:

He laboured for months to make that model.

他辛劳工作了几个月来制做那个模型。

They laboured for peace tirelessly.

他们为和平而不知疲倦地努力工作。

(6) *vi*. 艰难、缓慢地行进:

The old man laboured up the hill.

老人吃力地慢慢爬上小山。

(7) *vt*. 详细地做,详细说明:

There's no need to labour the point.

这一点无需详细说明。

练习答案 Key to written exercises

1. 关键句型练习答案

A See text.

B 1 I heard him *open the door and step into the room*.

2 I noticed *someone turn away from the crowd and take out a mobile phone*.

3 Did you see *anyone leave by the back door*?

C 1 They had laboured *for* three years...

2 *Since* 1628 few attempts had been made to salvage the *Vasa*.

3 *For* nearly three and a half centuries she lay...

D 1 In the deep dark forest *there lived* an old man who was said to be a hundred years old.

2 *There seemed* little point in speaking to him because he was obviously not going to change his mind.

E We all *went shopping* last Saturday.

Shall we *go swimming* this afternoon?

We won't *go sailing* again until next July.

2. 难点练习答案

A 1 *spread* = open out, stretch out

2 *spread* = make or become widely known

3 *Spread* = Put (a covering) on

4 *spread* = stretch out, so as to cover the table

B 1 *produce* = make by using skill and imagination

2 *produce* = show, bring out, or offer for examination

3 *produced* = prepared and brought before the public

4 *produce* = grow

C 1 *peeped* = came partly into view

2 *peered* = looked very carefully or hard, as if not able to see clearly

3 *glanced* = gave a quick short look

4 *caught a glimpse* = caught a quick look or incomplete view

3. 多项选择题答案

1	b	2	c	3	d	4	c	5	c	6	a
7	c	8	c	9	d	10	d	11	d	12	a

Lesson 28
Patients and doctors
病人与医生

课文详注 Further notes on the text

1. **This is a sceptical age, but although our faith in many of the things in which our forefathers fervently believed has weakened, our confidence in the curative properties of the bottle of medicine remains the same as theirs.**

   faith 与介词 in 搭配,表示"笃信"。in which 引导定语从句,由于从句中的动词 believe 也应与介词 in 搭配以表示"相信",所以该句中关系代词前用了介词 in, in 也可以置于该定语从句的句末。confidence 也与介词 in 搭配以表示"对……信任"。该句为了避免重复,分别使用了 faith in、confidence in 和 believe in 来表示"相信"、"信任"。theirs 指 our forefathers'。

2. **This modern faith ... the fact that the annual drug bill of the Health Services is mounting to astronomical figures and shows no signs at present of ceasing to rise.**

   that 引导的是同位语从句。astronomical figures 天文数字。表示很多,是夸张的说法。

3. **The majority of the patients attending the medical out-patients departments of our hospitals feel that they have not received adequate treatment unless ... in the shape of a bottle of medicine, ..., and the doctor in charge of the department is only too ready to provide them with these requirements.**

   attending the medical ... hospitals 为分词短语,作定语,修饰

the patients。out-patients departments 门诊部。that 引导一宾语从句，作动词 feel 的宾语。in the shape of 呈……形状。in charge of 为介词短语，作定语，修饰 doctor，意即“负责……的”。only too ready to do sth. 非常乐意做某事。英语中 too ... to ... 表示“太……以至于不能做……”，如：

I'm too tired to walk such a long way back home.

我太累了，不能走那么远的路回家。

但是如果在 too 前面用上 only，则表示“非常……能做……”的意思，如：

It's only too easy to say yes because your friends encourage you.

由于朋友们鼓励你，所以你说可以就非常容易。

4. **There is no quicker method of disposing of patients than ..., and the jar are almost always granted them.**

dispose of 处理，除掉，摆脱，如：

They must find a way to dispose of the opposition.

他们必须找出对付反对派的办法。

grant sb. sth./grant sth. to sb. 授予某人某物，如：

The government granted a pension to her./The government granted her a pension.

政府授予她一份养老金。

5. **Nor is it only the ignorant and ill-educated person who has such faith in the bottle of medicine.**

由于该句由否定词 Nor 开头，所以该句使用了倒装语序。此外，该句还是一个强调句。句中的 it 为强调句的形式主语，被强调的部分是 only the ignorant and ill-educated person。

6. **It is recounted of Thomas Carlyle that when he heard of the illness of his friend, Henry Taylor, he went off immediately to visit him, carrying with him in his pocket what remained of a**

bottle of medicine formerly prescribed for an indisposition of Mrs. Carlyle's.

It is recounted of Thomas Carlyle that ... 据说,托马斯·卡莱尔……(有下面这件事)。托马斯·卡莱尔是19世纪英国著名的散文作家和历史学家。It 为先行主语,真正的主语是由 that 引导的主语从句。when 引导的是该主语从句中的时间状语从句,该句中的主句是 he went off immediately ... Mrs. Carlyle's。carrying with him ... Mrs. Carlyle's 为现在分词短语,作伴随状语。of a bottle of medicine ... of Mrs. Carlyle's 作 what 的定语,意即"他妻子不舒服时吃剩下的一瓶药"。of Mrs. Carlyle's 是名词性所属格,如:a friend of hers(她的一个朋友),the car of Dr. Lee's(李医生的车)。

7. **Carlyle was entirely ignorant of what the bottle in his pocket contained, of the nature of the illness from which his friend was suffering, and of what had previously been wrong with his wife, but a medicine that had worked so well in one form of illness would surely be of equal benefit in another, and comforted by the thought of the help he was bringing to his friend, he hastened to Henry Taylor's house.**

be ignorant of 不知道,无知,如:

He is ignorant of the facts.

他不了解事实真相。

Thousands of children leaving school are ignorant of even basic skills.

成千上万辍学的孩子们连基本的技能都不了解。

该句中的3个 of 都是与 ignorant 相搭配的。what the bottle ... contained 以及 what had previously ... his wife 作介词 of 的宾语从句。but 连接并列句,后面省略了 he knew,意即"但是他只知道……"。that 引导定语从句,修饰 medicine。be of equal benefit 相当于 be equally beneficial,意即“同样有好处”。comforted by ... his friend 为过去分词短语,作原因状语,表示“由于想到能对朋友有所帮助,他感到欣慰”。

8. **History does not relate whether his friend accepted his medical help, but in all probability he did.**

relate 叙述,如:

She related the events of the past week to the police.

她向警察叙述了上一周发生的事情。

in all probability 很可能,如:

They realized too late that in all probability he was not guilty of the crime.

他们意识到他很可能没有犯罪,可是已经太晚了。

he did 指“他的朋友接受了他的药物治疗”。

9. **The great advantage of taking medicine is that it makes no demands on the taker beyond that of putting up for a moment with a disgusting taste, and that is what all patients demand of their doctors—to be cured at no inconvenience to themselves.**

that 引导的是表语从句。该从句中的 it 指 taking medicine。beyond that of ... taste 中 beyond 意为“除了”,that 代替 demand,意即“除了暂时忍受一下令人作呕的味道外”。put up with 忍受,如:

I can put up with the house being untidy, but I hate it if it's not clean.

我可以忍受房子里不整齐,但是我讨厌房子里不干净。

what 引导的是表语从句。破折号后面的 to be cured ... themselves 作 what 的同位语。at no inconvenience to themselves 作条件状语,修饰 to be cured。demand sth. of/from sb. 向某人要求某物,如:

His parents demanded an apology of him.

他父母要求他道歉。

语法 Grammar in use

动词不定式用法 (8)

带 to 的动词不定式的用法 (5)

(1) 动词 + 宾语 + to be 或其他带 to 的动词不定式

一些动词后可以跟随宾语 + to be 或其他若干通常为状态动词(如 have)的带 to 的动词不定式形式。常用的这类动词通常包括:acknowledge(承认)、assume(假定)、believe(相信)、calculate(估计)、consider(认为)、declare(声称)、discover(发现)、estimate(估计)、fancy(设想)、feel(感觉)、find(发现)、guess(猜想)、imagine(想像)、judge(判断)、know(知道)、maintain(主张)、proclaim(宣告)、prove(证明)、reckon(估计)、see(理解)、show(表明)、suppose(假设)、take(以为)、think(想)、understand(理解)等,如:

I consider him to be one of the best authorities in the country.

我认为他是这个国家中最好的权威人士之一。

She is known to have the best collection of stamps in the world.

她以藏有世界上最好的邮票而闻名。

此外,这些动词后还可以使用其他形式的不定式,如进行时或完成时形式,也可使用被动语态,如:

She is believed to be going/to have gone to the U.S.

人们确信她要去/已经去了美国。

He is thought to have been killed in an air crash.

人们认为他在一次空难中丧生了。

(2) 动词 + 带 to 的动词不定式或 that 从句

许多动词后可以直接使用带 to 的动词不定式或 that 从句。

常用的这类动词包括：agree（同意）、arrange（安排）、beg（乞求）、not care（不愿）、choose（愿意）、claim（宣称）、contrive（设法）、decide（决定）、demand（要求）、determine（决心）、expect（期待）、hope（希望）、intend（意欲）、learn（学习）、plan（计划）、prefer（宁愿）、pretend（假装）、promise（保证）、resolve（决心）、swear（发誓）、threaten（威胁）、wish（希望）等，如：

I decided to ask for my money back.

I decided that I would ask for my money back.

我决定把我的钱要回来。

因为这样的大多数动词都用来指未来，因此其后通常不能跟随不定式的完成时形式。然而，在表示意图、希望等的动词后却可以跟随动词不定式的完成时形式，如：

I hope to have finished by 12.

我希望在12点钟以前完成。

(3) 动词 + 疑问词 + 带 to 的动词不定式或从句

除 why 之外，所有的疑问词均可用于带 to 的动词不定式之前。在此结构中，如果后面跟随的是从句，则可以使用所有的疑问词，包括 why。可以与这种结构一同使用的动词除包括表示"询问"的动词外，通常还包括下述动词：consider（考虑）、decide（决定）、discover（发现）、explain（解释）、find out（发现）、forget（忘记）、hear（听到）、know（知道）、learn（学习）、observe（观察）、perceive（觉察）、remember（记住）、see（看到）、understand（理解）、wonder（想知道）等，如：

I don't know what/which/who(m) to choose.

我不知道该选择什么/哪一个/谁。

I wondered how/when/where to get in touch with them.

我想知道如何/何时/在何地同他们联系。

I don't know why the accident happened.

我不知道为什么发生了事故。

I didn't know that there had been an accident.

我不知道曾发生过一起事故。

在谈论取舍或表示怀疑时,可将 whether ... should 或 whether to 用于大多数上述动词之后。用动词 learn 表示“获得一种技能”时,其后可以使用 to 或 how to;而用其仅表示“向实践学习”时,其后则只能使用 to,如:

I haven't decided whether I should go/whether to go to Spain.

我还没决定是否去西班牙。

I learnt to/how to ride a bicycle when I was four.

我 4 岁时学会了骑自行车。

We soon learnt to do as we were told in his class!

我们很快就学会在他的课上照他的话行事!

(4) 动词 + 宾语 + 疑问词 + 带 to 的动词不定式或从句

仅有若干个动词可严格用于上述句子结构。它们是:advise(建议)、instruct(指示)、remind(提醒)、teach(教)和 tell(告诉),如:

He told us to run.

他叫我们快跑。

The receptionist told me where to wait.

接待员告诉我应当在哪儿等。

The union leader told the men when they should go back to work.

工会领导人告诉工人们应在什么时候去复工。

而在动词 persuade 和 warn 后,只能使用带 to 的动词不定式或 that 从句,但不能使用疑问词,如:

He warned me to stay away.

他警告我不要靠近。

He warned me (that) I was in danger.

他警告我处境危险。

在宾语后可以使用 whether +带 to 的动词不定式的常用动词是:advise(建议)、ask(要求)、show(表明)、teach(教)、tell(告诉),如:

Can you advise me whether to register this letter?

你能否告诉我这封信需要挂号吗?

You haven't told me whether to sign this form.

你没有告诉我是否应在这张表上签字。

词汇学习 Word study

1. believe (不用于进行时)

(1) *vt.* 相信:

The police didn't believe his account of the accident.

警方不相信他对那起事故的描述。

It's hard for you to believe that she's only 24.

简直让你难以相信她才 24 岁。

(2) *vt.* 认为,料想:

According to the poll, 65% of the public believes (that) the President's economic policies are right.

根据民意调查,65% 的公众认为总统的经济政策是正确的。

The banks are widely believed to be planning a cut in interest rates.

人们广泛认为银行正计划降低利率。

(3) *vi.* 笃信(宗教)

(4) believe in 相信……的存在,信任,信仰:

Do you believe in ghosts?

你信鬼吗?

I don't believe in all these so-called health foods.

我并不相信所有这些所谓的健康食物。

Christians believe in Jesus.

基督徒信仰耶稣。

2. mount

(1) *n*. (大写时用于名称中)山:

We climbed Mount Tai last summer.

去年夏天我们爬了泰山。

(2) *n*. 供骑用的动物:

The horse is not a good mount for a lady.

这匹马不适合女士骑。

(3) *n*. 厚纸板,托台,框:

I can't find the mount of this plate.

我找不到这个盘子的托架了。

(4) *vt*. 爬上,登上,骑上:

He was so tired that he could only mount the stairs with difficulty.

他非常累,上楼梯都很困难。

(5) *vt*. 扶上马或脚踏车:

They mounted the old man onto a mule.

他们扶老人骑到了骡子身上。

(6) *vt*. 加衬里,装框:

The little boy mounted his picture on a board, and gave it to his mother.

小男孩给自己的画衬上一块硬板,然后送给了妈妈。

(7) *vt*. 准备,开始(攻击),着手:

The soldiers were ready to mount an attack on the enemy.

战士们已经准备好向敌人发动攻击。

(8) *vi*. 上升,增加:

His debts now have mounted up to $20,000.

他的债务现在已经增加到 20,000 美元了。

3. attend

(1) *vt.* 出席,参加:

Will you be attending the meeting?

你将出席会议吗?

(2) *vt.* 伺候,护理,保护:

He was constantly attended by his bodyguard.

他一直受到贴身护卫的保护。

(3) *vt.* (正式)伴随:

The rescue attempt was attended by difficulties.

救援行动困难重重。

(4) *vi.* 出席,参加:

Please let us know if you are unable to attend.

如果你不能参加,请通知我们。

(5) *vi.* (on, upon) 伺候,护理,保护:

He has a good doctor attending on him.

他有一个很好的医生护理他。

(6) *vi.* (to)(正式)注意,倾听,专心于:

I wish I had attended his advice.

我要是听他的劝告就好了。

They should attend better to their research.

他们应当更专心于他们的研究。

(7) *vi.* (to) 对付,处理:

Excuse me, but I have an urgent matter to attend to.

对不起,我有一件紧急的事情要处理。

练习答案 Key to written exercises

1. 关键句型练习答案

A 1 These two words are spelled differently, but they are pronounced *the same as* each other.

2 John and James are twins, but in character they are quite *different from* each other.

B See text.

C See text.

D 1 *Not only* was he handsome, but he was also extremely intelligent.

2 *Never* have I been so embarrassed as I was that evening.

3 *Only now* is she beginning to realize how lucky she was not to be seriously injured in the accident.

E 1 There are a lot of people who don't *believe in* wasting a doctor's time.

2 They told me that they had every *confidence in* my ability to do the job.

3 The person *in charge of* our department is a very young man.

4 The Smiths have sold their shop and are now *disposing of* the contents.

5 We have asked our teacher to give us some *advice on* careers.

6 When John told me his news, he impressed on me *the need for* complete secrecy.

7 Aspirin is still *prescribed for* the relief of pain.

8 He was *ignorant of* even the basics of operating a computer.

9 A lot of British people *suffer from* colds in the autumn and winter.

10 Come on, get up: there's nothing *wrong with* you!

11 The scientist was sure that his invention would be of great *benefit in* lots of situations.

12 Expeditions of this nature *demand* a great deal *of* those that take part in them.

13 It won't cause any *inconvenience to* me if they cancel the meeting.

2. 难点练习答案

A 1 Note the difference in pronunciation between these two verbs: *cease* (/siːs/) and *seize* (/siːz/).

Cease means 'stop (especially an activity or state)': *The shop on the corner will cease trading from this weekend.*

Seize means 'take possession of, or take hold of eagerly, quickly or forcefully': *The army seized power in a coup. As he greeted me he seized my hand and shook it warmly.*

2 The verb *receive* means 'come into possession of (something that is given or sent), get': *Have you received an invitation to Stan's party yet?*

A basic meaning of the verb *take* is 'move or carry from one place or position to another': *Don't forget to take your bag when you go.* (The verb of course has many meanings, and students would be advised to note, and check with a dictionary, the many occasions on which they come across the word.)

3 The basic difference in use between the verbs *ask for* and *ask* is that *ask for* means 'request, hope to receive',

while ask means 'put a question to (someone), or call for an answer to a question'.

She asked me for my address. She asked a lot of stupid questions.

4 Again note the difference in pronunciation between the noun *advice* (/əd'vaɪs/) and the verb *advise* (/əd'vaɪz/). *Advice* is a noun which means 'the opinion given to someone about what they should do in a particular situation': *You should ask the doctor for her advice.*

Advise is the verb which means 'give, say or write advice': *The doctor has advised my father to have complete rest.*

5 The verb *prescribe* means 'say what medicine or treatment a sick person should or must have': *What did the doctor prescribe for the pain in your leg?*

Proscribe, on the other hand, is formal and means 'forbid, especially by law': *The law of the country proscribes the carrying of weapons.*

B 1 *in charge of* = responsible for

2 *charged at* = rushed in and attack at

3 *charged (with)* = a criminal charge was brought against him

4 *charge* = ask (someone) to pay

C 1 You would be *ill-advised* to buy that car: I've got a suspicion it's stolen.

2 You might have been told that I was in the bank that day, but you were *ill-informed*.

3 The defenders of the city were so *ill-prepared* that the

attackers took it in a few days.

3. 多项选择题答案

1	a	2	d	3	c	4	d	5	a	6	b
7	c	8	a	9	d	10	a	11	b	12	d

Lesson 29

The hovercraft

气垫船

课文详注 Further notes on the text

1. **Many strange new means ..., the strangest of them being perhaps the hovercraft.**

   the strangest of them being perhaps the hovercraft 是现在分词 being 的独立主格结构。

2. **In 1953, a former electronics engineer in his fifties, Christopher Cockerell, who had turned to boat-building on the Norfolk Broads, suggested an idea on which he had been working for many years ...**

   in his fifties 在他五十多岁的时候。who 引导的是非限定性定语从句,修饰 Christopher Cockerell。turn to 转而致力于,如:

   Finally she turned to the study of art.

   最终她转而研究艺术。

   Norfolk Broads 诺福克大沼泽区,位于英格兰东部。on which 引导定语从句,由于该从句中的动词 work 与介词 on 连用,表示"研究",所以将介词 on 置于关系代词之前。

3. **It was the idea of supporting a craft on a 'pad', or cushion, of low-pressure air, ringed with a curtain of higher pressure air.**

   of supporting ... cushion 为介词短语,作定语,修饰 idea。of low-pressure air 作定语,修饰 pad 和 cushion。ringed with ... air 为过去分词短语,作定语,也修饰 pad 和 cushion。ring ...

with/by ...用……围绕……，如：

The harbour is dangerous—it's ringed with rocks and reefs.

那个港口非常危险——它被岩石和暗礁所环绕。

4. Ever since, ...—for it is something in between a boat and an aircraft.

for 引导的是原因状语从句，说明为什么很难确定气垫船到底是属于轮船、飞机还是陆上交通工具的原因。in between 介于……之间。这是一种组合介词，常用的还有 from among（从中）、from under（来自下面）、in front of（在……前面）、up to（达到）等。

5. As a shipbuilder, ... a solution to the problem of the wave resistance which wastes a good deal of a surface ship's power and limits its speed.

of the wave resistance 作定语，修饰 the problem，意即“波浪阻力的问题”。which 引导定语从句，修饰 wave resistance。a surface ship 水面船只。

6. His answer was to lift the vessel out of the water by making it ride on a cushion of air, no more than one or two feet thick.

by making it ... air 作方式状语。no more than one or two feet thick 作非限定性定语从句，修饰 a cushion of air。

7. This is done by ...

This 指前句中的 to lift the vessel out of the water。

8. It 'flies', therefore, but it cannot fly higher—its action depends on the surface, water or ground, over which it rides.

It 'flies' 中的 it 指 the vessel。flies 用引号表明这是一种夸张的手法，形容它行进得非常快。破折号后面的部分是对该船的行进所作的进一步说明。water or ground 作 surface 的定语，意即“水面或地面”。over which it rides 作非限定性定语从句，修饰 surface。

9. **Later it crossed the Channel, riding smoothly over the waves, which presented no problem.**

the Channel 指英吉利海峡。riding smoothly over the waves 为现在分词短语，作方式状语，修饰动词 crossed。which presented no problem 作非限定性定语从句，修饰 waves，意即“波浪不再产生阻力”。

10. **Since that time, ... and taken up regular service.**

take up 开始从事，开始，如：

He's taken up a new job.

他开始从事一项新工作。

regular service 定期航行服务。

11. **... it can become a 'flying fruit-bowl', carrying bananas from the plantations to the ports; ...**

flying fruit-bowl 是比喻的说法，将气垫船比作“飞行的水果盘子”。carrying bananas ... ports 为现在分词短语，作定语，修饰 flying fruit-bowl。

12. **... and the railway of the future may well be the 'hovertrain', riding on its air cushion over a single rail, which it never touches, at speeds up to 300 m.p.h.— the possibilities appear unlimited.**

may well be 很可能是。hovertrain 用引号引上，表明当时尚没有这种“汽垫火车”。riding on its ... rail 作定语，修饰 hovertrain。which it never touches 作非限定性定语从句，修饰 rail。at speeds up to ... m.p.h. 为介词短语，作状语，修饰现在分词 riding，意即“时速可达每小时 300 英里”。m.p.h. 相当于 miles per hour(英里/小时)。破折号起到强调的作用，其后面的部分是对前面内容所作的补充说明。

语法 Grammar in use

动词不定式用法 (9)

形容词 + 带 to 的动词不定式的用法 (1)

(1) 主语 + be + 形容词 + 带 to 的动词不定式

1) 赞扬或批评某人时,可以使用此类型。常用于此类型结构的形容词包括:brave(勇敢的)、careless(粗心的)、clever(聪明的)、foolish(愚蠢的)、generous(慷慨的)、good(好的)、(un) kind(〈不〉仁慈的)、polite(礼貌的)、right(对的)、wrong(错的)、rude(粗鲁的)、(un) selfish(〈不〉自私的)、silly(愚蠢的)、wicked(邪恶的)等。这一类型主要包括两种结构:

a. 正常的主语结构,如:

The government would be brave to call an election now.

政府关于现在举行大选的决定很勇敢。

John was foolish not to accept their offer.

约翰不接受他们的建议是愚蠢的。

往往可以使用含有 so ... as to(正式)或 enough(非正式)的变体形式表达上述类型的句子,如:

Would you be so good as to/good enough to let me know as soon as possible?

你能费心让我尽早知道吗?

b. 由先行主语 it 引导的结构,如:

It was kind of her to help us.

她真好,帮了我们。

It was most selfish of him not to contribute anything.

他不捐献任何东西,太自私了。

使用先行主语 it 的结构也可视为上述结构的变体形式,较上述结构更为常用,尤其是在口语当中。当句子中的逻辑主语显而易见时,可以省略句型中的 of + 名词/代词部分。有时这一结构中还可使用诸如 seem、look 这样的动词。此外,除上述形容词外,此结构中还常常使用诸如 annoying(令人恼火的)、boring(令人生厌的)、trying(折磨人的)这类现在分词形式的形容词,如:

It was silly (of us) to believe him.

(我们)相信了他,真蠢。

It would look rude to refuse their invitation.

拒绝他们的邀请会显得无礼。

It was annoying of John to lose my keys.

约翰丢失了我的钥匙,真令我恼火。

将上述结构形式转换为感叹句进行表达的情况很普遍,如:

How kind of him to help us!

Wasn't he kind to help us!

Wasn't it kind of him to help us!

他帮助了我们,多好啊!

2) 当论述内容涉及某人对一种行为或情况的感情时,也可使用这一结构形式。虽然就结构而言,这一类与上一小节大体相同,但由于论述的内容不同,所使用的形容词也不相同,并且通常不能使用代词 it。其常用的形容词包括:afraid(害怕的)、anxious(焦急的)、ashamed(害臊的)、careful(小心的)、curious(好奇的)、determined(坚定的)、due(约定的)、eager(渴望的)、fit(合适的)、free(自由的)、frightened(害怕的)、glad(高兴的)、keen(热衷的)、prepared(有准备的)、quick(敏捷的)、ready(准备好的)、reluctant(不情愿的)、slow(缓慢的)、sorry(遗憾的)、willing(心甘情

愿的)等,如:

She's determined not to offend her mother-in-law.

她决心不冒犯她的婆婆。

She's anxious for her daughter to win the competition.

她盼望女儿赢得比赛。

可以将几个表示可能性的形容词,如 bound(一定)、certain(肯定)、(un)likely(〈不〉可能)、surc(一定)等包括在此类之中,但用这些形容词时可以使用先行主语 it,如:

He is bound/certain/likely/sure to sign the contract.

他必定/肯定/很可能/一定会签那份合同。

It's bound/sure to rain on our wedding day.

在我们婚礼的那一天一定会下雨。

当带 to 的动词不定式用来指对某人或物已经做了某事时,也可使用上述句型,并且可以使用以 it 作先行主语的结构。由于所要表达的语义不同,因此使用的形容词范围也不一样。这类形容词包括:agreeable(令人愉快的)、amusing(逗乐的)、boring(令人生厌的)、difficult(困难的)、easy(容易的)、hard(难的)、impossible(不可能的)、nice(美好的)等,如:

It is easy to please him.

他容易讨好。

She is amusing to be with.

跟她在一起很有趣。

Polyester is easy to iron.

聚酯纤维容易熨烫。

It is impossible not to offend her.

不冒犯她是不可能的。

词汇学习 Word study

1. develop

(1) *vi*. 发展,发达,生长:

Plants develop from seeds.

植物由种子发育而成。

Her writing skills were developing at a rapid pace.

她的写作技能在迅速提高。

(2) *vi*. 显现出,露出:

Large cracks have begun to develop in the wall of the house.

房子的墙上开始露出大裂缝。

(3) *vi*. 显影:

With this instant film, the picture develops in only one minute.

用这种即显胶卷,只用一分钟相片就能显影出来。

(4) *vt*. 使发展,使增长:

They have decided to develop their business.

他们决定发展他们的业务。

(5) *vt*. 开发:

They are drawing new plans to develop natural resources.

他们正在起草开发自然资源的新计划。

(6) *vt*. 使显影:

How long will it take to develop these pictures?

用多久能冲洗出这些相片?

2. suggest *vt*.

(1) 提出意见:

The teacher suggested several colleges for him to choose

from.

老师给他推荐了好几所大学供他选择。

He suggests that we set out immediately.

他建议我们立刻出发。

(2) 暗示,提示:

Your question suggests that you doubt my sincerity.

你提这个问题似乎表明你怀疑我的真诚。

(3) 使想起,联想到:

The music suggests a still night.

这段音乐使我联想到一个宁静的夜晚。

3. ride (rode, ridden)

(1) *n*. (可数) 骑,乘车:

The father is just giving the child a ride on the shoulders.

父亲正让小孩骑在肩上。

It's five penny ride on a bus.

乘公共汽车去需要5便士。

(2) *n*. 跑道(尤指供骑马用的林间小道):

The ride is not for vehicles.

这条林间道不能行车。

(3) *vt*. 骑;乘(坐):

He's riding a horse/car.

他正在骑马/乘(坐)小汽车。

(4) *vt*. 骑马(或驾车)进行(比赛等):

The girl is riding a race.

那个女孩正在赛马(或赛车)。

(5) *vt*. 让……骑/乘,搭载:

The old man is riding a child on his back.

那位老人正让孩子骑在背上。

(6) *vt*. 乘(风、浪);(喻)经受住:

Our boat rode the waves.

我们的船破浪前进。

The large ship rode the storm.

大船顶住了风暴。

(7) *vi*. (on) 骑马(或自行车),骑,乘:

He rode 50 miles on a horse.

他骑马行走了 50 英里。

You may ride there in/on a train/boat/plane.

你可以乘火车/船/飞机去那儿。

(8) *vi*. 适于乘/骑:

The car rides smoothly.

这车乘起来很平稳。

The ground rode hard after the frost.

霜后骑起马来觉得地面很硬。

(9) *vi*. (on) 漂浮;航行;停泊:

The ship rode on the waves.

船乘浪而进。

The ship rode at anchor in the harbour.

船停泊在港内。

练习答案 Key to written exercises

1. 关键句型练习答案

A 1 Many international exhibitions have been held, the most recent (one) *being in Tokyo*.

2 New York is full of skyscrapers, the ever tallest (one) *being the World Trade Centre*.

B See text.

C 1 among 2 between 3 between 4 between

D 1 *A great deal of* the information she gave me is incorrect.
2 She knows *a great many* famous people.
3 He's flown *a good many* times, but never really enjoyed it.
4 She has had *a good few* different jobs in the past ten years.

E 1 I made him *write a short letter of apology*.
2 The teacher made the class *do their homework again*.
3 He trained the team by making them *repeat the performance dozens of times*.

F 1 She *might well find* the accounts course too difficult.
2 The teacher *may well be* quite angry with a number of the students.

2. 难点练习答案

A 1 An *engineer* is 'a person who is professionally trained to plan the making of machines, roads, bridges, electrical equipment, etc.': *an electrical engineer, a mechanical engineer, an electronics engineer. One day that young man will be an excellent civil engineer.*

A *mechanic*, on the other hand, is 'a person who is skilled in using, repairing, etc. machinery': *That man employs a mechanic to look after the cars and lorries.*

2 A *solution* is 'an answer to a difficulty or problem': *There are no simple solutions to the unemployment problem.*

A *solvent* is 'a liquid able to turn a solid substance into liquid': *Alcohol and petrol are useful solvents for grease stains that will not come off in water.*

B 1 *turned to* = begun to do (as a change from his previous profession)

2 *turn off* = stop the flow of water by screwing the tap tight

3 *turned up* = arrived (at our house)

4 *turned about* = turned right around

C 1 The very first time I tried to *ride a horse*, I fell off.

2 Now that Andy's got a new bike, we can all *go for a ride* together.

3 If you're driving into town, can you *give me a ride*?

3. 多项选择题答案

1 c	2 c	3 a	4 d	5 d	6 c
7 c	8 a	9 d	10 a	11 b	12 c

Lesson 30
Exploring the sea-floor
海底勘探

课文详注 Further notes on the text

1. **Our knowledge of the oceans a hundred years ago was confined to the two-dimensional shape of the sea surface and the hazards of navigation presented by the irregularities in depth of the shallow water close to the land.**

   be confined to 被限制于，局限于，如：

   The lecturer confined herself to one topic.

   讲师把她讲课内容局限在一个主题内。

   presented by the irregularities 作定语，修饰 the hazards of navigation。in depth 深度的，作定语，修饰 the irregularities。of the shallow water 为介词短语，作定语，修饰 depth，意即"浅水区的深浅不一"。close to the land，作定语，修饰 the shallow water，意即"靠近陆地的浅水区"。

2. **The open sea was deep and mysterious, and anyone who gave more than a passing thought to the bottom confines of the oceans probably assumed that the sea bed was flat.**

   The open sea 无边际的大海。give a thought to 想，如：

   She doesn't give any thought to her appearance.

   她对自己的外表毫不在意。

   a passing thought 稍稍想过。该句主要由连词 and 连接的两个并列句构成。后一句的主语是 anyone，who 引导的是修饰 anyone 的定语从句。该句的谓语动词是 assumed。that 引导的是动词 assumed 的宾语从句。

3. **Sir James Clark Ross ... but it was not until 1869, when H. M. S. *Porcupine* was put at the disposal of the Royal Society for several cruises, that a series of deep soundings ... by dredging the bottom.**

连词 and 后面连接的是一个强调句,所强调的部分是 not until 1869, when 引导的是非限定性定语从句,修饰 1869。文中的 H. M. S. 是 Her Majesty's Ship (英国船舰)的缩略形式。at the disposal of 交由……支配,如:

If you want some help preparing for the party I can be at your disposal all day.

如果你需要人帮忙准备聚会的话,我一整天都可以由你支配。

Royal Society 皇家学会。

4. **Shortly after this the famous H. M. S. *Challenger* expedition established the study of the sea-floor as a subject worthy of the most qualified physicists and geologists.**

establish ... as 把……确立为,确认……为,如:

He established himself as the most popular minister in the new cabinet.

他已经成为新内阁中最受欢迎的部长。

The press established him as the leading contender.

报界认定他是主要的竞争者。

worthy of ... geologists 作定语,修饰 a subject,意即"值得一流物理学家和地质学家从事研究的课题"。worthy of 值得……的,如:

Two points in this report are especially worthy of notice.

这个报告中有两点值得特别注意。

5. **A burst of activity associated with the laying of submarine**

cables soon confirmed the *Challenger's* observation that many parts of the ocean were two to three miles deep, and the existence of underwater features of considerable magnitude.

A burst of activity 一阵行动，活动热潮。a burst of 一阵，又如：a burst of applause 一阵掌声。associated with ... cables 作定语，修饰 a burst of activity，意即"伴随着铺设海底电缆的热潮"。that many parts ... magnitude 是同位语从句，作 observation 的同位语。

6. **Since the sea covers ... it is quite reasonable to regard the sea floor as the basic form of the crust of the earth, with, superimposed upon it, the continents, together with the islands and other features of the oceans.**

it 是先行主语，真正的主语是动词不定式 to regard the sea floor as ... earth。with, superimposed upon it, the continents, together with ... oceans 是由介词 with 引导的过去分词独立主格结构。其逻辑主语是 the continents, together with ... oceans，由于该逻辑主语太长，所以将逻辑谓语部分 superimposed upon it 提前，构成倒装语序，意即"上面附加着大陆以及岛屿和海洋的其他形态"。

7. **From the shore line, out to a distance which may be anywhere from a few miles to a few hundred miles, runs the gentle slope of the continental shelf, geologically part of the continents.**

该句为倒装结构，按正常语序应该是：The gentle slope of the continental shelf, geologically part of the continents, runs from the shore line, out to a distance which ... miles. which 引导的是定语从句，修饰 a distance，意即"延伸几英里到几百英里的区域"。geologically part of the continents 是 the continental shelf 的同位语，对其作进一步的说明。

8. **This continental slope usually starts at a place somewhere near**

the 100-fathom mark and in the course of a few hundred miles reaches the true ocean floor at 2,500-3,500 fathoms.

somewhere near the 100-fathom 作定语,修饰 a place,其中的 somewhere 为副词,作状语,修饰介词短语 near the 100-fathom。in the course of a few hundred miles 为介词短语,作状语,修饰动词 reaches,意思是"延伸几百英里"。动词 reaches 与动词 starts 为并列谓语动词,共同的主语是 the continental slope。at 2,500-3,500 fathoms 作定语,修饰 the true ocean floor,意即"2,500 英寻到 3,500 英寻深处的真正洋底"。

9. **The slope averages about 1 in 30, but contains ..., and near its lower reaches there is a long tailing-off which is almost certainly the result of material transported out to deep water after being eroded from the continental masses.**

   1 in 30,1/30。which is almost certainly ... masses 为定语从句,修饰 a long tailing-off。transported out to ... masses 为过去分词,作定语,修饰 material。after being eroded from the continental masses 作时间状语,意即"从大陆块体上侵蚀下来后"。

语法 Grammar in use

动词不定式用法 (10)

形容词 + 带 to 的动词不定式的用法 (2)

(1) 作逻辑主语的带 to 的动词不定式与作形式主语的 it 连用

许多形容词都可以作补足语,用于其逻辑主语为一带 to 的动词不定式的句子当中。在此句子结构中,通常可以将作形式主语的 it 置于句首,而将作逻辑主语的带 to 的动词不定式置于形容词之后,放在表语的位置。比较:

To accept their offer would be foolish.（动词不定式作主语）

It would be foolish to accept their offer.（*it* 作主语）

接受他们的提议是愚蠢的。

带 to 的动词不定式有其逻辑主语时，通常在其前使用 for + 名词/代词结构，如：

It won't be easy for Tom to find a new job.

汤姆找个新工作不会是件容易的事。

(2) 表示顺序及最高级的词 + 带 to 的动词不定式

带 to 的动词不定式，可以用于表示顺序和表示最高级的词，如 the first（第 1）、the second（第 2）、the next（下一个）、the last（最后的）、the best（最好的）、the most suitable（最合适的）等之后，作定语。在这些词语后用不用名词或 one(s) 均可，如：

She is always the first to arrive and the last to leave.

她总是头一个来最后一个走。

Is a solicitor the best person to advise me about buying a house?

律师是我买房子的最好顾问吗？

但是，the only（惟一的）之后则必须用名词或 one(s)，如：

You're the only person (the only one) to complain.

你是惟一抱怨的人。

(3) too + 形容词/形容词 + enough + 带 to 的动词不定式

too 置于形容词之前，具有“过分”的含义。在其后使用动词不定式的结构中，too 通常具有否定的概念，如：

He is too weak to lift it.

他太弱，举不起它。

He is too heavy for me to lift.

他太重了，我举不起他。

注意上两个句子中的不同。在第 1 个句子中，主动词的主语也是动词不定式的逻辑主语；而在第2个句子中，主动词的主语则是动词不定式的宾语。当第2种情况时，在动词不定式之后绝不可跟随宾语，如不可说：

* *This bread is too stale for me to eat it.*

此外，一般来说，过去分词形式的形容词与人称主语搭配使用，而现在分词形式的形容词与非人称主语搭配使用，如：

I'm too tired to stay up longer.

我太累了，不能再熬夜了。

The race was almost too exciting to watch.

比赛紧张得几乎看不下去了。

enough需放在形容词之后，具有"达到必要的程度"的含义。同使用too时情况一样，含enough的结构可以用来表示两种概念。句子主动词的主语为动词不定式的宾语时，其后不能再跟宾语。比较：

He's strong enough to lift it.

他壮得足以举起它。(*He* 为 *lift* 的逻辑主语)

The pear is ripe enough to eat.

这梨熟得能吃了。(*The pear* 为 *eat* 的逻辑宾语)

同样，for+名词/代词结构可置于动词不定式之前，作它的逻辑主语，并且可以同too much、too little、not enough等连用，如：

The baby's too much for her to cope with.

照看婴儿对她来说可太难了。

There's too little work/not enough work for me to do.

供我做的工作太少/不够多。

词汇学习 Word study

1. confine

(1) *vt*. (to) 限制，限制在……范围之内：

Please confine your remarks to the subject under discussion.

请把你的讲话限制在我们正在讨论的话题上。

(2) *vt*. 关在室内;使闭门不出,监禁:

The heavy rain confined us to our house.

大雨使我们呆在家里。

They confined him to a mental institution.

他们将他关在精神病院。

(3) *n*. (可数,常用复数)界限,范围,疆界:

He stayed in the confines of the school.

他呆在校内。

2. establish *vt*.

(1) 成立,建立:

This school was established in 1877.

这所学校建于1877年。

(2) 确立,证实,确定:

The professor established himself as an expert of chemical engineering.

这个教授是大家公认的化工专家。

The coroner was able to establish that death took place at about eight o'clock.

验尸官能确定死亡发生在8点左右。

3. qualify

(1) *vt*. 使具有资格,使合格:

Her skills qualified her for the job.

她的技术使她有资格承担这一工作。

(2) *vt*. 限制,限定:

He wanted to qualify his last saying.

他想修正他最后说的话。

(3) *vt*. 把……称作：

We qualify him as a self-seeker.

我们把他称为自私自利者。

(4) *vi*. 取得资格，具备合格条件：

She clearly qualifies for the job.

她显然有资格做这项工作。

练习答案 Key to written exercises

1. 关键句型练习答案

A See text.

B 1 I didn't understand what had happened until I read the report in the newspaper./It was not until I read the report in the newspaper that I understood what had happened.

2 The plane will not take off again until the engine has been checked.

3 Tom didn't get home until four o'clock this morning.

4 I shan't return this book to the library until I have read it.

5 It wasn't until I had paid for the goods that the man agreed to deliver them.

C 1 *Since* the sun's shining, I think I'll go for a walk.

2 We've been waiting for them *since* six o'clock, and they still haven't arrived.

2. 难点练习答案

A 1 The adjective *flat* means 'smooth and level, not rounded or lumpy': *This beach is flat, but not level.*

Level, on the other hand, means 'flat and not tilted': *A football or rugby field must be level. Take a level teaspoonful of sugar.*

2 The noun *disposal* means 'the act of getting rid of something, removal': *They have called in a team of bomb disposal men.* However, it is also used in the expression 'at someone's disposal' to mean 'able to be used freely by someone': *Our car is at your disposal for the time you are here.*

Disposition means 'a particular tendency of character, behaviour, etc.': *The woman has always had a cheerful disposition.*

3 The adjective *worthy* means 'deserving', as in: *It was a performance worthy to be remembered.*

Valuable, on the other hand, means 'worth a lot of money': *I am sure that this is an extremely valuable painting.*

4 The verb *confirm* means 'give support or certainty to a fact, belief, statement, etc., e.g. by providing more proof or by stating that something is true or correct': *The new evidence confirmed our opinion that both men were lying.*

The verb *assure* means 'tell firmly and with confidence, with the aim of removing doubt': *She assured us that everything possible was being done for our father.* (Note that the verb is used in the patterns *assure someone of something*, *assure someone that...*)

5 Care must be taken with the pronunciation of these two adjectives: *rugged* (/ˈrʌgɪd/) and *ragged* (/ˈrægɪd/).

Rugged means 'having a rough uneven surface' and usually refers to land: *After crossing the plain, we eventually reached a range of rugged hills.*

Ragged means 'old and torn': *The man wore a ragged shirt*.

B 1 The little boat headed out into *the open sea* and was soon lost to view in the large waves.

2 Because the weather was so beautiful, we decided to have the party in *the open air*, not indoors.

C 1 *Mathematics* was my worst subject at school.

2 Here is *the news*.

3 *Physics* is a science concerned with natural forces such as light, heat, movement, and so on.

4 *Billiards* is not a game that I enjoy much.

D 1 The police and the ambulance arrived *shortly after* the accident happened.

2 *Shortly before* we were due to leave, we received a telephone call warning us not to go.

3 I know I'm already a little late, but I'll be there *shortly*.

E 1 *features* (ll.9-11) = typical or noticeable parts

2 *feature* (films) = full-length cinema (films) with an invented story and professional actors

3 *is featured* = is included as a major story

4 *features* = parts of the face

F 1 It is thought that about *1 in 10* of the population will have problems with their eyesight before they are 50.

2 The chances of your having an accident between home and school are about *1 in 1,000*.

3. 多项选择题答案

1 c	2 a	3 b	4 d	5 d	6 b
7 c	8 c	9 a	10 c	11 d	12 c

Lesson 31
The sculptor speaks
雕塑家的语言

课文详注 Further notes on the text

1. **Appreciation of sculpture depends upon the ability to respond to form in three dimensions.**

   Appreciation of sculpture 对雕塑的鉴赏。这里的介词 of 表示动宾关系，也就是说 appreciation 和 sculpture 虽然是两个名词，但 appreciation 是从动词 appreciate 派生出来的，sculpture 实际上是 appreciation 的逻辑宾语。to respond to form 为动词不定式，作定语，修饰 the ability，意即“对立体的反应能力”。in three dimensions 为介词短语，作定语，修饰 form，意即“三维的”。

2. **...; certainly it is more difficult than the arts which involve appreciation of flat forms, shape in only two dimensions.**

   shape in only two dimensions 作 flat forms 的同位语，意即“只有二维的形状”。

3. **Many more people are 'form-blind' than colour-blind.**

   form-blind 是作者仿照 colour-blind(色盲)生造的一个词，意即“形盲”，故用引号引上。

4. **The child learning to see, ...; it cannot judge distances, depths.**

   learning to see 作定语，修饰 the child。it 指 the child。

5. **Later, for its personal safety and practical needs, it has to develop (partly by means of touch) the ability to judge roughly**

three-dimensional distances.

for its personal ... needs 为介词短语,作目的状语。it 指 the child。括号中的内容是补充说明部分,说明孩子发展判断三维空间的能力是部分依赖触觉。by means of 用……方法,依靠,如:

She tried to explain by means of sign language.

她试图用手势语进行解释。

to judge ... 为动词不定式,作定语,修饰 ability,意即"粗略判断三维空间距离的能力"。

6. **But having satisfied the requirements of practical necessity, ... further.**

But having satisfied the requirements of practical necessity 为分词短语,作时间状语。

7. **Though they may attain considerable accuracy in the perception of flat form, they do not make the further intellectual and emotional effort needed to comprehend form in its full spatial existence.**

in the perception of flat form 在对平面的感觉方面。needed to comprehend form ... existence 为过去分词短语,作定语,修饰 effort。in its full spatial existence 为介词短语,作定语,修饰 form,意即"存在于空间的整个形态"。

8. **He must strive continually to think of, and use, form in its full spatial completeness.**

strive to do sth. 努力做某事,如:

All of us will continue striving to meet the very highest standards.

我们所有的人都应继续努力达到最高的标准。

form in its full spatial completeness 作动词 to think of 和 use 的宾语。其中的介词短语 in its full spatial completeness 作定语,

修饰 form,意即“想像并且利用形体在空间中的完整性”。

9. **He gets the solid shape, as it were, inside his head—he thinks of it, whatever its size, as if he were holding it completely enclosed in the hollow of his hand.**

as it were 可以说是,作插入语。破折号后面的 he thinks of it,为同位语,解释说明前面的文字。whatever its size 作让步状语从句,size 后面省略了 may be,意思是“不管其大小如何”。as if 引导的是方式状语从句。在正式文体中,由 as if 引导的方式状语从句多用 were,但在口语中也可用 was,如:

He looked at me as if I were mad.

他看着我,就好像我疯了似的。

enclosed in the hollow of his hand 作宾语补足语。

10. **He mentally visualizes a complex form *from all round* itself; ...**

from all round itself 从它的各个角度构想。该处介词用斜体,是为了强调。

11. **...; he knows while he looks at one side what the other side is like; ...**

while he looks at one side 是时间状语从句。what the other side is like 是动词 knows 的宾语从句。

12. **...; he identifies himself with its centre of gravity, its mass, its weight; ...**

该句的意思是“他把自身和物体中心、质量、重量融为一体”。identify ... with 与……认同,与……融为一体,如:

She always identifies him with the liberals.

她认为他与自由主义者有密切关系。

13. **...; he realizes its volume, as the space that the shape displaces in the air.**

as 为介词,逗号表示停顿,以强调 volume。that the shape displaces in the air 为定语从句,修饰 the space。

14. He must, for example, perceive an egg as a simple single solid shape, quite apart from its significance as food, or from the literary idea that it will become a bird.

perceive ... as 把……看作是,如:

I perceived her statement as a threat.

我把她的声明看作是一种威胁。

quite apart from its significance ... a bird 而完全抛开它的食用意义或它会变成鸟这样的文学概念来感觉。apart from 撇开,除……以外,如:

He works until nine o'clock every evening, and that's quite apart from the work he does over the weekend.

他每天晚上都工作到9点钟,还未算他在周末干的活。

Apart from you and me, I don't think there was anyone there under thirty.

除了你和我,我认为那儿的人没有在30岁以下的。

that it will become a bird 是 idea 的同位语从句。

15. And so with solids such as a shell, ... a bone.

so with solids 中的 so 指前面提到的 to feel shape simply as shape, not as description or reminiscence(把形体作为形体来感觉,不要靠描述和印象去感觉),意即"对于其他实体也应这样来感觉"。such as 用来列举一系列的实体。

语法 Grammar in use

动词不定式用法(11)

名词+带 to 的动词不定式的用法

(1) 作定语

当带 to 的动词不定式用于名词/代词之后时,通常起到定语的作用,修饰其前的名词/代词,如:

Our decision to wait was wise.

我们决定等待是明智的。

It's their wish to succeed.

成功是他们的希望。

It's fun to be here.

在这儿好玩。

It's a pity to leave so early.

这么早走真是遗憾。

The person to ask is Jan.

应该询问的人是简。

I've got an essay to write.

我有一篇作文要写。

I want something to eat.

我想吃些什么东西。

There was a lot to do/a lot to be done.

有大量的事要做。

然而,并非所有的名词都可以带动词不定式。有些名词的后面通常需要使用介词+动名词结构,如:

There's no hope of finding him.

没有找到他的希望。

Thank you for your generosity/kindness in contributing so much.

谢谢你如此慷慨/仁慈,给予这么多。

但有些则两者均可,如:

It's a pleasure to be with you.

跟你在一起是愉快的。

There's nothing to compare with the pleasure of being with you.

跟你在一起无比愉快。

(2) 形容词 + 名词 + 带 to 的动词不定式

在这样的句子结构中，主要应注意以下几种情况：

1）含 too 和 enough 时的使用方法

主要应注意不定冠词 a/an 的位置和作为数量词的 enough 在 there be 句子中修饰名词时的位置，如：

He's too clever a politician to say a thing like that in public.

他是一位非常聪明的政治家，绝不会在公开场合说那种话的。

He isn't a clever enough politician to have any original ideas.

他不是一位聪明得能有任何创见的政治家。

There is enough time / time enough to take care of everything.

有足够的时间料理一切事情。

2）含 so ... as to 和 such ... as to 时的使用方法

主要应注意不定冠词 a/an 的位置，如：

I'm not so stupid (a fool) as to put it in writing.

I'm not such a (stupid) fool as to put it in writing.

我不至于蠢到会把它写下来。

3）感叹句中冠词的位置

如下所示：

What an unkind thing to say!

这话说得多么不客气呵！

词汇学习　Word study

1. involve（常不用于进行时）　*vt.*

(1) 使陷入，使卷入：

Don't involve me in your quarrel.

不要把我卷入你们的争吵之中。

(2) 必然带来:

This job involves a lot of travelling.

这个工作需要经常旅行。

2. judge

(1) *vt*. 审判,审理:

The jury is judging the case.

陪审团正在审理这个案子。

(2) *vt*. 裁判:

He is going to judge the competition.

他将裁判这场比赛。

(3) *vt*. 判断,认为:

It's unfair to judge a man by his looks.

从外表来评判一个人是不公平的。

It is difficult to judge whether he was right or wrong.

很难判断他究竟是对是错。

He judged the plan to be impracticable./He judged that the plan was impracticable.

他认为计划是行不通的。

(4) *vi*. 裁判,判断,认为:

I'm not in a position to judge.

我无法作出判断。

(5) *n*.(可数) 审判官,法官,裁判,评判员:

The panel of judges consisted of a variety of famous people.

评判组由许多知名人士构成。

(6) *n*. 内行,鉴赏家:

He is a good judge of horses.

他善于相马。

3. hold (held)

(1) *vt*. 拿着,握住:

The dog held a newspaper in its mouth.

那只狗嘴里叼着一张报纸。

(2) *vt*. 保持(某种位置或状态):

Hold yourself still for a moment while I take your photograph.

我给你拍照时别动。

(3) *vt*. 容纳,装,盛:

This cinema can hold 1,500 people.

这个电影院可容纳 1,500 名观众。

(4) *vt*. 占有,担任(职务):

He holds 500 acres of land.

他拥有 500 英亩土地。

She holds the office of chairwoman.

她担任主席一职。

(5) *vt*. 支撑,承受:

The dam gave way, it was not strong enough to hold the flood waters.

水坝坍塌了,它的坚固程度不足以阻挡洪水。

(6) *vt*. 举行,召开:

They decided to hold a meeting next morning.

他们决定第 2 天早上召开一个会议。

(7) *vt*. (不用于进行时)持有(看法等),认为:

He held the opinion that the business was failing.

他认为生意正在走下坡路。

Therefore, I hold that Tom ought to be informed.

因此,我认为应该通知汤姆。

He holds gambling to be immoral.

他认为赌博是不道德的。

I hold parents responsible for their children's behaviour.

我认为父母应对子女的行为负责。

(8) *vi*. 保持某种状态,继续:

I fear this beautiful weather won't hold much longer.

恐怕这种好天气不会持续太久。

What he said still holds good.

他说的话依然有效。

(9) *n*. (可数,常用单数)握住,拿,托:

She kept a firm hold of her little boy's hand as they crossed the street.

过马路时,她紧紧牵着她的小男孩的手。

(10) *n*. (常用单数)影响,控制,掌握:

He has a tremendous hold over his younger brother.

他对他弟弟有极大的影响。

(11) *n*. 支撑物,可手攀的东西:

Can you find a hold for your hands so that you pull yourself up?

你能不能找到一个手抓得住的地方爬上去?

练习答案 Key to written exercises

1. 关键句型练习答案

A See text.

B 1 *Having asked her* to call me, I've decided not to call her.

2 *Having reached* a certain level in English, many students give up.

3 *Having read* his letter three times, I decided not to

answer it.

C See text.

D 1 He acted as if *he were the manager*. (Note: He wasn't the manager!)

2 He talked as if *he had a plum in his mouth*. (Note: He didn't have a plum in his mouth!)

3 It looked as if *it were snowing outside*. (Note: It might have looked like it, but it wasn't snowing!)

2. 难点练习答案

A 1 The noun *appreciation* means 'understanding of the good qualities or worth of something': *The audience showed their appreciation by applauding for a full five minutes.*

An *estimation* is an 'approximate calculation, judgment, esteem or opinion': *In my estimation, he is one of the best young sculptors we have.*

2 The verb *distinguish*, as used in the text, means 'see, hear, or notice as being separate or distinct, recognize clearly': *Can you distinguish the different buildings at such a distance?*

The verb *perceive* means '(come to) have knowledge of something through one of the senses or through the mind, become conscious of or understand': *The more they got to know each other, the more he perceived a change in her attitude towards him.*

3 *Depth* is the noun associated with the adjective *deep*, and is 'the state or degree of being deep': *They dived to a depth of twenty fathoms before they found parts of the wreck.*

The deep is a poetic word for the sea and can also be used in the plural 'the deeps' to mean the deep parts of the oceans: *Although we still know relatively little about the deeps, we know a lot more than we did fifty years ago.*

4 The verb *displace* means 'force out of the usual place': *He displaced a bone in his knee while playing football.*

Replace, on the other hand, means 'change (one person or thing) for another, often better, newer, etc.': *We've just replaced all our old computers with new ones.*

5 The adjective *single* refers to something as 'being the only one (of a possible number)': *A single tree offered shade from the sun.*

Unique, however, refers to something that is 'the only one of its type': *This glass goblet is unique: it was the only one ever produced to commemorate the 21st birthday of that famous writer.*

B 1 *forms* = shapes, outward appearances

2 *formed* = brought into existence, established

3 *form* = (school) class

4 *form* = degree of fitness or skill

5 *forms* = (wooden) benches

6 *form* = official paper or questionnaire

C 1 ... he knows while he looks at one side what the other side *is like*. = ... he can 'see' the appearance of the other side.

2 What *is* your new school *like*? = Is your new school big, small, interesting, enjoyable, etc.?

3 What *was* the weather *like* yesterday? = Was it dry, wet, cold, etc.?

3. 多项选择题答案

1	a	2	a	3	b	4	a	5	d	6	b
7	a	8	d	9	d	10	c	11	b	12	d

Lesson 32
Galileo reborn
伽利略的复生

课文详注 Further notes on the text

1. **In his own lifetime Galileo was the centre of violent controversy; but the scientific dust has long since settled, and today we can see even his famous clash with the Inquisition in something like its proper perspective.**

the scientific dust 科学纷争。指前面提到的 violent controversy。long since 作状语,表示"很久以前",如:

I've long since forgotten any Latin I ever learned.

我早就把我学过的拉丁语忘记了。

in something like its proper perspective 以正确的眼光或观点。something like 多少,大约,如:

There are something like 6 million people living in the capital.

大约有600万人口住在首都。

2. **But, in contrast, it is only in modern times that Galileo has become a problem child for historians of science.**

in/by contrast 形成对照。在句子中作插入语,如:

Their economy has expanded enormously in the last five years, whereas ours, by/in contrast, has declined.

他们的经济在过去的5年中得到巨大的发展,而与此形成对照的是,我们的经济则下降了。

该句为强调句,所强调的部分是 only in modern times。按正常语序应该是:Galileo has become a . . . only in modern times. a problem child 用在此处,是说将伽利略比作一个"问题儿童",这是一种比喻的手法,意思是"新出现的问题"。

3. **He was, above all, a man who experimented: who despised the prejudices and book learning of the Aristotelians, who put his questions to nature instead of to the ancients, and who drew his conclusions fearlessly.**

above all 作插入语,意即"首先"、"首要",如:

Above all, don't forget to write to me.

首要的是别忘记给我写信。

该句中一连用了 4 个由关系代词 who 引导的修饰 a man 的定语从句。这 4 个并列的定语从句构成排比结构(parallelism),起到加强语气的作用。put his questions to nature 他向自然界提出问题。draw a conclusion 得出结论。

4. **He had been the first . . ., and he had seen there evidence enough to overthrow Aristotle and Ptolemy together.**

there 指 in the sky。enough to overthrow . . . 作定语,修饰 evidence。Aristotle 亚里士多德,古希腊哲学家、科学家,亚历山大大帝的教师。Ptolemy 托勒密,公元 2 世纪时希腊天文学家、数学家及地理学家,提出太阳绕地球运行的学说。

5. **He was the man who climbed the Leaning Tower of Pisa and dropped various weights from the top, who rolled balls down inclined planes, and then generalized the results of his many experiments into the famous law of free fall.**

句子中的两个由关系代词 who 引导的从句都是定语从句,修饰 the man。from the top 后面省略了 of the Learning Tower of Pisa(比萨斜塔)。generalize . . . into 把……归纳成,如:

He generalized the results of his observations into a scientific theory.

他将观察结果归纳为一条科学理论。

the famous law of free fall 著名的自由落体定律。

6. **But a closer study of the evidence, supported by a deeper sense of the period, and particularly by a new consciousness of the philosophical undercurrents in the scientific revolution, has profoundly modified this view of Galileo.**

a closer study of the evidence 对那些证据的进一步研究。其中的 the evidence 指伽利略提出的证据。supported by ... revolution 作非限定性定语,修饰 a closer study。a deeper sense of the period 对那个时代更深的认识。a new consciousness of the philosophical undercurrents in the scientific revolution 科学革命中哲学潜流的新意识。该句的主语是 a closer study of the evidence, 其谓语部分是 has profoundly modified。this view of Galileo 对伽利略的看法。

7. **Today, although the old Galileo lives on in many popular writings, ...**

live on 继续活下去,如:

Long after he was dead, his name lived on because of his good deeds.

他去世很久以后,因为他的善行,他的名字仍然活在人们心中。

8. **His telescopic observations are justly immortal; they aroused great interest at the time, they had ..., and they provided a striking demonstration of the potentialities hidden in instruments and apparatus.**

句子中的 3 个 they 都指 his telescopic observations。at the time 当时。hidden in instruments and apparatus 为过去分词短语,作定语,修饰 potentialities,意即"仪表和仪器的潜在力量"。

9. **But can we blame those who looked and failed to see what Galileo saw, if we remember that to use a telescope at the limit of its powers calls for long experience and intimate familiarity with one's instrument?**

who looked and failed to see what Galileo saw 为定语从句,修饰 those。其中的 what Galileo saw 为动词不定式 to see 的宾语从句。if 引导的是该句的条件状语从句,that 引导的是该从句谓语动词 remember 的宾语从句。动词不定式 to use a telescope ... powers 为该宾语从句的主语,意即"用望远镜的极限功率",calls for 为其谓语动词。call for 需要,要求,如:

The position calls for an experienced engineer.

这个职位需要一位有经验的工程师。

10. **Was the philosopher who refused to look through Galileo's telescope more culpable than those who alleged that the spiral nebulae observed with Lord Rosse's great telescope in the eighteen-forties were scratches left by the grinder?**

who refused to ... telescope 为定语从句,修饰 the philosopher。more culpable 作该句的表语,意即"更应受谴责的"。than 引导的是比较状语从句。who ... eighteen-forties 作定语从句,修饰该比较状语从句中的主语 those。that the spiral nebulae ... eighteen-forties 作动词 alleged 的宾语从句,意即"在 19 世纪 40 年代用罗斯勋爵高倍望远镜观测到的螺旋状星云"。observed ... eighteen-forties 为过去分词短语,作定语,修饰 the spiral nebulae。该比较状语从句的谓语部分是 were scratches left by the grinder。left by the grinder 为过去分词短语,作定语,修饰 scratches,意即"望远镜镜片的磨工留下的划痕"。Lord Rosse 是英国天文学家,制造了 19 世纪最大的反射望远镜。allege that ... 断言,宣称,如:

It has been alleged that you stole the money.

据说你偷了那笔钱。

The two men alleged that the police forced them to make false confessions.

那两个男人声称警察强迫他们做假供。

11. We can perhaps ... if we recall that in his day, as for centuries before, curved glass was the popular contrivance for producing not truth but illusion, untruth; and if a single curved glass would distort nature, how much more would a pair of them?

该句中包含由两个 if 引导的条件状语从句。第 1 个条件状语从句中的 that 引导的是动词 recall 的宾语从句，in his day 为时间状语，his 指 Galileo's。as for centuries before 为插入语。as 为连词，表示“像”。后面跟介词短语 for centuries before，意即“正像几个世纪以前那样”。该处用 before 而未用 ago，原因在于：当表示距现在多久以前时用 ago，而表示从过去某个时间的多久以前时用 before。课文中是指在伽利略生活时代以前的几个世纪，所以用 before。试比较：

I met that woman in Scotland three years ago.
我 3 年前在苏格兰遇见那个女人。
When we got talking, I found out that I had been at school with her husband ten years before.
我们交谈时，我发现我曾在 10 年前与她的丈夫是同学。

该句中的交谈这个动作发生在过去，也就是在这个动作发生时的 10 年前，故用 before。curved glass was ... untruth 为 that 从句的主语和谓语部分。untruth 作 illusion 的同位语。a pair of them 指 a pair of curved glasses，后面省略了 distort nature。

语法 Grammar in use

动名词用法（1）

动名词的特征与一般用法

动名词由动词原形 + -ing 构成，既具有名词也具有动词的特征。它们既可以像名词那样作为不可数名词使用，也可以作为可数名词使用，并且在其前也可以像名词那样用限定词、物主代词和形容词等修饰，如：

Dancing is fun.

跳舞有趣。

Dickens often gave readings of his work.

狄更斯经常朗读他的作品。

He has made a new recording.

他又录制了一张新碟/盘音带。

同时，动名词还保留着动词的特征，即可以像动词那样被副词或副词短语修饰，可以有其自己的宾语，以及自己的完成时或被动形式，如：

Walking quickly/Walking in step is difficult.

快走/步调一致地走是很难的。（动名词分别被副词 *quickly* 和副词短语 *in step* 修饰）

Washing the car seems to be your main hobby.

擦汽车似乎是你的主要爱好。（*the car* 为动名词的宾语）

I'm sorry for having wasted your time.

我很抱歉浪费了你的时间。（*having wasted* 为动名词的完成时形式）

I can't forgive myself for having been taken by surprise.

我不能原谅自己吃了一惊。（*having been taken* 为动名词的被动形式）

动名词被副词或副词短语修饰或有自己的宾语时，所构成的结构

被称作动名词短语。动名词(短语)在句子中可以起到主语、表语和宾语的作用,如:

Being lost can be a terrifying experience.

迷路可能是一种可怕的经历。(作主语)

My favourite pastime is bird-watching.

我最喜欢的消遣是观察鸟类。(作表语)

He doesn't like not being taken seriously.

他不喜欢被人不当回事儿。(作宾语)

此外,动名词还有下述常见的几种用法:

(1) 用于 do + the + 动名词结构中,表示"做某种活",如:

Who does the cooking / the shopping / the washing-up here?

这儿谁做饭/买菜/洗碗?

(2) the + 动名词 + of 的使用规则如下:当动名词前无冠词时其后可以有直接宾语,但是当动名词前有冠词时则需使用上述结构,比较:

Lighting the fire used to be a daily chore in Victorian times.

在维多利亚时代,生火是一项家务。

The lighting of fires is forbidden.

禁止点火。

(3) 在禁令中,置于 no 后表示被禁止的行为,如:

No smoking here.

此处禁止吸烟。

No parking.

禁止停车。

(4) 用于 like 后,表示"例如"、"比如",如:

Why don't you find something to do, like cleaning the car for me?

你为什么不找点儿事干,比如给我擦擦汽车?

(5) 用于 for/for the purpose of 后,表示"为……目的",如:

It's a tool for making holes in metal.

它是一种用来在金属上凿洞的工具。

(6) 用于 what/how about 之后,表示"征求意见",如:

What/How about sending them a post card?

给他们寄张明信片怎么样?

词汇学习 Word study

1. settle

(1) *vt*. 安放:

She settled her baby in its crib.

她把婴儿放进童床上。

(2) *vt*. 使平静,调停:

Talking with strangers through the Internet can help you settle your nerves.

在网上与陌生人聊天可帮助你平缓紧张的神经。

(3) *vt*. 决定;解决:

The date of the examination has been settled.

考试的日期已经定下来了。

(4) *vt*. 结算:

He settled his bill without any delay.

他及时结了账。

(5) *vi*. 安定,安顿:

It is not easy to settle right away when you come to a new place.

初到一个新地方很快安顿下来可不容易。

(6) *vi*. 下沉,沉落:

The leaves are settling.

树叶正在落。

(7) *vi*. 安家,定居:

They had settled in Shanghai.

他们已经定居上海。

(8) settle down

1) *vi*. 定居下来:

They settled down in the countryside.

他们在农村定居下来。

2) *vi*. 安下心来;专心致力于:

He settled down and got back to work.

他安下心来,重新工作。

(9) settle in 习惯,适应:

He has settled in at the new school.

他已经适应了新学校。

(10) settle on 最终决定:

The couple settled on a name for the baby.

这对夫妇给这个小孩选定了名字。

2. blame

(1) *vt*. 指摘,责备,归咎:

Don't blame me if it doesn't work—it's not my fault.

要是它不能用可别责备我——那不是我的过错。

They blamed the failure of the talks on the other side.

他们把谈判的失败归咎于另一方。

They blamed the other side for the failure of the talks.

他们把谈判失败归咎于另一方。

If he fails the exam he's got only himself to blame.

如果他未能通过考试,那只能责怪他自己。

(2) *n*. (不可数)指摘,责备,归咎责任:

The judge laid / put the blame for the accident on the driver.

法官判定那个司机应对该事故负责。

We were ready to take / bear the blame for what had happened.

我们已经准备对所发生的事情承担责任。

3. fail

(1) *vi* 失败,没有能够,不及格:

The experiment failed.

实验失败了。

(2) *vi*. 衰弱,破产,倒闭:

My health is failing day by day.

我的身体一天不如一天。

(3) *vt*. 使失望,辜负期望,没起作用:

When I wanted his help, he failed me.

当我需要他的帮助时,他却让我失望。

(4) *vt*. 使不及格,不及格:

He failed five students this term.

他这学期给 5 个学生判了不及格。

I've failed the final examination.

我期末考试不及格。

They failed to finish the work within three days.

他们没能在 3 天内完成任务。

练习答案 Key to written exercises

1. 关键句型练习答案

A See text.

B See text.

C *To build* houses with the local stone was difficult.

(Note: This would sound better as 'It was difficult to build houses with the local stone'.)

Reading is one of the most important skills a young child must master.

To eat meat with your fingers is considered bad-mannered in that country.

Smoking is completely forbidden in many restaurants in Britain now.

2. 难点练习答案

A 1 The two nouns *plane* and *plain* are pronounced in exactly the same way: /pleɪn/.

As used in the text, the noun *plane* is a technical term (in geometry) meaning a completely flat surface: *If a rectangle is drawn at 90° to another rectangular plane, it can create an optical illusion.*

A *plain* is 'a large stretch of flat land': *They rode across the plain towards the distant mountains.*

2 The adjective *popular* means 'liked by many people': *Disneyworld is a popular holiday destination for many British people.*

The adjective *folk* refers to 'music or any other art that has grown up among working or country people as an important part of their way of life and that belongs to a particular area, trade, etc.': *I know a girl who wants to become a folk singer.*

3 *Sympathy* is 'sensitivity to and understanding of the sufferings of other people, often expressed in a willingness to give help': *The president sent a message of sympathy to the victims of the earthquake.*

Affection is 'a gentle lasting love, like that of a parent for a child': *She still has deep affection for some of her old school friends.*

4 The verb *blame* means 'consider (someone or something) responsible for (something bad)': *She blamed me for her exam results—as if I had anything to do with it!*

The verb *accuse* means 'charge someone with doing wrong or breaking the law': *Are you accusing me of cheating?*

5 The verb *refuse* means 'say no, express one's strong unwillingness to accept': *The prisoner refused to give his name.*

Deny, on the other hand, means 'declare untrue or refuse to accept as a fact': *He denied any involvement in the robbery.*

6 The noun *scratch* is 'a mark on a surface or a small wound on a person's skin made by rubbing with something pointed or rough': *There were some nasty scratches on the surface of the wooden table.*

A *scrape* is 'an act or sound of scraping, i.e. removing something from a surface by pulling or pushing an edge firmly across it repeatedly': *The sound of fingernails scraping across a blackboard makes my teeth go on edge.*

B 1 *settled down* = got used to living

2 *settled down* = sat comfortably

3 *settle* = pay

4 *settle* = solve

5 *settled* = went and lived

C 1 Whatever happens, the old man will *keep on* living in the farmhouse.

2 When my father retires, I am going to *carry on* the family business.

3 She doesn't want to *go on* being a secretary all her life.

4 After we had stopped for a rest, we *drove on* for another hour before we stopped again.

5 After crossing the bridge, we *walked on* until we reached a small hut on the side of the hill.

6 The book gets exciting at this point; just *read on*.

D 1 *calls for* = requires, needs

2 *call on* = pay a short visit to

3 *call you up* = telephone you

4 *call . . . off* = cancel

5 *call for* = collect

6 *call in* (a doctor) = ask (a doctor) to visit

3. 多项选择题答案

1	b	2	d	3	c	4	b	5	a	6	d
7	b	8	d	9	c	10	a	11	b	12	c

Lesson 33
Education
教育

课文详注 Further notes on the text

1. **A man without an education, many of us believe, is an unfortunate victim of adverse circumstances, deprived of one of the greatest twentieth-century opportunities.**

   many of us believe 作插入语,进行补充说明。deprived of ... 为过去分词短语,作定语,修饰 victim。deprive sb. of sth. 剥夺某人某物,如:

   This law will deprive us of our most basic rights.

   这条法律将剥夺我们最基本的权利。

2. **Convinced of the importance of education, modern states 'invest' in institutions of learning to get back 'interest' in the form of a large group of enlightened young men and women who are potential leaders.**

   Convinced of ... 作原因状语,用以说明'invest' in institutions of learning 的原因,即"由于深信教育的重要性"。convince of 使确信,如:

   He convinced me of his honesty.

   他使我确信他是诚实的。

   invest in 在……投资,如:

   He has invested heavily in bonds.

   他大量买进了债券。

   institutions of learning 教育机构。该句中的 invest 和 interest

用单引号表示该处是一种借喻的手法。用“投资”和“利息”这两个金融方面的词汇,表示对教育的投入以及由此培养出来大批的人才。in the form of 以……形式,作定语修饰interest,意即“以大批可望成为领导人的有知识的男女青年的形式取回利息”。

3. **Education, with its cycles ..., punctuated by textbooks ... without its benefits?**

该句中的 Education 和 punctuated 并不是一种主谓关系,因此这句话在语法上被称作单元句(one-member sentence)。有主谓结构的句子为双元句(two-member sentence)。只有单个或多个相互间没有主谓关系的词或词组的句子为单元句。该句中 with its cycles ... 和 punctuated by ... 都作定语,修饰education。破折号中间的内容 those purchasable wells of wisdom 是 textbooks 的同位语,对 textbooks 作进一步的说明,将 textbooks 比喻为 wells of wisdom。without its benefits 中的代词 its 指 education。

4. **So much is certain: that we would have doctors and preachers, lawyers and defendants, marriages and births—but our spiritual outlook would be different.**

So much is certain 处于段首,起着承上启下的作用:一方面回答了前一段最后一句的提问,另一方面开始列举没有教育将会给社会文明带来的影响。此外,so much 还是冒号后面的 that 引导的同位语从句的先行词。句子中的破折号用来强调其后的部分。

5. **We would lay less stress on ‘facts and figures’ and more on a good memory, on applied psychology, and on the capacity of a man to get along with his fellow-citizens.**

lay stress on 强调,重视,如:

Young people should lay stress on good manners.

年轻人应该重视举止。

more 后面省略了 stress。memory 后面的 on applied psychology, and on the capacity of a man 与 on a good memory 为并列关系。get along with 与……相处,如:

How does she get along with her mother-in-law?

她与她的婆婆相处得如何?

6. If our educational system were fashioned after its bookless past we would have the most democratic form of 'college' imaginable.

该句为虚拟语气。if 引导的是非真实性条件句。be fashioned after 按……做成。imaginable 为形容词,为后置定语,修饰 college。

7. Among tribal people all knowledge inherited by tradition is shared by all; it is taught to every member of the tribe so that in this respect everybody is equally equipped for life.

inherited by tradition 为过去分词短语,作定语,修饰 all knowledge,表示"由传统继承来的所有知识"。is shared 为该句谓语,表示"为所有人共享"。share 分享,共同具有,如:

The thieves shared the loot among themselves.

窃贼分赃。

分号后面的代词 it 代表 all knowledge。in this respect 在这方面,在这点上,指接受知识方面。be equipped for 为……而装备,如:

He was well equipped for the trip.

他为这次旅行装备充分。

8. It is the ideal condition of the 'equal start' which ...

It 指上一段中的最后一句话 Among ... for life。equal start 平等起步。

9. In primitive cultures the obligation to seek and to receive the

traditional instruction is binding to all.

to seek and to receive the traditional instruction 作定语,修饰名词 obligation。binding 为形容词,意即"有约束力的",后面可跟介词 to、on 或 upon,如:

The agreement is binding on you.

本协议对你有约束力。

10. There are no 'illiterates'—if the term can be applied to peoples without a script—while our own compulsory school attendance became law in Germany ..., and is still non-existent in a number of 'civilized' nations.

if the term can be applied to peoples without a script 为插入语,对 illiterates 作进一步的解释,term 指 illiterates。without a script 作定语,修饰 people,表示"没有文字的"。while 在此处表达的是"而"的意思。is still non-existent 的主语是 our own compulsory school attendance。

11. This shows how long it was before we deemed it necessary to make sure that all our children could share in the knowledge accumulated by the 'happy few' during the past centuries.

deem 认为,后面常跟 that 引导的宾语从句或与名词或形容词连用,如:

They deemed that he was no longer capable of managing his business.

他们认为他已经没有能力打理生意了。

We deem her worthy of support.

我们认为她值得支持。

it 为动词 deemed 的先行宾语,真正的宾语是 to make sure that all ... centuries。make sure 确保,后面跟 that 引导的宾语从句,如:

Please make sure that there will be enough light and heat.

请确保有足够的光和热。

share in 共同拥有,如:share in the profits(分享利润)。accumulated by 积累起来的,为过去分词短语,作定语修饰 knowledge。

12. **All are entitled to an equal start.**

be entitled to 对……有权的,有……资格的,如:

She is fully entitled to benefits.

她完全有资格领取救济金。

be entitled 后面也可以跟动词不定式,如:

They are entitled to attend all the lectures free.

他们有权免费听所有的讲座。

13. **There is none of the hurry which, in our society, often hampers the full development of a growing personality.**

which 引导的是定语从句,其先行词是 hurry,意即"我们社会中妨碍个性全面发展的匆忙生活"。hamper 束缚,阻碍,如:

We were hampered in the ice until noon.

我们一直被冰雪所困,直到中午。

14. **There, a child grows up under the ever-present attention of his parents; therefore the jungles and the savannahs know of no 'juvenile delinquency'.**

There 指 the wilderness,即"荒凉地区"。know of 听说,知道,如:

Do you know of any computer stores in this neighbourhood?

你听说这附近有电脑商店吗?

该句中 know of 的主语是无生命的 jungles and the savannahs,此处是拟人用法。juvenile delinquency 青少年犯罪。

15. **No necessity of making a living away from home results in neglect of children, and no father is confronted with his inability to 'buy' an education for his child.**

of making a living away from home 为定语,修饰 No necessity,

意即“没有必要离家谋生”。away from home 为状语，修饰 making a living。result in 结果导致，终于造成……结果，如：

The argument resulted in a fight.

争论最终导致大打出手。

confront with 使面对，与……对质，如：

I was confronted with the task of designing the building.

我面临的任务是设计大厦。

语法 Grammar in use

动名词用法 (2)

动词 + 动名词形式

在英语中，动词的用法比较复杂。如：某些动词后只能用动词不定式作宾语；有些动词后却只能用动名词作宾语；有些动词后既可以用动词不定式也可以用动名词作宾语而保持语义不变；而有些动词后虽然可以用动名词或动词不定式作宾语，但语义不同。因此，有必要对这样使用的动词进行比较详细的区分。

就其后使用动名词作宾语的某些动词而言，大体有 3 种类型：(1) 其后直接使用动名词作宾语的形式；(2) 其后使用宾格 + 动名词作宾语的形式；(3) 其后使用所有格 + 动名词的形式。

(1) 直接使用动名词作宾语的形式

在下述动词后只能使用动名词而不能使用动词不定式作宾语：admit(承认)、appreciate(欣赏)、avoid(避免)、celebrate(庆祝)、consider(考虑)、contemplate(注视)、defer(推迟)、delay(耽搁)、deny(否认)、detest(痛恨)、discontinue(停止)、dislike(不喜欢)、dispute(不同意)、enjoy(喜爱)、escape(逃脱)、excuse(原谅)、explain(解释)、fancy(喜爱)、feel like(想要)、finish(完成)、forgive(原谅)、can't help(不禁)、hinder(阻碍)、imagine(想像)、keep(保持)、loathe(厌恶)、mention(提及)、mind(介

意)、miss(错过,免于)、pardon(饶恕)、postpone(推迟)、practise(练习)、prevent(阻止)、racall(召回)、report(报告)、resent(怨恨)、resist(抵制)、risk(冒险)、suggest(建议)、understand(理解),如:

I don't fancy going for a walk in the rain.

我可不爱在雨中散步。

Imaging not knowing the answer to such an easy question!

真想不到竟会不知道如何回答这样一个简单的问题!

而在 deny(否认)和 regret(后悔)之后经常使用动名词的完成时形式,如:

Susan denies/regrets having said anything.

苏珊否认/后悔说过什么。

此外,这样使用时,注意下述两点的使用方法:

1) 动词 come 和 go 后的动名词形式

这两个动词后的动名词往往与户外活动有关,并通常表示提建议、进行邀请或进行叙事,如:

Why don't we go swimming?

为什么我们不去游泳呢?(建议)

Come dancing this evening.

今晚来跳舞吧。(邀请)

Yesterday we went sight-seeing.

昨天我们去游览了。(叙事)

2) 动词 need、want 和 require 后的动名词形式

这 3 个动词后的动名词通常具有被动的含义,且相当于被动的动词不定式形式,如:

He needs a lot of encouraging.

他需要多鼓励。

The front gate requires mending.

前门需要修理。

(2) 使用宾格 + 动名词作宾语的形式

下述动词与其后的动名词之间可加一个宾语：hear（听到）、keep（保持）、smell（闻）、start（开始）、stop（停止）、watch（观看）等，如：

When are you going to start him working ?

你打算什么时候让他开始工作？

而下述动词与动名词之间则必须加一个宾语：catch（抓住）、find（发现）、leave（留下）、notice（注意）、observe（观察）、perceive（觉察）、see（看）等，如：

I'd better not catch you doing that again !

最好别让我逮着你再干那件事！

(3) 使用所有格 + 动名词的形式

下述动词后可以只跟动名词形式或跟所有格 + 动名词形式：appreciate（欣赏）、avoid（避免）、consider（考虑）、defer（推迟）、delay（耽搁）、deny（否认）、enjoy（喜爱）、postpone（推迟）、risk（冒险）、suggest（建议）等，如：

I don't think the children enjoy your/his/John's teasing.

我认为孩子们不喜欢你的/他的/约翰的挑逗。

下述常用动词后既可以只使用动名词形式也可以使用宾格或所属格 + 动名词形式：anticipate（预期）、contemplate（注视）、detest（痛恨）、dislike（不喜欢）、dispute（不同意）、endure（忍耐）、escape（逃脱）、excuse（原谅）、(can't) face（〈不能〉面对）、fancy（喜爱）、forgive（饶恕）、hate（憎恨）、hinder（阻碍）、imagine（想像）、like（喜欢）、love（热爱）、mention（提及）、mind（介意）、miss（错过）、pardon（原谅）、prevent（阻止）、resent（怨恨）、resist（抵制）、understand（理解）、can't bear（不能忍受）、can't help（不禁）、can't stand（不能接受）等。

词汇学习 Word study

1. convince *vt.*

(1) 说服,使确信,使信服:

I finally convinced her of my innocence.

我最终使她相信我是无辜的。

The prosecutor could not convince the jurors that the defendant was guilty.

原告律师没能说服陪审员被告有罪。

I'm convinced that she is telling the truth.

我确信她说的是实话。

We finally convinced him to stay.

我们最终说服他留下来。

2. confront *vt.*

(1) (勇敢地)面对,面临:

Pronunciation is just one of the many problems that confront a language learner.

发音只是语言学习者要面临的许多问题中的一个。

As she left the court, she was confronted by angry crowds.

她离开法庭时,面对她的是愤怒的人群。

(2) 使对质,使对证:

They confronted him with the evidence.

他们将证据摆在他的面前。

3. teach (taught)

(1) *vt.* 教,讲授:

She teaches music at a middle school.

她在一所中学教音乐。

He's now teaching his child how to swim.

他正在教他的孩子游泳。

He teaches them English.

他教他们英语。

(2) *vt*. 教导:

He taught us to be responsible.

他教导我们要有责任心。

She taught me that most people can be trusted.

她教导我多数人是可以信任的。

(3) *vi*. 教书:

She teaches at middle school.

她在中学教书。

It's a book that teaches easily.

这是一本很容易教的。

练习答案 Key to written exercises

1. 关键句型练习答案

A See text.

B We use inverted commas (or quotation marks) around what is actually spoken, i.e. direct speech. We also enclose book and film titles in inverted commas. However, individual words and phrases are enclosed in inverted commas (or quotation marks) in English for a variety of other purposes.

The verb 'invest' (l.3), for example, is in inverted commas to indicate that the word is not being used in its normally defined meaning.

The phrase 'facts and figures' (l.8) is in inverted commas because again the author has extended the normal use of the phrase to suit his own purpose and to mean something like 'factual information'.

The phrase 'happy few' (l. 18) is a direct quotation from Shakespeare (*Henry V*, Act 4, Scene 3). There it refers to the small number of English soldiers that faced the French army. In the text it refers to the fortunate small number of extremely privileged people who received education in the past.

C 1 less 2 fewer 3 Fewer 4 less 5 fewer

D See text.

E 1 Most people would *consider* Chinese very difficult.
 2 I *find* it incredible that he still can't read at his age.
 3 He *thought* it funny that I had taken up chess.
 4 She *felt* it necessary to tell her best friend her news.
 5 I *believed* her incapable of doing any job properly.

2. 难点练习答案

A 1 The words *opportunity* and *chance* are very close in meaning and use in English.

An *opportunity* is 'a favourable moment or occasion (for doing something)': *You should go and see that film if you get the opportunity. I took the opportunity of visiting Ann while I was in London.*

Chance can also mean 'a time suitable for doing something you want to do': *I'll have a chance/an opportunity to go up the Eiffel Tower when I'm in Paris.*

However, only the word *chance* can be used to talk about possibility alone: *There is a chance* (= *possibility*) *that I'll see him later in the week.*

 2 The adjectives *potential* and *potent*, while they might look similar, are totally different in meaning.

Potential refers to something 'that may happen or become so, although not actually existing at present': *An ordinary kitchen is full of potential dangers, especially for young children.*

Potent, on the other hand, means 'very effective, convincing, or having great power': *She put forward a very potent argument for our moving house.*

3 Although both connected with the verb 'imagine', the adjectives *imaginable* and *imaginative* are very different in use. (A third adjective, *imaginary*, refers to something 'only existing in imagination': *Quite a lot of small children have imaginary friends.*)

Imaginable refers to something 'that can be imagined': *They tried every imaginable means/every means imaginable, but they couldn't wake her up.*

Imaginative refers to something 'that shows use of the imagination': *One of the students came up with an extremely imaginative design for the new college.*

4 A *tribe* is 'a social group of people made up of people of the same race, beliefs, customs, language, etc., living in a particular area often under the leadership of a chief': *Not long ago an English woman married a member of the Zulu tribe and brought him back to Britain.*

The word *race*, on the other hand, refers to 'the largest social group of humans, a group of the same colour and/or physical type': *The law forbids discrimination on the grounds of race or religion.*

5 Both adjective *compulsory* and *necessary* are connected to the idea of obligation.

Compulsory refers to something 'which must be done by law, by order, etc.': *Wearing a car seat belt is compulsory in Britain. Is it compulsory in China?*

Necessary refers to something 'that must be had, obtained or done': *Is it really necessary for all of us to go to the meeting?*

B 1 *outlook* = general point of view

2 *outburst* = sudden powerful expression of feeling

3 *outbreak* = sudden appearance or beginning of something bad

4 *outcome* = an effect or result

C 1 *All* knowledge... *is* shared by *all*. = The whole amount of knowledge (that exists)... is shared by everyone.

2 *All are* entitled to an equal start. = All people are... = Everyone is...

3. 多项选择题答案

1	b	2	d	3	b	4	a	5	d	6	b
7	c	8	c	9	d	10	c	11	b	12	a

Lesson 34
Adolescence
青春期

课文详注 Further notes on the text

1. Parents are often upset when their children praise the homes of their friends and regard it as a slur on ..., and often are foolish enough to let the adolescents ...

regard it as a slur on 中的 it 指 their children praise the homes of their friends。slur 诋毁。adolescents 指 their children。

2. They may even accuse them of disloyalty, ...

accuse of 指责,指控……犯有……,如:

He accused me of cheating.

他指责我作弊。

He was accused of murder.

他被控犯有谋杀罪。

them 指 their children。

3. Such a loss of dignity and descent into childish behaviour on the part of the adults ..., and makes them resolve that ...

on the part of 在……一方,作定语,修饰 Such a loss of dignity and descent into childish behaviour,意即"家长这种有失身份和孩子气的作法"。resolve 决心,后面可跟动词不定式或 that 引导的从句,如:

She resolved to study abroad.

她决心出国学习。

They resolved that they would resist to the end.

他们决心抵抗到底。

4. **Before very long the parents . . . , but they seldom realize that they have brought this on themselves.**

Before very long 不要很久。seldom 很少，副词，表达否定意思。they have brought this on themselves 他们这是咎由自取。this 指 the child is so secretive and never tells them anything。bring on 给……带来，如：

He brought trouble on himself.

他自找麻烦。

5. **Disillusionment with the parents, however good and adequate they may be both as parents and as individuals, is to some degree inevitable.**

Disillusionment with the parents 孩子对家长幻想的破灭。however good and adequate they may be both as parents and as individuals 为让步状语从句，they 指 parents，意即"作为父母和作为个人，无论他们多么好、多么合格"。to some degree 在某种程度上。

6. **Most children have such a high ideal of their parents, unless the parents themselves have been unsatisfactory, that it can hardly hope to stand up to a realistic evaluation.**

have such a high ideal of 对……期望如此高，将……如此理想化。unless 引导的是条件状语从句，意即"除非父母自身不能令人满意"。该句的整体结构是 such . . . that . . . 结构，that 引导的是结果状语从句。it 指 a high ideal of their parents。hardly 几乎不，否定词。stand up to 经受住，勇敢地面对，如：

This dam could not stand up to the big flood.

这个坝经受不住这样大的洪水。

If you stand up to that bully, he'll back down.

如果你勇敢地面对那个恶霸，他就会退缩。

7. **... how much belief their children usually have in their character and infallibility, ...**

have belief in 对……信仰,对……信任,如:

Do you have belief in God?

你信仰上帝吗?

8. **If parents were prepared for this adolescent reaction, and realized that it was a sign that the child ..., and therefore would not drive the child into opposition by resenting and resisting it.**

be prepared for 对……有准备的,如:

I'm not prepared for such a large bill.

我尚未准备足够的钱付如此大额的账单。

it 指 this adolescent reaction。drive into 驱使……处于某种状态,如:

Her son's death has driven her into despair.

儿子的死使她陷入绝望之中。

9. **The adolescent, with his passion for sincerity, always respects a parent who admits that ...**

with his passion for sincerity 由于酷爱真诚,介词短语,作原因状语。a passion for 对……的强烈爱好,如:

He has a passion for gambling.

他迷恋赌博。

who admits that...为定语从句,修饰 a parent。

10. **What the child cannot forgive is the parents' refusal to admit these charges if the child knows them to be true.**

What the child cannot forgive 是主语从句。to admit these charges 为动词不定式,作定语,修饰名词 refusal。these charges 指上文提到的 he is wrong, or ignorant, or even that he has been unfair or unjust。them 指 these charges。

11. Victorian parents believed that they kept their dignity by retreating behind an unreasoning authoritarian attitude; in fact they did nothing of the kind, but children were then too cowed to let them know how they really felt.

keep/maintain one's dignity 保持某人的尊严，如：

If you want to keep your dignity, you must obey the laws.

如果你要保持你的尊严，你必须遵纪守法。

retreat 撤退，退却，如：

Our troops retreated from the border to safer positions.

我们的队伍从边境撤退到较安全的地方。

of the kind 某一类的，含有轻蔑的意思。这里 the kind 指 kept their dignity。cow 吓唬，威胁，如：

I was cowed into agreeing with the boss.

我被吓得同意了老板的意见。

12. Today we tend to go to the other extreme, but on the whole this is a healthier attitude both for the child and the parent.

tend to do sth. 有做某事的倾向，如：

He tends to exaggerate.

他说话有夸张的倾向。

go to the other extreme 走向另一个极端。on the whole 总的看来，大体上，如：

The situation is, on the whole, satisfactory.

总的看来，形势是令人满意的。

13. It is always wiser and safer to face up to reality, however painful it may be at the moment.

face up to 勇敢地接受，如：

You must learn to face up to your responsibilities.

你必须学会勇于承担自己的责任。

however 引导的让步状语从句意即“尽管会有暂时的痛苦”。

语法 Grammar in use

动名词用法 (3)

形容词/名词 + 动名词形式

许多形容词和名词以及种种说法后可以跟动名词的主动和被动形式,如:

It's nice seeing him again.

再次见到他令人愉快。

It's fun being taken to the zoo.

被带到动物园真有意思。

(1) 形容词 + 动名词形式

形容词与动名词连用表达同一概念时,往往可以用两种形式表示,一是用动名词作主语,一是用先行词 it,如:

Finding work is difficult these days.

现在找工作很难。(动名词作主语)

It's difficult finding your way around in a strange city.

在一个陌生的城市里找路很困难。(先行词 *it* 结构)

此外,使用这一结构时,形容词之后可以跟宾格或所属格,以起到作其后动名词的逻辑主语的作用,如:

It's strange him/his behaving like that.

真奇怪,他的举止行动像那个样子。

但是,当动名词处于主语位置时,其前使用的通常仅为所属格,如:

His knowing I had returned home unexpectedly is strange.

奇怪的是他知道我突然回家。

在 it's/it was + 形容词 + of (sb.)结构后也可以使用动名词形

式,如:

It was rude of her interrupting you all the time.

她很无礼,总是打断你的话。

(2) 名词+动名词形式

动名词形式还可以用于 it's/it was+名词+动名词结构中。此结构中的名词既可以是可数名词,也可以是不可数名词,如:

It's a nightmare worrying where the children might be.

担心孩子可能到哪去,这是人们经常有的恐惧。

It's not fun having to do the same work over and over again.

一遍又一遍地不得不做同一件工作真没意思。

与形容词+动名词形式构成的句子一样,在名词后也可以用宾格或所属格作该动名词的逻辑主语,如:

It's a catastrophe their/them shutting all those factories.

他们关闭了所有那些工厂,这真是一场灾难。

在下述常见结构后,通常可以使用动名词形式:it's no good(无用)、it's no use(无用)、it's little use(没多大用)、it's hardly any use(几乎没有用)、it's not worth(没有价值)、it's hardly/scarcely worth(几乎没有价值)、it's worthwhile(值得)、spend money/time(花钱/时间)、there's no(无法)、there's no point in(毫无意义)、there's nothing worse than(没有比……更糟的)、what's the use /point(……有什么用/意义)等,如:

It's no good complaining.

抱怨是没有用的。

There's no telling what will happen.

谁也不知道会发生什么。

在某些上述结构之后,作动名词的逻辑主语也可以使用宾格或所属格形式,如:

It's no good his/him apologizing now the damage has been done.

损失既已造成,他道歉也没用了。

词汇学习 Word study

1. accuse *vt.* (of) 指控,控告,指责:

Are you accusing me of cheating?

你在指责我作弊吗?

He was accused of murder.

他被指控犯有谋杀罪。

2. respect

(1) *n.* (不可数)尊敬,尊重:

He has earned the respect of his students.

他赢得了学生们的尊敬。

Reporters should have respect for others' privacy.

记者应该尊重其他人的隐私。

(2) *n.* (可数)方面:

These two questions are similar in some respects.

这两个问题在某些方面有相似之处。

(3) *vt.* 尊敬,尊重:

We respect our supervisor very much.

我们非常尊敬我们的导师。

(4) with respect to 谈到,关联:

We must plan with respect to the future.

我们必须联系未来进行计划。

3. annoy *vt.* (由于琐碎烦心的事而)使恼怒,使生气,使烦恼:

Her complains annoyed me.

她的抱怨让我心烦。

I was annoyed at the attitude he had adopted.

我反感他采取的态度。

She was annoyed with him for his repeated interruptions.

他不断的打搅令她烦恼。

They were annoyed at not being allowed to attend the meeting.

他们因未被允许参加会议而生气。

It annoyed me to think how much time I had wasted.

一想起我浪费的那么多时间我就心烦。

练习答案 Key to written exercises

1. 关键句型练习答案

A 1 (Often) parents are (often) upset when their children (often) praise the homes of their friends.

2 Such a loss of dignity and descent into childish behaviour on the part of the adults (deeply) shocks the adolescents (deeply).

3 They (seldom) realize that they have brought this on themselves.

4 (Usually) parents would (usually) be (greatly) surprised and (deeply) touched if they realized how much belief their children (usually) have in their character and infallibility.

B 1 He's old *enough* to go on holiday on his own.

2 Have you got *enough* money for your bus fare?

C 1 They let us *use their bicycles for the weekend*.

2 We made them *wait for us*.

3 Will you let him *borrow your tennis racket?*

4 Why make me *address those letters when you could do them yourself?*

D See text.

E 1 *What* I most wanted to ask him was how he felt when his team won the championship.

2 *What* annoys me about him is the way he always knows the answers to questions in class.

3 *What* the girl wanted most for her birthday was a new computer.

2. 难点练习答案

A 1 When used with an adjective, the word *enough* means 'to the necessary degree': *She is old enough to know her own mind.*

The adverb *fairly*, on the other hand, means 'to some degree, rather, quite': *It was a fairly difficult exercise, but I managed to finish it.*

2 The noun *loss* (/lɒs/) comes from the verb *lose* (/luːz/) —and notice the difference in pronunciation.

Did you report the loss of the painting to the police?
When did you lose your wallet?

3 Notice first how these words are pronounced: *descent* (/dɪˈsent/) and *decent* (/ˈdiːsənt/).

The noun *descent* comes from *descend* and means 'the process of going down': *We watched the girl's descent from the tree.* It is also sometimes used figuratively, as in the text, and as here: *His friends watched his descent into a life of crime, not knowing what to do about it.*

The adjective *decent* means 'proper, socially acceptable': *Our neighbours are all very decent people.*

4 The noun *belief*, as used in the text, means 'a feeling that someone or something is good or can be depended on, trust or confidence': *The failure of the operation has shaken my belief in doctors.*

Loyalty is 'the feeling or quality of being loyal, faithful to friends, principles, country, etc.': *No one could ever doubt her loyalty to the team and her team-mates.*

5 *Grow up* and *grow* can easily be confused.

Grow up means 'develop from being a child to being a man or woman': *What do you want to be when you grow up?*

The verb *grow* means 'increase in size by natural development': *She doesn't like her hair short, so she's letting it grow.* (The verb can also be used transitively: *We grow all our own vegetables.*)

6 The verb *hurt* means 'cause physical pain and/or damage to': *She hurt her leg when she fell*; or 'cause a person to suffer pain of the mind': *I was deeply hurt by the way she just ignored me.*

The noun *pain*, however, means 'suffering, great discomfort of the body or mind': *His behaviour caused his parents a great deal of pain.*

7 The noun *refusal* (from the verb *refuse*) means '(the expression of) an unwillingness to accept': *My offer of help met with a polite refusal.* (=... was politely refused.)

The noun *denial* (from the verb *deny*) means 'the act or an example of saying that something is not true': *The government has issued a strong denial of this rumour.*

B 1 It was a mistake *on the part of* Jones (= Jones was mistaken) to sign the contract without reading it.

2 The firm agreed to refund one customer his money, and *before very long* hundreds of others were asking for refunds.

3 Most children learn quite early in life that they have *to stand up to* people who try to bully them.

4 The boy was accused of stealing a book from the shop, but he had done *nothing of the kind*.

5 '*On the whole*,' said the teacher, 'I'm very pleased with John's progress.'

6 In the end we all have *to face up to* our responsibilities.

7 I'm rather busy *at the moment*, but I promise I'll do it later.

3. 多项选择题答案

1	d	2	c	3	a	4	c	5	b	6	d
7	a	8	c	9	d	10	b	11	c	12	a

Lesson 35
Space odyssey
太空探索

课文详注 Further notes on the text

1. **The Moon is likely to become the industrial hub of the Solar System, supplying the rocket fuels for its ships, easily obtainable from the lunar rocks in the form of liquid oxygen.**

likely 可能的,不能单独使用,后面可以跟动词不定式或 that 引导的从句,如:

It is not likely to snow.

不大可能会下雪。

It is likely there will be more rain.

很可能还会下雨。

the industrial hub 工业中心。supplying the rocket fuels for its ships 为现在分词短语,作定语修饰 the industrial hub。easily obtainable from the lunar rocks 为形容词短语,作定语修饰 fuels,意即"很容易从月球的岩石中提炼的"。in the form of liquid oxygen 以液态氧的形式。

2. **The reason lies in its gravity.**

lie in 在于,如:

My real interest lies in developing a new sort of robot.

我真正的兴趣所在是开发一个新型的机器人。

The causes of the war lie in the greed and incompetence of politicians on both sides.

那场战争的原因是双方政客的贪婪和无能。

3. **Because the Moon has only an eightieth of the Earth's mass, it requires 97 per cent less energy to travel the quarter of a million miles from the Moon to Earth-orbit than the 200 mile-journey from Earth's surface into orbit!**

an eightieth of 1/80。to travel the quarter of a million ... 为动词不定式短语,作目的状语。the quarter of a million miles 25 万英里。连词 than 后面省略了 energy to travel。

4. **This may sound fantastic ...**

sound 在这里作系动词,后面跟形容词作表语,意即"听起来"。

5. **To escape from the Earth in a rocket, one must travel at seven miles per second.**

To escape from the Earth in a rocket 为动词不定式,作目的状语。

6. **The comparable speed from the Moon ...**

意为"从月球出发的相应的速度",这里指摆脱月球引力需达到的速度。

7. **Because the gravity on the Moon's surface is only a sixth of the Earth's (remember how easily the Apollo astronauts bounded along) ...**

the Earth's 后面省略了 surface。the Apollo astronauts 指 1969 年 7 月 20 日美国"阿波罗 11 号"宇宙飞船中第一次载人登月的宇航员。bound along 跳跃。

8. **Arthur C. Clark once suggested a revolutionary idea passes through three phases ...**

动词 suggested 后面省略了连词 that。当引述动词 suggest 为过去时时,其后的宾语从句中可以用情态助动词 should 或动词的过去时态或现在时态。该句使用的是动词的现在时态。

9. **The idea of colonising Mars—a world 160 times more distant than the Moon—will move decisively from the second phase to**

the third, when a significant number of people are living permanently in space.

a world 160 times more distant than the Moon 一个比月球远 160 倍的星球,是插入语,对 Mars 作进一步的说明。the third 后面省略了名词 phase。

10. **Mars has an extraordinary fascination for would-be voyagers.**

have a fascination for 对……具有魅力,如:

This ancient land has a great fascination for us.

这片古老的土地对我们具有极大的魅力。

11. **America, Russia and Europe are filled with enthusiasts—many of them serious and senior scientists—who dream of sending people to it.**

be filled with 充满了,如:

The large hall is filled with rows of desks.

那个大厅摆满了一排一排的办公桌。

many of them serious and senior scientists 作插入语,对 enthusiasts 作进一步的说明。dream of 梦想,如:

He dreamed of having a car.

他梦想有一辆汽车。

12. **It is the one world in the Solar System that is most like the Earth.**

one + 可数名词表示"惟一的",如:

She is the one person with enough medical knowledge to make it possible.

她是惟一一位具有丰富的医学知识而使其成为可能的人。

that is most like the Earth 为定语从句,修饰 the one world,即 Mars。

13. **It is a world of red sandy deserts (hence its name—the Red**

Planet) ...

hence 为副词,因此,由此,所以,如:

The stock market is jittery just now—hence my advice to avoid shares and to buy gold instead.

眼下股票市场极度不稳——因此我的意见是不要再购进股票而改买黄金。

该处的意思是"由此而得名"。

14. **... chasms wider than the Grand Canyon and at least one mountain more than twice as tall as Everest.**

Grand Canyon 指位于美国亚利桑那州西北部的科罗拉多河两岸的大峡谷。more than twice as tall as Everest 比珠穆朗玛峰高两倍多。

语法 Grammar in use

动名词用法 (4)

介词 + 动名词形式 (1)

介词后可以接所有的动名词形式,主动的和被动的均可。介词 + 动名词形式大体可以包括下述若干种形式:

(1) 一般形式

通常可以在其后使用动名词的介词有:about、after、by、for、instead of、to、without 等,如:

I have learnt a lot about gardening from my father.

我从我父亲那里学到了很多有关园艺的知识。

After changing some money, he went sight-seeing.

他换了一些钱后就去游览了。

Instead of making a fuss, you should have complained quietly.

你应当平静地申诉,而不应该大吵大闹。

You shouldn't try to leave the restaurant without paying.

你不应当试图不付账就离开饭店。

(2) 介词后的 there being 和 it being 形式

当介词后要使用 there be 结构和 it be 结构时,应当将 there be 结构变为 there being 形式,把 it be 结构变为 it being 形式,如:

Is there any chance of (there being) a vacancy in this hotel tomorrow?

这家旅馆明天会有空房吗?

If I bring in my suit for dry-cleaning, is there any chance of it being ready by tomorrow?

如果我把衣服拿来干洗,明天能洗好吗?

注意,介词后的 there being 可以省略。

(3) 形容词/名词 + 介词 + 动名词形式

许多形容词/名词后常常需用介词。这类介词后所用的动词需用动名词形式,如:

I'm interested in acting.

我对表演感兴趣。

He's good at skiing.

他擅长滑雪。

You can't be too sure of his/him agreeing.

你不能太肯定他会同意。

I'm surprised at your/you not having noticed.

我对你没有注意到感到惊奇。

(上述 4 例为形容词 + 介词 + 动名词结构)

She could never overcome her fear of flying.

她永远克服不了恐飞症。

His interest in hang-gliding proved to be fatal.

他对悬挂式滑翔的兴趣证明是令人致命的。

（上述两例为名词＋介词＋动名词结构）

词汇学习 Word study

1. supply

(1) *vt*. 供给，供应：

They have supplied necessary tools for the workers so that they could finish the task on time.

他们向工人提供了必要的工具，以使其能按时完成任务。

(2) *vt*. 满足需要，提供：

These foods supply the body with necessary vitamins and minerals.

这些食物为身体提供必要的维生素和矿物质。

They supplied needed water resources to the region.

他们为这一地区提供所需的水资源。

(3) *n*. （可数）供给，补给：

The storm cut off the city's water supply.

暴风雨中断了这个城市的供水。

(4) *n*. （可数）储备，储藏：

The store has a large supply of swimwear.

这家店贮藏了很多游泳用品。

(4) *n*. （不可数）供给（与需求相对）：

He told me something about the relation between supply and demand in the market.

他给我讲了讲市场上的供求关系。

(5) in short supply 供应不足，短缺：

Sorry, the umbrella is in short supply at the moment.

很抱歉，雨伞已经卖光了。

2. calculate

(1) *vt*. 计算,核算,估计,推测:

The government has to calculate the likely effects on revenues because of a big drop in the oil price.

政府不得不核算大幅下跌的油价可能对税收造成的影响。

The experts calculate that the market for these computers will expand by 200% in the next three years.

专家们预计,这些计算机的市场在未来的3年将要扩大200%。

The scientists calculated when the spacecraft would reach the moon.

科学家们计算了航天器到达月球的时间。

(2) *vt*. (常用被动形式)计划,打算;使适合:

The new regulations are deliberately calculated to make cheating impossible.

精心制定的新规定有意杜绝欺骗行为。

(3) *vi*. 计算,核算

(4) calculate on/upon 预期,指望:

We calculated on (making) an early start.

我们打算早早出发。

Don't calculate on him agreeing with you.

不要指望他会同意你的意见。

3. accelerate

(1) *vt*. 使加快,使增速:

Those policies accelerated unemployment.

那些政策加速了失业。

(2) *vt*. 促进,使……提早发生:

The government is carrying out a series of economic policies that have accelerated the decline of manufacturing industry.

该政府正在执行一系列促使制造业下滑的经济政策。

(3) *vi*. 加快,增速:

The unemployment rate accelerated.

失业率上升了。

(4) *vi*. 增长,增加:

The car accelerated.

汽车加了速。

✍ 练习答案 Key to written exercises

1. 关键句型练习答案

A See text.

B 1 It *feels* very hot today.

2 This chocolate *seems/tastes* very bitter.

3 You can see from her face that she *doesn't feel* well. (She *looks* unwell.)

4 The price *sounds/seems* about right, but I hope they can offer us a bigger discount.

5 How much did you say? That *sounds/seems* expensive!

2. 难点练习答案

A 1 The adjectives *industrial* and *industrious* are both derived from the noun *industry*, but are completely different in meaning.

Industrial means 'of industry and the people who work in it': *Germany has always been one of the major industrial nations in Europe*.

Industrious means 'hard-working': *If you have ever watched a colony of ants, you will realize how industrious they are.*

2 The verb *supply* means 'provide things to a person for use': *He has been supplying our restaurant with vegetables for years.*

The verb *provide* means 'cause or arrange for someone to have or use': *The course is free but you have to provide your own books.*

3 The adverb *less*, with adjectives and adverbs, means 'not so, not as, to a smaller degree': *I hope the next train will be less crowded than this one.*

The word *lesser* can be used as an adjective or an adverb and means 'not so great or so much as the other (of two) in worth, degree, size, etc.': *This is the lesser of two evils.*

4 The regular verb *bound* means 'move along quickly by jumping or leaping movements': *The dogs bounded across the field after the deer.*

The plural noun *bounds* means 'the furthest limits or edges of something, the limits beyond which it is impossible or undesirable to go': *His greed for power knows no bounds. The pub was out of bounds to the schoolboys.*

5 The irregular verb *bind* (*bound*, *bound*) means 'tie together, especially with rope': *The robbers bound the bank manager's hands together.*

The adjective phrase *bound for* means 'going to or intending to go to': *We boarded a plane that was bound for New York.*

6 The irregular verb *fly* (*flew*, *flown*) means 'control and

guide (an aircraft) in flight': *I'd love to learn to fly a helicopter.*

The regular verb *flow* (*flowed*, *flowed*) means 'move smoothly in a stream': *The river flowed right behind the back door of the farmhouse.*

7 An *idea* is 'a plan, thought, or suggestion for a possible course of action': *Has anyone got a good idea where to go this afternoon?*

An *ideal* is 'a perfect example': *That's my ideal of what a country cottage should be like.*

8 *At least* is an expression used for mentioning a small advantage that makes its disadvantage(s) seem not so bad: *The food wasn't good, but at least it was cheap.*

At last means 'in the end, after a long time': *At last we found out what had really happened.*

B 1 The Moon *could* become...

2 This *might* sound...

3 It takes *far* less energy...

C 1 which 2 which 3 which 4 who 5 who

3. 多项选择题答案

1 c 2 b 3 c 4 a 5 c 6 a

7 b 8 b 9 d 10 c 11 c 12 d

Lesson 36
The cost of government
政府的开支

课文详注 Further notes on the text

1. **If a nation is essentially disunited, it is left to the government to hold it together.**

   it 在此处是先行主语。动词不定式 to hold it together 是该句的真正主语。该动词不定式中的代词 it 所指的是 a nation。leave ... to 把……委托给,交由……来处理,如:

   I left the decision to your judgment.

   我让你根据自己的判断作出决定。

2. **... and reduces correspondingly the amount of economic resources that could be used for developing the country.**

   economic resources 经济实力。that could be used ... 为定语从句,修饰 economic resources。

3. **And it should not be forgotten how small those resources are in a poor and backward country.**

   it 在此处为先行主语,how small those resources are ... 为主语从句,是句子的真正主语。

4. **Where the cost of government is high, resources for development are correspondingly low.**

   句中 Where 引导的是地点状语从句。

5. **This may be illustrated by comparing the position of a nation with that of a private business enterprise.**

   that 指 the position。

6. **... in order to stay in business.**

stay in business 维持营业。

7. **... we are concerned only with one kind of cost ...**

be concerned with 对……感兴趣的,如:

We are more concerned with efficiency than expansion.

在效率和发展之间,我们对效率更感兴趣。

8. **Such administrative overheads in a business are analogous to the cost of government in a nation.**

administrative overheads 行政管理开支。be analogous to/with 和……相似的,和……可比拟的,如:

The two processes are not analogous with each other.

这两种过程彼此不相似。

9. **The administrative overheads of a business are low to the extent that everyone working in the business can be trusted to behave in a way that best promotes the interests of the firm.**

to the extent that ... 达到那样的程度。that 引导的是同位语从句。to the extent 及其同位语从句起到的作用类似于条件状语,意即"如果企业中的每个人都在真诚地为增加企业利润而工作"。in a way that best ... 为方式状语,其中 that 引导的是定语从句,修饰 a way。

10. **If they can each be trusted to take such responsibilities, and to exercise such initiative as falls within their sphere, then...**

as falls within their sphere 中的 as 为关系代词,引导定语从句,修饰名词 initiative,意即"属于他们份内的"。

11. **It will be low because it will be necessary to have only one man looking after each job, without having another man to check upon what he is doing, keep him in line, and report on him to someone else.**

have sb. doing sth. 使某人做某事,其中 doing sth. 作宾语补足

语，如：

We soon have them all laughing.

我们很快就使大伙儿都笑了起来。

without having another ... 为介词短语，作方式状语，修饰 looking after。这里应注意的是，在介词 without 后面的 having another man to check upon what he is doing 中，动词不定式短语 to check upon 作定语，置后，修饰 another man，而非表达"让某人做某事"的 have sb. do sth. 结构。to check upon, keep him in line 以及 report on him to someone else 这 3 个动词不定式为并列成分。check upon 检查。keep sb. in line 使某人规规矩矩。report on sb. 汇报某人的情况。

12. **But if no one can be trusted to act in a loyal and responsible manner towards his job, then the business will require armies of administrators, checkers ...**

act in ... job 为主语补足语。armies of 大批的。

13. **As administrative overheads rise, so the earnings ...; and the business will have less money to distribute as dividends or invest directly ...**

句首 As 引导的是时间状语从句。该句的主句是 so the earnings ...。so 在这里为副词，意思是"因此"。and 连接的虽然是并列句，但是在该句中所表达的是结果。to distribute 与其后的 invest 为并列的动词不定式，作定语，修饰 money。

14. **It is precisely the same with a nation.**

the same with 对……也是同样。

15. **To the extent that the people can be relied upon to behave ..., the government does not require armies of police and civil servants to keep them in order.**

to the extent that 见本课注 9，意即"如果……"。rely on/upon 依靠，信任，如：

You'd better rely on your parents for advice.

你最好依靠你父母亲的指点。

keep ... in order 使……规矩,如:

It is really very difficult for me to keep these naughty children in order.

对我来说,要使这些淘气的孩子们规规矩矩的实在是太难了。

16. ... the government cannot be sure that the actions of the people will be in the interests of the nation; and it will have to watch ...

in the interests of 符合……的利益,如:

in the interests of our organization 为了我们组织的利益

语法 Grammar in use

动名词用法(5)

介词+动名词形式(2)

动词+介词+动名词形式

许多动词在使用时往往需搭配使用相应的介词,从而构成动词+介词结构,如 apologize for(为……道歉)、insist on(坚持)、prevent sb./sth. from(阻止某人/某事……), thank sb. for(为……感谢某人)等,而动名词形式可以用于这类结构的介词之后,有时在该动名词前还可以使用一宾格或所属格来表示该动名词的逻辑主语,如:

I must insist on paying.

我必须坚持付钱。

I must insist on him/his paying.

我一定坚持他付钱。

I've given up smoking.

我已经戒烟了。

但是在使用 to 时应格外小心。因为 to 既可构成动词不定式的一部分,如在 I want to go home(我想回家)中;也可是其后应使用名词或动名词的介词 to,如在 I object to smoking(我反对吸烟)中。下述短语中使用的 to 均为介词:accustom (oneself) to(使〈自己〉习惯于)、be accustomed to(习惯于)、face up to(勇敢地面对)、in addition to(除……之外)、look forward to(期待)、object to(反对)、be reduced to(被缩小为)、resign oneself to(使听从于)、be resigned to(听命于)、resort to(诉诸于)、sink to(降低到)、be used to(习惯于)等,如:

I object to being kept waiting.

我对要我等待感到反感。

I'm used to doing shopping.

我已习惯于购物了。

在介词 to 与其后的动名词之间也可插入作为动名词逻辑主语的宾格或所属格,如:

I object to people/him/his smoking in restaurants.

我反对人们/他在饭店里吸烟。

一些名词和形容词之后也可使用上述的结构形式,如:alternative to(替代)、close/closeness to(接近于)、dedication/dedicated to(忠诚于)、opposition/opposed to(反对)、similarity/similar to(与……相似)等。

词汇学习 Word study

1. forget (forgot, forgotten)

(1) *vt.* 忘记,忘掉:

I am sorry, I've forgotten his name.

对不起，我忘了他的名字。

I forgot to ask him about it.

我忘了问他那件事了。

Don't forget we're going to a concert tonight.

别忘了我们今晚要去听音乐会。

I will never forget meeting you for the first time.

我永远忘不了第一次和你见面的情形。

(2) *vt*. 不要计较，别介意：

I'm sorry I broke your teapot.

真是抱歉，我把你的茶壶打碎了。

Forget it.

别放在心上。

(3) *vi*. 忘记，记不得：

You won't forget to write to me, will you?

你会记着给我写信吧？

No, I won't forget.

忘不了。

(4) *vi*. (about) 忘却，丢开：

Let's forget about our disagreements and be friends again.

让我们忘掉分歧，重新做朋友吧！

(5) forget oneself 失去理智，忘乎所以：

The little boy annoyed him so much that he forgot himself and hit him.

小男孩把他惹急了，使他失去理智动粗打了他。

(6) forget to do sth. 与 forget doing sth. 用法对比

在英语中，短语 forget to do sth. 是指“忘了要做某事”，如：She forgot to phone him.（她忘记给他打电话了。）而短语 forget doing sth. 却是指“忘记了曾经做过或发生过的某件事”，一般出现在否定陈述句中,表示“忘不了”,如:The children will never forget visiting this park.(孩子们永远不会忘记来这个公园玩过。)

2. compare

(1) *vt.* (with)比较,对照:

I compared the copy with the original, but there wasn't much difference.

我把副本同原件进行了比较,没有太大的不同。

(2) *vt.* (to)比作,比拟:

Life is often compared to a voyage.

人生常常被比作旅行。

(3) *vi.* 相比,比得上:

Artificial light cannot compare with daylight for general use.

在日常使用方面,人工照明无法与日光相比。

3. exercise

(1) *n.* (可数/不可数)运动;体操:

Walking and running are my favourite forms of exercise.

散步和跑步是我最喜欢的运动形式。

(2) *n.* (可数)练习(曲);(常用复数)演习:

Please do the translation exercise after class.

请在课后做翻译练习。

Military exercises are being carried out secretly.

正在秘密举行军事演习。

(3) *n.* (不可数)运用,行使:

You can only understand this story by the exercise of imagination.

只有发挥想像力才能明白这个故事。

(4) *vt.* 锻炼,训练:

Please exercise your muscles more regularly.

请更加有规律地训练肌肉。

(5) *vt*. 运用,行使:

Long distance race is a sport that exercises patience.

长跑是一项运用耐力的运动。

(6) *vi*. 运动,锻炼:

I exercise every afternoon.

我每天下午锻炼身体。

练习答案 Key to written exercises

1. 关键句型练习答案

A See text.

B See text.

C See text.

D 1 The book that *best illustrates* what I mean is *A Tale of Two Cities* by Charles Dickens.

2 'Selfish' is the word that *best describes* my uncle: he thinks of no one but himself.

3 The option that *best explains* what the sentence means is option 'A'.

2. 难点练习答案

A 1 *Earnings* (plural noun) is the money which is earned by working: *What are your take-home earnings after tax and other deductions?*

Profits, on the other hand, is the money gained by a trade or business: *Last week the company announced their profits for last year.*

2 The verb *watch*, as used in the text, means 'be careful with or pay attention to': *You'd better watch Smith; I*

think he's a thief.

The verb *follow* means 'move behind in the same direction': *The children followed the teacher out of the room*.

3 The verb *check* means 'test, examine, or mark to see if something is correct, true, in good condition, etc.': *Their bags were checked by security guards as they entered the building. She checked through the letter before sending it*.

The verb *control*, however, means 'have a directing influence over, have power over, rule': *Try to control yourself! The teacher just couldn't control his class. It is extremely difficult for more developing countries to control the growth of population*.

B 1 *Backward* (in *a backward country*) is a derogatory term for 'developing', i.e. a poor country that is trying to become richer and to improve the living conditions of its people.

2 *Backwards* (adverb) means 'in the opposite way to what is usual' or the opposite of 'forwards'.

3 *Backward* (in the phrase *backward children*) means 'behind in development'.

C 1 'We are concerned *only* with one kind of cost.'—The position of *only* here refers to 'one kind of cost'.

2 'We *only* are concerned.'—The position of *only* here implies that only we, and no other people, are concerned.

3 'We are concerned with *only* one kind of cost.'—This is the same as 1 above.

4 'We are concerned with one kind of cost *only*.'—The position of *only* here emphasizes or stresses 'one kind of cost'.

3. 多项选择题答案

1	a	2	c	3	b	4	c	5	c	6	a
7	c	8	c	9	d	10	b	11	a	12	c

Lesson 37

The process of ageing

衰老过程

课文详注 Further notes on the text

1. **..., the human body is at its most vigorous.**

   at its most vigorous 为介词 at + 形容词的最高级结构，表示“处于极点”，如：

   She is still at her best.

   她仍然精力充沛。

   science fiction at its most imaginative 最具想像力的科幻小说

2. **It has yet to reach its full size and strength, and its owner his or her full intelligence; but at this age the likelihood of death is least.**

   It 指 the human body。have yet to 在英语中表示 has/have not yet happened，即“尚未”，如：

   I have yet to meet a man I can trust.

   我尚未遇见一个我能够信任的男人。

   在 its owner his or her full intelligence 中，its owner 后面省略了 has yet to reach。its owner 指 the owner of the human body，该句的意思是“人的智力尚需完善”。

3. **Earlier, we were ...; later, we shall undergo a progressive loss of our vigour and resistance which, though imperceptible at first, will finally become so steep that we can live no longer, however well we look after ourselves, and however well society, and our doctors,**

look after us.

Earlier 指 12 岁以前,later 指 12 岁以后。which 引导的是一个定语从句,该定语从句中又包含了 3 个让步状语从句,即由 though 引导的是一个让步状语从句(该从句中省略了 it is, 这里指 a progressive loss of our vigour and resistance)以及两个由 however 引导的让步状语从句。

4. **This decline in vigour with the passing of time is called ageing.**

in vigour 作定语,修饰名词 decline,指“生命力方面的衰退”。with the passing of time 作定语,修饰 decline in vigour,意即“随着时间的流逝”。

5. **It is one of the most unpleasant discoveries which we all make that we *must* decline in this way, that if we escape wars, accidents and diseases we shall eventually 'die of old age', and that this happens at a rate which differs little from person to person, so that there are heavy odds in favour of our dying between the ages of sixty-five and eighty.**

3个由 that 引导的从句均是 discoveries 的同位语从句,即: that we must ..., that if we escape ..., and that this happens...。第 3 个从句中的 this 指 die of old age。so that 引导的是结果状语从句,修饰其前面的那个主语从句,意即“因此我们最可能死亡的年龄在 65 至 80 之间”。heavy odds 可能性极大。in favour of 作定语,修饰 heavy odds, 意即“有利于”、“赞成”。discoveries 后面的 which 引导一定语从句,修饰 discoveries。

6. **...., a few will live longer—on into a ninth or tenth decade.**

live on 继续活下去。该句中的破折号用以引出强调部分。

7. **But the chances are against it, ..., however lucky and robust we are.**

it 指 live longer。however 引导的是让步状语从句。

8. ...until they are reminded of it.

remind sb. of/about sth. 提醒某人某事，如：

Don't forget to remind her about the concert.

别忘记提醒她音乐会的事。

His secretary reminded him of two appointments.

他的秘书提醒他两个约会的事。

9. We are so familiar with the fact that man ages, that people have for years assumed that the process of losing vigour with time, of becoming more likely to die the older we get, was something self-evident, like the cooling of a hot kettle or the wearing-out of a pair of shoes.

be familiar with 对……熟悉，如：

I'm of course familiar with your work.

我当然了解你的工作。

句子中的第 1 个和第 2 个 that 引导的是两个并列的同位语从句。第 3 个 that 引导的是动词 assumed 的宾语从句。of losing vigour...和 of becoming more ...为并列的定语，修饰 the process。was something self-evident 是 that 引导的宾语从句的谓语部分。介词短语 like the cooling ...shoes 为状语，修饰整个宾语从句。

10. They have also assumed that ... must in the nature of things 'wear out'.

in the nature of things 从物质本质上来说。wear out 磨损，如：

Heavy traffic and variable weather can wear out the surface of a road.

繁忙的交通和变化的天气会损坏路面。

11. Most animals we commonly observe do in fact age as we do, if given the chance to live long enough; ...

we commonly observe 作定语从句，修饰 animals。do 在此用来

表示强调。as we do 为方式状语从句。if 引导的是条件状语，if 后面省略了 they are。

12. **... and mechanical systems like a wound watch, or the sun, do in fact run out of energy in accordance with ...**

do 起强调作用。run out of 耗尽，如：

She ran out of money.

她的钱用完了。

in accordance with 根据，按照，如：

In accordance with her wishes, she was buried in France.

依照她的愿望，她被埋葬在法国。

13. **But these are not analogous to what happens when man ages.**

be analogous to 与……相似，如：

The experience of mystic trance is in a sense analogous to sleep or drunkenness.

被催眠的经历在某种意义上讲与睡眠或喝醉十分相似。

14. **But a watch ..., which wears away by friction.**

wear away 逐渐磨损，逐渐消耗掉，如：

Water can wear away rock after a long time, even though rock is hard.

尽管岩石很坚硬，但久而久之，水能穿石。

by friction 由于摩擦。

15. **We could, at one time, repair ourselves—well enough, at least, to overcome all but the most instantly fatal illnesses and accidents.**

to overcome all but ... 为动词不定式短语，作 well enough 的结果状语。all but 除了，如：

Eventually, all but one of them promised to come to his farewell party.

最后，他们中除一个人以外都答应出席他的告别宴会。

16. **... an illness which at twelve would knock us over, at eighty**

can knock us out, and into our grave.

which at twelve would knock us over 为定语从句,修饰该句的主语 an illness。can knock 作该句的谓语。knock ... out 将……打晕,使……失去知觉;使……病倒,如:

She hit her head on the ceiling and knocked herself out.

她将头撞到天花板上,把自己给撞晕了。

If you carry on working like this, you'll knock yourself out.

如果你继续这么工作,你会使自己得病的。

and into our grave 是跟在动词 knock 之后的,省略了 us,意即"使我们进入坟墓"。

17. **If we could stay as vigorous as we are at twelve, it would take about 700 years for half of us to die, and another 700 for the survivors to be reduced by half again.**

if 引导的是非真实性条件句,所以主句使用的是虚拟结构 would take。因为人是不可能保持 12 岁时的旺盛精力,这只是一种假设。the survivors 指 700 年后活下来的那一半人。reduce by half 减少一半。by half 作动词不定式 to be reduced 的状语。

语法 Grammar in use

动名词用法 (6)

动词之后用动名词还是带 to 的动词不定式的区别 (1)

如前所述,一些动词后既可以跟随动名词也可以跟随带 to 的动词不定式。然而,句子有可能出现 3 种不同的情况:(1) 意义不变;(2) 意义有所变化;(3) 意义不同。

(1) 意义不变

下述动词后既可以使用带 to 的动词不定式,也可以使用动名词,语义没有太大变化或根本无变化:attempt(企图)、begin(开始)、can't bear(无法忍受)、cease(停止)、commence(开始)、continue(继续)、intend(意欲)、omit(省略)、start(开始)等,如:

I can't bear to see/seeing people suffering.

我不忍看人受折磨。

然而,当使用动词 begin、cease、continue 或 start 的进行时形式时,其后通常不使用动名词形式,而使用动词不定式形式,如:

He was beginning to recover when he had another attack.

他正开始恢复时,病又突然发作了。

但是,当该动词后不能使用动词不定式时,即使该动词本身使用的是-ing 形式,其后也可以跟随动名词形式,如:

We were considering catching an earlier train.

我们正考虑赶上较早的一班火车。

若这类动词后使用的是表示状态的动词如 know、understand 等时,状态动词通常不使用其-ing 形式,如:

I soon began to understand what was happening.

我很快开始明白正在发生什么事情。

(2) 意义有所变化

下述动词后既可以使用动名词也可以使用动词不定式形式,但是其意义略有不同。其后使用动名词时,通常表示目前正在进行的活动或一般所具有的行为;其后使用动词不定式时,通常表示特定的未来事件。这些常用动词是:dread(害怕)、hate(厌恶)、like(喜欢)、love(热爱)、prefer(喜欢,宁愿)等,如:

I hate to disturb you.

我很不愿打搅你。(含有"但我却要打搅你"之意)

I hate disturbing you.

我是很不愿打搅你的。(含有"我正在打搅你,我感到抱歉"之意)

I prefer to wait here.

我宁愿在这儿等。(含有"因此如果你不介意,我将等在这儿"之意)

I prefer waiting here.

我宁愿在这儿等着。(含有"我正在这儿等候,我喜欢这么做"之意)

正因为有上述语义的差异,因此在一定的场合其中的某一形式是不可用的,如不能说:

* *I dread thinking what has happened to him.*

(不可用来表达"我害怕去想他出了什么事"之意)

* *Would you like eating out?*

(不可用来表达"你愿意出去吃饭吗?"之意)

* *I prefer to swim to cycle.*

(不可用来表达"我喜欢游泳而不喜欢骑自行车"之意)

如前所述,可以使用动词不定式表达特定的未来事件,而动名词则用来表达正在进行中的活动。状态动词如第 1 例中的动词 think,通常不用动名词形式。因此,在前两个错句中,应当使用动词不定式表达语义。在第 3 例中,虽然在动词 prefer 后既可以用动名词形也可以用动词不定式形式,但用 prefer ... to ... 表达"喜欢……而不喜欢……"时,由于 to 为介词,其后只能使用动名词或名词,而不能使用动词不定式,因此该将句中的动词不定式改为动名词。

词汇学习 Word study

1. differ *vi.*

(1) (from)(不用于进行时)不同,相异,有差别:

My taste in music differs from hers.

我的音乐爱好与她的不同。

The whale differs from the fish.

鲸与鱼不同。

(2) 持不同意见:

His views differ considerably from those of his parents.

他的看法与父母的截然不同。

I differ with my wife sometimes, but we usually agree.

我与妻子有时观点不同,但是通常还是一致的。

2. tend

(1) *vt.* 照管,照料:

Her job is to tend the sick.

她的工作是照料病人。

(2) *vt.* 管理:

His responsibility is to tend a store.

他的责任是管理一家店铺。

(3) *vi.* (on, upon)服侍,招待:

The hostess is now busy tending upon the guests.

那位主妇正忙着招待客人。

(4) *vi.* (to)注意;照料:

She's very selfish and always tends only to her own affairs.

她非常自私,总是只顾自己的事情。

(5) *vi.* (to)趋向,走向:

The economy tends to recover.

经济在逐步复苏。

(6) *vi.* (to)倾向:

I tend to the simple style.

我倾向于简洁的风格。

3. familiar *adj.*

(1) 熟悉的,常见的:

Your name is very familiar to me.
你的名字我很熟悉。
He has become familiar with the street.
他已熟悉这条街道了。

(2)(罕)亲近的,随便的:

She has only two familiar friends.
她只有两个亲近的朋友。
The two managers are having a familiar conversation.
那两位经理正在随便地交谈。

练习答案 Key to written exercises

1. 关键句型练习答案

A 1 the 2 – 3 – 4 the 5 –

B 1 *However* rich you may be, it doesn't mean that you will be happy.

2 Living in the country has a lot of advantages. There are also, *however*, quite a few disadvantages.

C See text.

2. 难点练习答案

A 1 The noun *infant* is a rather formal word, often used in official English, meaning 'a very young child, especially one who has not yet learnt to speak or walk': *There is still an unacceptably high rate of infant mortality in that country.*

Baby is the commonest word to describe 'a very young child, especially one who has not yet learnt to speak or walk': *My memory is terrible: I don't remember anything from the time I was a baby.*

2 *Imperceptible* means 'not noticed because very small or slight': *There was an imperceptible movement in the tall grass and the soldier shot at it.*

Unperceived, on the other hand, means 'not known, observed or understood, or undiscovered': *At first the fraud was unperceived, and only came to light in the annual accounts.*

3 For notes on *alive* and *living*, with examples, see Lesson 26 (p.305).

B 1 *look after* = take care of, be responsible for

2 *Look out!* = Take care! Pay attention! Be careful!

3 *looking forward to* = expecting with pleasure

4 *looks on* = regards, considers

5 *look... up* = find...in a book

6 *looking up* = improving, getting better

7 *look up* = find and visit

8 *look in* = come here, pay a visit

C 1 *run out of* = be completely used up

2 *run in* = brought gradually and carefully into full use

3 *run over* = knocked down and driven over

4 *ran through* = spent fast and wastefully

5 *ran into* = met by chance

6 *ran into* = hit forcefully with a vehicle

D 1 *knock... over..., knock... out* = hit... down..., make...unconscious/go to sleep

2 *knock off* = finish, stop work (at a particular time)

3. 多项选择题答案

1	c	2	a	3	b	4	a	5	c	6	d
7	b	8	c	9	d	10	c	11	b	12	d

Lesson 38

Water and the traveller

水和旅行者

课文详注 Further notes on the text

1. Contamination of water supplies is usually due to poor sanitation close to water sources, ...

due to 归功于,归咎于,如:

Her absence was due to illness.

她缺席是因为生病的缘故。

close to 为定语,修饰 poor sanitation。poor sanitation, sewage disposal ..., leakage of ... 和 contamination with industrial ... 为并列成分。

2. Even if a piped water supply ..., it is not ...

句中 Even if 引导的是一个让步状语从句。

3. Intermittent tap-water supplies should be regarded as particularly suspect.

regard ... as 把……当作,如:

You shouldn't regard him as a friend.

你不应该把他视作朋友。

suspect 在该句中为形容词,意即"令人怀疑的"。

4. Travellers on short trips to areas with water supplies of uncertain quality should avoid drinking tap-water, or ...

on short trips 为介词短语,作定语,修饰 travellers。with water supplies ... 为介词短语,作定语,修饰 areas。avoid doing sth. 避免干某事,如:

She managed to avoid being punished.

她设法避免了受处罚。

5. It is best to keep to hot drinks, bottled or canned drinks of well-known brand names—international standards of water treatment are usually followed at bottling plants.

It 为先行主语,真正的主语是动词不定式短语 to keep to ...。keep to 局限于,保持,如:

She kept to her room.

她一直呆在自己的房间里。

of well-known brand names 为介词短语,作定语,修饰 bottled or canned drinks。破折号后面的部分是对前面的部分所作的进一步的说明。

6. Make sure that all bottles are opened in your presence, and that their rims are clean and dry.

该句为祈使句。in sb.'s presence 为方式状语,意即"当着某人的面"、"当某人在场时",如:

The play will be performed in the presence of the President.

总统将光临观看此剧。

7. Some hotels supply boiled water on request and this can be used for drinking, or for brushing teeth.

on/upon request 若提出要求,如:

Brochures are mailed out on request.

小册子承索即寄。

this 指 boiled water。

8. Portable boiling elements that can boil small quantities of water are useful when the right voltage of electricity is available.

that can boil ... 为定语从句,修饰 portable boiling elements。when the right ... 为条件状语从句。available 可获得的,可利

用的,如:

Portable boiling elements are not always easily available.

便携式热水装置并不总是容易获得的。

9. Ice is only as safe as the water from which it is made, . . .

本句意思为"冰块只是当制造冰块的水安全时才是安全的",from which it is made 为定语从句,修饰 water。

10. Drinks can be cooled by placing them on ice rather than adding ice to them.

by placing them . . . 为方式状语。rather than 宁愿,如:

I prefer walking rather than riding.

我宁愿步行而不愿乘车。

11. . . . , but should not be relied upon to sterilize water.

因为本句使用的是被动语态,因此原来应在主动语态中作宾语补足语的动词不定式 to sterilize water 现改在句子中作主语补足语。

12. . . . , below 20 per cent, its bactericidal action is negligible.

below 20 per cent 为介词短语,作条件状语,意即"如果乙醇浓度低于 20%"。

13. Spirits labelled 95 proof contain only about 47 per cent alcohol.

labelled 95 proof 为过去分词短语,作定语修饰 spirits。

14. Beware of methylated alcohol, which is very poisonous, and should never be added to drinking water.

该句为祈使句。beware of 当心,小心,只用于祈使句,如:

Beware of the dog!

当心有狗!

Beware of pick-pockets.

提防扒手。

which is very poisonous, and . . . 为非限定性定语从句,对

methylated alcohol 作进一步的说明。add to 添加，把……加上，如：

We added this amount to the bill.

我们把这笔数目加在账里了。

15. ..., tap water that is too hot to touch can be left to cool and ...

that is too hot to touch 为定语从句，修饰 tap water。leave sb. to do sth. 让某人做某事，如：

We left them to muddle through on their own.

我们让他们自己去过日子。

16. Those planning a trip to remote areas, or intending to live in countries where drinking water is not readily available, should know about the various possible methods for making water safe.

planning a trip..., or intending to ... 为现在分词短语，作定语，修饰 those。where drinking water ... 为定语从句，修饰 countries。know about/of 知道……情况，如：

We knew about the incident.

我们知道这件事的情况。

for making water safe 为介词短语，作定语，修饰 methods。

语法 Grammar in use

动名词用法 (7)

1. 动词之后用动名词还是带 to 的动词不定式的区别 (2)

某些动词后，虽然既可以使用动词不定式也可以使用动名词形式，但表达的语义完全不同。常用的这类动词有：remember、forget、try、stop、go on、regret 等。在这几个动词中，remember、forget、regret 后的动词不定式通常用来指未来的动作，而其后的动名词通常用来指已做过的动作，如：

I remembered to post the letters.
我想起了要去发那些信。
I remembered posting/having posted the letters.
我想起了我已发了那些信。

I forgot to ask Tom about it.
我忘记去问汤姆那件事了。
I forgot asking Tom about it.
我忘记已问过汤姆那件事了。

I regret to inform him that his account is overdrawn.
我遗憾地通知他他的账户已透支了。
I regret informing him that his account is overdrawn.
我为通知他他的账户已透支了而感到遗憾。

而动词 try 后使用动词不定式通常指“努力”,使用动名词时通常指“试验”、“实验”。动词 stop 后使用动词不定式通常指停止前一个动作而去做后一个动作,使用动名词时通常用来说明动宾关系。短语动词 go on 后使用动词不定式通常指做不同的事,使用动名词时通常指继续做同一件事,如:

You really must try to overcome your shyness.
你确实需要努力克服你的腼腆。
Trying holding your breath to stop sneezing.
试着屏住呼吸以止住打喷嚏。

On the way to the station, I stopped to buy a paper.
在去火车站的路上,我停下来买了一份报纸。
When he told us the story, we just couldn't stop laughing.
他给我们讲完故事后,我们不禁都笑个不停。

After approving the agenda, we went on to discuss finance.
通过了议事日程后,我们接着讨论财政问题。
We went on talking till after midnight.
我们继续谈话,一直到午夜以后。

2. 形容词/名词 + 动词不定式或 + 介词 + 动名词

一些形容词/名词之后既可以使用动词不定式形式也可以使用介词 + 动名词形式,有时它们在语义上没有太大的区别,但是有时则在语义上有区别,如:

I'm sorry (not) to mention it.
I'm sorry for (not) mentioning it.
(未)提及它我很抱歉。

I couldn't resist the opportunity to greet such a great actor.
I couldn't resist the opportunity of greeting such a great actor.
我不能放过这个向一位如此伟大的演员致意的机会。

I'm interested to hear your opinion.
我想听听你的意见。(表明将要做的动作)
I'm interested in emigrating to Canada.
我对移居加拿大感兴趣。(表明可能要发生的动作)

I'm sorry to interrupt.
对不起,我要打断你一下。(表明将要做的动作)
I'm sorry for interrupting.
对不起,打扰了。(表明已经发生的动作)

词汇学习 Word study

1. treat *vt.*

(1) 对待,看待,把……看作,处理:

Don't treat me as a child.

别把我当小孩对待。

You shouldn't treat it as a joke.

你不应当把它当作笑话。

(2) 医治,治疗:

The doctor is now treating the children for influenza.

那位大夫正在给孩子们进行流感治疗。

2. add

(1) *vt.* 增加,添加,附加:

Add a few more names to the list.

在名单上再加上几个名字。

Would you like to add anything to what I've said, John?

你还想对我所说的补充些什么吗,约翰?

(2) *vt.* 把……加起来,计算……的总和:

Add 6 to 4 and you get 10.

6 加 4 得 10。

(3) *vt.* 进一步说,又说:

Almost as an afterthought, he added that they were very pleased with the result.

就像又想起了什么,他接着说他们对结果非常满意。

(4) *vi.* 累积而成,加在一起:

Their remarks added together to build up the fact that she was innocent.

把他们的话综合起来,构成一个事实,即她是无辜的。

(5) add to 增加:

The rise in electricity bill has added to our difficulties.

电费的增加加重了我们的困难。

(6) add up(不用于进行时)言之有理,说得通:

The facts just don't add up.

这些事实硬是碰不到一块儿。

(7) add up to(不用于进行时)总计达;总括起来意味着:

What do all the arguments add up to?

所有的论据到底说明了什么?

3. beware

(1) *vi.*(用于祈使句或动词不定式中)当心,小心:

Beware of thieves!

当心小偷!

She was told to beware.

她被告知要小心。

(2) *vt.* 注意,提防:

Beware how you handle this dangerous substance.

要小心该如何处置这种危险物质。

练习答案 Key to written exercises

1. 关键句型练习答案

A 1 Drinking tap-water should be avoided.

2 Well-known brand names of bottled drinks should be preferred.

3 All bottles should be opened in your presence.

4 Boiled water should be requested in hotels.

5 Water should be boiled before drinking/being drunk.

B 1 Tap water shouldn't be drunk.

2 Bottles of water that haven't been opened in your presence shouldn't be accepted.

3 Ice shouldn't be put in drinks.

4 Alcohol shouldn't be relied on to sterilize water.

5 Methylated alcohol shouldn't be added to drinking water.

2. 难点练习答案

A 1 The word *drinking* here is a noun.

2 The phrase *bottling plants* here is a compound noun (i.e. plants where bottling takes place).

3 The phrase *drinking water* here is a compound noun (i.e. water for drinking).

4 The word *planning* here is a present participle (*Those planning*... = Those who are planning...).

5 The word *making* here is a noun.

6 The word *planning* here is again a present participle.

B 1 The word *regarded* here is a past participle.

2 The words *bottled* and *canned* here are adjectives.

3 The word *carbonated* here is an adjective.

4 The word *opened* here is a past participle.

5 The word *cooled* here is a past participle.

6 The word *labelled* here is a past participle, the rest of the passive construction (*which have been*) has been deleted.

3. 多项选择题答案

1	c	2	a	3	a	4	b	5	b	6	a
7	c	8	b	9	d	10	d	11	a	12	b

Lesson 39
What every writer wants
作家之所需

课文详注 Further notes on the text

1. **..., but those I have known, and whom I respect, confess at once that they have little idea where they are going when they first set pen to paper.**

   I have known, and whom I respect 为定语从句。I have known 前面省略了关系代词 whom。where they are going 为 idea 的同位语从句,意即"他们要写什么以及怎么写"。when they first set pen to paper 为时间状语从句。set pen to paper 开始写作。

2. **They have a character, perhaps two; they are in that condition of eager discomfort which passes for inspiration; all admit radical changes of destination once the journey has begun; ...**

   two 指 two characters。which passes for inspiration 为定语从句,修饰 that condition of eager discomfort。pass for/as 被认为,被错当作,但常指蒙骗、假冒,如:

   He can pass for/as a Frenchman.

   他会被错当作一个法国人。

   all 指所有的作家。admit sth. to sb. 向某人承认某事,如:

   The accused admitted his guilt to the police.

   被告向警察承认有罪。

   once 为连词,引导条件状语从句。该句采用比喻的手法,将写作过程比作旅行。

3. **...one, to my certain knowledge, ...**

one 指某作家。to my certain knowledge 为插入语,意即"就我所知"。

4. **I never heard of anyone making a 'skeleton', as we were taught at school.**

making a 'skeleton'为现在分词短语,作定语,修饰 anyone,意即"列提纲的"。as we were taught at school 中的 as 为关系代词,引导一个非限定性定语从句,意即"就像我们在学校学的那样"。

5. **..., the writer comes to discern things in his material which were not consciously in his mind when he began.**

come to do sth. 开始做某事,如:

They finally came to consider me a friend.

他们终于把我看作朋友了。

discern 领悟,辨明,如:

She could discern a faint light ahead in the forest.

她能看到前方森林里隐隐约约的灯光。

which 引导的是定语从句,修饰 material。

6. **This organic process, often leading to moments of extraordinary self-discovery, is of an indescribable fascination.**

This organic process 指前句中提到的 the breaking and remaking, the timing 等写作过程。often leading to ... 为非限定性定语从句,修饰 This organic process。be of 具有,如:

This book is of great importance.

这本书非常重要。

7. **A blurred image appears; he adds a brushstroke and another, and it is gone; but something was there, ...**

it 指 a blurred image。

8. **Sometimes the yeast within a writer outlives a book he has**

written.

outlive **活过,活得比……长,如:**

She outlived all her old classmates.

她比她所有的老同学都活得长。

该处表示"书写完后还激动不已"。

9. **... who read nothing but their own books; like adolescents they stand before the mirror, and still cannot fathom the exact outline of the vision before them.**

nothing but 仅,只,如:

I could see nothing but corn everywhere I looked.

我到处看到的只是玉米。

like adolescents 作状语,修饰 stand。该句中将其置于主语前面,用以起强调作用。意即"他们如同少年,站在镜前,不能辨认出自身的真面目"。此句出自古希腊的一则神话:有一漂亮少年,他热恋上了水中自身的影像,最后憔悴而死,化为水仙花。

10. **..., winkling out hidden meanings, super-imposing new ones, begging response from those around them.**

句子中的 3 个现在分词短语均作状语,表示伴随状况,修饰 talk about。new ones 指 new meanings。those around them 指他们周围的人。

11. **Of course a writer doing this is misunderstood: he might as well try to explain a crime or a love affair.**

doing this 为定语,修饰 a writer,意即"这么做的作家"。may/might as well do 还是干……为好。

12. **This temptation to cover the distance between himself and the reader, to study his image in the sight of those who do not know him, can be his undoing: he has begun to write to please.**

to cover ... 和 to study ... 这两个动词不定式短语均作定语，修饰主语 This temptation。句子的谓语部分是 can be his undoing，意即“会是他毁灭的原因”。冒号后面的部分是说明 undoing 的原因。in the sight of 从……角度来看。

13. **A young English writer made the pertinent observation a year or two back that the talent goes into the first draft, and the art into the drafts that follow.**

a year or two back 一两年前。that the talent goes into ... 是 observation 的同位语从句。the art 和 into 之间省略了动词 goes。that follow 为定语从句，修饰 drafts。

14. **For this reason also the writer, ..., no judgment from outside which can replace the judgment from within.**

also 为副词，通常置于主语的后面，但是该句的主语后面有插入语，故将 also 提前。outside 为名词，意即“局外人”。which 引导的是定语从句，修饰 judgment from outside。定语从句中的 within 也是名词，意即“内心”。

15. **A writer makes order out of the anarchy of his heart; he submits himself to a more ruthless discipline ...**

make order 理出头绪。submit oneself to 使自己屈从于，如：

We submitted ourselves to their wishes.

我们使自己屈从于他们的愿望。

16. **..., and when he flirts with fame, he is taking time off from living with himself, from the search for what his world contains at its inmost point.**

flirt with 不当回事，如：

She flirted with the idea of singing professionally.

她没把从事专业演唱的想法当回事儿。

take time off from 暂停。

语法 Grammar in use

先行主语和先行宾语 it 的用法 (1)

作先行主语的 it

在英语中,出现下述情况时,常常使用 it 作先行主语:

(1) 当主语是动词不定式时,通常将其置于句子的尾部,而将 it 置于主语的位置,如:

It's nice to talk to you.

同你谈话很有意思。(较 *To talk to you is nice* 更为自然)

再如:

It's important to book in advance.

提前订票很重要。

It's my ambition to run a marathon.

我的志向是跑一次马拉松。

It upsets me to hear people arguing all the time.

听到人们总是争吵使我很不安。

(2) 当主语是一名词性从句时,通常将其置于句子的尾部,而将 it 置于主语的位置,如:

It's probable that we'll be a little late.

很可能我们有点儿迟了。

It doesn't interest me what you think.

你怎么想我不感兴趣。

It's surprising how many unhappy marriages there are.

使人吃惊的是有那么多起不幸的婚姻。

It seems that he forgot to buy the tickets.

他好像忘了买票。

(3) 当主语是一动名词结构时,通常将其置于句子的尾部,而将 it 置于主语的位置,如:

It was nice seeing you.

见到你很高兴。

It's worth going to London if you have the time.

如果你有时间，去趟伦敦是值得的。

It's no use trying to explain—I'm not interested.

想解释也没有用——我不感兴趣。

It surprised me your not remembering my name.

你没记住我的名字使我感到吃惊。

(4) 用 it takes ... + 动词不定式结构表达“做某事花费多长时间”时，如：

It took me months to get to know her.

花了几个月的时间我才了解了她。

How long does it take to get to London from here?

从这儿到伦敦要用多长时间？

(5) 用 it 开头的且含 if、as if 和 as though 引导的从句，如：

It looks as if we're going to have trouble with Ann again.

好像我们又要同安有麻烦了。

It will be a pity if we have to ask her to leave.

如果我们不得不要她离开，那将是令人遗憾的事。

But it looks as though we may have to.

但是好像我们只能那样做。

(6) 在对句子的某一部分进行强调的分裂句中，将 it 作先行主语，比较：

It was my aunt who took Peter to London yesterday, not my mother.

是我姑妈昨天带彼特去了伦敦，而不是我妈。

It was Peter that my aunt took to London yesterday, not Lucy.

我姑妈昨天带着去伦敦的是彼特，而不是露茜。

(7) 在某些用被动语态表达的动词结构中，这些用被动形式表示的动词后通常为名词性从句，如：

It was thought that she was a spy.

人们认为她是个间谍。

It is said that his company is in trouble.

据说他的公司陷入了困境。

词汇学习 Word study

1. confess

(1) *vt.* 认罪，交代，供认，承认：

He confessed his guilt to the police.

他向警察承认自己有罪。

He confessed (that) he was the killer.

他供认自己就是凶手。

I must confess that I haven't finished my homework.

我得承认我还没有完成作业。

(2) *vi.* (to)承认，认错，坦白：

He confessed to the murder.

他对谋杀供认不讳。

2. replace *vt.*

(1) 把……放回(原处)：

Please replace the magazines after reading.

阅后请把杂志放回原处。

(2) 取代，以……代替：

English has replaced Russian as the first foreign language in this country.

英语已代替了俄语，成为这个国家的第一外语。

3. submit (submitted) *vt.*

(1) 屈服，服从，忍受：

We submitted ourselves to their wishes.

我们屈从于他们的意愿。

(2) 呈送,提请,提出:

I tried my best to submit the report to the manager yesterday.

我昨天尽了最大努力将那份报告呈递给了经理。

(3) 申述,建议,认为:

I submit that he is mistaken.

我认为他错了。

I submit he should provide complete documentation of his complaint.

我认为他应该提供完整的申诉书。

练习答案 Key to written exercises

1. 关键句型练习答案

A See text.

B 1 He had *little expectation* of passing the exam.

2 They seem to have *little appreciation* of the good things in life.

3 There has been *little improvement* in the school since I left over ten years ago.

C 1 This organic process, *often leading* to moments...

2 I have often heard of writers *reading* nothing but...

3 A writer *doing* this is misunderstood.

D 1 There's no point in trying to persuade him: you *might as well* shout at the moon.

2 If you've got nothing better to do, you *may as well* mend that electric lamp.

E 1 We went to Scotland for a short holiday a month or so *back*.

2 I was in London a little while *back* when I met a very old friend of mine from university.

2. 难点练习答案

A 1 A *destination* is 'a place to which someone is going or to which something is sent, especially at the end of a long journey': *The parcel was unfortunately sent to the wrong destination*.

Destiny is another word for 'fate, what must happen and cannot be changed or controlled': *It was the great man's destiny to lead his country to freedom*.

2 The adjective *indescribable* means 'impossible to describe, either because extremely good or extremely bad, or because description is too difficult to attempt': *The scene of devastation after the earthquake was almost indescribable*.

Undescribed, on the other hand, simply means 'not described': *The final meeting between the boy and his long-lost father was left undescribed*.

3 The verb *capture* means 'take a person (or animal) prisoner': *They managed to capture the tiger alive so that they could treat it*.

The verb *arrest* means 'seize by the power of the law': *The man was arrested on suspicion of murder and taken to the nearest police station*.

4 *Misunderstood* means 'understood wrongly': *She misunderstood what I said and went on Saturday, not Sunday*.

Not understood: *The new regulations are clearly not understood by all the workers, so I want to explain them again.*

5 The words *draft* and *draught* are pronounced in exactly the same way: (/drɑːft/).

A *draft* is 'the first rough and incomplete form of something written, drawn or planned': *I've made a first draft of my speech for Friday, but it still needs a lot of work.*

A *draught* is 'a current of cold air flowing through a room': *You'll catch cold if you sit in a draught.* (This is also spelt *draft* in American English.)

6 The word *judgment* (also *judgement*) is used to describe 'an opinion or an official decision given by a judge or a court of law': *In my judgment, we should accept the employer's offer. After four days, he passed judgment on the man.*

Criticism, on the other hand, is 'unfavourable judgment or expression of disapproval': *The new road scheme has come in for (= received) a lot of criticism.*

B 1 Literally, a *brushstroke* is the stroke of the brush while you are painting (artistic or decorating).

2 Literally, *yeast* is 'a form of very small plant life that is used for producing alcohol in beer and wine and for making bread light and soft'.

3 Literally, the verb *fathom* means 'get at the true meaning of, come to understand'.

4 Literally, the verb *flirt with* means 'behave with a member of the opposite sex in a way that attracts interest

and attention'.

3. 多项选择题答案

1	b	2	c	3	a	4	d	5	a	6	b
7	d	8	d	9	b	10	d	11	b	12	c

Lesson 40
Waves
海浪

课文详注 Further notes on the text

1. **Waves are the children of the struggle between ocean and atmosphere, the ongoing signatures of infinity.**
the ongoing signatures of infinity 是 waves 的同位语，对 waves 作进一步的说明。
2. **..., awakening it to flow, to movement, to rhythm, to life.**
awakening it to flow, ... life 为现在分词短语，作状语，表示伴随状况。it 指 the atmosphere of the earth。短语中的 3 个由介词 to 引导的介词短语为并列成分。awaken ... to ... 使……意识到，使……醒来。该句中采用拟人手法，将 the atmosphere of the earth 视作有生命的物体，阳光使它流动，产生节奏，获得生命。
3. **The wind then speaks the message of the sun to the sea and the sea transmits it on through waves—an ancient, exquisite, powerful message.**
该句通过使用 speaks the message of the sun 和 transmits it on through waves 这类的词语，将风和海洋都赋予了生命，使文章更为生动形象。speak ... to 向……传递。transmit ... on 继续传送。破折号后面的部分是 it 的同位语，it 指 the message。
4. **The basic features include a crest (the highest point of the wave), a trough (...), ...and a period (which is the time it takes a wave crest to travel one wave length).**

该句中各括号部分是对该括号前的名词的具体说明。to travel one wave length 作动词 takes 的宾语 a wave crest 的补足语。

5. **Although an ocean wave gives the impression of a wall of water moving in your direction, in actuality waves move through the water leaving the water about where it was.**

Although 引导让步状语从句。give the impression of 给人……印象。moving in your direction 为现在分词短语,作定语,修饰 a wall of water。in actuality 为介词短语,作状语。leaving the water about where it was 为现在分词短语,作伴随状语。

6. **..., the ocean and everything on it would be racing in to the shore with obviously catastrophic results.**

it 指 ocean。race in to 冲向,如:

The angry crowd raced in to the city hall.

愤怒的人群冲进市政厅。

7. **An ocean wave passing through deep water causes a particle on the surface to move in a roughly circular orbit, drawing the particle first towards the advancing wave, then up into the wave, then forward with it and then—as the wave leaves the particles behind—back to its starting point again.**

passing through deep water 为现在分词短语,作定语,修饰 wave。on the surface 为介词短语,作定语,修饰 particle。to move in a roughly circular orbit 为动词不定式短语,作宾语 a particle 的补足语。现在分词 drawing 引导的短语作状语,表示伴随状况。该分词短语中分别用 towards、up into、forward with 和 back to 等介词和副词引导并列成分,生动地将微粒在海浪作用下的运动规律完整地描述出来。破折号后面的部分为时间状语从句,对波浪的运动作具体的说明。

8. **From both maturity to death, a wave is subject to the same**

laws as any other 'living' thing.

From both maturity to death 为介词短语,作时间状语。作者在文中一直采用拟人的手法。此处也不例外。将波浪的运动过程比作"从成熟到死亡"。

be subject to 受……的支配,服从于,如:

We are subject to the rules and regulations in effect.

我们遵守各项已生效的规章制度。

the same ... as 与……相同的,如:

I want a shirt that's the same as the one in the window.

我想买一件和橱窗里那件一样的衬衫。

living 加引号表示这是一种比喻的用法,因为 wave 本身是没有生命的。

9. **For a time it assumes a miraculous individuality that, in the end, is reasorbed into the great ocean of life.**

for a time 一度,曾经。assume 装做,好像是,如:

He assumed a humble manner.

他装出一副谦卑的样子。

that 引导一定语从句,修饰 a miraculous individuality。absorb into 把……吞并,把……融入,如:

The small firms were absorbed into large cartels.

小公司被并入大的联合企业。

All the houses were absorbed into the flood.

所有的房屋都被洪水吞没了。

10. **Once waves have been generated, gravity is the force that drives them in a continual attempt to restore the ocean surface to a flat plain.**

Once waves have been generated 为时间状语,意即"一旦波浪形成"。that 引导的是定语从句。in a continual attempt 作方式状语,意即"持续不断地"。to restore the ocean surface to a flat plain 为动词不定式，作目的状语。restore ... to ... 把……归还，使……复职，使……复原，如：

She was restored to her former position.

她被复职了。

The stolen goods must be restored to the owners.

被盗物品必须归还给失主。

语法 Grammar in use

先行主语和先行宾语 it 的用法 (2)

作先行宾语的 it

在英语中，出现下述情况时，常常使用 it 作先行宾语：

(1) 当动词的宾语为一带有形容词或名词补足语的动词不定式或名词性从句时，如：

I find it difficult to talk to you.

我感到很难同你谈话。

My blister made it a problem to walk.

我脚上的水泡使我走路成了问题。

I thought it strange that she hadn't written.

她没有来信，我觉得很奇怪。

George made it clear what he wanted.

乔治明白地表示了他想要什么。

注意，当没有作补足语的形容词或名词时，通常不使用这种结构，如：

I cannot bear to see people crying.

我不能忍受看人们哭。(不说：* *I cannot bear it to see ...*)

I remember that we were very happy.

我记得我们非常高兴。(不说：* *I remember it that ...*)

(2) 当动词的宾语为一带有补足语的动名词结构时，如：

I find it interesting talking to you.

我觉得同你谈话有意思。

(3) 在 would appreciate 后代替作宾语的 if 从句,如:

I would appreciate it if you would keep me informed.

如果你随时让我知道情况,我会很感激的。

(4) 在 owe it to sb. to do sth. 和 leave it to sb. to do sth. 结构中代替动词不定式,如:

We owe it to society to make our country a better place.

把国家建设得更美好是我们对社会应尽的责任。

I'll leave it to you to decide.

我让你去决定吧。

词汇学习 Word study

1. excite *vt.*

(1) 使兴奋,使激动:

The news so excited me that I could not sleep.

这消息让我激动得睡不着觉。

(2) 引起,激起:

The professor's lecture excited our interest.

教授的讲座引起了我们的兴趣。

2. awake (awoke/awaked, awoken/awaked)

(1) *vt.* 唤醒,使醒来:

The noise awoke them all.

那响声把他们都吵醒了。

(2) *vt.* 唤起,引起,勾起:

The old photo awoke her some bad experiences.

那张旧照片勾起她一些不快的经历。

(3) *vi.* 醒,醒来:

He awoke only to find himself alone.

当他醒来时发现只有他孑身一人。

(4) *vi.* (to) 认识到,意识到:

They awoke to the danger of the situation too late to do anything about it.

当他们意识到形势的危险性时已经为时太晚了。

(5) *adj.* (作补足语)醒着的:

She lay awake for hours thinking about him.

她醒着躺了几个小时,思念着他。

(6) *adj.* (to) 意识到的,认识到的:

The government is fully awake to the seriousness of the situation.

政府已充分认识到形势的严重性。

3. subject

(1) *n.* /ˈsʌbdʒikt/ (可数) 题目,主题:

He raised a subject for discussion.

他提出一个讨论的主题。

(2) *n.* /ˈsʌbdʒikt/ 科目,学科:

Which subjects are you taking this semester?

你这学期上哪些课程?

(3) *n.* /ˈsʌbdʒikt/ 主语:

Could you tell me the subject of the sentence?

你能告诉我这个句子的主语吗?

(4) *adj.* /ˈsʌbdʒikt/ (to)隶属的,受支配的:

We are also subject to the rules and regulations.

我们也受制度和法规的约束。

(5) *adj.* /ˈsʌbdʒikt/ (to)易受(伤害)的,常遭……的:

The region is subject to earthquake.

这个地区经常发生地震。

(6) *vt*. /səb'dʒekt/ 使隶属,使服从:

The tribe is subjected by another race.

这个部落受另外一个种族的控制。

(7) *vt*. /səb'dʒekt/ 使遭受,使受到:

The workers subjected the metal to intense heat.

工人们使该金属受高温的灼烧。

(8) subject to 使遭受,使经受:

The project is subject to his approval.

这个项目需要经过他的同意。

练习答案 Key to written exercises

1. 关键句型练习答案

A See text.

B See text.

2. 难点练习答案

A Words of foreign origin in English (especially from Greek and Latin) can create problems when we come to form plurals. There is a natural tendency to make all nouns conform to the regular rules for the pronunciation and spelling of English plurals. However, many retain their foreign plurals. These nouns can be put into three main groups.

- nouns of foreign origin with anglicized plurals: *album—albums*, *genius—geniuses*
- nouns with both foreign and anglicized plurals: *cactus—cacti/cactuses*, *antenna—antennae/antennas*, *index—indices/indexes*, *automaton—automata/automatons*
- nouns with foreign plurals only: *phenomenon—phenomena*,

alumus—alumni, *stratum—strata*, *analysis—analyses*

index—indices/indexes

automaton—automata/automatons

appendix—appendices

alumnus—alumni

stratum—strata

analysis—analyses

criterion—criteria

B 1 the others 2 The others 3 The other

4 others 5 other

C excite—excitement live—life move—movement

generate—generation restore—restoration

3. 多项选择题答案

1 d 2 c 3 d 4 a 5 c 6 a

7 d 8 d 9 d 10 a 11 d 12 b

Lesson 41
Training elephants
训练大象

课文详注 Further notes on the text

1. **..., which we may call respectively the tough and the gentle.**
which 引导的是非限定性定语从句,修饰 techniques。the tough 和 the gentle 后面省略了 techniques。

2. **The former method simply consists of setting an elephant to work and beating him until he does what is expected of him.**
The former method 指 the tough technique。consist of 包括,由……组成,如:

    Our state consists of thirty counties.
    我们州由 30 个县组成。

    set sb. to do sth. 使某人做某事,如:

    She set them to write reports.
    她让他们写报告。

    until 引导的是时间状语从句,意即"直到它做人们期望它做的事为止"。expect sth. of/from sb. 期待某人某事物,如:

    We expected more of/from him.
    我们对他有更大的期待。

3. **Apart from any moral considerations this is a stupid method of training, for it produces a resentful animal who at a later stage may well turn man-killer.**
apart from 除……以外,且不说,如:

    It's a good piece of work, apart from a few faults.

除了几个错误之外，这是一件很不错的作品。

Apart from being too large, this dress just doesn't suit me.

除了太大之外，这件礼裙对我就是不合适。

for 引导的是原因状语从句。who 引导的是定语从句，修饰 a resentful animal。at a later stage 在以后的某个阶段。may well 很可能。turn 在该句中的意思是“成为”，作系动词，其后可以跟名词，但该名词前不用冠词，如：

He had turned traitor and told the police where to find his fellow gang members.

他成了叛徒，告诉警察在哪儿能找到他的同伙。

4. ... is to assign to the animal a single mahout who ...

assign sth. to sb./assign sb. sth. 给某人分派某物，给某人指定某物，如：

They assigned a very difficult mission to us./ They assigned us a very difficult mission.

他们给我们分配了一项非常困难的任务。

5. ... when by some unavoidable circumstance they have been deprived of their own trainer.

by some unavoidable circumstance 由于某些不可避免的情况。deprive sb. of sth. 夺去某人某物，剥夺某人某物，如：

She thought she had been deprived of everything.

她认为她被剥夺了一切。

6. ... be taken with a grain of salt, but they do underline the general principle that the relationship ...

take sth. with a grain of salt 对某事采取保留的态度。but they do underline ... 中的助动词 do 起强调作用。that 引导的是 principle 的同位语从句。

7. ..., for it is then almost ready to undertake heavy work and

can begin to earn its keep straight away.

for 引导的是原因状语从句。earn one's keep 挣得某人的生活费，意即"小象能很快地挣回饲养它的花费"。straight away 立即，马上。

8. **..., and a very firm hand must be employed in the early stages.**

a very firm hand 一个强有力的人。hand 可以指"工人"，也可以指"专业人员"、"行家"，如：a hired hand(一个雇工)，an old hand at sth.(处理某事的能手)。

9. **The captive elephant, still roped to a tree, plunges and screams every time a man approaches, and for several days will probably refuse all food through anger and fear.**

still roped to a tree 为过去分词短语，作定语，修饰 The captive elephant。plunges and screams 和 will probably refuse 为该句的并列谓语。every time 在这里为连词，引导时间状语从句，等于 whenever。through anger and fear 为状语，表示原因，意即"因为愤怒和恐惧"。

10. **Sometimes a tame elephant is tethered nearby to give the wild one confidence, and in most cases the captive gradually quietens down and begins to accept its food.**

to give the wild one confidence 作目的状语。the wild one 指尚未被驯服的象。in most cases 在大多数情况下。the captive 被捕获的大象。quieten down 安静下来。

11. **The next stage is to get the elephant to the training establishment, a ticklish business which is achieved with the aid of two tame elephants roped to the captive on either side.**

get sb. to some place 将某人送到某处，如：

We'd better get him to a hospital.

我们最好把他送到一所医院去。

the training establishment 训练场所。a ticklish business ...是 to get the elephant to the training establishment 的同位语。which is achieved ...为定语从句,修饰 a ticklish business。with the aid of 在……帮助下,如:

With the aid of the PLA soldiers, the people in the flooded area soon rebuilt their houses.

在解放军的帮助下,水灾地区的人们很快就重新建起了房子。

roped to the captive on either side 为过去分词短语,作定语,修饰 two tame elephants。

12. ..., it is customary for the new arrival to be placed between ...

it 为先行主语,真正的主语是 for the new arrival to be placed ...。

13. It is then left completely undisturbed with plenty of food and water so that it ... and see that nothing particularly alarming ...

It 指新来的大象。leave sb. with sth. 把某物留给某人,如:

They left the children with her mother.

他们把孩子们留给她母亲照看。

completely undisturbed 作表语。so that 引导的是目的状语从句。particularly alarming 作 nothing 的定语。

14. The trainer stands ... holding a long stick with a sharp metal point.

holding a long stick ...为分词短语,作方式状语。with a sharp metal point 为定语,修饰 a long stick。

15. Two assistants, mounted on tame elephants, ..., while others rub their hands over his skin to the accompaniment of a monotonous and soothing chant.

mounted on tame elephants 作定语,修饰 Two assistants。others 指其他的驯象助手。his 指大象的。to the accompaniment of a monotonous and soothing chant 伴随着单调并且起镇定作用的歌声。

16. This is supposed to induce pleasurable sensations in the elephant, and its effects ...

This is supposed 据说。This 指前句中提到的"其他驯象助手的抚摸和单调的歌声"。induce ... in ... 使……产生……,如:

The unsuccessful job interview induced a sense of failure in him.

不成功的求职面试使他产生了失败的感觉。

its 所指与句首的 This 相同。

17. The elephant is not immediately susceptible to ...

be susceptible to 对……敏感的,如:

She is susceptible to cold.

她对寒冷非常敏感。

18. These movements ...

These movements 指象鼻子猛烈地向各个方向甩动。

语法 Grammar in use

修辞疑问句的使用

疑问句并非总是用来征询信息,有时仅仅被用来唤起对某事的注意。因此,这样的疑问句形式并不要求回答。这样使用的疑问句被称作"修辞疑问句",如:

Do you know what time it is?

你知道几点了吗?

Who's a lovely baby?

谁是那个可爱的小家伙呀?

I can't find my coat.
我找不到我的外衣了。
What's this, then?
那么这是什么?

当上述疑问句作为修辞疑问句使用时,并不要求回答,而往往根据语境分别表达出诸如“你已经迟到啦”、“你就是那个可爱的小家伙呀”和“就在这儿嘛,真笨”这样的含义。修辞疑问句还经常用来引起对一否定情况即答案显而易见是否定的情况的注意,如:

What's the use of asking her?
问她有什么用?(即“问她也没用”之意)

How do you expect me to find milk on a Sunday night? Where am I going to find a shop open?
你怎么能指望我在星期天夜里搞到牛奶呢?我在哪儿去找一家开门的商店呀?(即“你指望我在星期天夜里搞到牛奶是没道理的:哪家商店也不会开门的”之意)

此外,还有一种由 Why/How should? 形式的不要求回答的疑问句。这通常用于拒绝某一建议、要求和指示,如:

Ann's very unhappy.
安很不痛快。
Why should I care?
关我什么事儿?

Could your wife help us in the office tomorrow?
你妻子明天能到办公室帮帮我们忙吗?
Why should she? She doesn't work for you.
她凭什么?她又不为你干活。

How should I know?
我凭什么要知道?

还有一种暗示肯定情况而无需回答的一般否定疑问句也属于此

类，如：

Haven't I done enough for you?

我给你干得还不够多吗？（即"我给你干得已足够了"之意）

Didn't I tell you it would rain?

我没跟你说要下雨吗？（即"我告诉过你要下雨的"之意）

Don't touch that!
别摸那东西！
Why shouldn't I?
我凭什么不摸？（即"我完全有权利摸它"之意）

词汇学习 Word study

1. apart *adv.*

(1) 分开，分离：

The boxers stood apart, waiting for the signal to start fighting.

拳击手分开站立，等候比赛开始的信号。

The two sides in the dispute are still a long way apart and it is unlikely that any agreement will be reached.

争论双方之间还有很大的距离，达成协议的可能性微乎其微。

He took the clock apart to repair it.

他把那只钟拆开修理。

(2) apart from

1) 除……以外(别无)，不仅

Apart from being too large, it just doesn't suit me.

除了太大外，它也不适合我。

2) 除……之外(尚)：

It is, apart from a few slight faults, a good piece of work.

除了几处小毛病外，这活儿还干得不错。

2. assign *vt.*

(1) 分配，布置：

I've been assigned the job of looking after the new students.

我被分配去照顾新生。

They've assigned the job to me.

他们把这一工作分配给了我。

(2) 指定，定出：

They assigned the date for their meeting.

他们确定了开会的日期。

The manager assigned me to take notes.

经理指定我做记录。

(3) 转让：

She assigned her whole estate to a charity organization.

她将其所有财产都转让给了一个慈善组织。

3. induce *vt.*

(1) 引诱，劝使：

Nothing could induce him to betray his country.

没有什么可以诱使他背叛祖国。

(2) 导致，招致：

Overuse of computer may induce eye disease.

过多使用电脑会导致眼疾。

练习答案 Key to written exercises

1. 关键句型练习答案

A 1 That's the famous cross-eyed lion *who* was in all those films.

2 The couple just did not know how to thank the dog *who* had pulled their daughter out of the water and saved her life.

B See text.

2. 难点练习答案

A 1 The verb *train* means 'give or be given a course of instruction or practice, especially in a profession or skill': *She trained as an opera singer. These dogs have all been trained to detect drugs.*

Educate, on the other hand, means 'teach or train, especially through formal instruction at a school or college': *She was born in the U.S.A. but educated in England.*

2 The phrase *apart from* means 'without considering': *Apart from a few small errors, it's a good piece of work.*

Apart from can also mean 'as well as': *Apart from being too large, this sweater just doesn't suit me.*

Except, as a conjunction + verb, means 'apart from': *He can do everything around the house except cook.* As a preposition, *except* means 'not including, leaving out, but not': *Everyone was tired except John.*

3 The noun *degree*, as used in the text, means 'a point on an imaginary line used for measuring or comparing qualities, feelings, abilities, etc.': *The minister expressed a degree of optimism about the economic situation.*

Rank refers to 'a level of relative value, ability, importance, etc. on a scale, especially the official position one holds in the army, navy, etc.': *After two years he reached the rank of sergeant.*

4 *Afterwards* is an adverb meaning 'after that, later': *We went for a swim. Afterwards, we lay and sunbathed.* *After* is a preposition meaning 'following in time, later than': *We'll leave after breakfast.*

B 1 Because she tells so many lies, everything she says *must be taken with a grain of salt.*

2 Getting my father to lend me money was always *a ticklish business*: he wanted to know exactly how much I wanted, why I wanted it, when he could have it back, and so on.

3. 多项选择题答案

1	a	2	c	3	a	4	c	5	d	6	c
7	b	8	b	9	b	10	d	11	b	12	c

Lesson 42
Recording an earthquake
记录地震

课文详注 Further notes on the text

1. **An earthquake comes like a thief in the night, without warning.**
   此处将地震比喻成深夜偷偷溜进来的小偷。此句采用的是明喻的手法。
2. **It was necessary, therefore, to invent instruments that neither slumbered nor slept.**
   It 为先行主语, to invent instruments ... 为句子的真正主语。that 引导的是定语从句,修饰 instruments。
3. **... which would stand up on end like ninepins.**
   stand on end 竖立着。
4. **..., it shook the rigid table upon which these stood.**
   it 指 a shock。upon which these stood 为定语从句,修饰 table。these 指 rods of various lengths and thicknesses。
5. **If it were gentle, ... If it were severe, they all fell.**
   这两个句子中的 it 均指 a shock。they 指 rods of various lengths and thicknesses。
6. **Thus the rods, by falling, and by the direction in which they fell, recorded for the slumbering scientist the strength of a shock that was too weak to waken him, and the direction from which it came.**
   by falling, and by the direction ... 为并列方式状语,表示"通

过跌倒和跌倒的方向”。in which they fell 为定语从句，修饰 the direction。for the slumbering scientist 表示“为那些睡觉的科学家记录”。the strength of a shock ..., and the direction ... 为动词 recorded 的并列宾语。

7. **But instruments far more delicate than that were needed if ... was to be made.**

far more delicate than that 作定语，修饰 instruments。be to do sth. 表示“想要做某事”、“计划做某事”。

8. **The ideal to be aimed at was to devise an instrument ..., the movements of the ground or of the table as the quake passed by.**

to be aimed at 为动词不定式，作定语，修饰 The ideal。to devise an instrument ... 为动词不定式短语，作表语。the movements of ... 作 record 的宾语。of the ground or of the table 作定语，修饰 the movements。as the quake passed by 为时间状语从句，修饰 that could record ...。

9. **With practice, no doubt, I could in time learn to write by holding the pen still ...**

With practice 作状语，表示“通过练习”。in time 最终，迟早，如：

In time everything will be forgotten.

迟早一切都会被忘记的。

by holding the pen still ... 为方式状语。

10. **That sounds a silly suggestion, ... the idea adopted in some of ... for recording earthquake waves.**

That 指前句所提到的“笔不动而纸移动的书写方式”。sounds 在此处为系动词，a silly suggestion 为表语。adopted in some of ... 为过去分词短语，作定语，修饰 the idea。for recording ... 作定语，修饰 instruments。

11. A simple experiment will help us a little further.

help us a little further 帮助我们进一步搞清这个问题。

12. With the hand held high in the air, hold the string so that the weight nearly touches the ground.

该句为祈使句,谓语动词是 hold。With the hand ... 作方式状语,修饰 hold。so that 引导目的状语从句。

13. Now move the hand to and fro ...

to and fro 作方式状语,意即"来来回回地"。

14. It will be found that the weight moves but slightly or not at all.

It 作先行主语,that 引导的从句为真正的主语。but slightly or not at all 但动得很小,甚至没动。

15. Imagine a pen attached to the weight in such a way that its point rests upon a piece of paper on the floor.

attached to the weight 为过去分词短语,作定语,修饰 a pen。in such a way 为介词短语,作方式状语,修饰 attached。that 引导的是定语从句,修饰 such a way。rest upon/on 支撑在,搁在,如:

The statue rests upon a pedestal.

那座雕像放在基座上。

16. Imagine ...shaking the floor, ...

shaking ...为宾语补足语。

17. In the midst of ...

为"在……之中"之意。

18. It was upon this principle that the first instruments were made, ...

该句为强调结构。强调部分是 upon this principle。该句依正常语序为:The first instruments were made upon this principle.

19. The apparatus thus described, however, records ..., which

is, in fact, much more complicated.

thus described 作定语,修饰 The apparatus。which 引导非限定性定语从句,修饰 the horizontal component。

20. **... it would be more like that of a bluebottle buzzing round the room.**

that 指 the path。buzzing round the room 为现在分词短语,作定语,修饰 a bluebottle。

21. **... that all three elements can be recorded in different graphs.**

all three elements 指 up and down, to and fro and from side to side。

22. **..., the graphic record shows three waves arriving one after the other at short intervals.**

arriving one after the other 作宾语补足语。one after the other 一个接一个地,作方式状语。at short intervals 相隔不久,作状语,修饰 arriving。

23. **The first ... The second ...**

The first 和 The second 后面均省略了 wave。

24. **These two have ...**

These two 后面省略了 waves。

25. **It was from the study of these that so much was learnt about the interior of the earth.**

该句为强调句。强调部分是 from the study of these。these 指前文提到的两种 waves。该句依正常语序为:So much was learnt about the interior of the earth from the study of these.

语法 Grammar in use

英语中经常使用的强调形式 (1)

语音强调形式

在英语中,我们经常对某一单词或短语给予强调,其目的主要有两

个:(1)想对所说内容表现出强烈情感时,用于“情感强调”;(2)想对两个事物/状况进行说明时,用于“对比强调”,如:

You do look nice today!

你今天看起来的确漂亮!(情感强调)

Your hair looks so good like that.

你的那种发型真好看。(情感强调)

Why weren't you at the meeting?

你为什么没有参加会议?

I was at the meeting.

我参加了会议。(对比强调)

I don't have much contact with my family, but I do see my mother occasionally.

我同家人没有太多联系,但我确实时常见到母亲。(对比强调)

在口语中,可以通过对某些词进行重读或利用升调,对所要强调的部分给予强调。比较:

***Mary** phoned me yesterday.*

玛丽昨天给我打了电话。(而非他人)

*Mary **phoned** me yesterday.*

玛丽昨天给我打了电话。(而非通过其他手段)

*Mary phoned **me** yesterday.*

玛丽昨天给我打了电话。(而非给他人)

*Mary phoned me **yesterday**.*

玛丽昨天给我打了电话。(而非其他时间)

在含 be 动词、助动词或情态助动词的句子中,通常可以通过重读这些词而使句子得到强调,如:

It was a nice party!

那是个很好的聚会!

You have grown!

你已经长大啦！

I am telling the truth—you must believe me !

我在说实话——你得相信我！

而在没有上述词的句子中，强调通常可以通过在句子中加进助动词 do 表示，如：

Do sit down .

快坐下。

She does like you .

她真的喜欢你。

If he does decide to come , let me know , will you ?

如果他真的决定来，告诉我，行吗？

有时可以通过重读句中使用的诸如 so、such、really、just、last、ever、on earth 等词语来表示强调，如：

This is the last opportunity .

这是最后的机会。

Thank you so much . It was such a lovely party . I really enjoyed it .

太谢谢你啦。这么好的一个聚会。我真的过得很愉快。

What on earth is she doing here ?

她到底正在这儿做什么？

词汇学习 Word study

1. warn *vt .*

(1) 警告，告诫：

He warned us that the roads were icy .

他警告我们路上结冰了。

I warned them not to go skating on such thin ice .

我警告他们别在这么薄的冰上滑冰。

He warned me of danger.

他警告我有危险。

I was warned against him.

我得到忠告,要提防他。

(2) 预先通知:

The weather station warned that a storm was coming.

气象台预报暴风雨即将来临。

2. invent *vt.*

(1) 发明,创造:

The light bulb was invented by Edison.

电灯泡是爱迪生发明的。

(2) 虚构,杜撰:

She tried to invent an excuse, but no one believed her.

她想编造个借口,但是没人相信她。

3. shake (shook, shaken)

(1) *vt.* 摇,(猛力)摇动,使震动:

They shook hands and said good-bye.

他们握手道别。

The earthquake shook the house.

地震摇动着房子。

(2) *vt.* 晃动:

He shook his fist at her.

他向她挥动着拳头。

The boy shook the apples from the tree.

那个男孩把苹果从树上摇了下来。

(3) *vi.* 震动,颤动,发抖:

He was shaking because of the cold.

他冷得发抖。

His voice shook with rage.

他愤怒得声音都发颤。

(4) *vi*. 摇,晃动:

Shake well before use.

用前摇匀。

(5) *n*. (可数)摇动,震动:

Give the bottle a good shake before you drink.

喝之前好好摇一下瓶子。

(6) *n*. (口)地震:

There comes the shake of the earth.

地震开始了。

(7) *n*. 奶昔(即牛奶或鸡蛋等和冰淇淋搅成的饮品):

I ordered a shake.

我要了一份混合饮料。

(8) shake off 摆脱:

She can't shake off a feeling of despair.

她无法摆脱失望的感觉。

练习答案 Key to written exercises

1. 关键句型练习答案

A See text.

B See text.

2. 难点练习答案

A 1 For notes on *device* and *devise*, with examples, see Lesson 21 (p.251).

2 The verb *travel* means 'go from one place to another, especially to a distant place': *If I had a lot of money, I'd travel all over the world.*

A *trip* (noun) is 'a journey, especially a short one for

pleasure or for a particular purpose (e.g. business)': *We took all the old people in our village on a day trip to London.*

3 Although they look alike, the verbs *adopt* and *adapt*, are quite different in meaning.

The verb *adopt* means 'take and use as one's own': *It has taken a time, but we have finally adopted the methods that our competitors have found so successful.*

The verb *adapt* means 'make or become suitable for new needs, different conditions, etc.': *He adapted an old car engine to fit his boat.*

B 1 Noun *export*: What are your main exports? — Oil and wool.

Verb *export*: They have always exported a lot of oil to neighbouring countries.

2 Noun *import*: Oil is this country's most important import.

Verb *import*: Many of their cars are imported from Japan.

3 Noun *produce*: Our neighbours sell their own produce in the market.

Verb *produce*: When children are learning to play the violin, they produce some strange noises!

4 Noun *conduct*: That boy's conduct is excellent.

Verb *conduct*: I'd love to conduct a large orchestra.

3. 多项选择题答案

1 b 2 c 3 c 4 b 5 d 6 b
7 d 8 a 9 d 10 c 11 a 12 c

Lesson 43
Are there strangers in space?
宇宙中有外星人吗?

课文详注 Further notes on the text

1. **We must conclude ..., that given a planet only approximately like our own, life is almost certain to start.**
   that 引导的是动词 conclude 的宾语从句。从句中的 given 引导的是条件状语,意即"如果与我们所在的行星大致相同的话"。given 相当于 if,如:
   Given A and B are true, C follows. (= *If A and B are true, then so is C.*)
   如果 A 和 B 是正确的,那么 C 也是正确的。
2. **Of all the planets ..., the Earth is the only one on which life can survive.** 为
   Of all the planets ...为介词短语,作定语,修饰 one。on which life can survive 为定语从句,修饰 the only one。
3. **,... and poor in oxygen, Venus far too hot, and so is Mercury, ...**
   be poor in 在……方面贫乏的,如:
   The country is poor in natural resources.
   那个国家自然资源贫乏。
   Venus 后面省略了 is。
4. **But other suns, stars as the astronomers call them, are bound to have ..., and as the number of stars ..., this possibility becomes ...**

stars as ...为 other suns 的同位语。as 为关系代词。them 指 stars。be bound to do sth. 一定/必然会做某事,如:

She is bound to find out.

她一定会发现的。

It is bound to happen.

这事必定会发生。

as the number of stars ...为原因状语从句。this possibility 指 to have planets like our own。

5. So the number of stars that we know exist is now estimated at ...

that 引导的是定语从句,从句中的谓语动词是 exist。该定语从句修饰 stars。we know 为插入语。estimate sth. at 估计某物为,如:

His parents estimated the cost at about $5,000.

他父母亲估计费用在 5,000 美元左右。

6. Although perhaps ... will develop into highly complex ..., so vast is the number of planets, that intelligent life is bound ...

Although 引导的是让步状语从句。该句的主句是 so vast ...。so vast is the number of planets 为倒装结构,按正常语序为:the number of planets is so vast。that intelligent life is bound ...为结果状语从句。

7. ..., and found our then prevailing primitive state completely uninteresting to their own advanced knowledge.

then 为形容词,意即"当时的"。completely uninteresting to their own advanced knowledge 为宾语补足语,意即"同他们先进的知识相比是索然无味的"。

8. Professor Ronald Bracewell, a leading American radio astronomer, argued in *Nature* that ..., on a visit to our own solar system, may have left an automatic messenger behind ...

a leading American radio astronomer 是 Professor Ronald Bracewell 的同位语。*Nature* 之所以用斜体是因为是杂志名。on a visit to ...作状语,意即"在访问我们太阳系的时候"。该处用情态助动词+现在完成时结构 may have left,表示这只是一种对过去情况的猜测。leave ... behind 将……留下。

9. **..., receiving our radio and ..., might well ..., although what impression any other civilization would thus get from us is best left unsaid.**

receiving our radio and ...作时间状语,意即"收到我们的无线电和电视信号后"。might well 很可能。although 引导让步状语从句。what impression any other civilization would thus get from us 为该让步状语从句中的主语从句。is best left unsaid 最好不去说。

10. **But here we come up against the most difficult of all obstacles to contact with people on other planets—the astronomical distances which separate us.**

come up against 碰到,如:

They come up against opposition.

他们突然遇到抵抗。

to contact with people ...作定语,修饰 obstacles。破折号后面的部分为 obstacles 的同位语。

11. **..., and assuming such an ... of the 1920's, ...**

assuming 作连词,引导条件状语从句。

12. **..., though good enough to orbit men, ..., four light years away, let alone distances of tens or hundreds of light years.**

though 引导的是让步状语从句,其后省略了从句中的主语和谓语动词 they are。four light years away 是 the nearest other star 的非限定性定语从句。let/leave alone 更不用说,如:

I'm too tired to walk, let alone run.

我累得走都走不动了,更不用说跑了。

13. ..., as Walter Sullivan has put it in his excellent book, *We Are Not Alone*.

as引导的是方式状语从句。put it 所说。*We Are Not Alone* 是 Walter Sullivan 所写的书名,意即《我们并不孤独》。

14. ...; it must be known to any kind of radio astronomer in the universe.

be known to 为……所知的,如:

This is known to everyone.

这件事众所周知。

15. ..., it was not long before its use as ... was suggested.

its use 指 the use of this wave-length。as 为介词,意即"当作"。was suggested 的主语是 its use。

16. Without something of this kind, searching for intelligences on other planets would be like trying to meet a friend ... and absurdly wandering the streets in the hope of a chance encounter.

searching for ... planets 作句子的主语。trying to meet a friend ...和 absurdly wandering the streets ...是介词 like 的并列宾语。in the hope of ...作 wandering the streets 的目的状语,意即"怀着……希望",如:

We returned to the park in the hope of finding his wallet.

我们返回公园,指望找到他的钱夹子。

语法 Grammar in use

英语中经常使用的强调形式 (2)

结构强调形式 (1)

(1) 前置句子中的某些词语,如:

That film—what did you think of it?

那部影片——你认为它怎么样?

Asleep, then, were you?

睡啦,哦,是吗?

I knew he was going to cause trouble, and cause trouble he did!

我知道他打算找麻烦,他还就真的找了麻烦!

Strange people they are!

他们可真是些怪人!

(2) 用某些词强调句子中的某一成分,如:

1) 用 do 强调肯定句中的动词,如:

She does seem to be trying.

她真的像是在试。

Do come in.

快进来吧。

2) 用反身代词强调名词或人称代词,如:

I did it myself.

我自己做的这件事。

I got a letter from the Director himself.

我收到了主任亲自回的信。

3) 用 indeed 强调修饰一形容词或副词的 very,如:

I was very surprised indeed.

我的确很吃惊。

That car runs very fast indeed.

那辆车的确跑得非常快。

4) 用 very 强调最高级形式及 next、last、first、和 same 等,如:

I'd like a bottle of your very best wine.

我想要一瓶你最好的那种酒。

The letter arrived on the very next day.

就在第2天那封信到了。

We were born in the very same street in the very same year.

我们就在那同一年同一条街上出生。

(3) 用重复法强调,如:

She looks much, much older than she used to.

她可比过去显得老得多得多了。

He could do it very, very fast.

他可以特别特别快地把这件事做完。

词汇学习 Word study

1. conclude

(1) *vt*. 结束,终了:

He concluded the speech by reminding us of our responsibility.

他结束讲话时提醒我们注意自己的职责。

(2) *vt*. 缔结,议定:

The two countries concluded an agreement on trade.

这两个国家缔结了一项贸易协定。

(3) *vt*. 推断出,断定,决定:

From her smile I concluded that the news was good.

从她的笑容我断定那是个好消息。

What have you concluded from the data?

从那些数据中你得出什么结论?

(4) *vi*. 结束,终了:

The meeting concluded at 10 o'clock.

会议10点钟结束。

2. certain

(1) *adj*. 确定的,无疑的:

There is no certain cure for this illness at present.
现在对这种病还没有一定的治疗方法。

(2) *adj*. (作补足语)确信的，明确无误的：

She was quite certain about/of it.
她对此毫不怀疑。

I'm almost certain that she saw me yesterday.
我几乎可以肯定她昨天看到了我。

We are not certain where he lives.
我们不能确定他住在哪里。

He's certain to pass the exam.
他肯定能通过考试。

(3) *adj*. (作定语)某(一)，某种，一定的：

It's not a beautiful building, but it has a certain charm.
虽然它并不是座漂亮的建筑，但是还有着一定的魅力。

When the water reaches a certain level, the pump switches itself off.
当水达到一定高度时，泵就会自动关闭。

A certain Ms. Jones phoned you today.
一个名叫琼斯的女士今天给你打了个电话。

I agree with you to a certain extent.
在某种程度上我是赞成你的。

(4) *pron*. (正式)某几个，某些：

Certain of these questions have never been answered.
这些问题中的某些问题从未得到答复。

(5) for certain 肯定地；确切地：

I know for certain that he's there, but he won't answer me.
我明明知道他就在那儿，但是他就是不回答我。

(6) make certain 弄清楚，搞明白：

Make certain (that) you know when the train arrives, please.

请务必弄清楚火车到达的时间。

3. bound *adj.*

(1) 很可能的,肯定的:

It's bound to rain soon.

肯定很快就会下雨的。

There are bound to be such accidents.

必然会发生这样的事故的。

(2) 受约束的,有义务的:

You're not legally bound to answer these questions.

你没有法律义务来回答这些问题。

(3) (in) 装有封面的:

That's a book bound in leather.

那是一本皮面装帧的书。

(4) bound up in 忙于;对……极感兴趣:

She's bound up in her own problems.

她正忙于处理自己的问题。

(5) bound up with 有赖于,与……有关联:

Our future is closely bound up with that of the company.

我们的前途同公司的紧密地联系在一起。

练习答案 Key to written exercises

1. 关键句型练习答案

A 1 It's an excellent film—you're *sure to* enjoy it.

2 I was just *about to* leave the house when the telephone rang.

3 The concert was *due to* begin at 7.30, but it was delayed

for half an hour.

B See text.

2. 难点练习答案

A 1 A *planet* is 'a large body in space that moves round a star, especially round the sun': *Mars is sometimes called the 'Red Planet'.*

A *star*, on the other hand, is 'a very large mass of burning gas in space, especially one that can be seen as a small bright point of light in a clear sky at night': *When it is dark, the stars come out.*

2 The verb *estimate* means 'judge or calculate the nature, value, size, amount, etc., of something, especially roughly': *The film cost an estimated $25 million to make.*

Esteemed means 'respected and admired': *The old teacher was much loved and highly esteemed.*

3 The adjective *natural*, as used in the text, means 'of or being what exists or happens ordinarily in the world': *The country's natural resources include forests, coal and oil.*

The adjective *physical* means 'of or for the body': *You should take a lot more physical exercise.*

4 The adjective *unsaid* means '(thought of but) not spoken' and is usually used in the phrase 'left unsaid': *Whatever you might have thought, it would have been better left unsaid.*

Untold, however, is an adjective that usually means 'too great to be counted or measured, limitless': *She has done untold damage to our chances of winning the election.*

It can also mean 'not told or expressed' as in: *The full true story of his part in the resistance movement remains untold*.

5 The verbs *search for* and *search* are very close in meaning, and can be confusing.

Search for means 'look for': *They have searched for him everywhere, but they haven't found him. Scientists are still searching for a cure to the common cold.*

Search means 'look at, through, into, etc., or examine carefully and thoroughly to try to find something': *They searched the house from top to bottom. When the boy went missing, they searched the nearby woods first. The police searched the man when they arrested him.*

Look at these sentences using *search x for y*: *They searched the woods for the children. She searched the man for drugs. We will have to search the building for weapons.*

B 1 He's incapable of adding up a simple list of figures, let alone *doing his annual accounts for the Inland Revenue*.

2 He doesn't earn enough to support himself, let alone *a wife and children*.

3. 多项选择题答案

1	d	2	b	3	a	4	b	5	c	6	c
7	d	8	d	9	a	10	c	11	b	12	b

Lesson 44
Patterns of culture
文化的模式

课文详注　Further notes on the text

1. **The inner workings of our own brains we feel to be uniquely worthy of investigation, but custom, we have a way of thinking, is behaviour at its most commonplace.**

   The inner workings of our own brains 是动词 feel 的宾语，为了强调而把其提前。to be uniquely worthy of investigation 是该宾语的补足语。we have a way of thinking 是插入语，意即"我们认为"。at its most commonplace 作定语，修饰 behaviour。

2. **..., it is the other way around.**

   it is the other way around 是固定词组，意即"正好相反"。

3. **Traditional custom, taken the world over, is a mass of detailed behaviour more astonishing than what any one person can ever evolve in individual actions, no matter how aberrant.**

   taken the world over 是过去分词短语，作 Traditional custom 的定语。taken 前面省略了 it is，意即"被全世界所接受的"。a mass of 一大堆，如：a mass of sand（一大堆沙子）。more astonishing than ... actions 作 behaviour 的定语。no matter how aberrant 作让步状语，省略了 they may be，这里 they 指 individual actions。

4. **The fact of first-rate importance is the predominant role that custom plays in experience and in belief, and the very great varieties it may manifest.**

that 引导的是定语从句,修饰 the predominant role。and the very great varieties it may manifest 与 the predominant role 同为该句的主语。it may manifest 作 varieties 的定语,意即“它所表现出的极其丰富多彩的形式”,it 指 custom。

5. **He sees it edited by a definite set of ...**

edited 作 it 的定语。it 指 the world,而 He 指 man。该句采用暗喻的手法,用动词 edit(编辑,剪辑)来描述人们透过特定的习俗、制度和思维方式来看待世界。

6. **... he cannot go behind these stereotypes; his very concepts of the true and the false will still have reference to his particular traditional customs.**

go behind these stereotypes 摆脱这些旧框框。go behind 摆脱。his very concepts 中的 very 为形容词,用于加强语气。have reference to 与……有关,参照。

7. **John Dewey has said in all seriousness that the part played by custom in shaping the behaviour of the individual, as against any way in which he can affect traditional custom, is as the proportion of the total vocabulary of his mother tongue against those words of his own baby talk that are taken up into the vernacular of his family.**

in all seriousness 十分严肃地,作动词 said 的状语。that 引导的是动词 said 的宾语从句。played by custom in shaping the behaviour of the individual 为过去分词短语,作定语,修饰宾语从句中的主语 the part,意即“在形成个人行为方面所起到的作用”。as against ... is as ... against ... 与……相比较就如同……与……相比。in which 引导定语从句,修饰 any way。is 及其后面的部分是 that 引导的宾语从句中的谓语部分。that 作 baby talk 的定语从句。take up 接纳,采纳,如:

I'd like to take up your offer of a ride into town.

我愿意接受你的建议,坐你的车进城。

8. **When one ..., the figure becomes no more than an exact and matter-of-fact observation.**

the figure 指“杜威的比喻”,即前句中杜威所说的话。

9. **The life history ... is first and foremost an accommodation to the patterns and standards traditionally handed down in his community.**

first and foremost 首先。an accommodation to 适应(某种情况)。如:make an accommodation to wartime conditions(适应战时环境)。traditionally handed down in his community 作 the patterns and standards 的定语,意即“他的社团世代相传的”。

10. **From the moment of his birth, the customs into which he is born ...**

into which he is born 为定语从句,修饰 the customs。

11. **By the time ..., by the time he is grown and able to take part in its activities, its habits are his habits, its beliefs his beliefs, its impossibilities his impossibilities.**

句子中的两个 by the time 引导时间状语从句。该句中的 4 个 its 都指 the culture's。its beliefs 和 its impossibilities 后面都省略了系动词 are。

12. **Every child that is born into his group will share them with him, and no child born into one on the opposite side of the globe can ever achieve the thousandth part.**

that is born into his group 是 every child 的定语从句,意即“诞生在他的社团的”。them 指前句中的 activities、habits、beliefs 和 impossibilities。born into ... 为定语从句,修饰 no child。on the opposite side of the globe 是 one 的定语,意即“诞生在地球另一边某社团的”。one 指 his group。the thousandth part 后面省略了 of the customs。

13. There is no social problem it is more incumbent upon us to understand than this of the role of custom.

it is . . . custom 作 problem 的定语从句,it 前面省略了关系代词 that。定语从句中的 it 是先行主语,而真正的主语是 to understand。this 代替 problem。be incumbent upon/on 义不容辞的。形容词 incumbent 不能单独使用,如:

It's incumbent on you to warn them.

你有责任提醒他们。

14. Until we are intelligent as to its laws and varieties, . . .

be intelligent as to 对……可以理解。its 指 custom's。

15. In the first place, any scientific study requires that there be no . . . items in the series it selects for its consideration.

动词 require 后面可以跟 that 引导的宾语从句。从句中的动词可以用动词原形或情态助动词 should + 动词原形(即虚拟语气结构), 如:

She required that everyone attend / should attend the meeting.

她要求全体人员出席会议。

in the series 作 items 的定语。it selects . . . 是 the series 的定语从句,it 指 scientific study。

16. . . . and to take note of . . .

take note of 注意到,如:

We'd better take note of all possibilities.

我们最好要注意到所有的可能性。

17. In this way, we have learned all that we know of the laws of astronomy, or of the habits of the social insects, let us say.

that 引导的是定语从句,修饰 all。关系代词 that 在从句中作 know 的宾语。of astronomy, or of the habits of the social insects 作 that 的定语。let us say 作插入语,意即"譬如说"。

18. It is only in the study of man himself that the major social sciences have substituted the study of one local variation, that of Western civilization.

该句为强调结构。所强调的部分是 in the study of man himself。该句依正常语序为:The major social sciences have substituted ... only in the study of man himself. that of Western civilization 作 variation 的同位语。

19. ..., as long as ..., held sway over people's minds.

as long as 引导的是条件状语从句。hold/have sway over 统治,支配,如:

He still holds sway over a large bureaucracy.

他仍然控制着一个庞大的官僚机构。

20. ... that degree of sophistication where we no longer set our own belief against our neighbour's superstition.

where 作 that degree of sophistication 的定语从句。set ... against 使与……对立,反对,如:

He managed to set brother against brother.

他得兄弟之间不和。

21. It was necessary to recognize that these institutions which are based on the same premises, let us say the supernatural, must be considered together, our own among the rest.

that 作动词 recognize 的宾语。which 引导的定语从句修饰 these institutions,意即"这些建立在相同前提下的风俗"。let us say the supernatural 作插入语,表示举例,说明 premises。must be considered together 是 that 引导的宾语从句的谓语部分。our own among the rest 作方式状语,our own 和 the rest 后面省略了 institutions。

语法 Grammar in use

英语中经常使用的强调形式(3)

结构强调形式(2)

可以使用由 it、what 等构成的分裂句对句子中的某一部分进行强调。分裂句大体包括下述几种形式:

(1) be 动词+关系从句(the person who 或 the thing that 等)形式

假定要分别对 Mary keeps a pig in the garden shed(玛丽在花园工具棚养了只猪)的相应部分进行强调,则可分别用如下形式:

Mary is the person who keeps a pig in the garden shed.
玛丽就是在花园工具棚养了只猪的那个人。
The person who keeps a pig in the garden shed is Mary.
在花园工具棚养了只猪的那个人是玛丽。
(上述两个句子对主语 *Mary* 进行强调)

A pig is what Mary keeps in the garden shed.
玛丽在花园工具棚养的是只猪。
What Mary keeps in the garden shed is a pig.
(同上)
(上述两个句子对宾语 *a pig* 进行强调)

The garden shed is (the place) where Mary keeps a pig.
花园工具棚是玛丽养了只猪的地方。
(The place) where Mary keeps a pig is the garden shed.
玛丽养了只猪的地方是花园工具棚。
(上述两个句子对地点状语进行强调)

注意:

用 what 从句作主语构成分裂句时其后通常使用动词单数形式,但动词后如为复数名词时也可使用动词复数形式,如:

What we want is/are some of those cakes.

我们想要的是那些蛋糕中的一部分。

(2) 强调动词的形式

通常可以用 what ... do 结构对句子中的动词进行强调;如动词后还有其他成分,也可视为既对动词也对动词后的其他成分的强调,如:

He screamed.

他尖叫。

What he did *was* (*to*) *scream/screamed.*

他所做的就是尖叫。

She writes science fiction.

她写科幻小说。

What she does is (*to*) *write/writes science fiction.*

她所做的就是写科幻小说。

(3) 强调整个句子的形式

通常可以用 what happen 结构对整个句子进行强调,如:

The car broke down.

车坏了。

What happened was (*that*) *the car broke down.*

发生的事情是车坏了。

(4) 由先行词 it 引导的强调形式

见本册第 39 课语法相关部分。

(5) 其他常见强调形式

All I want is a home somewhere.

我所想要的就是在哪儿有个家。

All you need is love.

你所需要的就是爱。

The only thing I remember is a terrible pain in my head.

我所记得的惟一一件事就是我头上的剧痛。

The first thing was to make some coffee.

头一件要做的事情就是煮些咖啡。

It was not until I met you that I knew real happiness.

直到见到你,我才知道真正的幸福。

It was only when I read her letter that I realized what was happening.

只有在看了她的信后,我才知道发生了什么事情。

That's where we live.

那就是我们住的地方。

词汇学习 Word study

1. worthy *adj.*

(1)(作定语)有价值的;可尊敬的:

We are now carrying out a worthy cause.

我们正从事着正义的事业。

(2)(常作补足语)值得的,配得上的,相称的:

That's the problem worthy to be considered.

那是值得考虑的问题。

That's a beautiful city worthy of its name.

那是一座名符其实的美丽城市。

2. probe

(1) *n.*(可数)刺探,探索,查究,彻底调查:

The workers are working on a probe to find the causes of the accident.

工人们正在对事故的原因进行调查。

(2) *n.* 探针,探测器:

The plane is flying high up in the sky, carrying a space probe.

那架飞机正携带着一个空间探测器在高空飞行。

(3) *vt*. 用探针(或探测器)探查,探测:

The doctor probed the cut on her head.

医生探查她头上的伤口。

(4) *vt*. 查究,彻底调查:

The researchers spent a lot of time probing the roots of war.

研究人员花费大量时间探究战争的根源。

(5) *vi*. 探查,探索:

The representatives from both countries are probing for ways to find mutual agreements.

两国代表正在寻求双方达成协议的途径。

3. shape

(1) *n*. (可数) 形状:

An egg is an oval shape.

鸡蛋的形状是椭圆的。

(2) *n*. 体型:

She has a good shape.

她体型很好。

(3) *n*. 体现,具体化:

We have a shape of the ideas.

我们的想法已成形。

(4) *vt*. 使成形,使具有……形状,形成:

She used a wooden comb to shape her hair.

她用一把木梳把头发梳成形。

(5) *vt*. 影响:

We are all shaped by the modern life style.

我们都受到现代生活方式的影响。

(6) *vi*. 成长,发展:

Everything seems to be shaping up nicely.
一切都似乎进展顺利。

✍ 练习答案 Key to written exercises

1. 关键句型练习答案

See text.

2. 难点练习答案

A 1 The noun *custom* means 'an established and habitual practice, especially of a religious or a social kind, that is typical of a particular group of people': *Social customs vary greatly from country to country.*

A *habit*, on the other hand, is 'a tendency to behave in a particular way or do particular things, especially regularly and repeatedly over a long period': *She has an annoying habit of biting her fingernails.*

2 The noun *aspect* means 'a particular side of a many-sided situation, idea, plan, etc.': *The training programme covers every aspect of the job.*

A *view*, on the other hand, is 'something seen from a particular place, especially a stretch of pleasant country; a scene': *I'd like a room with a view over the harbour, please.*

3 A *proportion* is 'the compared relationship between two things in regard to size, amount, importance, etc.': *Your income tax will increase in proportion to the amount you earn.*

A *percentage*, on the other hand, is 'an amount stated as if it is part of a whole which is 100': *What percentage of the population now takes an annual holiday abroad ?*

4 The adjective *unintelligible* is the opposite of *intelligible*, which means 'can not be understood': *His argument was completely unintelligible.*

Unintelligent is the opposite of *intelligent*: *The new employee wasn't unintelligent, but he wasn't particularly clever, either.*

5 The adjective *controversial* means 'causing much argument or disagreement': *The council's decision to close the town centre to traffic was extremely controversial.*

The adjective *argumentative* is used to describe people and means 'liking to argue': *I wouldn't bother to discuss the question with her: she's just an argumentative old lady.*

B 1 The *accommodation* in the local inn was very comfortable indeed.

2 What kind of a *creature* is a panda? —I think it's a bear, but I'm not sure.

3 In her hand the little girl held a small glass *globe* full of liquid which gave the impression of a snowstorm when she shook it.

4 That young man is extremely *intelligent*, I think he will do very well at university.

3. 多项选择题答案

1 a　2 a　3 a　4 a　5 b　6 b

7 b　8 b　9 d　10 c　11 b　12 a

Lesson 45

Of men and galaxies

人和星系

课文详注 Further notes on the text

1. **In man's early days, competition with other creatures must have been critical.**

   must have been 为典型的情态助动词 must + 动词的现在完成时形式,表示对过去情况的推测,如:

   We went to Rome last month.

   上个月我们去了罗马。

   That must have been nice.

   那一定很有意思。

   critical 意即"关键的"、"决定性的"。

2. **Indeed, we lack practice and experience nowadays in dealing with primitive conditions.**

   lack 缺乏,如:

   You lack common sense.

   你缺乏常识。

   He lacks three votes to win.

   他距获胜只差 3 票。

   lack 还可以作不及物动词,后面跟介词 for,表示"缺少",如:

   She will never lack for friends.

   她永远不会缺少朋友。

   此外,lack 还可以作名词,意即"缺乏",如:

   For lack of fuel, their planes were grounded.

他们的飞机因缺乏燃料而被迫停飞。

nowadays 为副词,意即"现如今",如:

Nowadays I hardly ever see her.

现在我几乎见不到她。

nowadays 还可以作名词,如:

The kitchens of nowadays are more efficient than those of yesterday.

现在的厨房比过去的方便多了。

in dealing with primitive conditions 该介词短语作状语,意即"在对付原始环境方面"。

3. I am sure that, without modern weapons, I would make a very poor show of disputing ..., and in this I do not think that I stand alone.

that 引导的是宾语从句。without modern weapons 作该从句中的条件状语,意即"如果没有现代化武器"。make a very poor show 出丑。in this 指"在这方面"。stand alone 孤立,孑然一身。

4. The last creature to compete with man was the mosquito.

last 有"极不可能"的意思,如:

He's the last man I want to see.

他是我最不想看到的人。

to compete with man 作定语,修饰 creature,意即"与人竞争的"。

5. But even the mosquito has been subdued by attention to drainage and by chemical sprays.

subdue 制服,征服,如:

The Japanese invaders were subdued by the Chinese people.

日本侵略者被中国人民打败了。

by attention to drainage 和 by chemical sprays 为并列状语,表示方式。attention to 对……的注意,如:meticulous attention to detail(对细节的细心注意)。

6. **Competition between ourselves, person against person, community against community, still persists, ...**

person against person 和 community against community 为并列短语,作定语,修饰 Competition,意即"人与人、团体与团体的竞争"。persist 坚持,如:

People persist in thinking that standards are going down.

人们坚持认为水准在下降。

7. **But the competition ... not the simple process envisioned in biology.**

envisioned in biology 为过去分词短语,作定语,修饰 process,意即"生物学中想像的"。envision 想像,设想,如:

We envision this dictionary as a handbook for serious students.

我们设想这本词典是供认真学习的学生的使用手册。

8. **It is not a simple competition for a fixed amount of food determined by the physical environment, ...**

for a fixed amount of food 为介词短语,作定语,修饰 competition,意即"为争夺有限的食物的"。determined by the physical environment 为过去分词短语,作定语,修饰 food,意即"由物质环境所决定的"。

9. **Morocco and California ..., both on the west coasts of continents with similar climates, and probably with rather similar natural resources.**

both 指 Morocco and California,其引导的部分作插入语,对 Morocco 和 California 作进一步的说明。with similar climates 和 with rather similar natural resources 为并列成分,作定语,修

饰 continents。

10. Yet their present development ..., not so much because of different people even, but because of the different thoughts that exist in the minds of their inhabitants.

their 指 Morocco 和 California 的。even 作副词,表示"更确切地",如:

I find some of his habits rather unpleasant, disgusting even.

我觉得他的一些习惯十分不好,甚至令人讨厌。

that exist ...为定语从句,修饰 thoughts。not so much ...为该句的原因状语。

11. It is well known that where the white man has invaded a primitive culture, the most destructive effects ...

It 为先行主语,that 引导的从句为真正的主语。从句中的 where 引导的是地点状语从句,从句中的主句是 the most destructive effects ...。

12. The Holy Office knew this full well when it caused heretics to be burned in days gone by.

The Holy Office 指罗马天主教的宗教法庭。this 指前一句 Ideas are dangerous。full well 中的 full 为副词,表示"十分",意即"十分清楚"。it 指 The Holy Office。gone by 为过去分词短语,作定语,修饰 days,意即"逝去的日子"。

13. ... to such a degree that it is very difficult to conceive of anything really destructive.

such a degree 作程度状语,意即"达到这样一种程度"。that 引导的是 degree 的同位语从句。从句中的 it 为先行主语,真正的主语是动词不定式 to conceive of ...。really destructive 作定语,修饰 anything。conceive of 设想,如:

Can you conceive of such cruelty?

你能想像得出有这样残酷的事情吗？

14. **It is only someone looking on from outside that can inject the dangerous thoughts.**

该句为强调结构。被强调部分是句子的主语 only someone looking on from outside，其中现在分词短语 looking on from outside 作定语，修饰 someone。

15. **I do not doubt that it would be possible to inject ideas into the modern world that would utterly destroy us.**

that 引导的是动词 doubt 的宾语从句。从句中 it 为从句的先行主语，动词不定式短语 to inject ideas ... 为从句的真正主语。that would utterly destroy us 作名词 ideas 的定语。

16. **Perhaps it will suffice to mention the nuclear bomb.**

it 为先行主语，真正的主语是动词不定式 to mention the nuclear bomb。suffice 足够，满足……需要，如：

My salary suffices for our basic needs.

我的工资能满足我们生活的基本需要。

17. **Imagine the effect on a reasonably advanced technological society, one that still does not possess the bomb, of making it aware of the possibility, of supplying sufficient details to enable the thing to be constructed.**

该句为祈使句。one 指 society。that 引导的是定语从句，修饰 one。of making ... 和 of supplying ... 同为 effect 的定语。of making it ... 中的 it 指 a reasonably advanced technological society。of supplying ... 中的 the thing 指 nuclear bomb。to be constructed 作宾语补足语。

18. **... around the year 1925 would have been sufficient to change the course of world history.**

would have been 表示“虽然在过去没有发生但有可能发生”。

19. **It is a strange thought, but I believe a correct one, that ...**

在 believe 和 correct one 中间省略了 it is。that 引导的是 a strange thought 的同位语从句。

20. I have often tried to conceive of what those pages might contain, but of course I cannot do so because ...

what 引导的是动词 conceive of 的宾语从句。关系代词 what 在从句中作动词 contain 的宾语。do so 中的 so 指 conceive of what those pages might contain。

21. We cannot think outside the particular patterns that our brains are conditioned to, or, to be more accurate, ..., and then only if we are very original.

that 引导定语从句,修饰 patterns。condition to 使习惯于,如:

The boy was finally conditioned to life in the jungle.

那个男孩子终于习惯了丛林中的生活。

to be more accurate 作插入语,意即"更确切地说"。and then only if we are very original 作条件状语从句,意即"即使这样也需要我们有独创思想"。

语法 Grammar in use

感叹句的表达形式

英语中的感叹句通常由带有 how 和 what 或带有 so 和 such 的句子构成,而使用否定形式表达的感叹句也是常见的。

1. 用 how 构成的感叹句

常见的用 how 构成的感叹句有下述 3 种形式:

(1) 由 how + 形容词构成,如:

Strawberries! How nice!

草莓! 多棒哪!

(2) 由 how + 形容词/副词 + 主语 + 动词构成,如:

How cold it is!

天好冷啊！

How beautifully you sing!

你唱歌多好听啊！

(3) 由 how + 主语 + 动词构成，如：

How you've grown!

你长得真快！

2. 用 what 构成的感叹句

常见的用 what 构成的感叹句有下述 3 种形式：

(1) 由 what a/an + (形容词) + 单数可数名词构成，如：

What a rude man!

多粗鲁的一个人啊！

What a surprise!

多令人吃惊啊！

(2) 由 what + (形容词) + 不可数/复数名词构成，如：

What beautiful weather!

多好的天气啊！

What lovely flowers!

多可爱的花啊！

(3) 由 what + 宾语 + 主语 + 动词构成，如：

What a beautiful smile your younger sister has!

你妹妹的微笑多美啊！

3. 用 so 和 such 构成的感叹句

常见的用 so 和 such 构成的感叹句有下述 3 种形式：

(1) 由 so + 形容词构成，如：

You're so kind!

你的心太好了！

(2) 由 such a/an + (形容词) + 单数可数名词构成，如：

He's such a nice boy!

他是多么可爱的小男孩呀！

(3) 由 such＋(形容词)＋不可数/复数名词构成，如：

They talk such rubbish!

他们竟这样胡说八道！

They're such kind people!

他们就是这种心地善良的人！

4. 用否定疑问句形式构成的感叹句

可以使用否定疑问句形式构成感叹句，但一般在美国英语中而且有时在英国英语中也用疑问句表达感叹，如：

Isn't the weather nice!

天气多好啊！

Hasn't she grown!

她长这么大了！

Am I hungry!

我饿坏啦！

Wow, did she make a mistake!

哇，她做错啦！

词汇学习 Word study

1. critical *adj.*

(1) 挑剔的，苛求的：

Don't say any more critical remarks to her.

别再对她说苛刻的话了。

How can I have any self-confidence when you're always so critical of me?

你对我总是那么挑剔，我怎么会有自信心？

(2) 评论的，批评的，批判的：

His articles are full of the critical spirit of Marxism.

他的文章中充满了马克思主义的批判精神。

(3) 重要的，关键的：

This is a critical moment in American politics.

这是美国政治中的关键时刻。

(4) 危急的，危险的：

Be aware of the present critical situation.

要认识到当前危险的局势。

Both drivers are in a critical condition after the crash.

撞车之后，两个驾驶员都处于危险之中。

2. sure (surer, surest)

(1) *adj.* (of, about) 对……有把握的：

Are you sure about this?

你对这件事有把握吗？

I was sure that he had told her.

我确信他已经告诉她了。

(2) *adj.* (of) 自信的：

They felt sure of success.

他们对胜利充满信心。

(3) *adj.* (of) 不容争辩的，无可怀疑的：

Be sure of his honesty.

要相信他的诚实。

(4) *adj.* 肯定的，当然的：

It is sure to happen.

事情肯定会发生。

(5) *adj.* 坚定的：

They, with a sure aim, began their work.

他们目标坚定地开始工作。

(6) *adv.* 确实地：

She sure acts funny sometimes.

她有时的举动的确有点怪。

(7) make sure 确定：

Make sure that you set the alarm o'clock.

你要保证将闹钟上好。

(8) for sure 当然，确实：

We'd like to know for sure that you're on our side.

我们要确认你的确是站在我们这边。

3. conceive

(1) *vt*. 想出，设想，想像：

He conceived the project while on vacation.

他在假期中构想出这个计划。

I can't conceive that it would be of any use.

我想像不出它有什么用处。

(2) *vt*. 把……看作：

He conceived (*of*) *me as the author of the book.*

他把我看作是那本书的作者了。

(3) *vt*. 怀孕：

Their son was conceived during their stay in America.

他们的儿子是他们在美国期间怀上的。

(4) *vi*. (of) 想出，设想，想像：

I couldn't conceive of living without electricity.

我无法想像没有电的生活。

(5) *vi*. 怀孕：

After three years of treatment she finally conceived.

经过 3 年的治疗，她终于怀孕了。

练习答案 Key to written exercises

1. 关键句型练习答案

A 1 She *must have been* brilliant to get that job so easily.

2 A few years ago, you *had to be* academically brilliant or simply rich to go to university.

B See text.

2. 难点练习答案

1 In the past she has been very *critical* of the art college, but she has recently changed her mind.

2 That country is now an independent *state* with its own president and its own parliament.

3 You get a *free* weekend magazine with most Sunday newspapers in the UK.

3. 多项选择题答案

1 c 2 a 3 d 4 a 5 c 6 c

7 a 8 c 9 d 10 c 11 d 12 c

Lesson 46
Hobbies
业余爱好

课文详注 Further notes on the text

1. **... the mind catches hold of something and will not let it go.**

   catch/get/take hold of 抓住，如：

   At last the policeman caught hold of the thief.

   警察最终逮住了那个小偷。

   let ... go 放掉，让……走，如：

   We cannot let them go.

   我们不能让他们走。

2. **It is useless to argue with the mind in this condition.**

   It 为先行主语，真正的主语是动词不定式短语 to argue with ...。

3. **The stronger the will, the more futile the task.**

   该句使用的是 the more ..., the more... 比较结构。the will 后面省略了 is, the task 后面省略了 will be。the task 指 to argue with the mind。

4. **One can only gently insinuate something else into its convulsive grasp.**

   insinuate ... into... 使……巧妙地进入/取得……，如：

   She insinuated herself into his good graces.

   她巧妙地取得了他的好感。

   its 指 the mind 的。

5. **..., if it is really attended by the illumination of another field**

of interest, gradually, . . . , the old undue grip relaxes and . . .

it 指 the mind。attend 照顾,照料,料理,如:

The nurse was attending her patient.

那位护士正在照看她的病人。

the old undue grip 原先不适当的紧张。

6. **The seeds must be carefully chosen; they must fall on good ground; they must be sedulously tended, if the vivifying fruits are to be at hand when needed.**

该句将精神上多种情趣的培养过程比作植物的生长过程,即从选种、种植到护理的过程。if 引导的是该句的条件状语从句。the vivifying fruits 比喻培养成熟的情趣。are to be at hand 中的 be to do sth. 结构表示"计划或安排的",如:

The President is to visit Japan next month.

总统下月将访问日本。

We are to get a 10 per cent wage rise in June.

6月份我们的工资将提高10%。

at hand 在手边,如:

When I read, I want my dictionary near at hand.

我读书时,希望词典近在眼前。

when needed 作该条件状语从句中的时间状语,when 后面省略了 they are。

7. **To be really happy and really safe, . . .**

To be really happy and really safe 作目的状语,意即"要想真正感到幸福和平安"。

8. **It is no use starting late in life to say: 'I will take an interest in this or that.'**

It 作先行主语,而真正的主语是动名词短语 starting late in life to say。其中 late in life 作状语,修饰动名词 starting。动词不定式 to say 作动名词 starting 的宾语。take an interest in sth.

对某事感兴趣，如：

She took a keen interest in the project.

她对这个项目极感兴趣。

9. **A man may acquire great knowledge of topics unconnected with his daily work, ...**

unconnected with his daily work 为过去分词短语，作定语，修饰 great knowledge of topics。

10. **It is no use doing what you like.**

It 作先行主语，真正的主语是动名词短语 doing what you like。what you like 作动名词 doing 的宾语。

11. **Broadly speaking, human beings may be divided into three classes: those who are toiled to death, those who are worried to death, and those who are bored to death.**

Broadly speaking 作插入语，意即"泛泛地说"。句子中的 3 个 those 指前面提到的 3 类人，作 three classes 的同位语。3 个 those 后面跟随的是定语从句。

12. **It is no use offering the manual labourer, tired out with a hard week's sweat and effort, the chance of playing a game of football or baseball on Saturday afternoon.**

It 作先行主语，真正的主语是动名词短语 offering ... on Saturday afternoon。the manual labourer 作 offering 的间接宾语，the chance of playing ...作 offering 的直接宾语。tired out with ...为过去分词短语，作定语，修饰 labourer。

13. **It is no use inviting the politician or the professional or business man, who has been working or worrying about serious things for six days, to work or worry about trifling things at the weekend.**

who 引导非限定性定语从句，修饰 the politician or the professional or business man。to work or worry about ...此动

词不定式结构作宾语补足语。

14. As for the ..., who can gratify every caprice and lay their hands on almost every object of desire—for them a new pleasure, a new excitement is only an additional satiation.

as for 至于。常用于句首,用来介绍新话题或对已谈过的事情作进一步的说明,如:

I've invited Andy, Bob and Mark. As for Stephen, I don't care if I never see him again in my life.

我已经邀请了安迪、鲍勃和马克。至于斯蒂芬嘛,我可不在乎这辈子是否再也见不到他。

lay one's hands on 得到,抓住,如:

Where can I lay my hands on a good second-hand car?

我在哪儿能得到一部好的二手车?

破折号后面的部分用来对该种人作进一步的说明。

15. In vain they rush frantically round from place to place, trying to escape from avenging boredom by mere clatter and motion.

in vain 徒劳地,作状语。trying to escape from ...为现在分词短语,作目的状语。by mere clatter and motion 作方式状语,修饰 escape,意即"仅以闲聊和乱窜来摆脱"。

16. Of these the former are the majority.

Of these 作定语,修饰 the former,意即"这两类人中的前一类"。

17. But Fortune's favoured children belong to the second class.

Fortune 指"命运女神",故大写。

18. ..., and ordinary holidays, when they come, are grudged as enforced interruptions in an absorbing vocation.

they 指 ordinary holidays。grudge 怨恨。

19. Yet to both classes, the need of an alternative outlook, of a change of atmosphere, of a diversion of effort, is essential.

3 个 of 介词短语作定语,修饰 the need。to both classes 被提前了,该句按正常语序为:Yet the need of ..., of ..., of ..., is essential to both classes. be essential to/for 对……非常重要的,如:

Right timing is essential for our project.

时间选得恰当对我们的方案来说是很重要的。

20. ..., it may well be that those whose work is their pleasure are those who most need the means of banishing it at intervals from their minds.

may well be 非常可能。that 引导的是表语从句。whose 引导的是定语从句,修饰 those。who 引导定语从句,修饰 those。of banishing it ...为介词短语,作定语,修饰 the means。其中的 it 指 work。banish ... from ...把……逐出……,如:

She was banished from the country.

她被驱逐出境。

at intervals 每隔一段时间,如:

They visit us at regular intervals.

他们每隔一定的时间就来看我们。

语法 Grammar in use

英语中常见的几种倒装形式 (1)

英语中的倒装形式可以大体分为两类。一类是将助动词和非助动词 have/be 用于主语之前,另一类是将整个动词用于主语之前。

助动词和非助动词 have/be 置于主语之前的情况 (1)

(1) 疑问句,如:

Have your father and mother arrived?

你父母到了吗?

Where is the concert taking place?

音乐会在哪儿开呀？

(2) 感叹句和用 may 构成的祝愿，如：

Isn't it cold!

天真冷啊！

Hasn't she got lovely eyes!

她的眼睛真动人哇！

Am I fed up!

我腻烦死了！

How beautiful are the flowers!

这些花真美！

May all your wishes come true!

愿你所有愿望成真！

May she rest in peace!

愿她平安长眠！

(3) so、neither、nor 构成的简短答语或类似语，如：

I'm hungry.
我饿了。
So am I.
我也饿了。

I don't like opera.
我不喜欢歌剧。
Neither/Nor do I.
我也不喜欢。

(4) 在否定和限定短语后

当否定副词(短语)置于句首进行强调时，其后通常使用倒装语序，如：

Under no circumstances can we cash cheques.

在任何情况下我们都不能把支票兑换成现金。

Not until much later did she learn who her real father

was.

没过多久,她就知道亲生父亲是谁了。

Hardly had I arrived when trouble started.

我刚一到麻烦就来了。

Seldom have I seen such a remarkable creature.

我很少见到这样奇异的东西。

Only then did I understand what she meant.

只是到那会儿我才明白她是什么意思。

Not only did we lose our money, but we were nearly killed.

我们不仅丢了钱,还几乎丧了命。

(5) 在 as、than 和 so 后

文学作品中,有时在 as、than 和表示强调的 so 之后用倒装语序,如:

She was very religious, as were most of her friends.

她是个十分虔诚的信教者,就像她的大多数朋友那样。

City dwellers have a higher death rate than do country people.

城市居民的死亡率要比农村人的高。

So ridiculous did she look that everybody burst out laughing.

她看起来太可笑了,以至于所有的人都大笑起来。

(6) 条件从句

在正式和文学作品中,有时将助动词置于主语之前,省略引导条件状语从句的连词 if,如:

Were she my daughter ...

如果她是我的女儿……

Had I realized what you intended ...

假如我明白你想些什么……

Had we not spent all our money already ...

如果我们还没有把所有的钱花完……

词汇学习 Word study

1. use

(1) *vt*. 用,使用,应用:

May I use your car?

我能用一下你的车吗?

(2) *vt*. 发挥,使出,行使,运用:

They used all their efforts to fulfil the task.

他们使出浑身解数来完成任务。

Use your head when you deal with mathematical problems.

做数学题时动动脑子。

(3) *vt*. 耗费,消费,耗尽:

They use a ton of coal every week.

他们每周用掉一吨煤。

He has used up all his energy.

他已筋疲力尽了。

(4) *vt*. 利用:

You should use every opportunity well.

你应当利用好每次机会。

(5) *n*. (不可数)使用,运用,利用:

For use only in case of fire!

只供火警时使用!

Is this dictionary in use?

在用这本词典吗?

(6) *n*. (可数/不可数)用途,用处,用法;好处:

He's put his dictionary to (a) good use.

他善用他的词典。

That's a tool with several uses.

那是一台多用途工具。

What's the use of this?

这有什么用?

I have no use for this car.

我用不着这车。

There is no use in complaining.

抱怨没有用。

Is this of any use to you?

这东西对你有任何用处吗?

(7) come into use 开始被使用:

The method has only recently come into use.

这一方法刚被采用。

(8) make use of 利用:

You should make the best use of everything.

你应当使物尽其用。

(9) of use 有用:

It is of great use for my work.

这对我的工作非常有用。

2. benefit

(1) *n*. (不可数)益处,裨益,优势:

His holiday wasn't much of benefit to him.

假期对他没有太大的好处。

(2) *n*. (可数)义演,义赛,义卖:

They held a benefit for old actors.

他们为老演员举行了一次义演。

(3) *vt*. 有益于,对……有好处:

It's an expensive investment but will benefit the company

in the long run.

这是一次高昂的投资，但从长远的观点来看对公司是有利的。

(4) *vi*. (from) 得益，得到好处：

These small businesses have benefited greatly from the fall in interest rates.

这些小企业从这次降息中得到极大好处。

3. essential

(1) *adj*. 本质的，重要的，必不可少的：

Books are essential to students.

书对于学生来说是必不可少的。

What is the essential difference between the Democratic Party and the Republic Party?

民主党和共和党的主要区别是什么？

(2) *n*. (可数) 必需品：

The room was furnished with the simplest essentials: a bed, a chair, and a table.

这个房间摆放着最简单的必需品：一张床、一把椅子和一张桌子。

练习答案 Key to written exercises

1. 关键句型练习答案

A See text.

B See text.

2. 难点练习答案

A 1 The plane took off *late*.

I haven't seen old Mr. James *lately*.

2 We have *hardly* slept at all since we arrived in the city.

That boy works extremely *hard* and deserves to do well.

3 The adjective *alternative* means 'different from what is usual or traditional': *We are gradually beginning to use alternative sources of energy more, wave power and wind power, for example.*

Alternating, on the other hand, means 'following by turns': *She treated him with alternating affection and contempt. They wore the spy down with alternating periods of kindness and cruelty.*

B 1 It was clear that the government's actions were sowing the *seeds* of rebellion.

2 The man sadly died before he could enjoy the *fruits* of all his hard work.

3 All I want to do after a hard day's *sweat* is to soak in a long hot bath.

C 1 *Broadly speaking*, the British education system can be divided into two main sections: public and private.

2 'Jane can have the bed in the spare room,' my aunt said. '*As for* you, you can sleep on the sofa.'

3 Of the two proposals put forward by the committee, *the former* had the best chance of succeeding.

3. 多项选择题答案

1	b	2	b	3	d	4	b	5	d	6	a
7	b	8	c	9	d	10	a	11	b	12	d

Lesson 47
The great escape
大逃亡

课文详注 Further notes on the text

1. **Economy is one ..., since after the ...**

   该句为复合句。since 引导的是原因状语从句,用来说明为什么露营的主要动机是为了省钱。

2. **But, contrary to a popular assumption, it is far from being the only one, or even the greatest.**

   contrary to a popular assumption 作插入语,意即"和一般的看法相反"。此处,contrary 为形容词,但该形容词不能单独使用,一般和介词 to 连用,表示"相反的"、"对抗的",如:

   His actions are contrary to the rules.

   他的行为是违背规章的。

   it is far from ... 远不是……。it 指 economy。one 指 motive。greatest 后面省略了 one 或 motive。

3. **The man who manoeuvres carelessly into his twenty pounds' worth of space at one of Europe's myriad permanent sites may find himself bumping a Bentley.**

   manoeuvre into 设法进入。该词的美式拼写是 maneuver。该词常用来表示"调动军队",如:

   The troops manoeuvred for position.

   部队调动以取得有利阵地。

   twenty pounds' worth of space 价值 20 英镑的空地。此处 worth 为名词,意即"价值",如:true worth(真正的价值),

books of great worth(有巨大价值的书)。bump 的原义是“撞”、“碰”,如:

She bumped her arm against the table.

她将手臂撞到桌子上了。

而在此处,该词的意思是“碰上”而不是“撞”的意思,如:

She bumped into her teacher in high school.

她偶然遇见了她中学的老师。

Bentley(本特利)以及下一句中的 Ford Escort(福特·康索尔)、Renault(雷诺)、Mercedes(梅塞迪斯)都是汽车品牌。

4. **... will be hub to hub with ..., but rarely with bicycles made for two.**

hub to hub with 中 hub 为名词,在此处意即“车轴”,表示“车轴与……车轴相接”,也就是说这些车“并排停放着”。rarely 后省略了 be hub to hub。made for two 为过去分词短语,作定语,修饰 bicycles,意即“双人自行车”。

5. **That the equipment of modern camping becomes yearly more sophisticated is an entertaining paradox for the cynic, a brighter promise for the hopeful traveller who has sworn to get away from it all.**

That 引导的是一个主语从句,该句的谓语动词是 becomes。yearly 是副词,意即“一年比一年地”。is 是整个句子的谓语动词。an entertaining ... 和 a brighter promise ... 是该句的表语。who 引导定语从句,修饰 traveller。get away from it all 是个固定词组,意即“用出走的方法来摆脱烦恼”。

6. **It also provides—and some student sociologist might care to base his thesis upon the phenomenon—an escape of another kind.**

It 指 camping。两个破折号中间的部分是插入语。some student sociologist 指“学社会学的大学生”。care to do sth. 想

做某事，愿意做某事，如：

I don't care to attend.

我不想出席。

Would you care to dance?

你想跳舞吗？

base ... on/upon ... 以……为……的依据，如：

We based our conclusions on facts.

我们的结论是以事实为依据的。

He based the book on his own life.

他依据自己的生活写的这本书。

7. ... a man who dislikes the Splendide and the Bellavista, not because he cannot afford, or shuns their material comforts, ...

the Splendide and the Bellavista 是两个大酒店的名字。their 指上述两个大酒店的。shun 避开，如：

She shunned her family and refused to return to her home village.

她避开她的家人，并拒绝返回家乡。

8. Affluent he may be, but he is by no means sure ...

Affluent he may be 作让步状语从句，该从句省略了 however，意即“不管他有多么富有”。by no means 与 in no way 同义，意即“决不”、“决非”，如：

It is by no means certain.

还不能肯定。

9. Master in his own house, he has little idea of when to say boo to a *maître d'hôtel*.

该句的结构与前一句结构相同。Master in his own house 为让步状语，该句省略了 Although he is a，意即“虽然他在自己家里是主人”。have little idea of 不知道。when to say ... 为介词 of 的宾语从句。say boo to a *maître d'hôtel* 对酒店的经理

表示不满。say boo to a *maître d'hôtel* 是从 not say boo to a goose(非常胆小,不敢得罪)演变而来的。在这个成语中,a goose 常被人们幽默地换成其他字眼。boo 为名词,意即"不满"、"不赞成"。

10. **From all such fears camping releases him.**

该句为倒装句。状语 From all such fears 置于句首,用以起强调作用。release ... from 从……释放,从……解放出来,如:

He has been released from prison.

他被释放出狱了。

11. **Granted, a snobbery of camping itself, based upon equipment and techniques, already exists; but it is of a kind that, if he meets it, he can readily understand and deal with.**

整个句子的主体结构是 Granted..., but ..., 表示"虽然……,但是……"。这种句型中 granted 总放在句首,意思是"是的"、"诚然",相当于连接副词,引导让步状语从句。a snobbery of camping itself 作主语,谓语动词是 exists。based upon equipment and techniques 为过去分词短语,作定语,修饰 a snobbery of camping itself。that 引导的是 kind 的同位语从句。if he meets it 作该同位语从句中的条件状语从句。he 指 modern traveller 。it 指 a snobbery of camping。

12. **There is no superior 'they' in the shape of managements and hotel hierarchies to darken his holiday days.**

they 用引号特指酒店中的管理阶层的那些"趾高气昂"的人。in the shape of ... 以……形式出现的,作定语,修饰 they。darken 使……沮丧,如:

Those setbacks darkened his mood.

那些挫折使他十分沮丧。

13. **To such motives, yet another must be added.**

该句为倒装句,To such motives 作状语,置于句首,表示强调。

14. ... is to be explained not least by the sense of independence and freedom that ownership entails.

is to be explained 可以得到解释。to be 后面跟动词不定式可表示可能性。not least 重要地,主要地,如:

They refused to admit her, not least because she hadn't got her membership card with her.

他们拒绝让她进入,主要是因为她没带会员卡。

entail 需要,必然伴有,如:

This job would entail your learning how to use a computer.

这项工作需要你学会使用电脑。

15. To this pleasure camping gives an exquisite refinement.

该句和本段第1句的结构相同,为倒装句。To this pleasure 作状语,提至句首是为了强调。句子按正常语序为:Camping gives an exquisite refinement to this pleasure. 意即:"露营给这种快乐增加了一种优雅意境。"

16. From one's own front door to home or foreign hills or sands and back again, everything is to hand.

home 和 foreign 作定语,修饰 hills 和 sands,意即"国内和国外的山区或沙滩"。be to hand 唾手可得,在手边。

17. Not only are the means of arriving at the holiday paradise entirely within one's own command and keeping, but ... from holiday hell (if the beach proves too crowded, the local weather too inclement) are there, outside—or, as likely, part of—the tent.

该句的主体结构是 not only ..., but ...。该句的第1个分句为倒装句。在英语中,以否定词开头的句子要倒装。这类的否定词有:no、neither、not only、hardly、rarely、barely 等。该分句按正常语序为:The means of arriving at the holiday paradise are not only entirely within one's own command and keeping ... keeping 为不可数名词,意即"看管"、"照管",如:

The papers are in my keeping.

文件由我保管。

为了形成鲜明的对比,作者采用了对照的手法,即同时采用两个相反的词组,the holiday paradise 和 holiday hell 形成反差,分别形容给游客带来快乐的假日和给游客带来烦恼的假日。括号中的内容是对 holiday hell 的具体说明。the local weather 后面省略了 proves。outside ... the tent 作 there 的同位语。破折号中间的部分为补充说明。as likely 很可能。

18. Idealists have objected to the practice of camping, as to the package tour, that the traveller abroad thereby denies himself the opportunity of getting to know the people of the country visited.

object 因……而反对,之后的 that 引导的是宾语从句,如:

She objected that the accusation was based on hearsay.

她提出反对,说指控是根据道听途说而做出的。

Our offer was $3 million, but they objected that they had paid $4 million for the property in the first place.

我们出 300 万美元,但是他们反对说首先他们已经为这个产业支付了 400 万美元。

deny oneself sth. 使自己得不到某物,如:

He denies himself nothing.

他从不克制自己的欲求。

visited 为过去分词,作定语,修饰 country。

19. Insularity and self-containment, it is argued, go hand in hand.

it is argued 作插入语,意即"人们争辩说"。go hand in hand 相当于 go together,携手并进,如:

Prosperity goes hand in hand with investment.

Prosperity and investment go hand in hand.

繁荣与投资是分不开的。

20. Holiday hotels tend to cater for one nationality of visitors especially, ...

cater for/to 迎合,如:

This restaurant caters to all tastes.

这家餐馆迎合各种口味。

21. Camping sites, by contrast, are ...

by contrast 相形之下,相比之下。

22. Granted, a preponderance of Germans ...; but as yet there is no ...

该句的结构与注释 11 的结构相同。as yet 至今,到目前为止。

23. Notices forbidding ... for car washing, ..., or those inviting ... a boat trip are printed not only in French or ..., ... and Dutch.

forbidding ... for car washing 作定语,修饰 notices。those 指 notices。inviting ... a boat trip 作定语,修饰 those。该句的谓语部分是 are printed not only in French or ..., ... and Dutch。

24. At meal times the odour of sauerkraut vies with that of garlic.

vie with/against 跟……竞争,跟……争,如:

Car dealers are vying with each other to attract customers by offering discounts.

车商正在以打折的方式吸引顾客互相竞争。

The streets were full of cars vying with each other for parking spaces.

街道上挤满了互相争停车位的车辆。

此句是比喻的用法,意思是"德国泡菜味和大蒜味争相散发"。

that 代替 the odour。

25. The Frenchman's breakfast coffee competes with the Englishman's bacon and eggs.

该句中的 competes with 同前句相同,也是比喻的用法,意思是"法国人的早点咖啡和英国人的咸肉煎蛋竞相比美"。

26. Whether the remarkable growth ... is hard to say.

Whether 引导的是主语从句,主句的谓语部分是 is hard to say。

27. Police are wary of itinerants who cannot be traced ... to four walls.

be wary of 提防,如:

Be wary of strangers.

提防陌生人。

who 引导定语从句,修饰 itinerants,意即"查不出有固定营地或住处的游荡者"。four walls 在这里指"住所"、"房子"。to trace to 追踪到,如:

The letter was traced to its sender.

查到了那封信的寄信人。

28. ... how many heath fires they cause; how much litter they leave; in short, whether or not they wholly alienate landowners and those who live in the countryside.

该句为 3 个并列成分,列举具体事例,说明为什么重要的是露营者自己。alienate 使疏远,如:

She was alienated from her family.

她与家庭疏远了。

those who live in the countryside 中的 those 与 landowners 都是动词 alienate 的宾语。who 引导定语从句,修饰 those。

29. Only good scouting is likely to preserve the freedoms so dear to the heart of the eternal Boy Scout.

good scouting 指童子军进行的露营,也即“纪律良好的露营”。so dear to . . . Boy Scout 作定语,修饰 freedoms,意即“不朽的童子军所衷心热爱的各项自由”。Boy Scout 童子军,英国军官贝登堡在 1908 年创建的一种对儿童进行军事化训练的组织。露营是童子军训练的一个项目。

语法 Grammar in use

英语中常见的几种倒装形式 (2)

将整个动词置于主语之前的情况

(1) 用于地点状语短语之后,如:

Under a tree was lying one of the biggest men I had ever seen.

在树下正躺着我从未见到过的巨人中的一个。

On the grass sat an enormous frog.

一只巨大的青蛙伏在草地上。

Directly in front of them stood a great castle.

就在他们面前矗立着一座巨大的城堡。

Along the road came a strange procession.

沿路走来一奇怪的队列。

这种结构在文学和描述性文字中很常见。将表示地点或方位状语的部分置于句首并且引入一新的非限定主语且主动词为不及物动词时,经常使用上述结构。口语中,当表示地点的状语为 here、there 和其他较短的副词(短语)时,也常用这样的结构,如:

Here comes the bus.

公共汽车来了。

There goes your brother.

你兄弟走啦。

I stopped the car, and up walked a policeman.

我把车刚停下来,一个警察就走了过来。

但注意,当主语为代词时,该代词则需置于动词之前,如:

Here she comes.

她来啦。

Off we go!

我们走啦!

(2) 在叙述故事中,主语通常置于引用言语动词之后,如:

'What do you mean?' asked Henry.

"你是什么意思?"亨利问。

'I love you,' whispered Mary.

"我爱你,"玛丽喃喃说道。

但是,当主语为代词时,该代词通常置于动词之前,如:

'What do you mean?' he asked.

"你是什么意思?"他问道。

词汇学习 Word study

1. hire

(1) *vt.* 雇用;租用:

We need to hire some shop assistants for the Spring Festival rush.

春节繁忙时,我们需要雇用几个店员。

During the holidays we hired a boat and went fishing.

假期里,我们租了一条小船去钓鱼。

(2) *vi.* (out) 出租:

We hire out our vans by the day.

我们按天出租客货车。

(3) *n.* (不可数) 租用,雇用:

These cars are for hire.

这些汽车是供租用的。

Bicycles on hire, two dollars an hour.

出租自行车,每小时收费两美元。

2. care

(1) *n*. (不可数) 照顾,照料,护理:

These disabled children need special care.

这些残疾儿童需要特殊照料。

This article offers advice on skin and hair care.

这篇文章就皮肤和头发的护理提出建议。

(2) *n*. (可数/不可数) 忧虑,烦恼,挂念:

She's free from all care.

她无忧无虑。

She has all the cares of the world.

她有无数烦心的事。

She hasn't a care in the world.

她没有丝毫烦恼。

(3) *n*. (不可数) 小心,谨慎,注意:

Try to do your work with a bit more care.

做工作时尽可能更仔细些。

Cross the road with care.

过马路时要小心。

Take care not to drop the glass.

当心,别把杯子打碎了。

(4) *vi*. (about)(不用于进行时)关心,介意:

The only thing he cares about is money.

他惟一关心的就是钱。

(5) *vt*. (不用于进行时) 关心,介意:

I really care whether we win or lose.

我真的很在意我们的输赢。

As if I cared whether he comes or not!

就好像我多么在意他来不来似的!

(6) *vt*. 喜欢,愿意:

Would you care to go for a walk?

你愿意去散会儿步吗?

(7) *vt*. (for) 照顾,照料:

I'm glad to see that you are being well cared for.

我很高兴你受到很好的照顾。

(8) *vt*. (常用于疑问句和否定句)喜欢,对……中意:

I don't really care for tea; I like coffee better.

我不是特别喜欢喝茶;我更喜欢喝咖啡。

(9) take care of 照顾,照料:

Who will take care of the dog while we're away?

我们不在时谁来照料这只狗呢?

3. object

(1) *n*. /ˈɔbdʒikt/ (可数) 物品,物体,东西:

Can you name that object?

你能说出那个东西的名字吗?

(2) *n*. /ˈɔbdʒikt/ 对象,目的物;目的,目标:

In his whole life, he worked with the object of becoming someone famous.

他一辈子工作的目标就是成为名人。

(3) *n*. /ˈɔbdʒikt/ 样子怪异的人或物:

He looks an object in that funny suit.

他穿着那身可笑的西装真是太滑稽了。

(4) *vi*. /əbˈdʒekt/ (to) 不赞成,反对:

He objected to teaching in that way.

他反对用那种方法教学生。

练习答案 Key to written exercises

1. 关键句型练习答案

See text.

2. 难点练习答案

A 1 The adjective *initial* means 'which is (at) the beginning': *After she had overcome her initial shyness, she became very friendly.*

The adjective *primary* means 'chief, main, or principal': *The primary purpose of his visit is to discuss the local housing problem.* (It is also used to describe education for children between 5 and 11 years old: *He still goes to a primary school. She has been a primary school teacher for 30 years.*)

2 The verb *hire* means 'get the use of something for a special occasion or a limited time on payment of a sum of money': *We hired a car for a week when we were in Canada.*

While we usually *hire* something for a short time, we *rent* things for a longer period. *Rent* also means 'pay money for the use of', therefore, but usually refers to a room, house, television set, etc.: *Mrs. Smith rents rooms to students. They rent their rooms from her.*

3 *Total* means 'being a total, considered as a complete amount': *The total number of cars produced in the period was 5,500.*

Whole, on the other hand, means 'all (the), the full amount of': *When she was ill last year, she spent a whole month in hospital. He spent the whole evening watching television.*

4 The verb *shun* means 'avoid with determination, or keep away from': *He was a shy man who always shunned publicity.*

Avoid means 'prevent something from happening, or stop oneself from doing something': *He did everything he could to avoid answering my questions.*

5 The two nouns *worship* and *warship* are close in spelling and pronunciation, but very different in meaning.

The uncountable noun *worship* (/ˈwɜːʃɪp/) is 'strong, usually religious feelings of love, respect and admiration, especially when shown to God or a god': *Some societies practise ancestor worship.*

A *warship* (/ˈwɔːʃɪp/) is 'a naval ship used for war, especially one armed with guns': *They sent four warships to guard the convoy of twenty cargo boats.*

6 The phrase *by contrast* means 'in comparison with objects or situations that are dissimilar, especially to show differences': *The coastal areas have mild winters, but by contrast the central plains become extremely cold.*

The noun *opposite*, often in the phrase 'the complete opposite to', means 'a person or thing that is as different as possible from another': *She's rather quiet, the complete opposite to her sister, who is bubbly and full of life.*

B 1 The circulation of the magazine has been *bumping* along for some time at about 30,000.

2 After years of slow and careful negotiations, the island was finally *granted* its independence.

3 The usual *custom* there is for a bride to wear a white dress.

3. 多项选择题答案

1	c	2	a	3	a	4	d	5	b	6	c
7	a	8	c	9	d	10	b	11	b	12	c

Lesson 48
Planning a share portfolio
规划股份投资

课文详注 Further notes on the text

1. **There is no shortage of tipsters around offering ‘get-rich-quick’ opportunities.**

   offering ‘get-rich-quick’ opportunities 为现在分词短语，作定语，修饰 tipsters，意即“提供迅速发财致富的机遇的情报贩子”。

2. **..., leave the Las Vegas mentality to those with money to fritter.**

   Las Vegas 是美国西部的赌城，全城布满了各式各样的赌场，所以作者将想迅速发财致富的心态比作拉斯韦加斯心态。

3. **The serious investor needs a proper ‘portfolio’—a well-planned selection of investments, with a definite structure and a clear aim.**

   破折号后面的部分是 portfolio 的同位语，对其作具体说明。with a definite structure and a clear aim 作定语，修饰 portfolio，也即“有投资结构和明确目标的投资组合表”。

4. **But exactly how does a newcomer to the stock market go about achieving that?**

   go about 从事，做，如：

   It's time you went about your business.

   你该干自己的事了。

   achieving that 为现在分词短语，作目的状语，修饰 go about。

5. **...,—even if you give all the relevant information ...**

破折号后面的部分为让步状语从句,置于破折号后面起强调作用。

6. **Moral?**

这是个省略疑问句,意即"这是个道德问题吗?"

7. **There is no one 'right' way to structure a portfolio.**

one 在此处表示"惟一的",如:

She's the one person I can trust.

她是惟一我可以信任的人。

to structure a portfolio 为动词不定式,作定语,修饰 way,意即"排列这种投资组合的方法"。

8. **...would have suggested sinking all (or perhaps any) of your money into Periwigs.**

sink ... into ... 此处为比喻用法,该短语动词的原义是"使……深入",如:sink one's teeth into a good steak(大口地咬美味的牛排)。Periwigs 是一个假想的公司的名字。

9. **We'll assume that you have sorted out the basics—like mortgages, pensions, insurance and access to sufficient cash reserves.**

sort out 整理,分选,如:

She is trying to sort things out at home.

她在家里正竭力整理东西。

the basics 基本情况,基本要素。破折号后面的部分列举出具体的基本情况是什么。access to 有接近/进入/使用……的机会或权利,如:

We gained access to the files.

我们获得了查阅档案的权利。

We got access to the building.

我们获准进入这幢大楼。

10. **These are partly a matter of personal circumstances, partly a**

matter of psychology.

a matter of... ……的事情，如：

a matter of great importance 一件至关重要的事情

a matter of a few minutes 在几分钟内就可以解决的事情

a matter of personal opinion 个人看法的问题

11. **..., and you may well wish to boost your pension income.**

to boost 作动词 wish 的宾语，意即“提高”。另如：

boost price 提高物价

12. **So preserving your capital and generating extra income are your main priorities.**

preserving ... and generating ...为两个并列的动名词短语，作主语。

13. **..., you'd probably construct a portfolio with some shares (but not high risk ones), along with gilts, ...**

with some shares 作宾语 a portfolio 的补足语。括号中的内容是对 shares 的补充说明。along with gilts ...作状语。

14. **If you are younger, and in a solid financial position, you may decide to take an aggressive approach—but only if you're blessed with a sanguine disposition and won't suffer sleepless nights over share prices.**

If 引导条件状语从句，and 后面省略了 if you are。to take an aggressive approach 作动词 decide 的宾语。破折号后面的部分也是条件状语从句，破折号起强调的作用。

15. **If you recognize yourself in this description, ...**

If 引导的是条件状语从句，该从句的意思是“如果你觉得你的情况是这样的话”。this description 指前一句所描述的那样。

16. **Once you have decided on your investment aims, you can then decide where to put your money.**

Once 引导的是时间状语从句。where to put your money 作动词 decide 的宾语。动词不定式可以置于疑问词如 who、what、where、when、whether 等后面(除 why 外),作动词宾语,如:

I wonder who to invite.

我不知道该邀请谁。

Can you tell me how to get to the airport?

你能告诉我怎么去机场吗?

I don't know where to park the car.

我不知道该把车停在哪儿。

Tell me when to pay.

告诉我什么时候付款。

17. The golden rule is spread your risk—if you put ..., you're setting yourself up as a hostage to fortune.

spread your risk 为动词不定式,作表语,省略了动词不定式前面的符号 to。破折号后面的部分从反面说明为什么要分散投资风险。if 引导条件状语从句。set ... up as 使……成为,如:

His father lent him some money to set him up as a shoemaker.

他父亲借给他一些钱使他成为一个鞋匠。

语法 Grammar in use

进行时的几种其他常见用法

1. 表示经常性的进行时

当进行时同 always、continually 和类似的副词一同使用时,通常并非表示进行时,而表达"非常经常的"且往往是"意想不到的"含义,如:

I'm always losing my keys.

我总是丢钥匙。

Granny's nice. She's always giving people little presents.

祖母心地很善良。她总是给人一些小礼物。

I'm continually running into Tom these days.

这些天我总是碰到汤姆。

Her mother was always arranging little surprise picnics and outings.

她母亲过去总是安排一些小型的意外野餐和郊游。

2. 动词不定式的进行时形式

像其他进行时形式那样,动词不定式的进行时形式用来表示动作和事件现在正在/过去正在/将来正在所述时间左右进行,如:

It's nice to be sitting here with you.

这会儿同你坐在这儿很惬意。

I noticed that she seemed to be smoking a lot.

我注意到她好像一直抽了不少烟。

Why's she so late? She can't still be working.

她为什么会这么迟呢?她不可能还在工作呀。

3. 动词 be 的进行时形式

这一形式通常由 be + being + 形容词/名词构成。这样的结构一般不用来说明状态,而用来说明与所述形容词或名词相关的动作或行为,如:

You're being stupid.

你在做傻事。

I was being very careful.

我那会儿正认真做事。

Who's being a silly baby, then?

那么,谁是那个在做傻事的孩子呀?

词汇学习 Word study

1. sort

(1) *n*. (可数)类,种类:

What sort of music do you like best?

你最爱听什么音乐?

(2) sort of 稍微,有点:

It's sort of long and thin, a bit like sausage.

那个东西好像是细长的,有点像香肠。

(3) *vt*. 把事情分类:

The machine sorts the eggs into big and small ones.

这台机器把鸡蛋分成大、小两种。

(4) sort out 整理:

He sorted out his clothes and put old ones in a bag.

他把衣服整理了一下,把旧的放在袋子里。

2. access *n*.

(1) (to) 通道,入口:

The only means of access to the building is along a muddy track.

只有沿着那条泥泞的小道才能进入该幢大楼。

(2) 接近的机会,使用/接近/获得权利:

Students need easy access to books.

书籍应当便于学生使用。

3. solid

(1) *adj*. 固体的:

Liquid and solid waste is collected in the tank.

液体和固体垃圾放在箱中收取。

(2) *adj*. (物质结构)紧密的,坚固的,实心的:

That bicycle has solid rubber tyres.

那辆自行车的轮胎是实心的。

(3) *adj*. 立体的：

A sphere is a solid figure.

球形是立体形。

(4) *adj*. 纯质的：

He carries a solid gold watch.

他带着块纯金表。

(5) *adj*. 连续的：

I am compiling the dictionary for a solid day.

一整天我都在编字典。

(6) *n*. (可数)固体：

At what temperature does that kind of liquid become a solid?

那种液体在多高温度下会变成固体?

练习答案 Key to written exercises

1. 关键句型练习答案

A See text.

B See text.

2. 难点练习答案

See text.

3. 多项选择题答案

1 c	2 c	3 b	4 c	5 c	6 c
7 c	8 d	9 b	10 a	11 a	12 b